Library of
Davidson College

MONEY IN GREAT BRITAIN AND IRELAND

C. R. JOSSET

Illustrated by Gaynor A. Barnes

CHARLES E. TUTTLE COMPANY : PUBLISHERS
RUTLAND, VERMONT

For my wife

332.49
J84m

Published by the Charles E. Tuttle Company, Inc.
of Rutland, Vermont & Tokyo, Japan
with editorial offices at
Suido 1-chome, 2-6, Bunkyo-ku, Tokyo, Japan

COPYRIGHT NOTICE

© C. R. JOSSET 1971

All rights reserved. No part of this publication may be reproduced, stored in a retrieval system, or transmitted, in any form or by any means, electronic, mechanical, photocopying, recording or otherwise, without the prior permission of the publishers

All rights reserved
First edition 1971
LOC 70-170671
ISBN 0-8048-1011-7

73-3838

Printed in Great Britain

CONTENTS

		page
	List of Illustrations	7
	Foreword	13
	Introduction	15

Chapter

1	Pre-Roman and Roman	17
2	Anglo-Saxon and Danes	27
3	Norman Rule	39
4	The Plantagenets	46
5	Lancaster and York	65
6	The Tudors	77
7	Stuart and Commonwealth	107
8	Restoration and Change	131
9	Hanover to Victoria	152
10	Twentieth-Century Monarchs	203
11	The Channel Isles and the Isle of Man	239
	Bibliography	268
	Acknowledgements	271

Appendices

Catalogue of British and English Coins	272
Catalogue of Scottish Coins	306
Catalogue of Irish Coins	327
Catalogue of Irish Free State Coins	351
Catalogue of Eire Coins	351
Catalogue of Isle of Man Coins	354
Catalogue of Channel Isles Coins	356
Catalogue of Jersey Coins	356
Specimen Set Catalogue	364
Printed Note Issues in Great Britain	368
Translations of Mottoes on Coins	381
Index	385

LIST OF ILLUSTRATIONS

Plates

	page
Bars of iron *(courtesy: the Sunday Times)*	33
Early coining tools *(courtesy: the Royal Mint)*	33
The Master of the mint *(courtesy: Thames Television Ltd)*	34
The earliest known specimen of a goldsmith's receipt *(courtesy: Williams & Glyn's Bank Ltd)*	51
A goldsmith's note *(courtesy: Williams & Glyn's Bank Ltd)*	51
A drawn note *(courtesy: Williams & Glyn's Bank Ltd)*	52
A receipt from Nell Gwyn *(courtesy: Williams & Glyn's Bank Ltd)*	52
A drawn note of Barbara, Duchess of Cleveland *(courtesy: Williams & Glyn's Bank Ltd)*	69
A drawn note of the first Duke of Bolton *(courtesy: Williams & Glyn's Bank Ltd)*	69
Eighteenth-century exchequer tallies *(courtesy: Thames Television Ltd)*	70
The Cruikshank note *(courtesy: Coins Weekly)*	70
The Royal Mint, London *(Crown copyright)*	87
Nineteenth-century country banknotes *(courtesy: Williams & Glyn's Bank Ltd)*	88
Nineteenth-century specimen banknotes *(courtesy: Institute of Bankers)*	121
Selection of banknotes *(courtesy: Institute of Bankers and the Bank of England)*	122
The £5 note of the Royal Bank of Scotland *(courtesy: The Sport and General Press Agency Ltd)*	139
Newly minted cupro-nickel coins being scrutinised for faults *(courtesy: Coins Weekly)*	140
The Royal Mint, Llantrisant, South Wales *(Crown copyright)*	140
Victorian decimal patterns *(courtesy: HMSO)*	157
Finished coins being collected by conveyor *(Crown copyright)*	158

	page
The coining room at The Royal Mint, Llantrisant *(Crown copyright)*	158
Blanks arriving at the coining room by conveyor *(courtesy: Coins Weekly)*	175
Obverse for all decimal currency coins *(Crown copyright)*	175
The Isle of Man 50 new pence note *(courtesy: Keystone Press Agency Ltd)*	176
The first Isle of Man gold coinage *(courtesy: The Sport and General Press Agency Ltd)*	176

List of Illustrations in Text

Philippi of Philip of Macedon	25
'Bellovaci' gold stater	25
Whaddon Chase type gold stater	25
Roman Empire silver denarius of Augustus	25
Classical style stater of Tincommius	25
Gold stater of Cunobelinus	25
An uninscribed Iceni silver stater	25
Silver penny of Sihtric III	25
Brass sestertius of Antonius Pius	25
Roman Empire bronze follis of Diocletian	26
Silver penny of Offa	37
Dinar of Offa	37
Silver penny of Coenwulf	37
Silver penny of Alfred the Great	38
Silver penny of Aethelred II	38
The 'Agnus Dei' silver penny	38
Silver penny of Edward the Confessor	38
Silver penny of Harold II	38
The 'Pax' type silver penny of William the Conqueror	45
The 'Two Star' type silver penny of William the Conqueror	45
Silver penny of William II (mule)	45
Silver penny of Henry I (mule)	45
The 'Sceptre' type silver penny of Henry I	45
Another 'Sceptre' type silver penny of Henry I	45

List of Illustrations 9

	page
Silver penny of Stephen	45
Silver penny of Stephen and Matilda	45
Silver penny of Baron Eustace Fitzjohn	45
Henry II silver short cross penny	63
Richard I short cross silver penny	63
Richard I silver denier of Aquitaine	63
Short cross silver penny of King John	63
Henry III long cross silver penny c 1248	63
The first English gold penny, Henry III c 1257	63
Scottish silver sterling of Alexander III	63
Edward I silver penny c 1280 Lincoln	64
English silver groat (4d) c 1279 London	64
Edward III English gold half florin c 1344	64
Edward III gold noble	64
Edward III Aquitaine guiennois, Anglo-Gallic c 1360	64
Henry VI gold salute c 1446 Rouen	75
Lion of James II of Scotland	75
Henry VI gold angel Bristol	75
Edward IV Irish silver double groat	75
Edward IV 'Anonymous Issue'	76
Richard III Irish silver groat	76
James III rider	76
James III unicorn	76
Sovereign of Henry VII	102
Henry VII silver testoon c 1508	102
Gold crown of the double rose	102
The base testoon of Henry VIII	102
Edward VI countermarked testoon	103
Silver crown of Edward VI	103
Mary's silver groat	103
Silver shilling of Philip and Mary	103
The Mary Queen of Scots testoon 1561	103
Elizabeth I gold half pound	104
Elizabeth I silver crown	104
James VI of Scotland twenty pound piece c 1576	104
James I gold unite	127
James I second coinage silver crown 1604	127

List of Illustrations

	page
James I second spur-ryal	127
Oval Harrington farthing	127
Tower Mint variety of silver crown, Charles I	127
Shrewsbury type declaration crown 1642	128
Gold triple unite Charles I	128
Oxford crown	128
Truro crown	128
Newark 'siege piece'	129
Scarborough 'siege pieces'	129
Carlisle 'siege piece'	129
Octagonal shilling 'siege piece' of Pontefract	129
Crown piece, octagonal Inchiquin money	129
'Blacksmith's money' half crown	130
Commonwealth crown	130
Commonwealth shilling	130
Commonwealth penny	130
The Cromwell pattern crown	130
The 'hammered' shilling of Charles II	149
Charles II first 'milled' crown	149
Thomas Simon's petition crown	149
Early 'milled' shilling of Charles II	149
The first issue turner of Charles II	149
New copper halfpenny	150
Charles II's 'St Patrick's Coinage' halfpenny	150
James II crown	150
'Gun money'	150
Sixty shilling piece of James II	150
The William and Mary crown	151
William III crown	151
The Scottish crown of Anne	151
George I silver crown	197
'Wood's Halfpenny'	197
'Young Head' George II five guineas	197
George II 'Young Head' crown	197
George II 'Old Head' crown. LIMA	197
The Irish halfpenny	198
'Voce Populi' token halfpenny	198

List of Illustrations

	page
George III gold guinea of 1761	198
George III 'Spade' guinea	198
Countermarked dollar of Charles III of Spain	198
Overstamped Spanish American 8 reals, Bank of England dollar	198
First crown of the 1816 recoinage	199
Token copper halfpenny of Coventry—Lady Godiva	199
Twopenny copper 'Cartwheel'	199
'Cronebane Halfpenny'	199
Silver crown of George IV, first type	199
Silver crown of George IV, second type	199
The 1826 shilling	200
Proof crown of William IV dated 1831	200
'Cumberland Jack', political counter	200
The 'Young Head' Victorian crown	200
The Gothic crown	200
Decimal currency pattern pieces	201
£5 piece, Una and the Lion	201
The Gothic florin	201
The four shilling 'Jubilee' piece (double florin)	201
The five shilling piece	202
The 'Old Head' crown	202
The 1890 sixpence	202
Victorian farthing	202
The Edward VII half crown	234
The Edward VII florin	234
Edward VII's 1902 crown	234
1910 pattern crown of George V	234
1911 florin	234
Trial half crown of George V	235
Lion shilling	235
Wreath crown of George V	235
The Jubilee crown	235
The 1933 penny	235
Edward VIII twelve-sided nickel brass threepence	236
George VI florin	236
Maundy fourpence	236
English shilling	236

List of Illustrations

	page
Scottish shilling	236
George VI nickel brass threepence	236
1937 George VI crown	236
1952 halfpenny	236
Cupro-nickel 1951 crown	236
Elizabeth II coronation crown	237
The 1954 florin	237
The nickel brass threepence	237
The 1960 crown	237
The Churchill crown	237
50 new pence	238
10 new pence	238
5 new pence	238
2 new pence	238
1 new penny	238
½ new penny	238
Armorican billon stater c 75-50 BC	265
Token silver five shilling piece	265
The Jersey silver token for eighteen pence	265
Token penny of 1813	265
The ⅓ shilling copper piece	265
The Liberation bronze penny of 1949	265
The Guernsey threepence	265
The Guernsey eight doubles	265
The Guernsey four doubles	265
Elizabeth II Guernsey ten shilling piece	265
The Sark Arms	265
The John Murrey penny	266
The 'Butcher's Halfpence'	266
The 1732 halfpenny of James Stanley, Earl of Derby	266
James Murray, Second Duke of Athol coin	266
Monarch's head coinage	266
A token coin, early and mid-nineteenth century	266
A token card of 1815	266
Bowstead's 2/6d card	266
Ramsey & Isle of Man Banknote	267
A Victorian 1839 penny	267

FOREWORD

What is the difference between a groat and a testoon, a guinea and a 'broad', or a Treasury and a Bank of England note? The answers to many questions of this nature will be found in these pages.

During the past two decades the hobby of coin collecting has achieved great popularity, particularly in the years leading up to decimalization. More recently there has been a growing interest in paper money.

Mr Josset has broken new ground with this study of money in Britain, for not only does he give a historical account of English coinage showing the relationship to it of the contemporary coinages of Scotland, Ireland and the smaller British islands, but he also discusses the 'tally' system of accountancy, the growth of banking institutions in the British Isles and the development of their banknotes. In doing so he has performed a service to those of us who have been inclined to separate coin and paper into watertight compartments. He has shown the relationship between all kinds of money and discusses some of the factors which have resulted in changes in our currency.

Even old hands at coin or note collecting will learn something from this book and newcomers to the hobby will discover the fascinations of the historical study of money, be it ancient or modern, metal or paper.

PETER SEABY

INTRODUCTION

> This royal throne of kings, this scepter'd isle,
> This earth of majesty, this seat of Mars,
> This other Eden, demi-paradise;
> This fortress built by nature for herself
> Against infection and the hand of war;
> This happy breed of men, this little world;
> This precious stone set in the silver sea,
> Which serves it in the office of a wall
> Or as a moat defensive to a house,
> Against the envy of less happier lands;
> This blessed plot, this earth, this realm, this England . . .
> —Shakespeare: *Richard II* (Act II Scene I)

This England, or in a wider context, this British Isles, is indeed a land rich in history, with which is interwoven a fascinating coinage, in use since before the Roman invasion and a paradise for the serious numismatist.

If we pause and glance briefly into past history it will be sufficient to give a vivid impression on how some outstanding events and even those of a comparatively minor nature have shaped our lives. Before the highly developed modern financial machinery of today, coins and perhaps at a later date paper money, were an all-important factor of public life governing the development of trade. Thomas Violet in 1651 wrote: 'Money is the public means to set a price upon all things between man and man, and experience has sufficiently proved in all ages that small money is so needful to the poorer sort that all nations have endeavoured to have it'.

The intensely interesting study of numismatics has been sadly neglected in the past though the few collector enthusiasts and a very small number of writers have kept the interest alive. Fortunately today there has been a great upsurge of public interest with a realisation of the great contribution that past issues of coins have made in uncovering obscure history. Robertson in his *Historical Disquisition on India* sums up past apathy, which, though intended for artistic pursuits generally, may accurately be applied to numismatology.

> It is a cruel mortification in searching for what is instructive in the history of past times, to find that the exploits of conquerors who have desolated the earth, and the freaks of tyrants who have rendered nations unhappy, are recorded with minute and often disgusting accuracy, while the discovery of useful arts and the progress of the most beneficial branches of commerce are passed over in silence, and suffered to sink into oblivion.

I
PRE-ROMAN AND ROMAN

British Tribal Money

The earliest Britons were a primitive people who lived by agriculture in small self-contained settlements, bartering their livestock and goods with their neighbours, and possibly using gold and silver as currency in the shape of rings, which we know as 'ring money'. Some of the larger rings may have been worn by chiefs as emblems of rank. For the purposes of exchange the commodity employed had to satisfy certain practical demands. It had to be conveniently divisible and portable, and its value and quality had to be consistent. One can imagine that ring money would meet the latter two requirements, with the added attraction of being decorative. There is evidence, however, that, at the same time, coining was practised by native chiefs, the coins being mainly imitations of those used in Gaul in the fourth century BC. These, in turn, were copies made by the native Belgic people of the gold stater of Philip of Macedon (*Fig 1*). Named after their prototype they are called 'Philippi'. Their introduction into Massilia (Marseilles), then a Greek colony, was the result of trading and also due to the journeying of Philip's son, Alexander the Great. The stater (*Fig 2*) itself originated in Lydia (now western Turkey). As early as 1100 BC bean-shaped lumps of electrum, a natural alloy of gold and silver, had been used in this area as a means of exchange. The stater, which appeared about 700 BC, followed a natural progression by now having simple and meaningful incuse designs. The Belgic invasion brought Belgic copies over to Britain.

    The coinage of a civilisation records both the progress and character of that civilisation. As Greece comprised a number of individual nation states, it needed a more sophisticated coinage for trade than a small country having to satisfy only internal requirements. Its coins also demonstrate the Greek consciousness of the need for beauty and delight in mythology. The Roman coins display a more utilitarian and political approach. The effect of these two influences is visible in the early money in Britain.

When Julius Caesar invaded Britain in 55 and 54 BC he inflicted a number of defeats on the combined tribes of the south-east, who were led by Cassivellaunus, King of the Catuvellauni tribe, which occupied an area to the north of the Thames and whose main town was Verulamium (St Albans). From these tribes Caesar exacted a yearly tribute. The large hoard of gold staters found at Narbury, Buckinghamshire, and known as the Whaddon Chase hoard (*Fig 3*), may have been this tribute stolen by robbers. In the winter of 54 BC Caesar mentioned the existence of a gold coinage and of dies being used, but this coinage may have consisted of Gaulish staters brought over about 75 BC in the first Belgic invasion.

Most of the documentary evidence about the early currencies of the British Isles is found in Caesar's *De Bello Gallico*, where iron rings and bars are referred to as money used in Britain. Bars of iron, similar to crudely fashioned sword-blades, have been found buried in ancient British camps of the first century BC. The most recent find, considered to be the most important Iron Age currency ever discovered, was in 1969 at Danbury Hill Fort, 3 miles from Stockbridge in Hampshire. There were twenty-one sword-shaped iron bars 2½ ft in length, which had been buried for over 2,000 years behind the inner ramparts of this Celtic fort.

In a second Belgic invasion the Atrebates and Regni tribes landed on the south coast in the vicinity of what is now Southampton, settling in a large area of Hampshire, Sussex, Berkshire and Surrey. These tribes also used gold staters and quarter staters as currency, many of them bearing the name of their King, Commius (35-20 BC), who had previously been sent as an envoy by Caesar from Gaul to assess the strength of the tribes before his invasions.

The earlier types of these gold staters were uninscribed, but later ones bore inscriptions after the Roman style, some with the name of Commius. Silver and bronze coins mainly copied the Roman types, popular coins being the Roman silver denarii (*Fig 4*), which

Pre-Roman and Roman

were circulated early in the Belgic occupation, augmenting the scanty supply of native coin; nevertheless the native tribes must have resorted to much barter to overcome currency shortages.

Tincommius (20 BC - 5 AD), who was one of Commius' sons and succeeded to part of his kingdom, struck silver as well as gold coins (*Fig 5*); these showed the same Roman influence, probably because he had fled earlier from his tribe and was believed to have aided the Emperor Augustus.

Verulamium (St Albans) was the main mint for supplying Tasciovanus (20 BC - 10 AD), king of the Catuvellauni, though several other mints were probably striking coins of gold, silver and bronze, one of these being the mint at Camulodunum (Colchester), on occasions the capital of the Trinovantes tribe. In the following reign Cunobelinus (10-40 AD), whom many will know better as Shakespeare's 'Cymbeline', had many coins struck by the Camulodunum mint. These were gold staters (*Fig 6*) and quarter staters, as well as silver and bronze coins, all of native design, though there were indications that coin designs were being more and more influenced by the Romans across the Channel. Possibly Cunobelinus employed Gaulish craftsmen. This would account for the excellent workmanship and the variety of attractive designs on his coins. Many of them display those weird beasts peculiar to Roman mythology: the centaur, the griffin and the winged horse Pegasus. Also Roman deities, the personifications of abstract virtues, are celebrated here. At the height of his power Cunobelinus was overlord of the Cantii tribe of Kent and later virtually all of south-east England. After the conquest by the Emperor Claudius, which began in 43 AD and soon over-ran the south-east, the coinage in general became more romanised and regular supplies of Roman coin circulated.

The coins of the Cantii (East Kent) were very like those of the Catuvellauni under Tasciovanus, but neither the Durotriges (Dorset, Wiltshire and east Hampshire) nor the Dobuni (Somerset, Gloucestershire and parts of Oxfordshire and Worcestershire) had any coinage worthy of comment. The Durotriges struck crude quarter staters and base silver and copper coins, while the Dobuni struck gold coins similar to those of the Atrebates and Regni, who had virtually merged to form a combined state radiating from the Solent.

Kent was the only part of Britain that Caesar considered to be civilised. The coins of the Brigantes (Yorkshire and Lincolnshire) were of crude workmanship; some were quite blank on the obverse side, probably because worn dies had been used. There was no bronze coinage and the gold was mostly debased. It is difficult to think that these coins were descended from the finely executed fourth-century philippus, but it shows how the non-Belgic tribes of Celtic origin had clung to the traditional Apollo and horse patterns.

It is known that Cartimandua, queen of the Brigantes, produced a small number of coins, but she is better known for turning out her husband Venutius, the warrior leader of her tribe, in favour of her standard-bearer Vellocatus, and handing over Caractacus, the son of Cunobelinus, to the Romans, after he had been defeated by them in North Wales and had fled to her for refuge. Caractacus was granted honourable retirement in Rome. Two of his coins only are known. The main design depicts an eagle seizing a snake. The Romans finally invaded the Brigantes in 71 AD and occupied their country after several years of fighting.

The Coritani (Leicestershire and Nottinghamshire), which dwelt just to the south of their more powerful neighbours the Brigantes, convey no information on their coins. Possibly they struck some of the unidentified uninscribed ones.

The Iceni (Norfolk, Suffolk and parts of Cambridgeshire) were of non-Belgic origin like their lesser neighbours, the Trinovantes (Essex and parts of Suffolk), but little was known of them until they submitted to Claudius soon after the invasion. He reported that they were a powerful tribe unbroken by war, following the pattern of non-Belgic tribes with their gold and silver coins, which were mostly uninscribed and crude (*Fig 7*). One inscribed coin is known, bearing the monogram ANTED, and providing an enigmatic link with the Dobuni (west of the Catuvellauni), whose coinage shares this feature. No evidence is available to explain this connection, though they may have united under a common leader to fight a common foe. The most famous Iceni ruler was Queen Boadicea, whose brave revolt resulted in defeat and death.

After the Claudian invasion Roman coinage gradually replaced

Pre-Roman and Roman

Celtic. The conquest is celebrated on the Claudian denarius, which depicts a triumphal arch inscribed with the island's name DE BRITANN. Septimius Severus had a denarius designed to the same effect, showing a winged Victory on the reverse.

The Roman Occupation

The Roman campaign continued further north after the subjugation of the Brigantes, and Agricola penetrated into Caledonia between 80 and 83 AD and finally defeated the Picts in a great battle and established a legionary fortress at Inchtuthil, where the rivers Tay and Isla unite. Agricola's fleet also sailed round the north of Scotland and established that Britain was a large island. Evidence of the advance to the north of Perth is found in a hoard of early gold staters that could hardly have been buried by the local tribes, as they did not use money at that period.

Scotland had been conquered but the troops necessary to hold it were withdrawn and eventually the Emperor Hadrian settled the northern frontier by building Hadrian's Wall from the Tyne to the Solway, which was completed about 127 AD. In 140-42 AD, however, the district north of Hadrian's Wall to the line of the Firths of Forth and Clyde was conquered, and the Antonine Wall, named after the Emperor Antonius Pius, was built—a rampart studded with forts stretching from sea to sea. The legions occupied the lowlands of Scotland until about 184 AD, when the Antonine Wall was overrun and they retreated to Hadrian's Wall, which was more or less the northern frontier of the Brigantes. There is little evidence to show that a currency was used north of the Wall at this time.

The Roman invasion of Britain drove many of the natives to Ireland, where other immigrants from Scandinavia and eastern Europe (descendants of the Menapii, Belgic and Chauci tribes) had already settled, but were continually skirmishing with the native tribes. Ireland remained permanently outside the rule of Rome, though Agricola was invited by an Irish provincial king to invade his country—probably for personal reasons. It is known, however, that a king of Ireland, Niall of the Nine Hostages (379-405), carried out raids on Britain towards the end of Roman occupation. Slave traders are mentioned by Bede as having visited the Irish coast as well as Britain as early as 679. These early contacts must have conveyed the knowledge that currencies existed in Britain and on the Continent, but there appears to have been no coinage except rings of gold and silver, which also served as ornaments among the chieftains of the tribes. The earliest coins which can be assigned to Ireland are those of the Hiberno-Norse princes, though it is claimed that ring money in graduated weights, representing different values, was in use before this period. From about 870 until 1177, when Henry II's son John was appointed Lord of Ireland, crude silver pennies were in use. Although the kings of the provinces of Dublin, Limerick and Waterford are believed to have struck coins, the only king we are reasonably sure of is Sihtric (989-1029), who struck them in Dublin (*Fig 8*).

The Romans, with their numerous emperors and still more numerous commemorative events, used to the full the art of advertising on their coins. Much abbreviation in the lettering was used on the obverses, in order that the full rank and titles of those who struck the coins could be included. The reverses are equally interesting, as they record victories and major events, together with the virtues of the respective emperors. The coin which presents an interesting link with today's coinage is the brass sestertius of Antonius Pius (138-61), the reverse of which represents Britannia seated, and symbolises the conquest of Britain as far north as the Clyde (*Fig 9*). The same device, slightly modified, is seen on the modern 50 pence piece.

During the early part of the Roman occupation British native coins continued to be used, but as these went out of circulation Roman coins at varying periods took their place. Roman currency differed from the native coinage, the highest denomination being a gold aureus (nearly the weight of a modern sovereign). The following is a list of some of the comparative values of Roman coins.

1 gold aureus = 25 silver denarii
1 half aureus (quinarius) gold = 12½ silver denarii
1 denarius = 4 brass sestertii
1 silver quinarius = 2 brass sestertii

Pre-Roman and Roman

    1 sestertius = 4 copper asses
    1 dupondi = 2 copper asses
    1 as = 2 copper semii = 4 copper quadrans

Throughout almost 400 years of Roman occupation the purchasing power of coins in Britain varied and the names of coins were sometimes transferred from one metal to another. At varying periods the quinarii were issued in all three metals—gold, silver and copper. At another period copper asses were also known as dupondii.

During the reign of Claudius 42 gold aurei and 84 silver denarii both equalled 1lb in weight, but in AD 63 (under Nero) these were increased to 45 and 96 respectively. Caracalla (211-17) introduced a silver coin called an antoninianus, with a value of two denarii, but it was not long before it became debased, with only a silver film covering the surface of base metal. At the same time the bronze denominations either ceased or were considerably curtailed.

In 286 Carausius seized power and as commander of the Roman fleet in British waters resisted and defeated a fleet sent against him by Rome. He became joint emperor in 287, his reign ending in 293, when he was murdered and succeeded by Allectus. Carausius, who came from the Menapians, a seafaring people from the Low Countries, did much in his short reign to improve the quality of the coinage. It is probable that the denarii he struck were from silver obtained from the rich deposits in Britain; alternatively, coins may have been restruck from previous issues. This issue was terminated in the reign of Allectus. Carausius is known to have established mints in London and Colchester, the latter possibly having been an earlier British mint; and as his realm included parts of Gaul it is believed that he struck coin there too, probably at Rouen. Diocletian, his co-emperor, introduced two new coins, the follis and the argenteus (*Fig 10*).

When Britain again became part of the Roman Empire under the reign of Constantine I, the Colchester mint was closed. Commemoration of this event resulted in the beautiful gold medallion equivalent in value to ten aurei. It portrays the emperor on the obverse and the conqueror entering the gates of London on the reverse. The legend reads 'Restorer of Eternal Light'. Constantine struck a number of bronze coins of unknown values throughout his reign.

The original Roman unit was a copper or bronze as, but this was superseded by the silver denarius, from which the 'd' of our modern penny was derived. This had ten times the purchasing power of the as and originally weighed 60 grains, but in later years weighed only 52½ grains. In comparison our modern sixpence weighs 43.6 grains.

Roman influence on our coinage is seen by the Latin word for a pound in weight of silver—*libra*—from which our £ sign is descended; and again in the solidus of Constantine I—the original coin from which our 's' for silver is derived—which weighed 24 carats and was of pure gold. The sole issue of the London mint was the follis, a bronze coin coated with silver. After Constantine's death in 337 the London mint closed down, causing urgently needed coins to be imported from Gaul. Two new coins were introduced in the mid-fourth century—the siliqua and the miliarense, both replacing the argenteus.

The size of the bronze coins again suffered a reduction at this time, a sign that the barbarians from central Europe were interrupting the supply of metal from Britain to Rome. An attempt to overcome the shortage of coins in Britain was made by producing crude bronze coins which are known as 'minimi' because of their smallness.

Metal shortages and the difficulty of keeping clear the trade routes to Britain indicated that the grip of Rome was loosening, a fact which was to become more apparent in the next century.

1 Obverse of a philippi, Philip of Macedon 359-36 BC
  Actual size of coin showing the traditional Apollo and horse pattern on reverse
2 'Bellovaci' gold stater c 130-80 BC imitating the Macedonian stater
3 Whaddon Chase type gold stater 45-20 BC. Spirited horse on reverse
4 Roman Empire silver denarius, Augustus 14 BC
5 Classical style stater, Tincommius 20 BC - 5 AD
6 Gold stater, Cunobelinus 10-40 AD (Shakespeare's Cymbeline)
7 An uninscribed Iceni silver stater, showing a boar and a horse on opposite sides
8 Silver penny, Sihtric III 989-1029—the first coin attributed with any certainty to an Irish ruler
9 Brass sestertius, Antoninus Pius 138-61 AD, the coin from which the Britannia of today originated

25

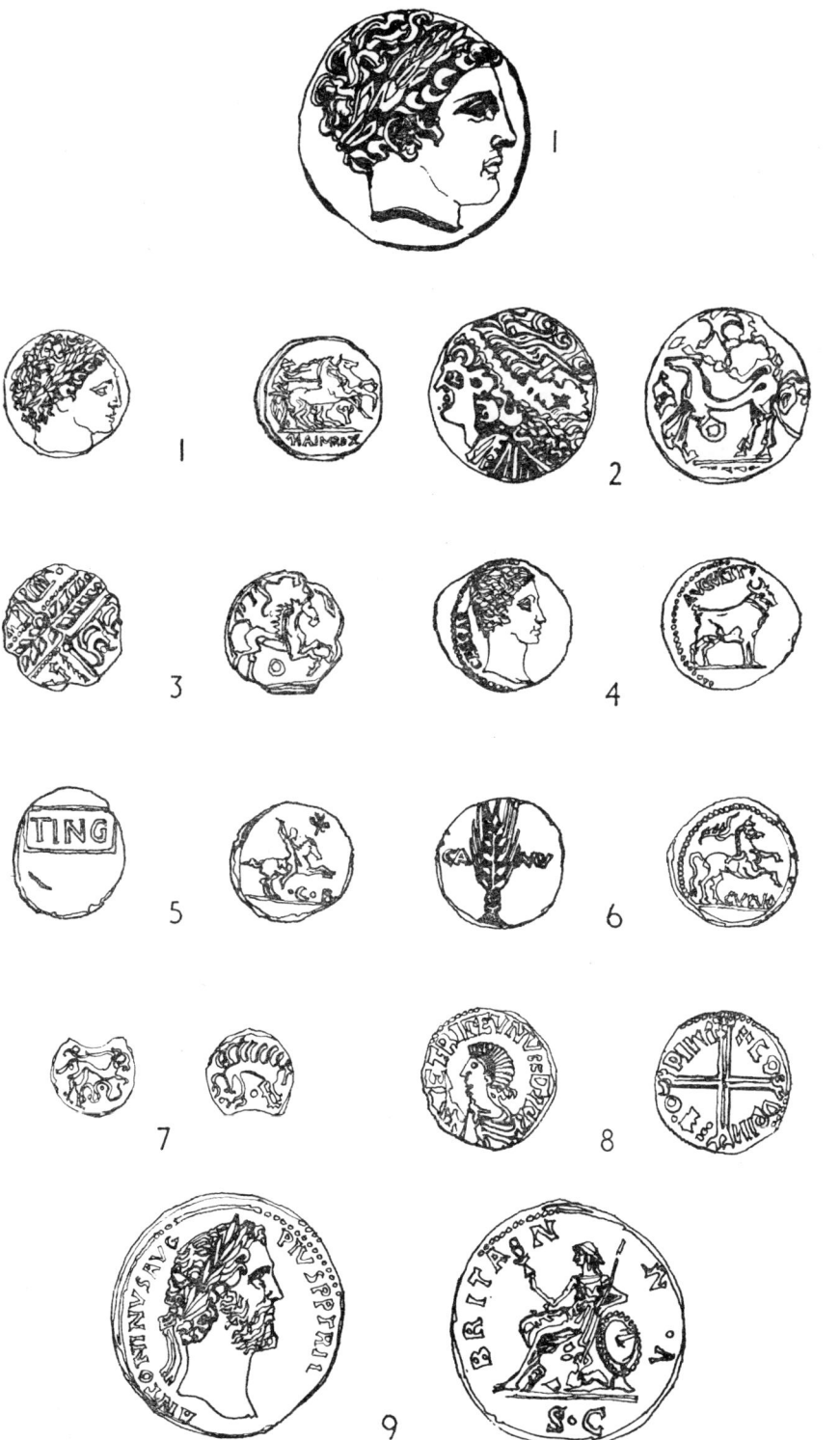

10 Roman Empire bronze follis, Diocletian 284-305. The mint mark is clearly visible (twice diameter of coin)

II
ANGLO-SAXONS AND DANES

The Roman forces in Britain had been slowly diminishing since 380, and had gradually taken the coinage with them. In 388 came the death of Magnus Maximus, the last of the Roman emperors to strike coins in Britain. By the early fifth century very little of the coinage was left. The mints in Gaul had ceased production and no evidence exists of the economic conditions inside Britain. One assumes that the inhabitants lived by barter among themselves and by a certain amount of barter overseas. Nevertheless, discoveries of a few isolated hoards of tiny bronze coins, which because of their size should surely have been called minimissimi, suggest that the use of metal money may have persisted to some extent.

Early Settlers

From the middle of the fifth century Angles, Saxons and Jutes began to occupy parts of eastern England. The first signs of reviving trade, however, appeared in the south-east, and gold coins called tremisses began to find their way there from the Merovingian kingdom in Gaul. About 600 a mint at Canterbury began producing coins which may be considered Anglo-Saxon; these coins are extremely rare. They were made of gold, weighed a little over 20 grains troy and were referred to in Anglo-Saxon documents as thrymsas; they remained in circulation until late in the eighth century. Although they bore legends, these are incomprehensible and primitive. They were replaced by silver coins called sceats (or sciattae), which circulated from the middle of the seventh century, and were approximately the same size and weight as the thrymsas; many later issues were made in copper, though initially they were silver, and it is here that we find the moneyer's name inscribed for the first time.

The first known coins of this period belong to Ecfrith, last of the powerful Northumbrian kings (670-85) of the seventh century. The lettering is in the Roman style, and only one of the three common types bears a legend and traces of the Runic alphabet of Scandinavian origin. The other two classified styles are the Frankish and the Native art style. Northumbrian sceats were not only struck for royalty but also in the name of leading ecclesiastics, particularly the Archbishops of York.

By the end of the eighth century the sceats gave way to silver pennies. The first silver penny came into existence under Heabert, King of Kent, c 765, and remained in use until the reign of Henry III in the middle of the thirteenth century. They weighed about 20 to 25 grains, according to the period. The idea of a coin bearing only a portrait and the mint name, on the obverse and reverse respectively, originated from Pepin, father of the Frankish ruler Charlemagne, though the name penny may have come from coins struck by King Penda of Mercia in the seventh century.

Offa and the Supremacy of Mercia

Offa, King of Mercia (757-96), was overlord of England. After he had imposed his rule on Kent after about 785, it seems that he used the mint at Canterbury to issue a particularly attractive series of portrait coins, probably influenced by the example of Charlemagne and trade with the Frankish empire. These coins were by far the most attractive of the earlier Saxon and Norman coins, if not of the whole coinage of England (*Fig 1*). Several coins bear the portrait in profile of Offa's wife Cynefrith. He traded with the caliphs of the East, and struck some copies of Arabian dinars, probably for the Arab traders. Unfortunately only one specimen is known to exist today, the dinar of Caliph Al-Mansur of Bagdad. 'Offa Rex' is engraved upside down in relation to the Arabic lettering (*Fig 2*).

There seems little doubt that the mint at Canterbury was striking coins for Offa as overlord, as well as for kings of Kent and archbishops of Canterbury. A second mint in East Anglia is believed to have been established by Offa's successor Coenwulf (796-822), where he struck pennies (*Fig 3*). Though equally varied in types these coins show a marked fall in standard, a state of affairs which continued as the power of Mercia diminished.

The supremacy of Mercia, with Kent as a puppet state, came to an end in 825 when the King of Wessex, Ecgberht (802-38), defeated the Mercians at the Battle of Ellendun, annexing Kent and at the same time driving out King Baldred (807-25) who was Kent's last king. Most of the coins of the Mercian King Wiglaf (828-39)— Mercia now being a puppet state of Wessex—closely resembled the previous coins of King Ecgberht in bearing a head without a bust. Wiglaf's earlier coins were struck by the Canterbury mint but the later ones were struck in London. Ecgberht's successor Aethelwulf struck coins at Winchester as well as Canterbury.

The reduction of the power of Mercia coincided with the increase in the frequency of raids by the Danes, until in 866 they culminated in an invasion, when the kingdom of Northumbria was occupied, and the issues of crude copper and base silver coins by the Northumbrian kings ceased.

Expansion in Wessex meant that mints were established at Gloucester, London, Oxford and Exeter, though not all mint marks were shown. Half and third pennies were struck; pennies fell into two categories, those with portraits and those without.

Alfred and the Kings of Wessex

The first pennies struck by Alfred (871-900), youngest son of Aethelwulf, had a poorly executed bust within a circle of beads with the moneyer's name in three lines on the reverse, probably issued before 874 (*Fig 4*). The second issue had an equally poor bust with the circle omitted, the reverse showing a diamond shape with crosses at each corner. The date of these is considered to be 874 or 875. There is a third issue of which only one coin is known. This has a London monogram design, the obverse showing two seated emperors with Victory above them. While there is a possibility that this was an issue of Ceolwulf II or Halfdan, the Danish leader, from whom Alfred was constantly under attack, its quality is probably superior to anything that the Danes produced. Further confirmation of this is the lettering REX ANGLORUM, the first statement of this kind to be found on a coin.

Throughout their sojourn in Britain most of the Danish kings struck coins approximate in size and quality to the Anglo-Saxon silver penny; nevertheless they produced nothing of distinction except the coins of Halfdan, which are regarded by some as copies of Alfred's originals.

Edward the Elder (900-25) succeeded Alfred and produced a limited number of artistic coins worthy of comment. Though lacking in finish and hardly approaching Offa's, they had originality, and the flower designs on them showed artistry, ingenuity and grace. Unfortunately very few of them have been found.

At a period when communications and transport were uncertain and hazardous, it was convenient, if not essential, for the manufacture of money to be carried on in a number of centres throughout the country, and when Aethelstan (925-39) came to the throne, twenty-eight mints were in existence. He became overlord of Anglo-Saxons and Danes alike, and on his coins called himself not only REX but also REX TOTIS BRITANNIAR.

Aethelstan is the first king who may be given credit for reforming the law governing our coinage. He ordained in 928 that a single coin only was to be current and that moneyers attempting forgery should be punished by the loss of a hand, a provision which suggests that the evil was widespread. The number of moneyers for each mint was fixed: London was allowed eight, Canterbury seven, Winchester six, Rochester three, a few more important mints two, and the smallest one each. The mints of the archbishops continued to function, but the clergy themselves were now denied the privilege of placing their names on the coinage. The prerogative was confined to royalty. Moneyers were usually men of some social standing, personally responsible to the king for the running of the mint. They lived rent free, and had to obtain their dies from the official goldsmith in London whenever the coinage changed.

Of the coins of Aethelstan and of the kings who succeeded him,

Anglo-Saxons and Danes

Edmund (939-46), Edred (946-55), Edwig (955-9) and Edgar (959-75), only a few scarce examples in each reign bear portraits, while the first known portrait coins struck in larger numbers are those of Edward the Martyr (975-9), murdered at the age of 17. From that time to the present day almost all silver coins have borne an image of the king's head. From Edward the Elder down to Edward the Martyr there were efforts to improve the design of coins, but attempts to produce portraits were seldom successful.

Seventy mints were in operation to produce the enormous output in coinage of the next reign, Aethelred II (979-1016), and for the first time the king appears holding the sceptre (Fig 5). The amount of money in circulation showed how much more wealth the country had accumulated, but the hoards of British coins found in Denmark and Scandinavia generally suggest that much of this currency was used in an attempt to buy off the Danish raiders, who were again a constant menace (Fig 6).

Danish Conquest

The massacre of the Danish settlers in 1002 merely aggravated the warfare between Anglo-Saxons and Danes, and in 1003-6 King Sweyn of Denmark landed an army and ravaged the country. The English king, Edmund Ironside, continued the fight against Sweyn's son Canute. At the Treaty of Alney (1016) they agreed to divide England, Edmund ruling the land south of the Thames and Canute the rest, but Edmund died in the same year and Canute was accepted as king by the whole country. Neither Sweyn nor Edmund issued coins, but Canute seems to have issued a number of types, including a crowned portrait, changing his dies frequently. Two other main types show him wearing a helmet and a diadem, the last issue being the jewelled cross type. Harthacnut should have succeeded his father Canute, but though he became king of the Danish Empire his half-brother Harold I (1035-40) seized the English throne in spite of two years' opposition from the south, who favoured the elder son.

On his half-brother's death in 1040 Harthacnut became king, but lived for only another two years. On his death the Saxon line was restored when the throne was given to Aethelred's son Edward the Confessor (1042-66). None of these kings produced any interesting coins, as Canute, Harold and Harthacnut all copied Aethelred's, though there was an increase in the number of mints. Edward struck numerous coins, and increased the number of mints working for him to seventy. For the first time the full-face portrait was seen. One coin worthy of comment was the penny, showing the king seated on the throne with the orb and sceptre. This coin we know as the 'sovereign' type, as it is believed to have been inspired by the Roman gold solidus (*Fig 7*). On Edward's death, his brother-in-law the Earl of Wessex, Harold Godwinson, became king as Harold II, and during his short reign an appreciable number of coins were struck as there were then still many mints in existence (*Fig 8*). His death in 1066 at the Battle of Hastings, when the English were defeated by William I, brought an end to the Saxon rule. On Christmas Day 1066, William was crowned in London.

Mints and Minting

At one time during this period there were as many as seventy-three mints. This may be attributed partly to the revenue the king derived from them. Each mint paid fees for its dies to the central mint in London, and fairly frequent changes in the dies made this a substantial source of income.

An English mint of this period was usually a workshop adjoining a furnace with pots to contain the molten metal, which was poured out on a slab for cooling and then beaten out on an anvil to the correct thickness before being cut up into suitably sized circular blanks. These blanks were then placed on the lower die, which was fixed to a solid wooden block and secured so that it could not be driven in further; the lower die contained the obverse pattern of the coin and was known as a pile, standard or staple. The die containing the reverse side of the coin was contained in the end of a puncheon or trussel, which could be easily handled by the operator. This fitted on the lower die, on which a metal blank was placed, before the puncheon was struck several times with a hammer to

Page 33 (*above*) Bars of iron—Iron Age currency (British) found at Danbury Hill Fort excavations near Stockbridge, Hampshire, 1969; (*below*) early coining tools—a fourteenth-century pile and trussel

Page 34 The Master of a sixteenth-century mint, seen using a pile and trussel

obtain a clear impression from both pile and puncheon. It was usual to make two puncheon dies to one pile, because of the greater wear on the former from the additional shock of the hammer blows. For the same reason the more important obverse side, where the design of the head required more skill, was on the pile.

In those early days it was the moneyer who struck the coins, showing his name as an acknowledgment of his responsibility for the impression, quality and correct weight of the coin. Engraving was not attempted in the way dies are made today, but the pattern was built up by different sized punch holes and gauges. One can only marvel that sufficient furnace heat was obtained, and that the slow and arduous methods employed were able to produce the required number of coins.

1 Silver pennies of Offa 759-96. The first real attempt at portraiture. (Three obverses and one reverse)
2 The unique dinar of Offa, demonstrating eastern influence
3 Silver penny, Coenwulf 796-822. Canterbury

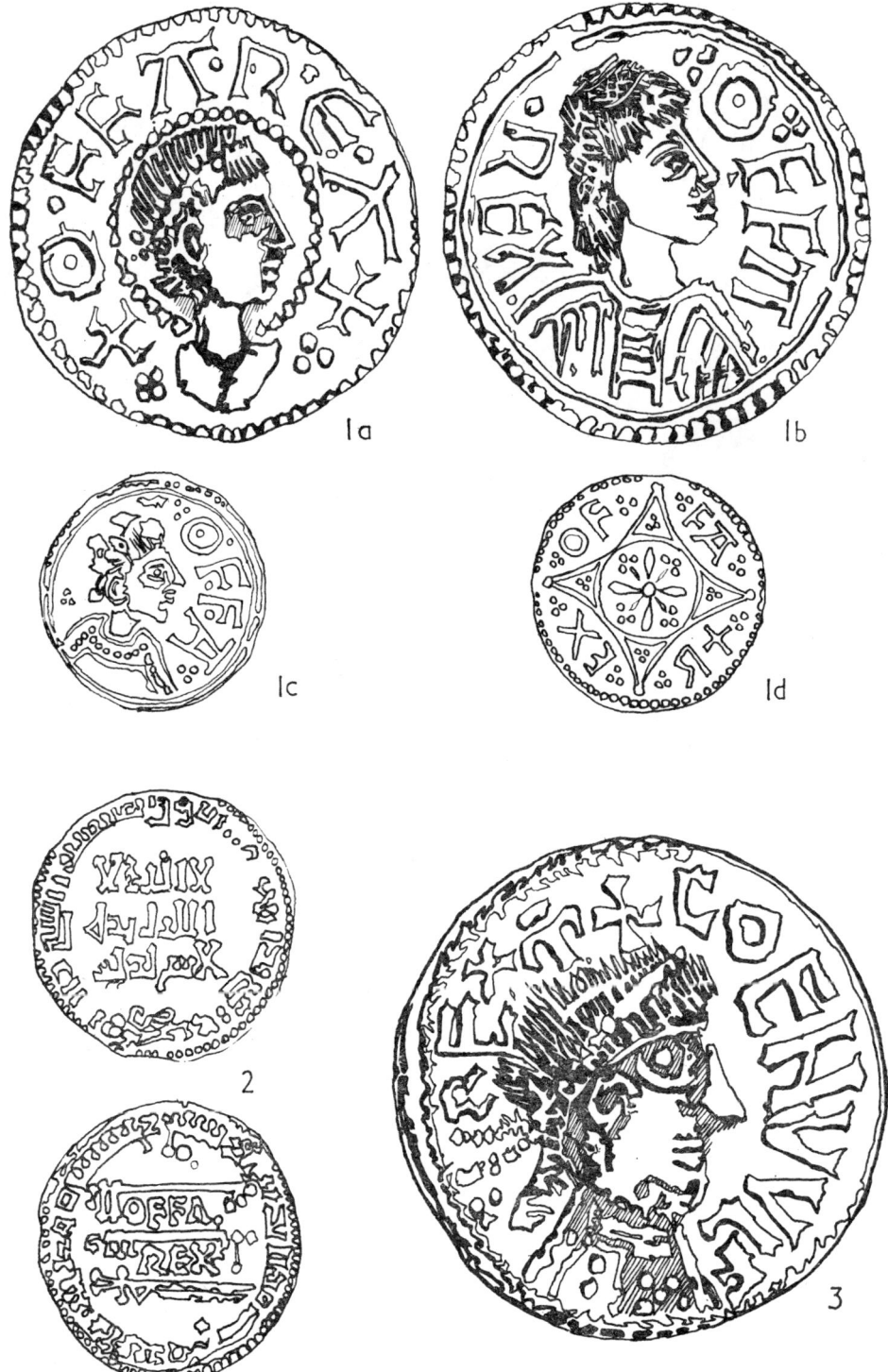

4 Silver penny, Alfred the Great 871-900, showing the London monogram and moneyer's name
5 Silver penny. Aethelred II 979-1016. Hand giving benediction (reverse)
6 Silver penny with the symbolic sacrificial lamb and dove, commemorating a thousand years of Christianity. 'Agnus Dei'
7 Silver penny, Edward the Confessor 1042-66
8 Silver penny of Harold II's short reign

III
NORMAN RULE

Norman Establishment

After the Norman conquest, William I (1066-87) did not attempt to replace the Anglo-Saxon moneyers, probably because English coinage had such a good reputation in Normandy and elsewhere on the Continent that moneyers from abroad could hardly have improved it. William collected his revenue from the mints in the same way as the late Anglo-Saxon kings: the moneyer paid 20s to the king's dues for a die whenever it was changed, and frequent die-changing meant a good portion of the profits being diverted to the king. The moneyer had also to pay the graver for the die. In 1373 there is a record of the graver charging 7s a dozen for his dies.

A common moneyer's trick was to retain the old die for economy, and use it in conjunction with a new die. In this way 'mules' were struck, having the obverse of one period with the reverse of another. Today they often give us great assistance in classifying types.

When the Normans came to England they found that the silver penny—a much thinner coin than the Roman denarius—weighed $22\frac{1}{2}$ grains, a 240th part of the accepted Tower pound (ie 5,400 grains). It remained this weight for many years, for at the time of the early Plantagenets it was still the same, being about the size of a modern sixpence, but very much thinner.

Both William I (*Figs 1 and* 2) and William II retained the silver penny as the sole coinage, the former having eight different issues and the latter five. The eight types of William I penny are as follows: 'Profile Left', 'Bonnet', 'Canopy', 'Two Sceptres', 'Two Stars', 'Sword', 'Profile Right' and 'Pax'. It is of interest to note that of these eight, six show a full-face portrait. The name William is lettered with the Saxon P appearing as PILLEM REX or PILLELM

REX. There is a general distinction to be made between the coins of the two reigns in that those of William Rufus are, in general, technically inferior, marking a decline which was to reach its nadir in the times of Henry I, and lacking originality of any sort.

The known seventy-three mints of Edward the Confessor had gradually shrunk to fifty-seven, but William I had opened another ten during his reign and Rufus added another, making sixty-eight at the time of his death in 1100. William Rufus ended an inglorious reign by dying a dramatic death in the New Forest, being mortally wounded by an arrow while hunting (*Fig 3*).

As the quality of the striking and the metals was poor, forgeries continued to be a problem. Moneyers, in spite of punishment that was brutal by modern standards, resorted to numerous tricks in evading detection. Dies were altered to remove the lettering on the reverse and attempts to change a moneyer's name have even been traced. In 1125 forgery reached such a pitch that Henry I asked the Bishop of Durham to adopt drastic measures to combat it. All the moneyers were thereupon summoned to Winchester and found guilty, and the savage sentence of mutilation, ie cutting off the right hand, is said to have been passed on them. One report, however, states that only ninety-four of them suffered this treatment.

The coins of Henry I's reign (1100-35) have perhaps more originality than those of the Williams, numbering fifteen different types in all (*Figs 4 and 5*). One unique ½d exists—a denomination that was not adopted until Edward I's reign. Contemporary records suggest that control over coin output slackened, a fact which is supported by the number of base coins circulated. Nicks have been observed on some of the coins—no doubt caused by traders testing them for baseness. The public refused to accept the marked coins, which often had the appearance of being cracked, so an official order was given to the mints to nick all coins, producing the absurdity of mints defacing their own coins even before issuing them (*Fig 6*).

Wood Tally System

Henry I was the first king to introduce the wood tally system.

The king's treasurers issued them as receipts for payment made to the king or his officials, and they became known as exchequer tallies. Old records show that by the middle of the twelfth century there was an organised and well understood system of tally cutting and distribution at the Exchequer; as a means of exchange the tally was very adaptable, light in weight, small in size and difficult to use fraudulently. The tally stick or rod was four-sided, usually made of hazelwood; early types were from 6 to 9in long and up to 1in thick. An early twelfth century type is described as follows:

> The accepted length of an early tally was from the tip of the index finger to the tip of the extended thumb, and at one end it was pierced with a small hole. Before it was issued by the Exchequer it was cut lengthways into two parts, the cut running through top and bottom for about two-thirds to three-quarters of the total length. At the end opposite to the small hole a complete cut across was made at an approximate angle of 45deg; another cut at the same angle, parallel to this end cut, was made to meet the end of the cut running down the centre until it divided the tally into two pieces. The larger of these was known as the 'stock' and the smaller part was called the 'foil'. Before being issued, an identical cut on both 'foil' and 'stock' was made at the Exchequer to record the amount of the transaction. The 'stock' was then handed over as a form of receipt for the money paid.

The great advantage of the tally system, from the Exchequer's point of view, was that they could cancel out a creditor or debtor to themselves by transferring the transaction, an arrangement which was legally permitted. An example of this is as follows: Alwine owed Winlf £5 and Winlf owed Baldwin £5; Winlf took an iou from Alwine and gave it to Baldwin, who did not hand it to Alwine until he was paid. When the Exchequer is substituted for Winlf it is easy to understand how the unfortunate Baldwin could be made to collect a government debt. From this it can be seen that the tally, which may be considered a receipt, was frequently used as a type of cheque payable to bearer. It also enabled the bulk of the Exchequer business to be transacted without using money.

There is an interesting record about a certain William Trente, a butler of Edward I, who was greatly in need of money. He was given a tally representing part of a large sum owed to the Exchequer by the citizens of London, from whom the butler was to obtain payment before handing over the tally. The citizens were notified that part of their debt had been transferred to the king's butler.

Forgeries were made difficult by the retained foil, which was matched when the tally was returned—usually by the sheriffs, who collected them for taxes due to the king. One recorded instance of forgery, however, occurred in 1297 when William de Boochose was entrusted by the sheriffs with 60s in cash and a tally recording 5 marks (an unspecified amount which had already been paid to the Exchequer). He pocketed the cash and added the equivalent notches for 60s to the tally; but his dishonesty was discovered and he was sentenced to prison for a year and a day.

On the face and back of each tally, transverse notches of varying size and type were cut, each representing a fixed amount of money. Writing, too, on both vertical sides helped the Exchequer in identifying each transaction as well as to distinguish the tally face from the back. The larger amounts were always cut on the top of the tally while smaller amounts of 1s or 1d were to be found cut underneath. The width of the cut decided its value. An old record gives the following measurements and their equivalent in money:

The thickness of a hand	£1,000
The breadth of a thumb	£100
The width of a little finger	£20
The thickness of a ripe grain of barley	£1
Two narrow converging notches	1s
A single cut with no wood removed (obliquely cut)	1d
A single cut with no wood removed, but on upper side centrally placed (straight cut)	'gold penny'

Unfortunately the value of the 'gold penny' is not given. We must therefore assume that this is the gold florin introduced from Florence in 1257. Such coins were fractionally heavier than our current sixpence and had a value of 20d.

It is regrettable that no precise description exists on the production of tallies, but the lack of uniformity and probable secrecy on the part of the Exchequer has caused the writers on this subject to be vague. It is surprising how few 'foils' have been found compared to the number of 'stocks'. Presumably when the two halves had been matched the Exchequer destroyed the 'foils' but retained the

Norman Rule

'stocks' for future record. One cannot help wondering what sort of filing cabinet would be needed if tallies were in use today!

The origin of the English 'tally' or the French 'taille' is sometimes given as a derivation of the verb 'tailler' (to cut). This is only partially correct. 'Tailler' is from the Latin 'taliare', meaning to cut.

Private tallies were also known to circulate. These were popularised by the sheriffs who collected small sums for the Exchequer, giving the debtor a tally which would clear him of the debt. There is also evidence of private tallies being issued by wealthy landowners, who probably issued them in payment for services rendered. These would have circulated in a very limited area.

Examples of later tallies vary considerably in size, some being as long as 4ft. The one unsplit tally still in existence (ie with no detached foil) is a faggot cutter's tally on which twenty 1s shaped notches are cut. These are narrow converging cuts. There are several other tallies, which were used as payment to the hop-pickers in the Kent hopfields, and probably date from the eighteenth century.

During Henry I's reign twelve mints were closed and two were opened. One of the latter was the border mint of Carlisle, which struck coins at various periods for England and Scotland. The coins struck for the King of Scotland, David I, were the first Scottish coins to be used. The moneyer who controlled this mint was named Erebald; he was the head of a wealthy family who leased the Cumberland mines in which the silver ore was worked for the mint.

Henry I's daughter Matilda, designated as heir on his death, was not acceptable to many of the barons, who were biased against a sovereign queen, so William I's grandson Stephen (1135-54) was invited to be king (*Fig 7*). Matilda's supporters—the Angevins—staged a revolt in 1139 with the aid of King David of Scotland (1124-53), and civil war continued intermittently for the remainder of Stephen's reign (*Fig 8*).

The Carlisle mint struck coins for both Stephen and David at different times; but many of the provincial mints appear to have lost contact with the central control because of the civil war, and used their own resources for making dies and coining money. This would explain the scarcity and poor quality of many of the coins in Stephen's reign. Not only were most of the legends illegible, but some were quite incomprehensible. In one instance, in place of the usual names STEFNI, STEIFNE, STEFN, STEIFNEI, STEIN, occurs the name PERERIC! Perhaps it was an alias.

It was natural that David should copy the English coinage, as he had spent his early life at the English court; his sister had married Henry I, he had married a widow of one of the English barons, and he had no previous Scottish coinage on which to base his own. He struck just one denomination—the silver penny or sterling—which was the same as the English in weight and fineness.

In 1141 Stephen was captured by the Angevins and Matilda was crowned queen at Winchester, but Stephen was released shortly afterwards. Matilda eventually abandoned her claim to the throne in 1142 in favour of her son Henry, then Duke of Anjou and Normandy, but not before coins had been struck in her name and in that of her son. The most common of the three types issued by Stephen was the Watford type of 1141. The second and third issues were struck in the east and west of England, respectively, the one at a time when fortune favoured him, the other after the death of Eustace his son which, combined with defeat, rendered Stephen's cause futile. Having no heir, Stephen made peace in the Treaty of Wallingford in 1153, accepting Matilda's son Henry of Anjou as heir. Stephen survived only one year after this treaty.

Of particular interest here is the York penny, thought to have been struck during Stephen's captivity. Two upright figures support a tall central sceptre. Seaby's classify this as the 'double figure type'.

Many of the barons during this disorderly reign set up mints in their own castles and struck their own coins. One such showed the unconventional but decorative armed figure of Eustace Fitzjohn, a staunch adversary of Stephen (*Fig 9*). In many cases where barons took it upon themselves to make their own money, the moneyers took the natural precaution of omitting any incriminating evidence that might be held against them by the opposite side.

1 The 'Pax' type silver penny of William the Conqueror
2 The 'Two Star' type silver penny of William the Conqueror
3 Silver penny, William II 1087-1100 (mule). Crowned bust facing with sword and cross within quadrilobe (reverse)
4 Silver penny. Henry I 1100-35. Example of a mule
5 Silver penny of Henry I with crowned bust and sceptre
6 Another example of Henry I 'sceptre' type silver penny
7 Silver penny, Stephen 1135-54. Sceptred crowned bust facing right. Moline type cross reverse
8 The silver penny of Stephen and Matilda, struck by the York mint (twice diameter of coin)
9 Silver penny, Baron Eustace Fitzjohn. Armoured figure standing (obverse)

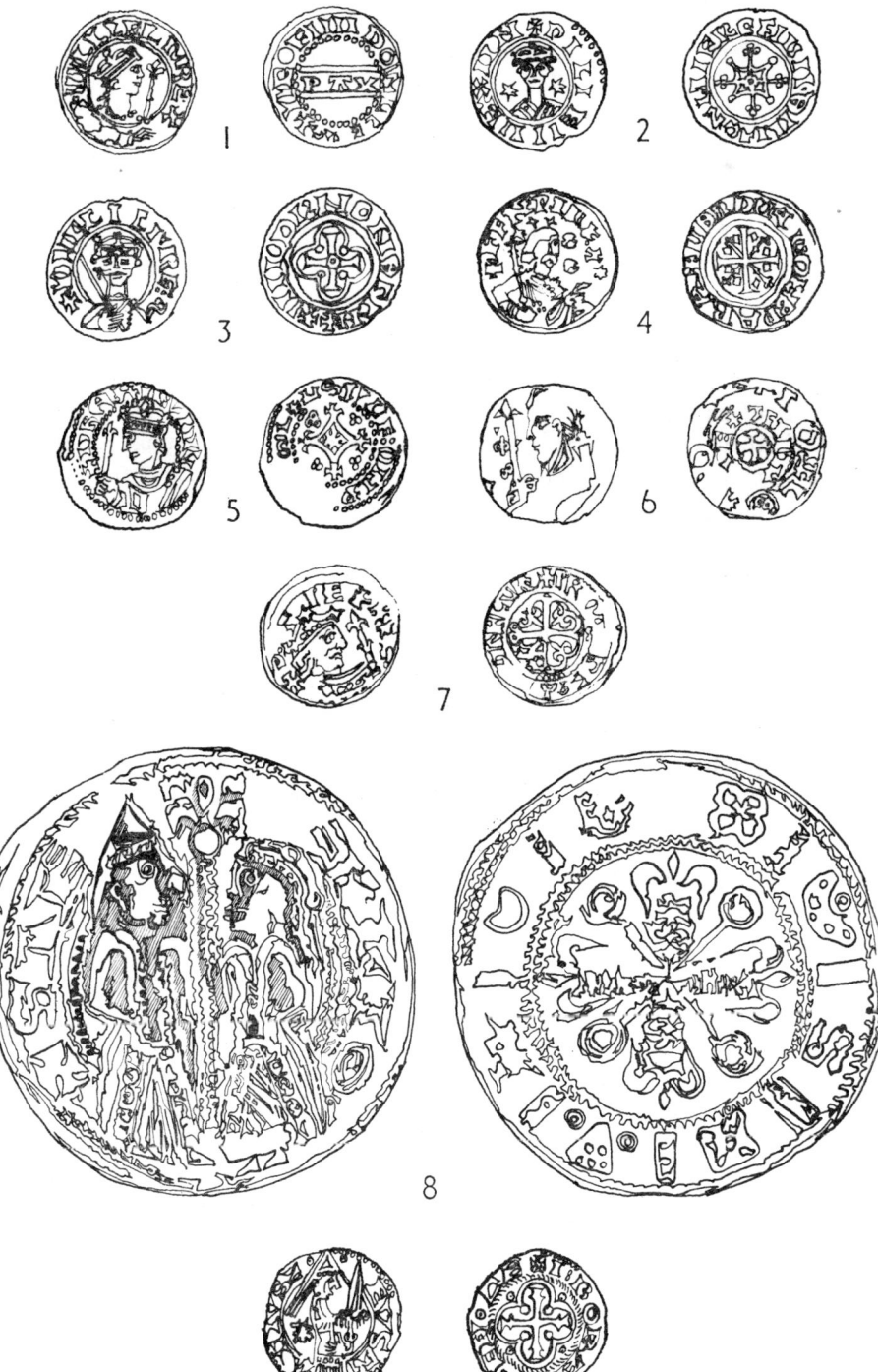

IV
THE PLANTAGENETS

On the death of Stephen in 1154, Henry of Anjou became Henry II of England (1154-89). He struck his first coins in 1158, and though they were even more unattractive and crude than those of the previous reign, they were used until 1180 (*Fig 1*). They are commonly referred to as the 'Tealby' type since the discovery in the nineteenth century of 5,700 such coins in the village of Tealby in Lincolnshire. With this issue came an order that the coinage was the 'sole currency' of the realm, meaning that the numerous types struck in the previous reigns would not be continued. This caused a big reduction in mints (to thirty) with a considerable loss in revenue to the king; but he must have recouped himself in some other way, probably by reducing the number of moneyers and collecting the profits himself. There is some evidence of this in the fact that a number of moneyers left the country about that time.

Ireland under the English

In Ireland, Richard Strongbow, Earl of Pembroke, seized an opportunity of assisting a deposed provincial king of Leinster by landing at Waterford in 1169, defeating the Irish, and becoming master of Leinster himself. King Henry then decided to land a strong army in Ireland with the declared intention of assisting Strongbow, who had wisely done homage for Leinster, but really fearing the creation of a second Norman state under leaders who were of Norman extraction. Henry was acclaimed king in Dublin and some Irish kings and bishops paid homage to him there. His younger son John was ap-

The Plantagenets

pointed Lord of Ireland (1177-99), thus uniting Ireland to the English crown. To Henry must be given the credit of being the first king to establish a civil government.

When John de Courcy, self-styled 'Lord of Ulster', was accepted by Henry in 1185, he struck halfpennies and farthings (Patrick farthings) locally. By 1189 he was removed from his office, but was allowed to return to his earldom until, in 1204 he finally left Ireland.

Following this period there were circulating in Ireland some interesting silver coins which we know as Bracteate coins. These were unofficial coins struck by native princes of the late eleventh or early twelfth centuries, copying the reverses of coins of the English kings Harold I, William I and Henry I; they were struck on one side only, and were very thin, weighing only 7 to 10 grains.

John, in his capacity as Lord of Ireland, struck halfpennies and farthings, the former bearing a profile portrait and the latter a portrait said to be that of John the Baptist; the farthing was the first round coin of this denomination to be produced. Both were struck at Waterford, Dublin and Limerick.

Henry II and Richard I

After 1180, when a new improved coinage known as the Short Cross coinage was introduced, the English mints were reduced further to eleven. It was the practice—originally adopted by Edward the Confessor—to cut coins in halves and quarters when money of lesser value was required, the half being a halfpenny and the quarter being a farthing. The word farthing means a fourth part, and comes from the Anglo-Saxon word *feorthing*. The cross on the reverse, with deep voiding running along the centre, enabled the coins to be divided evenly when required. Eleven mints produced these pennies, which were designed by Philip Aimery, a goldsmith from Anjou. Those actually coined by the designer are of a good standard and may be recognised by their inscription FIL AIMER OM LUND. Following his departure the standard declined noticeably.

During the next four reigns the short cross coinage continued in the name of HENRICUS; the type and inscription remained unaltered. One could make an allowance, perhaps, in the case of Richard, who, in all his ten years of kingship, passed but nine months in England itself.

Henry II, by his marriage to Eleanor, Duchess of Aquitaine, acquired the provinces of Aquitaine and Poitou, to which other provinces were added later. Both Henry and his wife struck deniers in French towns. This coinage was the beginning of the Anglo-Gallic coinage which was to continue, if in name only, until the reign of William and Mary.

Richard I's reign (1189-99) had no effect on the English coinage except that the number of moneyers was reduced from about sixty to thirty, though the same number of mints were working (*Fig 2*). This reduction tends to confirm the belief that the authority of the moneyers had been shifted to a central control. The coins were identical with those of the previous reign. The king was absent most of the time in the Holy Land, fighting a crusade, and in his French provinces, where he struck deniers (equivalent to the English penny) and half deniers in Aquitaine and deniers in Poitou and Normandy (*Fig 3*). The treatment of these coins was heavy handed.

Scotland and Sterling

In Scotland, David's grandsons, Malcolm IV (1153-65) and William the Lion (1165-1214), both hoped to join Northumbria to the Scottish crown. Unfortunately for William he was captured by Henry II in 1174 while assisting English rebels against the English king, which ended his aspirations for the time. But in the same year William was released by the Treaty of Falaise, on condition that he swore allegiance to the English crown—an agreement from which William was released by the next English monarch, Richard I, who received payment in return. Both Malcolm and William continued to strike pennies, or sterlings as they were called, which were similar to those of David, though the effigy of the former is full-faced whereas that of the latter is in profile.

The word sterling (from the £ sterling) appears during the Norman period and is probably an abbreviation of Easterling—the name of a body of merchants from eastern Europe. The coins with which they were associated became known as 'Esterlins' or 'Easterlings', which later became 'sterlings'.

Some of the legends on William's coins have peculiarities and others show a short double cross in place of the earlier single cross. On some of the obverses is the legend LE REI WILLAME (or WILLAM), revealing the probable presence of French coiners. There were three issues, with Roxburgh mint issuing some of the first two and all the last issue, while Edinburgh and Perth produced some of the first two issues. There is also a rarity struck by the Berwick mint.

John and Henry III

When John became King of England in 1199, a coinage similar to that of his father, Henry II, was continued, as in his brother's reign, but it was of even cruder workmanship (*Fig 4*). One may suppose that John retained the coinage for economic reasons and because it was accepted as popular and reliable by Continental traders, who had become accustomed to it as an established part of good trade relations from the time of Henry. It did not matter that the portrait it bore looked more like a ferocious halfwit than a king. Ultimately an inquiry into the methods of working in the mints resulted in a new and much improved coinage, with the establishment of four new mints and the appointment of fifty additional moneyers. Pennies of this issue were well executed. In 1204 new dies for the Irish coinage were produced in pennies, halfpennies and farthings and a new issue was made available in Ireland.

The early coins of Henry III were very similar to those of his father John, being still short cross, but they were altered slightly around 1218 to 1223, and the number of mints was reduced to six, under the control of William Marshall. With each mint was an exchange office whose duty was to purchase the necessary bullion and to distribute the coin to the public throughout the district. The custodian of the exchange was responsible to the king for the weight and standard of the coins and the true imprint on them. The moneyers of the mint were men of some authority who lived rent-free: Henry III was known to have given three of these appointments to his surgeon, goldsmith and tailor. Their incomes came from the profits to be got from issuing the coins, after paying the king's due and deducting labour costs.

The prevalence of clipping brought to an end the short cross coinage. This practice of clipping pieces of metal off the edge of a hammered coin was pursued by profiteers in order to collect small portions of metal. A new issue, known as the Long Cross coinage because of the long cross on the reverse, designed as a deterrent to clipping, was circulated in 1247 (*Fig 5*).

The first gold coins since the Norman kings came to the throne were produced in 1257. Although there were very few, each was of pure gold, 24 carats fine, well designed and well struck. The value of each was 20d, giving a gold ratio of ten to one with silver, a value which lasted until 1265, when the equivalent was altered to 24d. Undoubtedly this coin owed its existence to the great popularity of a Continental gold coin which was struck at Florence five years earlier and named a florin. Its prototype may have been the gold bezant of Constantinople, which bore the image of Christ. Henry III appears to have used this design, substituting himself for the Saviour, seated on an ornamental throne. This is the only gold penny of the English coinage, and there are only a few examples which exist today (*Fig 6*).

In Ireland, Henry III issued no coins before 1248. Dies of a new type were sent to the Dublin and Canterbury mints and in 1251 pennies were circulating; the profit, however, from those struck in Ireland was used to pay the large and frequent subsidies exacted by the Pope, Innocent IV. Under Henry a central government in Dublin was steadily built up and some attempt made to spread English law.

It is probable that during this reign the number of 240 pennies to a £ was fixed. The pound sterling was once an actual pound weight in silver, with 240 pennies each weighing one pennyweight. There are records showing that in Henry III's reign there were 243 pennies to a Mint pound, but calculation must have been difficult and the more convenient figure of 240 pennies to the £ came to be used.

Page 51 (*above*) A goldsmith's receipt—the goldsmith gave a receipt for money deposited which took the form of a 'promise to pay on demand', the forerunner of the modern banknote. This example, dated 1684, is the earliest known specimen still in existence; (*below*) a goldsmith's note, drawn by the Earl of Aran, dated 1687

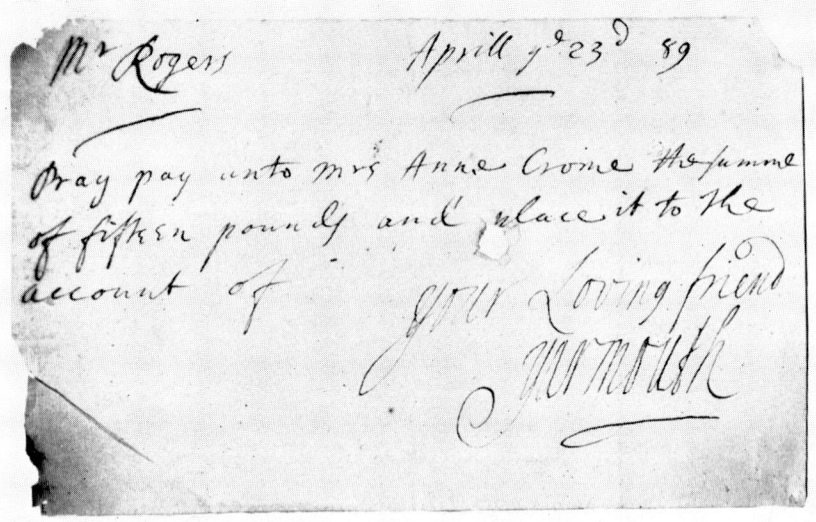

Page 52 (*above*) A drawn note of the Earl of Yarmouth, dated 1689, signed as many such documents were, 'Your loving friend'; (*below*) a receipt of Eleanor (Nell) Gwyn, dated 1686. Although a famous beauty of the time, she could not write as is seen by her mark 'EG'

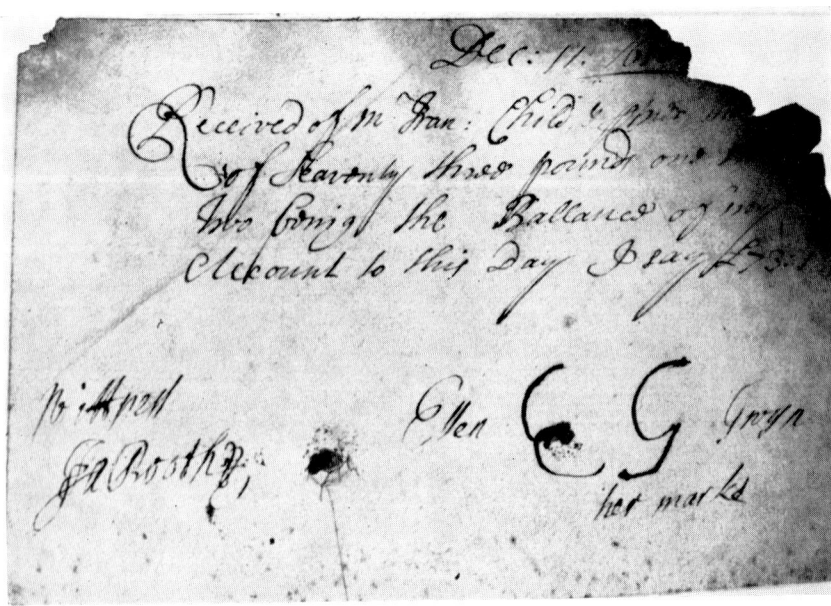

The Plantagenets

Peace in Scotland

William the Lion's son, Alexander II of Scotland (1214-49), not only followed his father in the types of coin which he struck—though later in his reign he altered the designs to correspond to those of the English coins of Henry III—but he also continued to cherish a desire to annex Northumbria. During the struggle following the grant of Magna Carta (1215) he unsuccessfully tried to seize that part of England. His coins, which are silver pennies only, have a frequently misspelt legend, ie ALEXANDE, ALEXSANDER or ALEXSAMDER. In the last years of his rule Scotland enjoyed peace and prosperity, which continued during the reign of his son —Alexander III (1249-86). To meet the need for a greater volume of money, which inevitably accompanies growing prosperity, Alexander III increased the number of mints to sixteen and issued pennies, halfpennies and farthings (*Fig 7*). The pennies were in two issues, and to the legend of the later issue he added DEI GRATIA, a form which the English kings did not adopt for many years.

The Western Isles, where Scandinavians had dwelt since the ninth century, were recovered from the Norsemen after the Battle of Largs (1263), and three years later the Hebrides were returned by Norway in exchange for a sum of money. The Scots were at peace with England; Alexander, who had married Margaret, sister of Edward I, was on friendly terms with his brother-in-law, and the border was quiet.

Unfortunately, Alexander was killed in an accident and left a grand-daughter as heir to the throne. Edward I, in a statesmanlike scheme, proposed her marriage—she was daughter of the Norwegian king—to his son. Misfortune again intervened, however, and the child died at sea on its way from Norway to Scotland.

Edwards I, II, III

The persistent malpractice of coin-clipping in England caused Edward I (1272-1307) to try and improve the coinage. To satisfy an indignant public, scapegoats were found and a number of Jews were prosecuted, and all who would not renounce their faith were expelled from the country.

Until 1280 the old issues of coins from the previous reign were continued (*Fig 8*); but from this date a new coinage with three new denominations was struck, consisting of groats (4d pieces), pennies, rounded halfpennies and rounded farthings (*Fig 9*). The groats were probably not intended for general circulation, as so few of them existed. Their design, probably based on the French *gros tournois*, was a great improvement on previous issues and for many years English designs were based on them; their influence was seen even on the Continent. In the inscription the Latin words *Dei Gratia* (By the Grace of God) made their first appearance, while the titles *Dominus Hiberniae et Dux Aquitaniae* (Lord of Ireland and Duke of Aquitaine) were used for the first time in abbreviated form.

With the new issue of 1280 the sole responsibility for all the mints was given to William de Turnemire, who was called the Master Moneyer. He had been employed at the Marseilles mint, from which he brought to England a new process of coining money. This method was to cast the metal into long bars whose cross-section was a square with rounded corners, equal in area to that of a coin. Blanks cut from these bars by shears were heated and hammered into a round shape. Oxide was then removed from them by a process called blanching, and they were ready to be placed between the dies and struck.

Although certain ecclesiastics were allowed rights in minting, it was Edward's intention to centralise mint control, thus abolishing the moneyers. Until this time the Mint was in the Treasury Buildings in Westminster, but in 1300 it moved to the Tower of London, where there was more space for expansion. With the growth of foreign trade the constitution of the Mint changed and it became more and more important. Increasing quantities of foreign coins and bullion were brought into the country and it became necessary to create some system for changing foreign currency into English coin.

Many foreign coins from the Low Countries, often base and underweight, found their way illegally into the coinage. With the good English silver disappearing from circulation (probably finding its way to the Continent), economic difficulties were encountered,

The Plantagenets 55

and in an endeavour to check these the penalty of hanging and quartering was imposed upon those found importing money.

In 1292 Edward I, as overlord of Scotland, after examining the claimants to the Scottish throne, chose John Baliol, a descendant of William the Lion; Baliol, after four years as a vassal king to the English throne, rebelled and formed an alliance with the French, but was soon defeated and deposed. His coins, silver pennies and halfpennies in two issues, were very similar to those of Alexander III. Those struck at St Andrew's, however, have the name of the mint on the reverse.

For ten years Scotland had no king and lost even vassal status, but the English were guilty of indiscretion and unnecessarily stirred up bad feeling by garrison outrages. On the death of the Scottish leader William Wallace, who was captured and cruelly put to death, Robert Bruce (1306-29) was accepted and crowned king by the Scots. However, he had alienated the support of many of them by murdering one of their own leaders. After a number of misfortunes—he spent much time as a fugitive—he returned and won a victory at Loudon Hill. Edward took an army north with the object of overwhelming Bruce, but died before he achieved this object. His successor abandoned the campaign. Bruce's coins were pennies, halfpennies and farthings, without any appreciable alteration from the previous coinage.

In Ireland, Edward I made a second attempt to create a real central authority and a series of justiciars reduced the feudal liberties to some extent. A considerable number of silver pennies, halfpennies and farthings were struck in the Cork, Dublin and Waterford mints to provide a much needed supply, though the two smaller denominations did not appear until 1297. In this year a parliament was summoned, in which knights and common clergy were included. Nine shires and five liberties sent representatives. In 1310 the towns also sent deputies. This legislative representation was the beginning of a parliament which remained until 1800.

In 1315 Edward Bruce, brother of the King of Scotland, landed at Larne with an army, and with Irish support defeated Richard, Earl of Ulster, at Connor. In the following year Edward Bruce was crowned King of Ireland. The Irish, however, then lost a battle at

Athenry, and Bruce failed to take Dublin. The newly appointed viceroy, Roger Mortimer, revived a lifeless government, and finally overwhelmed Bruce at Dundalk in 1318. Thus the hope of Scottish sovereignty over Ireland failed, but Edward II certainly did not deserve to retain a kingdom when he had failed entirely to maintain it; neither did he gain the loyalty of the Irish, who made a steady revival in arms, language, law and civilisation.

Edward II's coins (1307-27) were similar to those of his father and differed in minor detail only. His reign was marred by domestic strife in his own court, a situation which led to his dethronement in 1326; whereupon, after being kept a prisoner in Berkeley Castle, he was murdered.

When the Scots, permanently divided by feud, presented an excellent opportunity for attack, he failed to follow up his father's campaign. He was finally driven to take an army to Scotland in 1314, but at Bannockburn the English suffered their worst defeat. For many years after this Bruce carried on guerilla raids in the north of England, creating terror among the population and doing considerable damage. Not until after the death of Edward II in 1327 did the regents of Edward III make peace with Scotland and recognise its independence.

A period of prosperity marked Edward III's reign (1327-77). The wool trade flourished and the amount of coinage increased. For the first eight years the coinage was similar to that of the previous reign, but after 1335 there was a shortage of silver metal, which became acute in the following years, aggravated by the illegal export of silver coins to the Continent. At the same time base silver coins named 'lusshebournes', a product of Luxembourg, were imported and circulated with the good silver coinage, being almost indistinguishable from the genuine product.

Chaucer wrote of these base coins in the 'Monkes Prologue' in the *Canterbury Tales*:

> This maketh that our wives wol assaye
> Religious folk, for they moun better paye
> Of Venus paymentes than mowen we:
> God wot, no LUSSHEBURGHES payen ye.

From this period the coinage began to take on a more interesting

The Plantagenets 57

appearance both from a numismatic and an historical viewpoint. After the public's indifference to the discarded Henry III gold florin of 1257 and the attractive silver groat of 1279 it had become increasingly important to match the country's growing prosperity. Gold nobles, half nobles, quarter nobles, silver groats, half groats, as well as pennies, halfpennies and farthings were struck. Following the general tendency for a gold coinage to be used over all Europe, in 1337 Edward III struck gold florins in Aquitaine imitating the St John the Baptist design. Similar coins were struck in 1344 in England—the first permanent gold currency to be established—as well as half and quarter florins (*Fig 10*). As the rare 1297 groat was probably only a pattern the groat and its half, first issued in 1351, may also be considered the first coins in these denominations. These three coins were known as 'double leopards', 'leopards' and 'helms' respectively and filled a need for coins of greater value. They were soon withdrawn, as their value was not proportionate to that of the silver coins—the florin was valued at 6s—and were supplanted by gold nobles having a ratio of twelve to one with silver, and a value of 6s 8d. In an effort to check clipping, these gold coins had scriptural texts around the reverses, simulating amulets; it was hoped that people would be deterred from removing metal from the coins' edges and clipping away the holy texts as well.

The wars with France caused new innovations in the coinage (*Fig 11*). The design on the noble (it depicts a king in a ship) may have been the result of the English naval victory at the Battle of Sluys in 1340, during which two French admirals and about 30,000 men were slain and over 230 large French ships captured with little loss to the English. There is a verse about this battle written in *The Libel of English Policie*.

> For foure things our noble sheweth to me—
> King, ship, and swerd and power of the see.

The same writer, referring to the siege of Calais and Edward's power at sea, writes:

> But King Edward made a siege royall,
> And wanne the town, and in speciall
> The sea was kept, and thereof he was lord;
> Thus made he nobles coined of record.

On the death of the French King Charles IV, who had no son, Edward claimed the French throne in 1337 and, having proclaimed himself King of France, struck gold coins with the lettering 'Rex Anglie et Francie', but after the Treaty of Bretigny in 1361 he agreed to omit his French title.

Earlier in the war with France, Edward III had captured Calais, which he turned into an English port by expelling all the French and encouraging the English to settle there. In 1363 a Calais mint started to strike English coins for Edward; both gold and silver coins were produced, but the shortage of silver, and to a lesser extent of gold, caused delays in production, which at times ceased altogether. Records show that the yearly average dropped from £2,000 of silver to less than £500.

After the treaty had been broken by the French the king's title on the larger coins was again adjusted to contain the kingdoms of England, France and the duchies of Ireland and Aquitaine. In the last-named province and adjoining possessions he struck fine gold and silver coins (*Fig 12*). Later he appointed his eldest son Edward, the Black Prince, Prince of Aquitaine and he, in turn, struck coins under this title. He died in 1376, a year before his father.

When Bruce of Scotland died in 1329 his son David II (1329-71) became king. Meanwhile many of those who had disputed Bruce's claim to the throne had fled to England to join forces with Edward Baliol—the son of John Baliol—who, with Edward III's permission invaded Scotland and won a victory; before Edward could assist him, however, he was driven out. Soon the English king claimed the throne of France and lost interest in Baliol, with the result that the Scots regained large areas of southern Scotland and their king, young David II, returned from France.

But in 1346 David was captured when attacking the north of England as an ally of the French, a defeat which cost the Scots much territory in southern Scotland, just as the Battle of Crécy in the same year was to cost the French much territory. In 1357 David was released, but the heavy ransom demanded kept the Scots impoverished for many years.

David's coins were pennies, halfpennies and farthings in his first issue. One issue of farthings, known as the Moneta farthings, has a curious inscription. On the obverse the letter D is an abbreviation of the name David, but the remainder of the name, 'AVID', is on the reverse. The second issue in 1357 included new denominations—groats and half groats—as well as pennies. These two new coins resembled the English groats. Another issue followed but this was of cruder workmanship. The outstanding coins of this reign were the gold nobles—the first gold coins of Scotland.

In Dublin, Edward III struck a small issue of halfpennies, of which only two specimens are known to exist, and these were the only Irish coins he issued. During this period the country suffered much from unrest and discontent. From 1361 to 1367 Lionel, Duke of Clarence, was sent over as viceroy and the English forced the Irish to adopt more English customs and even to take English names, on pain of outlawry.

At this time there was a test in the mints called the 'Trial of the Pyx'. It was the duty of the master to retain a specimen of each journeyweight of coins (720oz troy in weight) and place it in a pyx (or box), which at the end of three months was sealed and sent to an appointed place for the purpose of testing for quality, weight, etc. The three-month interval between each testing was necessary because the master had to change the secret mark or privy seal on the coins at the end of such a period. The 'trial' was by no means repeated regularly, for old records often make no mention of this custom for years at a time. During the years 1351-60 the small alterations in the legends were numerous. Sometimes it was a missing stop, or an additional one, or perhaps the shape of the letters. Undoubtedly these alterations were intended as indications of the period in which a coin was issued or by whom, etc, and the 'Trial of the Pyx' was designed to check forgery. The 'Trial' today is a regular event, two coins being set aside before the issue of the 'journey', one for testing by the mint assayer and the other for production at the close of the year when a jury drawn from the Goldsmiths Company tests these coins. When the Trial of the Pyx originated is unknown, but a trial carried out in a similar manner is recorded around 1250. It may be that tests of this nature were carried out even before this, as secret marks, which must have served some purpose, have been traced on earlier coins.

Richard II

When Richard II (1377-99) came to the throne he was only eleven years of age. With the French wars continuing interminably and the heavy cost of maintaining an army abroad, the country encountered financial difficulties. In addition, as English silver was still undervalued in comparison with Continental prices, very little was imported, but a large quantity of silver coins managed to find their way abroad. So Richard's silver coinage is rarely found, in spite of the continued striking by the ecclesiastical mints of York and Durham. Confirmation of this can be seen in the 'Stamford Find' (Lincs) in which 2,940 groats, dating from 1360 to 1465, were excavated in 1866. Only two of these showed Richard's name, the majority being attributable to Edward III, his grandfather. Further confirmation is seen in the Balcombe (Sussex) find of 1897 when only six coins were found belonging to Richard with 321 belonging to Edward III. The gold coins, which were not so scarce, were struck in nobles, half nobles and quarter nobles; the silver coins were groats, half groats, pennies, halfpennies and farthings. The two mints in use were those of London and, to a lesser extent, Calais, though most of the French possessions were once again in the hands of the French, with only small areas near the coast—including Calais and Bordeaux—under English rule. The continued shortage of small silver in the change caused much inconvenience and some hardship; a number of petitions was presented by Parliament, with the result that more halfpence were put into circulation.

In 1394 Richard II landed in Ireland at Waterford with a large army and remained there until the following year, securing the homage of all. But his authority departed with his army. No coins were struck in Ireland by Richard or his two successors, Henry IV and Henry V.

Richard's reign came abruptly to an end after he had seized the estate of the deceased John of Gaunt, Duke of Lancaster. This was the signal for the Duke's eldest son Henry, who had been banished from the country by Richard on a charge of treason, to return with the support of the nobles. Richard was dethroned and imprisoned; he died in prison a few months later, and the way was clear for

The Plantagenets

Henry IV, first Lancastrian king, to mount the English throne.

When David II of Scotland died in 1371 a weak and futile reign came to an end and his nephew Robert II (1371-90) became king, the first monarch of the House of Stuart. He spent most of his reign in dispute with the English, but took no part in active warfare at that time. By renewing their alliance with the French the Scots involved themselves in the Anglo-French struggle, and for expelling the English from southern Scotland, they were invaded first by John of Gaunt and then by Richard II, with nothing gained but devastation to Scottish soil. The next heir to the Scottish throne was Robert III (1390-1406), who was—in his own words—'the worst of kings and the most wretched of men'. Scotland was mainly ruled by his brother, the Earl of Fife; but in 1399 the King's eldest son ousted his uncle. A bitter feud followed ending with the King's son dying mysteriously, for which, of course, tradition blamed the uncle. After this Robert III sent his remaining son James to be educated in France, but when he was captured at sea by the English the shock killed his father. Although James I was accepted as king, his rule was only nominal until he was released from captivity in England in 1424.

The coinages of Robert II and III have been frequently confused in the past; both kings struck groats and half groats (though the later king struck groats in two different weights), pennies and halfpennies. Until recent years numismatists have been unable to decide which of these kings struck the issues of the gold coins known as st andrews (lions) and demi-lions (demies). Today, however, it is considered that they belong to Robert III, with the larger coins weighing about 60 grains during the 'heavy' coinage and 38 grains in the 'light' coinage (their value in both cases being 5s), and the demi-lions weighing 30 and 19 grains respectively. The first name is derived from the figure of St Andrew with arms extended which is shown on the reverse, while the name lion is derived from the obverse, which displays a lion rampant over the shield of Scotland. While the coins of the earlier reign were similar to David II's, those of Robert III have the King's head crowned and full-face. It was during the latter King's reign that the Scottish coins became devalued in relation to those of England, the ratio being two to one.

Until about 1357 the two coinages had been equal but David II's ransom caused the Scottish coinage steadily to deteriorate until the reign of James VI. The mints existing in Robert II's reign were at Dundee, Edinburgh and Perth, while those of his successor were at Aberdeen, Edinburgh, Perth, Dumbarton and Inverness.

1 Henry II silver short cross penny. King's name displayed with crowned bust
2 Richard I short cross silver penny
3 Richard I silver denier of Aquitaine
4 John short cross silver penny. Full-face portrait
5 Henry III long cross silver penny c 1248. Moneyer: William of Northampton
6 The first English gold penny (24 carat) Henry III c 1257. Moneyer: William of London (twice diameter of coin)
7 Alexander III Scottish silver sterling
8 Edward I silver penny c 1280 Lincoln
9 English silver groat (4d) c 1279 London (twice diameter of coin)
10 Edward III English gold half florin c 1344 London. Crowned leopard with banner. Otherwise known as leopard (twice diameter of coin)
11 Edward III gold noble. King in ship (twice diameter of coin)
12 Edward III Aquitaine guiennois, Anglo-Gallic c 1360 (twice diameter of coin)

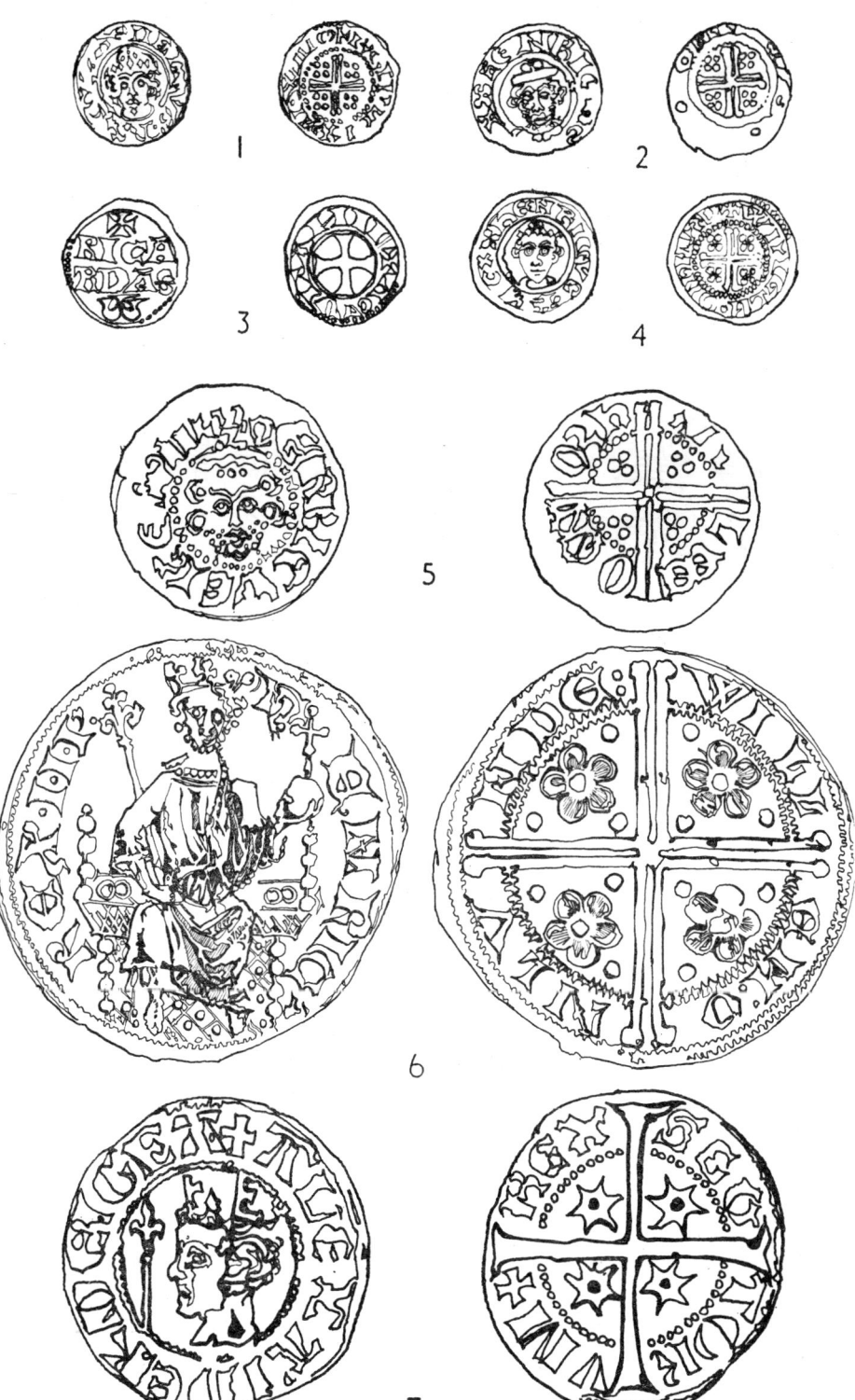

64

V
LANCASTER AND YORK

When Henry IV (1399-1413) became King of England the economic state of the country was bad, but conditions became progressively worse. Attempts at reform were made but the real cause was neglected. The undervaluing of silver and gold by comparison with Continental standards was the root of the trouble and supplies of these metals practically ceased. The application of import and export duties and the prohibition of coin exports did little to improve the situation and merely checked trade. After twelve years of economic chaos steps were taken to reduce the weights of coins while retaining their values: in 1412 the weight of the gold nobles was reduced from 120 grains to 108, and the silver pennies dropped from 18 to 15. This had the desired effect of checking the drift of precious metals to the Continent. The Calais mint issued none of the new coinage and was closed down.

The coinage was in two issues, the first being known as the Heavy Coinage (1399-1412) and the second as the Light Coinage (1412-13). The first issue consisted of gold nobles, half nobles, quarter nobles, silver half groats, pennies, halfpennies and farthings, distinguishable as the 'heavy type' by their symbols of coronet, crescent, the star and pellet. The second issue was similar except for the addition of the groats, the trefoil and amulet on the ships' side being the symbol.

After eighteen years of captivity, James I of Scotland (1406-37) was released by the English in 1424. There was a full range of coins during his reign; the gold coins consisting of demies and half demies, also known as lions and half lions. The groats were made of silver but the pennies and halfpennies were of billon.

Henry V and Henry VI

After Henry IV's death in 1413 his son Henry V (1413-22) became King of England. The complete range of coins as in the previous reign was struck and in considerably greater quantities, with the ecclesiastical mints of York and Durham continuing their output of pence. The only obvious change to be noted here is that on the new portrait of the groat, Henry sports two extra wild side locks, which protrude from under the crown rim. This remains the norm in presentation until Henry VII's portrait appears in profile. Shortly before the king's death in 1422 a petition was put before him that both the Calais mint and the royal mint at York should reopen; but it was not until 1423 that the Royal York mint opened and it was a year later before coins came from Calais again. It seems that the custom was for the ecclesiastical mint at York to cease production whenever a royal mint was producing in that city; accordingly the archbishop struck no further coins, and the ecclesiastical mint was closed until 1465.

It was not long before the gold supply began to fail. Henry VI (1422-61) gave encouragement to alchemists in the vain hope that from the Calais mint they would solve this problem (*Fig 1*). From 1428 the gold coins, which bore a C in the ship's flag, ceased. The blame for this rested on the Duke of Burgundy, who after the defeat of the English in France, formed an alliance with the French and refused to allow gold bullion, in payment for wool exported from England, to pass through his territory. As a result of this loss of bullion, London gold coin production almost ceased.

There was a full range of coins including nobles, half nobles and quarter nobles, groats and half groats, pennies, halfpennies and farthings, which were put out in eleven different issues of gold and silver, all recognisable by their privy marks, which were to be found sometimes in the coin field, but mostly as ornate stops in the legend. Also a variety of crosses indicated the beginning of the legend. The Calais mint produced a considerable proportion of these, even though it was closed finally in 1440; its last issue was of groats.

At this stage the rose was to become a regular feature on the coinage, having more than usual symbolic significance; it typifies the period better known as the Wars of the Roses, during which two rival houses struggled bitterly for supremacy, dividing the nation in the process.

Wars of the Roses

The quarrel between the two rival houses of York and Lancaster as to who should rule the country developed, in 1450, into civil war, an internal strife in England which was to last for the following twenty-one years. In 1460 at the Battle of Wakefield the Duke of York was killed, but his son Edward, the Earl of March, defeated the Lancastrians at the Battle of Mortimer's Cross, marched on London and became king, as Edward IV. Henry VI was eventually captured by Yorkist sympathisers and suffered nine years' imprisonment in the Tower of London.

In the Wars of Succession the Irish almost completely favoured the rose of York and regarded the Lancastrians as usurpers. From this time on three Irish earls ruled Ireland, in effect, though the Dublin government was theoretically in control. These three worked together and virtually dominated the official authority in spite of its English support.

Three years after he became king, Henry VI struck pennies in Ireland to alleviate the acute shortage, but it was not until 1460 that a new Irish coinage of groats and pennies was planned. It is recorded that at that time the parliament held at Drogheda enacted that 'a proper coin separate from the coin of England was with more convenience agreed to be had in Ireland'; a further statement added that there should be one issue 'having imprinted on one part of it a crown, and on the other part a cross, called a Patrick, of which eight shall pass for one Denier'. This refers undoubtedly to the copper half farthings called Patricks. As a result of the decisions at Drogheda it is probable that Edward IV struck the Anonymous Issue (1461-3) after he had seized power. This issue of groats and pennies was so called because of the absence of a name in the legend of the coins. The Dublin mint was responsible for its issue as it was for the 1425-6 issue of Henry VI pennies.

For the short period in 1470-71 (3 October to 11 April) during Henry's restoration no coins were struck for Ireland.

Scottish Feud, Douglas v Crown

The Scottish king James II (1437-60) was a child of six when he came to the throne. Much of the new strength gained by the central government under his father was lost until he reached his majority. The great House of Douglas at this time was so powerful that it endangered the supremacy of the Crown. During a personal interview with the King, the Earl of Douglas refused to break a league he had entered into with his brother and the Earl of Crawford, and in the fight that ensued he was fatally wounded. This murder started the final conflict between the Crown and the House of Douglas in which the Crown was victorious and the 9th Earl fled for his life to England. During the Wars of the Roses, James II took the opportunity of recapturing some of southern Scotland from the English, but while he was besieging the English-held Roxburgh Castle in 1460, he was accidentally killed. The throne was left to his son, James III, and once again Scotland had a boy king.

James II's coins were, like those of his father, James I, struck in gold, silver and billon. His first issue of gold demies was struck from 1437 until 1451; and his second gold issue, consisting of st andrews and half st andrews, was continued from 1451 until the end of his reign (Fig 2). The first silver coins issued up to and including the year 1450 were groats similar to those of James I. From the time of this issue Scottish coins began to lose value rapidly; in 1451 the English coins were two and a half times the value of the Scots', and five years later the gap had widened to three to one. A second issue during and after 1451 included groats and half groats, which continued until the end of the reign in 1460. Billon pennies were also struck, being made of two-thirds silver and one-third alloy.

Mr Rogers pray paye fifty
ginnyes to the barer and
plase it to my acount

Aprell the
12: 1689

Cleaveland

Page 69 (*above*) A drawn note, dated 1689, of Barbara, Duchess of Cleveland (a rival of Nell Gwyn); (*below*) a drawn note of the 1st Duke of Bolton, dated 1689, in favour of the famous Titus Oates, whose endorsement can be seen

July 30 1689

On Sight hereof pray pay
unto ye Reverend Doctor Tytus
Oats or his Ordr the Sume of
fifty pounds And place ye same
to the Account of

50 £

Yo. Assured friend

To Mr Fra. Child
at Temple Barre

Bolton

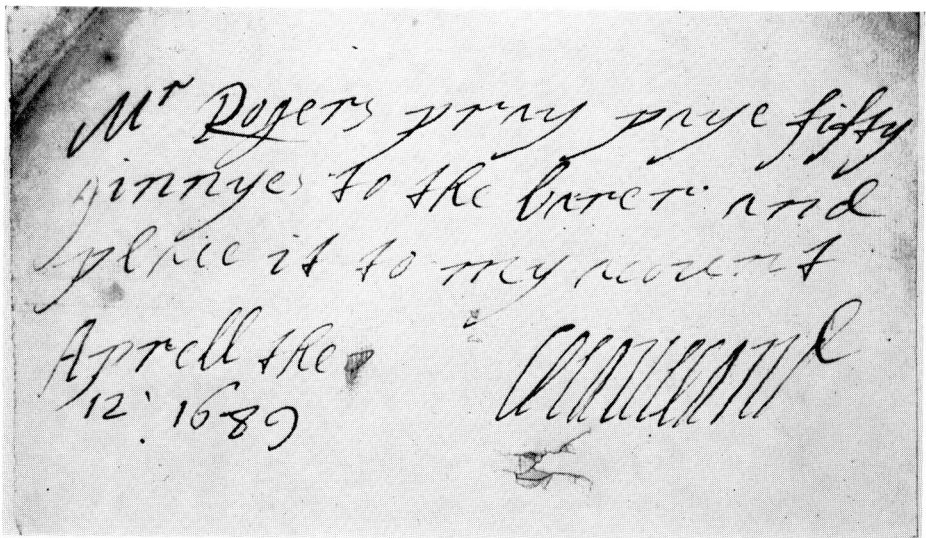

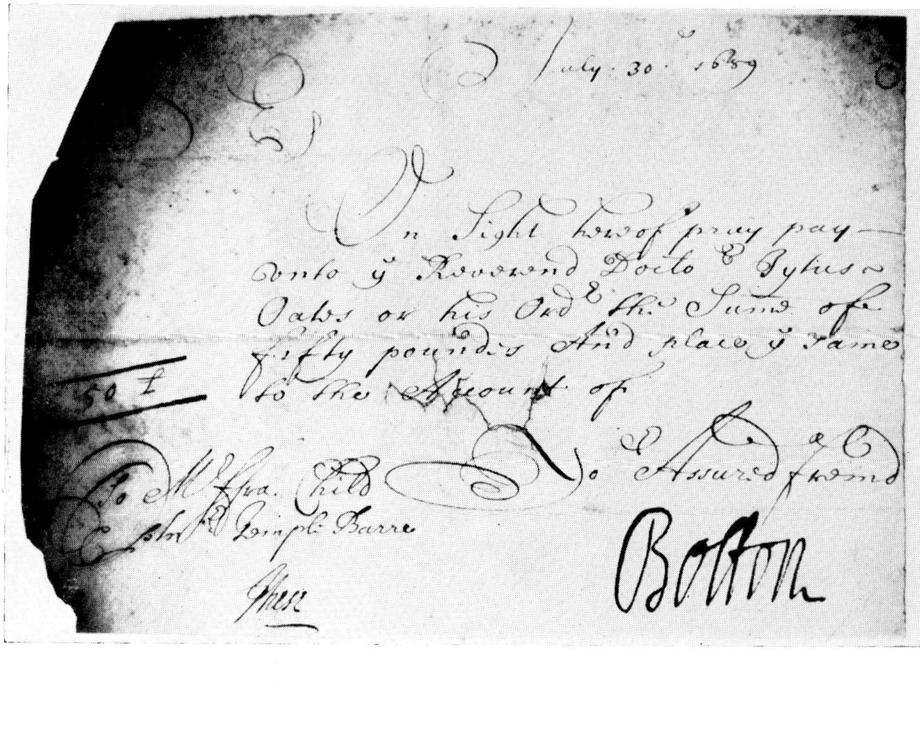

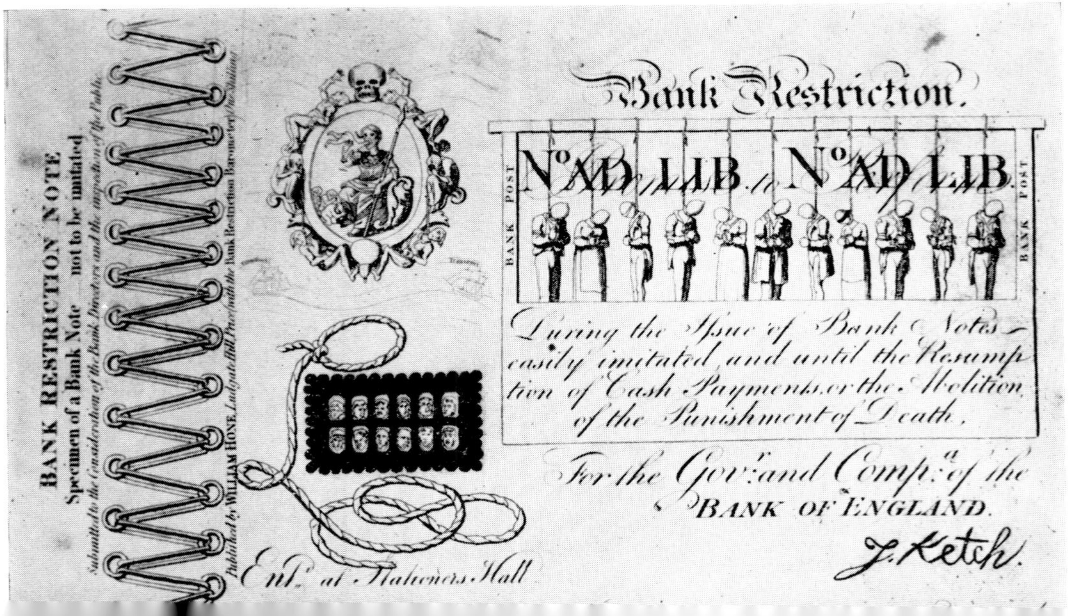

Page 70 (*above*) Examples of eighteenth-century exchequer tallies; (*left*) the Cruikshank note, designed in the eighteenth century by George Cruikshank to advertise the injustice of hanging passers of forged notes

The House of York

When Edward IV (1461-83) came to the English throne the production of the gold coinage was almost at a standstill. Although the silver coin supplies had been sufficient since 1449 Edward's concern was to increase production. Thus in 1464 he ordered the silver penny to be reduced from 15 to 12 grains and allowed the mint to pay as much as 33s per lb instead of 29s. The ratio of silver to gold was kept the same, at 9 to 100, by raising the value of the gold noble from 6s 8d to 8s 4d. New gold coins, ryals (or rose nobles), valued at 10s followed immediately, with the half ryals and quarter ryals in addition. As the noble had been raised in value, another new gold coin, the angel valued at 6s 8d, took its place, with its half angel (or angelet) in addition. This coin takes its name from its design on the obverse depicting the Archangel Michael slaying the dragon. A feature on the gold coins which identifies them as Edward's is the placement of the legend, which begins from the top left position and not the top right as its forerunners.

This reform of the coinage had the desired effect and large quantities of gold and silver bullion came to London from the Continent. In 1465 the York and Canterbury mints were reopened, with three new provincial mints in Bristol, Coventry and Norwich, to cope with the extra output. These adjustments caused the coins of 1461-4 to be quite separate from the later issues, with distinct differences in weight and type. The reign also marked the beginning of an orderly continuation of mint marks, which is apparent on all denominations and gives added historical interest to the coins.

Edward's personal badge, the sun in splendour, displayed with sixteen rays on his Rose noble, has a real historical background. The Battle of Mortimer's Cross was preceded by a dense fog on the morning of the conflict, and as the fog lifted it caused the appearance of a freak sunrise giving the illusion of three suns. When this phenomenon merged into a normal sunrise, the Yorkists went into battle and won a great victory.

In 1470 Richard, Earl of Warwick, 'the Kingmaker', forsook his allegiance to Edward, defeated him, and restored Henry VI to the throne for a few months.

The supplies of bullion remained plentiful after Henry's restoration and as was to be expected a new master of the mint was appointed. After 1470 the ryals, which had never been popular, ceased to be struck, though a few exceptional issues were produced in the reigns of the Tudors. The only gold coins were angels and half angels, while silver groats, half groats, pennies and halfpennies continued as before struck by the London, Bristol and York mints (*Fig 3*).

With the aid of the Duke of Burgundy, Edward VI returned in 1471 with an army and defeated the Lancastrians at the Battle of Barnet, in which the Earl of Warwick was killed, and at Tewkesbury. Henry VI was again committed to the Tower of London where he died mysteriously and conveniently.

In Ireland so little coin had been struck during the previous century that there was a great shortage in Edward IV's reign. No doubt the doubled value of coins in Henry VI's last year influenced the striking of new ones named doubles, which were given a current value of 8d (*Fig 4*). The remaining silver coins were groats, half groats, pennies and halfpennies in seven different issues. There were also copper issues of farthings and half farthings as well as one billon issue of farthings. In 1472 English groats, half groats and pennies of Edward III, Richard II, Henry IV and Henry VI were all revalued in Ireland; the groats passed for 5d, with the smaller denominations in proportion, until 1475; then their value was raised to 6d, while the contemporary English groats remained current at 5d.

The seven silver coinages can be divided into distinct types, the periods in which they were issued being as follows:

1. 1461-63
2. 1463-65
3. 1465-67
4. 1467-70
5. 1470-73
6. 1473-78
7. 1478-83

The copper coins were in four issues, including one billon issue, namely 1461 half farthings; 1463-5 farthings and half farthings; c 1467-70 farthings, some of which may have been struck in brass; and 1462, when there was an issue of billon farthings. Twelve mints —Dublin, Trim, Galway, Waterford, Limerick, Carlingford, Drogheda, Cork, Youghal, Kinsale, Kilmallock and Wexford—were responsible for producing the coinage during this period (*Fig 5*).

The initial marks of the legends which are shown on the coins of Edward IV assist considerably in dividing the various issues into groups. For a number of reigns these marks had been used as a means of distinguishing mints, engravers, etc, acting as an excellent guide for present-day collectors. At one time a cross would be seen, later its place would be taken by a crown or a fleur-de-lis, and in Edward IV's reign emblems such as a rose, sun, annulet or perhaps a particular type of cross were used.

When the twelve-year-old son of Edward IV became king as Edward V, his uncle, the unscrupulous Richard, Duke of Gloucester, became guardian and protector of the Realm. Ambitious for the kingship, Richard had no difficulty in imprisoning and probably murdering the unfortunate boy king and his young brother, and assuming the crown. The angels and groats sometimes attributed to Edward V (9 April to 26 June 1483) were ordered by his uncle Richard while he was regent, as can be seen from the mint mark— a boar's head—Richard's personal badge. Many numismatists consider that these belong exclusively to Richard's coinage. But some very rare examples of Edward V's coin are known with his father's mint marks on them. They are angels, half angels and groats. Dies for these may have been prepared and the coins struck just before Richard became the young king's guardian on 7 May, at which time he was able to substitute his own badge as mint mark.

Richard III (1483-5) did not live long to enjoy the results of his scheming. One rebellion by the Duke of Buckingham was successfully suppressed, but a second, led by Henry Tudor, Earl of Richmond, a great-great-grandson of John of Gaunt, defeated and killed Richard at the Battle of Bosworth. The coins of Richard III were angels and angelets in gold, and groats, half groats, pennies and halfpennies in silver. In Ireland he struck groats, half groats and pennies only, in three issues (*Fig 6*); his proclamation in 1483 that money coined for Ireland should have a 'clear and express difference' from the English money was disregarded in the first two issues but put into practice in the third. This proclamation dated 18 July required that all dies previously used must be destroyed, with only the Dublin and Waterford mints left functioning. On the new coins the arms of England were to be displayed on one side and three crowns on the other.

James III of Scotland

While James III of Scotland (1460-88) was in his minority, England was fully occupied in a civil war, which the Scots used to their advantage. Margaret, wife of Henry VI, ceded the border town of Berwick to the Scots in exchange for assistance to the Lancastrian cause; but in spite of their intrigue with the Lancastrians the Scots made peace with the Yorkists in 1464. On reaching his majority James ascended the throne in 1469 in an atmosphere of peace. His nobles, however, did not approve of his intellectual and artistic pursuits and would have preferred his brother the Duke of Albany. Albany and the king quarrelled, causing the former to leave the country, only to return later with an English army and regain Berwick-on-Tweed, which from that time became permanently English. Later Albany and the exiled Earl of Douglas were defeated together with their small English army; a few years later James III was killed in conflict with some of his nobles.

James' coinage consisted of gold, silver, billon and copper coins. The gold coins were two new denominations called riders (80 grains) and unicorns (59 grains) (*Figs 7 and 8*), with half riders, quarter riders and half unicorns. The riders were issued in 1475 and received their name from the reverse, which depicts the figure of the king seated on a galloping horse. Unicorns were issued in 1486 and derive their name from the design of a unicorn, having a crown around its neck from which to hang a ring and chain and supporting a shield of arms. With the issue of these gold coins the ratio of gold coin values compared with those of England again increased to one to four. Although affecting the Scots adversely, the small number of gold coins minted could have hardly affected the economy as a whole.

The silver coins were in six issues of groats, half groats and pennies, with some of these issues varying considerably in design. Billon coins were in pennies, placks and half placks. The placks were first given a value of 3d but were later reduced to 2d. They take

Lancaster and York

their name from the French *plaque*, a thin piece of metal. Copper farthings were also a new denomination, popularly known as 'black farthings' from the colour of the metal.

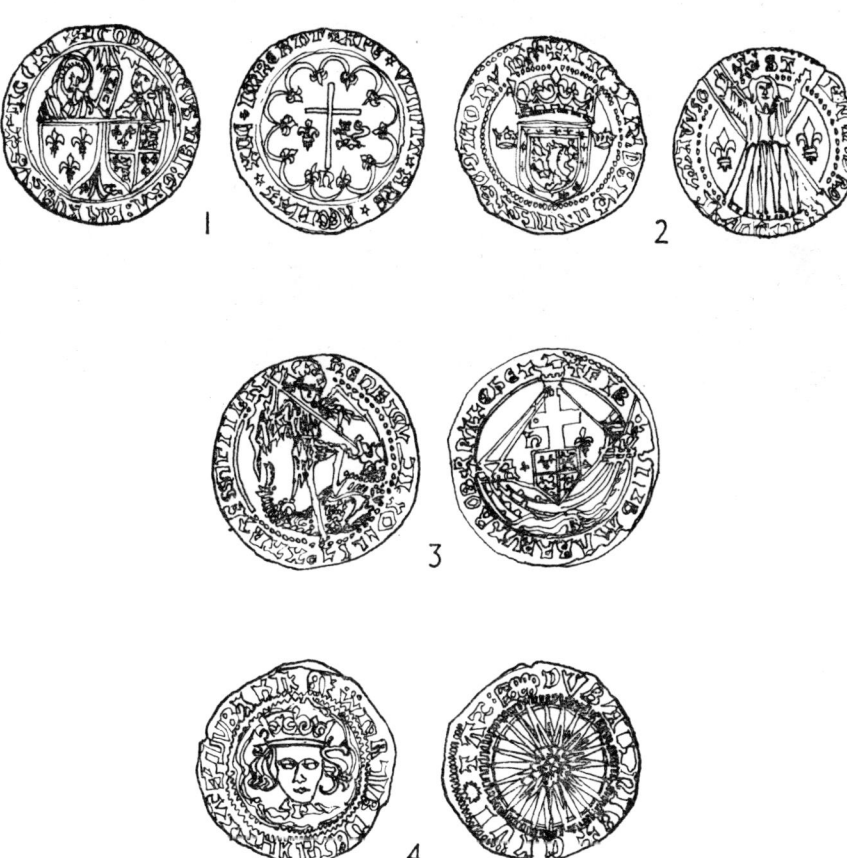

1 Henry VI gold salute c 1446 Rouen. Virgin and angels over two shields
2 James II Lion. Lion in crowned shield, St Andrew's cross (reverse)
3 Henry VI Restored. Gold angel c ? Bristol. St Michael slaying the dragon, cross and arms on ship
4 Edward IV Irish silver double groat. Dublin. Rose in centre of radiate sun (reverse).

5 The first silver groat of Ireland. Edward IV 'Anonymous Issue'
6 Richard III Irish silver groat. Dublin. Shield obverse and vertical Irish three-crown design
7 James III rider. King on horseback. Shield in centre of long cross (reverse)
8 James III unicorn. Reverse, star with wavy rays

VI
THE
TUDORS

The accession of Henry VII (1485-1509) to the throne marked the end of our medieval currency. The new king took a great personal interest in the coinage. He introduced an artistic portrait for the silver, redesigned the royal coat of arms and changed the conventional methods of coining, which had existed for the previous 200 years.

One important improvement took place under Henry VII—the first real attempt at portraiture on English coins, if one excludes the designs of Offa, King of Mercia. Offa's coins, though revealing considerable talent in this field, lacked the necessary technical knowledge to produce results comparable to Henry VII's. The engraver cut the complete design of the coin in steel, in relief so that when transferred to the die (an action performed in the same manner as the die striking a blank) it was in incuse, which of course was essential if the pattern was to appear in relief on the actual coin. This same method, greatly improved, is still used today. Thus the old patterns, built up by means of small lines, curves and dots, were replaced by real portraits.

In 1489 new gold coins, the first English 20s pieces, were created and called double ryals (*Fig 1*). Being large coins (over 1½ in across and having twice the amount of gold as the modern sovereigns) they offered ample scope for the magnificent Tudor design; it is generally agreed that these coins, at least in their earlier issues, are the most artistic achievement in our English coinage. They bear the French arms on the reverse, a comment on Henry's aspirations in that direction. The king bestowed the name sovereign on them and gave to his new large man-of-war, the second of a revived navy, a similar name, *Sovereign of the Seas*, associating them both with the dignity of the throne.

Later in Henry VII's reign the graver Alexander of Brugsal achieved great success with the portrait coinage in silver. No graver since has exhibited such artistry on our coinage, with the possible exception of Simon in his portrait of Charles II. Henry's were the first profile portraits to appear since Stephen's reign.

In 1504 new silver coins were produced named 'testoons', valued at 12d (*Fig 2*). This name comes from the first French coin to bear the head of a monarch—the old French word being *teste*, the modern French being *tête*, meaning 'head'. They displayed a fine profile portrait of Henry VII and were the first silver coins to have a lifelike portrait of a reigning monarch. Their name was soon changed to shilling, though the first mention of a shilling in our history was in Anglo-Saxon laws when it was used as a money of account (ie a value used only in calculations but with no corresponding coin, similar to our guinea of today). The name 'scilling' meaning 'a piece cut off', was a Saxon word for pieces of broken silver that were used to make up the loss in weight of worn coins when payment was by weight. The origin of its nickname is lost, but the 'bob' appears in 1812 in the *Flash Dictionary* by J. H. Vaux, who refers to 'bob' or 'bobstick' as a shilling. Dickens used the word in both *Pickwick Papers* and *Oliver Twist*. The remaining gold coins struck during this reign were ryals, angels and angelets—the last two having slightly modified designs—while the rest of the coins were silver groats, half groats, pennies, halfpennies and farthings.

Henry VII greatly strengthened his position on the throne by marrying Elizabeth, daughter of Edward IV, thereby joining the Houses of York and Lancaster, an event which he commemorated on his coinage by a double Tudor rose made up of the emblems of both Houses. Through his statesmanlike and energetic approach to affairs, the country became one of the great commercial powers of the world.

In the Ireland of 1485, however, the victor of Bosworth seemed a usurper, as a restoration of the royal line of Plantagenets, descendants of the Angevin house, had been thought a possibility. Soon Henry VII decided that he was strong enough to attack the Anglo-

The Tudors

Irish oligarchy. In 1494 he substituted Sir Edward Poynings for the Earl of Kildare as Governor and then proceeded to restore the power of the English crown. It was then that the famous 'Poynings Law' was passed, stating that no parliament might meet in Ireland until the King gave consent. Eventually these ambitious measures were abandoned; Kildare was restored in 1496 and a general pardon issued.

Henry's coins in Ireland were in three periods. The first was divided into four 'Three Crown' issues, so called because the reverses displayed a three-crowns design. These included groats, half groats, pennies and halfpennies. The third issue, in groats only, is unusual in that it bears the additional arms of the Fitzgeralds on either side of the royal arms, evidence of the Yorkist plot to oust Henry from the throne and replace him by Lambert Simnel, who posed as the murdered Duke of York. The head of the Fitzgeralds—the Earl of Kildare—supported this rebellion, which caused the Earl to be replaced as Governor of Ireland by Sir Edward Poynings. The second and third periods, both with two issues, showed portrait obverses of the king; the former period consisted of groats only and the latter of groats, half groats and pennies in the first issue, and groats in the second issue.

The lack of documentary information regarding Henry's Irish coinage makes for some uncertainty when attempting to date these four issues.

Union and Peace in Scotland

The King of Scotland, James IV (1488-1513), was an able and strong ruler who firmly suppressed his rebellious barons and thereby obtained complete control. In 1503 he accepted Henry VII's daughter Margaret in marriage, thus promoting friendship between England and Scotland; such a friendship had been considered an impossibility by those Scots who regarded England as Scotland's natural enemy. But it brought about a period of peace for Scotland, which greatly increased her commercial prosperity, though James clearly showed his father-in-law, by the continued building of his large navy, that he had no intention of being ruled by the English. When Henry VIII (his brother-in-law) became King of England it was soon made plain to James that he must choose between the friendship of England and France. James, in mistaken alarm for the safety of France, bound himself to the French cause against the advice of his counsellors. Eventually he was defeated and killed at the Battle of Flodden in 1513 and his infant son became king, leaving Scotland once again to deal with the problem of a minority. His navy was purchased by the French and the country lost the prosperity which had marked his reign.

The Scottish coinage was of gold, silver and billon, with the gold in two issues of st andrews (or lions) and half st andrews (or half lions), unicorns and half unicorns. These coins followed closely the types of James III. The silver coinage was in six issues made up of groats, half groats and pennies, with the first, third and fifth issues of groats and half groats, the second and sixth issues of groats only, and the fourth issue of groats, half groats and pence. The first three issues were dated 1488, 1489 and 1490 respectively, but the dates of the last three issues are uncertain. The billon coinage was made up pennies, placks and half placks in two issues.

Henry VIII

Henry VIII (1509-47) inherited his father's great wealth, which was said to be over 5 million pounds sterling, as well as all his jewels, robes, etc; it took Henry, for all his lavish spending, several years to squander this money, which was an enormous sum in those days. For the first sixteen years he was content to continue the coinage with his father's portrait, the numeral in the king's title being changed from VII to VIII. Long before this period elapsed, however, coins were struck for the town of Tournai in France, following the invasion by Henry in 1513. These were followed in England in a first issue (1509-26), which included new types of farthings in 1523 to avoid the confusion caused by a similarity between halfpennies and farthings. The new coins showed a portcullis—the badge of the Tudors—in the place of the king's head,

The Tudors

and displayed a cross with a central rose on the reverse side.

As the profit from the coinage belonged to the king and the kings of the past were always in need of money, dishonesty on the part of royalty was frequent and coins of certain value steadily had their valuable metal content replaced by base metal. His father had struck a new coin, the shilling, of which $37\frac{1}{2}$ made a Tower pound of silver; Henry made 48 from the same amount with the changed troy weights and when his finances dwindled he made 150 shillings to the troy pound of silver. The Tower pound was originally known as the Saxon pound. It was changed to troy weight, which was adopted as the legal weight for gold and silver in 1527; 40 of Henry VII's shillings were worth a troy pound. The pound avoirdupois, which is used for general purposes, has been in continuous use since the fourteenth century, though its weight has been slightly modified from time to time. Henry VIII achieved lasting notoriety by his debasement of the gold coinage to 20 carats.

In 1526 Cardinal Wolsey, Henry's Chancellor, was directed to reduce the value of the gold in English coins to parity with those of the Continent, in order that English gold should not be shipped overseas to be sold at a profit and to check the importing of Flemish and French gold. After a committee of experts had deliberated on this, sovereigns were revalued at 22s 6d, angels at 7s 6d and angelets at 3s 9d. This revaluation was followed by the issue of several new coins to fill the gaps created by these increased values. The first of these were the crowns of the double rose with a value of 5s (*Fig 3*). They were the first coins to be made of 22 carat gold, which became known as crown gold. From this date until 1634 gold coins varied in content, but since then all gold coins have been made of crown gold, pure gold being far too soft a metal for practical purposes. Other new coins were George nobles value at 6s 8d, and the crowns of the rose valued at 4s 6d, the latter copied from the French *ecu de soleil*. This coin also claims additional historical interest as it was the first gold coin to be struck below English standard fineness; it is also the first of the crown denomination. In the next reign of Edward VI it passed into the silver coin series, becoming the first crown issue in silver. These three coins were struck for a short period only and are almost unknown today.

In the meantime the silver coins of this issue retained the same fineness as before but were reduced in weight from 12 grains to 10⅔ per penny unit. At the time of these changes it was decided to replace the pound Tower (equivalent to 5,400 grains troy) by the pound troy of 5,760 grains, a measure which is used to the present day.

The reverse of the crown of the rose bore the sort of self-righteous legend that could only have been conjured up by a man as conceited as Henry. His monomania was himself. HENRICUS RUTILANS ROSA SINE SPINA—Henry, the dazzling rose without a thorn. The legend was retained on the reverse of the crown of the double rose, while the obverse ironically proved that this statement could not be more untrue! With each new issue it recorded the ever-changing fancies—especially the wives—of this man.

His first marriage to his brother's widow—Katharine of Aragon—lasted the longest. He had been granted dispensation by the Pope to marry his brother's widow but in 1533 he questioned the validity of the dispensation in order to get the marriage decreed null and void, which in reality it was since he had already married Anne Boleyn in 1532. In 1536 Henry married Jane Seymour, the day after Anne had been beheaded. By October 1537 Henry had a son and heir, Edward VI, and within two days he was a widower. By 1540 Henry had taken Anne of Cleves as wife only to divorce her six months later, in July; before the month of August was out Henry had married for the fifth time. As Katherine Howard was of no particular importance it was less trouble for Henry to have her beheaded than to go through a tedious divorce. He married his last wife Katherine Parr in 1543; here he met his match for she had herself, apart from Henry, had two other husbands and one more after his death.

The king, having found that debasing the coinage was profitable and that his father's large fortune was fast disappearing, decided to debase it further, reducing the gold coins from 23 carat 3½ grains (standard gold) to 23 carat, and the silver coinage from 11oz 2dwt fine silver to 10oz (12oz troy equals 1lb). At first Parliament refused to sanction these reductions, but in 1544 the necessary proclamation was given with the silver debased even further to 9oz. Another new coin, the quarter angel, then appeared, based on an 8s valuation of

The Tudors

the angel, which gave a new valuation to gold coins.

In 1545 one would have expected the lowest limit to have been reached when sovereigns were reduced in weight to 192 grains (their original weight was 240 grains) and silver was debased to 6oz; but in 1546 gold was debased to 20 carats with the same weights and values, and silver to a low level of 4oz. Testoons also reappeared in 1544, for one year only, but it was long enough for many derogatory remarks to be made regarding their quality (*Fig 4*). Being large coins with a full-faced portrait of the king, they showed more clearly than the smaller coins the appearance of base metals as they became slightly worn; this was particularly pronounced round the nose of the portrait, which took on a coppery hue. The following is one of the many rhymes by contemporary writers ridiculing them:

These Testoons looke redde, how like you the same?
'Tis a token of grace; they blush for shame.

As a result of this Henry was often referred to as 'Old Coppernose'.

Henry, King of Ireland

When Henry VIII declared himself supreme head of the Church in England, he also became head of the Church in Ireland, whether inside or outside the Pale. In 1541 Parliament and six Gaelic chiefs passed an act making him King of Ireland. Soon afterwards he renounced the Pope's authority over Ireland, while his dissolution of the abbeys did nothing to improve relations between the Crown and the Irish people.

None of Henry VIII's Irish coins were issued until 1534, though it is recorded that there were many other types and varieties of coin in circulation. All coin came from the English mints, as there was no regal mint in Ireland during Henry VIII's reign. The first issue was in groats and half groats, with the inscription 'Dominus Hibernie'. During the second issue in 1541 the inscription was changed to 'Hibernie Rex', with only groats issued. These were the first Irish coins to use the design of the harp. The third issue continued with the REX title, while the fourth, fifth and sixth issues of 1544, 1544-6 and 1546-7 issued new sixpenny groats; though the coins had the name 'Dublin' on them, they were actually struck in London. The 1544 issue contained less alloy than the English money; in spite of this the Irish sixpence was the same weight as the English fourpence (groat) and the Irish threepence similar in weight to the English twopence. Finally, in 1546 billon sixpences were issued so debased that they contained only 3oz of silver, ie 25 per cent.

In 1544 the mint in the Tower was completely reorganised. Sir Edmund Peckham became treasurer in place of a warden, with two under-treasurers replacing the former master workers. Sir William Sharington as under-treasurer at Bristol was authorised to strike coins in both metals, a privilege which he later abused by making counterfeit coins for Lord Seymour of Sudeley, an offence which landed him in the Tower until he could free himself by paying a heavy fine.

By the end of Henry's reign, Roman lettering had replaced the medieval Lombardic lettering. For four years after his death in 1547 base silver and gold coins were struck in his name.

Edward VI

To reform the much debased coinage of Henry VIII was an enormous task which the economic state of the country would not permit except by easy stages. With a nine-year-old boy as king, Edward VI (1547-53), the country was ruled by a Council of Regency, headed by the Duke of Somerset. The many coins in circulation, varying in their metal content to a considerable degree, gave ample scope to the forger and many of the finer quality coins disappeared.

In the earlier part of his reign Edward VI issued coins in the name of his father. Half sovereigns, with the young king's profile but bearing his father's name, were struck, as well as a large output of other denominations with the late king's head, but with these it is impossible to tell which are Henry's and which are Edward's. They are classed as Henry VIII's posthumous coinage.

In 1549 gold coins were improved, being made of 22 carat gold

The Tudors

instead of 20 carat. Sovereigns, half sovereigns, gold crowns and half crowns were struck in Edward's name. Silver shillings were made in two sizes, the larger of silver 6oz fine and the smaller of silver 8oz fine. Base shillings were also struck in 4oz fine silver with the portrait of Henry on them. Finally in 1550 new base silver shillings made of silver only 3oz fine were foisted on the public (*Fig 5*). These were the basest silver coins ever circulated by a government in this country (excluding, of course, our present day coinage of cupro-nickel, which is not intended to be of more than token value).

The following year an attempt was made to restore the coinage to its previous high level of value. The sovereigns and angels were struck in $23\frac{1}{2}$ carat gold and revalued at 30s and 10s respectively; while smaller sovereigns and half sovereigns valued at 20s and 10s, as well as gold crowns and half crowns, were struck from 22 carat gold; then followed the first silver crowns (*Fig 6*) together with half crowns, shillings, sixpences, threepences and pennies all struck in 11oz fine silver. The smaller silver denominations of pennies, half-pennies and farthings continued to be struck in base silver. Although many of the base shillings were withdrawn from circulation, there were such a large proportion left that the public soon became suspicious of them and began to refuse them at their face value.

No evidence exists as to whether Edward VI issued any coins for Ireland other than the testoon (or shilling) of 1552 with the young king's effigy and the harp mint mark. Some numismatists claim that a mint in Dublin existed in his reign. In support of their argument they point to the fact that English fine silver testoons began in 1551; but coins of this date and 1552 circulated in Ireland with very little silver content. If these were from the Royal Mint they were unrecorded and specially detached for circulation in Ireland.

The public in Edward's reign must indeed have been troubled with the complicated currency. With so many coins of different metal value circulating at the same time with the same face value, much profit was undoubtedly made from trafficking in coins, until it was made illegal to pass a coin at more than its current value. In spite of his premature death at the age of fifteen, Edward VI did much in his short reign to restore the gold and silver coinage to its earlier fineness though the work must have been done by his Council.

James V of Scotland

The reign of James V of Scotland (1513-42) was disturbed by political intrigue. While he was a minor, his mother, Margaret, who had forfeited any claim to being regent by her remarriage to the Earl of Angus, often acted in support of Catholic France with the backing of the regent, the Duke of Albany; meanwhile her husband, with whom she had quarrelled, supported her brother Henry VIII and the Protestant English. Nevertheless both factions were anxious to obtain an alliance with countries in opposition to one another.

For a short period, during which James escaped from his stepfather's control, the Earl of Angus governed Scotland. After his mother had obtained her divorce by special consent of the Pope, his uncle, Henry VIII, with whom James was on friendly terms, endeavoured to persuade the young Scottish king to support him. Henry tempted James to isolate himself from the influence of Rome and enrich himself with the spoils of the monasteries. In the meantime James complicated matters by marrying a French princess, who unfortunately died shortly afterwards. He then married another Frenchwoman, Mary of Guise, who was the widow of the Duc de Longueville. Henry also tried to detach his nephew from the French alliance and the Scottish Church Party. Finally the English king lost his patience and broke off friendly relations, reviving the claim of homage and dispatching an army to Scotland. James's various conflicts with his nobles had alienated their loyalty, and so with an army raised only by the Church Party, James was defeated at Solway Moss in November 1542. Shortly afterwards he died, leaving a six-day-old daughter, Mary, as heiress to the throne.

The first gold coins of James V were unicorns and half unicorns, identical to those of James IV. These were followed by two types of *écu* (or crown) and a third issue of gold in some new coins known as ducats (or 'bonnet pieces'—for obvious reasons), with a two-third and one-third ducat. According to the writer Burns, 'These coins were made of native gold, obtained from Crawford Muir and the

Page 87 The Royal Mint, London, an exterior view

Page 88 Examples of nineteenth-century country banknotes

The Tudors

lands of Coxehead', and were the first Scottish coins to bear a date, preceding English coins in this respect by some years. The silver coinage was in four issues of groats, and third groats, the first named being popularly known as 'Douglas groats'.

As well as placks, new coins were struck in billon named bawbees and half bawbees. The bawbees, which were first struck in 1542, are considered by some to have derived their name from the French *bas billon* or *bas pièce*, but a more probable explanation is that they take their name from Alexander Orrok, Lord of Sillebawbye, who is said to have struck them.

Henry VIII failed to take advantage of his position after the death of James V, and by demanding too much drove the opposing Scottish parties together. He then sent the Earl of Hertford with an army to ravage the southern part of the country. With the assistance of the French the Scots continued the struggle until 1551, when peace was made with England; the French, however, were determined still to gain control of Scotland. A strong movement grew up and championed the cause of protestantism against the catholics and French; this cause was further strengthened by the unpopularity of Mary Queen of Scot's marriage to the Dauphin of France in 1558.

When the Earl of Caithness began building the Castle of Mey in 1568—now 'Barrogill', the beautiful home of the Queen Mother—he took precautions very necessary in those days to provide a secret 'escape route' which could be used for escape by land in the case of invasion by sea, or for escape by sea if his attackers came by land. This secret route was rediscovered during World War II when an army lorry caused the tunnel to collapse. The earl died before the completion of the castle, which was continued by his grandson. This grandson, who also inherited the title, was very short of money and seeking a way to repair his financial embarrassment, found a coiner serving a sentence in the Edinburgh jail. The earl took the coiner away to his castle, provided him with the necessary implements and from a secret room gold and silver coins were provided for the earl, who prospered accordingly. We are not told whether or not the coins were of pure metal, but the odds must have been greatly against this.

Lady Jane Grey

When Edward VI died at the age of fifteen, the Duke of Northumberland, leader of the Council of Regency, advanced his own daughter-in-law, Lady Jane Grey, to the throne. Her claim was that she was Henry VII's great-granddaughter, but Mary, the daughter of Henry VIII and Katharine of Aragon (the first of his six wives), was the rightful successor and so obtained strong support. After nine days as queen, the unfortunate Lady Jane Grey was deposed, and later was taken to the Tower and executed. No coins, of course, were struck in such a short period.

Bloody Mary

Mary's coinage (1553-8) comprised two distinct issues, the first before her marriage to Philip of Spain, and the second after.

She proclaimed shortly after her accession that she would restore the coinage to its previous fineness in both gold and silver. All her gold coins were of standard gold (23 carat 3½ grains), while her silver was of 11oz fine except for the base pennies, which she continued to issue alongside the fine pennies, undoubtedly as token coins to augment the supplies. They were made from the melted metal of the base testoons and half groats.

Some of Mary's early gold sovereigns, which were valued at 30s, were the first gold English coins to bear a date, some with MDLIII and others with MDLIV. The obverse was both intricate and beautiful in design. Mary, in full regal gown, is enthroned on a delicately worked high-backed throne, and a portcullis lies beneath her feet. Mary's pre-marriage coins show, in the inscription, the pomegranate, the badge of her mother, Katharine of Aragon. Ryals, angels and angelets were struck, but in small quantities, while the early silver coins were groats, half groats and pennies (*Fig 7*). Base pennies were also struck at a weight 50 per cent above the 'fine' ones.

When Philip of Spain (later King Philip II of Spain after his father's abdication) married Mary in 1554 the marriage was generally unpopular with the English people; nevertheless, it was made an event by the issue of a new set of coins. Philip brought with him a vast mass of wealth from Spain, of which a detailed report is available from old records: 540 chests of bullion, each over 1yd long, were loaded on to twenty carts, followed by ninety-nine horses and two carts loaded with gold and silver coins. This great procession of wealth was driven to the Tower mint, where it was placed in safe keeping. Philip, however, was not impressed with his wife or with the English people, who did not receive him well, and after a few months returned to Spain on his father's abdication. The only gold coins issued after Mary's marriage were angels and angelets of the same standard. The designs of the silver coins were altered, the shillings and half shillings having the portraits of Mary and Philip facing one another—a fashion introduced into Spain by Philip's great-grandfather, King Ferdinand (*Fig 8*). The pennies continued to be struck as before in fine and base silver. Half crowns existed but these are thought to have been patterns only. The groats and half groats continued with the crowned bust of Mary, but with a different legend to the first issue. Mary retained her title as Queen of Ireland and in some degree religious unity was achieved; there was, however, no real peace. Her early Irish coins were shillings, groats, half groats and pennies, while after her marriage shillings and groats were struck from 1554 to 1558. The base rose pennies that were struck by Henry VIII and Edward VI were forbidden for use in England after September 1556, but were sent to Ireland, where they remained current.

Elizabeth — Last of the Great Tudors

When Mary died in 1558 and her protestant half-sister Elizabeth —the daughter of Henry VIII's second wife, Anne Boleyn—became queen, the Scottish protestants immediately saw the opportunity of an ally against the roman catholics. At the same time the catholic Henry II of France openly denounced Elizabeth as being illegitimate, since the catholics did not recognise divorce, not acknowledging any of Henry VIII's marriages except the first. An alliance which marked the end of the Franco-Scottish league was formed between the Scottish protestants and Elizabeth. The Scottish Parliament then denounced roman catholicism and secured the establishment of protestantism in 1560.

Mary Queen of Scots

Meanwhile Mary, the catholic Scottish queen had lost her husband the Dauphin of France and was obliged the following year to return to Scotland, where protestantism was now all-powerful. In 1565 she married her cousin, Lord Darnley, son of the Earl of Lennox. On her own initiative she bestowed on him the title of king, thereby giving him the authority to issue proclamations. In the troubles that followed, Mary obtained public support and gained two successes which alarmed the protestants, but after the birth of Prince James in 1566 the parents had a violent quarrel which left a permanent rift between them. This was utilised by their enemies, who saw an opportunity of destroying them both. Darnley was murdered in 1567. Finally the insurgents forced Mary into England, where she was imprisoned by Elizabeth I, and placed her son James VI of Scotland, who later became James I of England, on the throne.

The coinage of Mary Queen of Scots reveals many periods of her life, but it may be divided into two distinct parts—those before and after her first marriage, with the latter divided still further into four issues, namely: (1) Francis and Mary, (2) Mary (first widowhood), (3) Henry and Mary, (4) Mary (second widowhood). The gold coins were *écus d'or* (abbey crowns), lions (or 44s pieces), half lions, ryals (three-pound pieces), half ryals and 20s pieces. The silver coins were testoons (value 5s) (*Fig 9*), half testoons, silver ryals, two-third ryals, and one-third ryals, while base metal coins were billon bawbees and half bawbees, billon lions (or hardheads, value 1½d), pennies, placks and nonsunts (12d groats). The gold coins of the first and second issues were *écus d'or* and 20s pieces, both struck in 1543, the former being the only coin of Mary without a date on it. In the year following this issue, the Scottish silver and bronze coinage was devalued to one to four in ratio with the English coinage so that it was in line with gold. This ratio lasted until 1560 when, on the death of

Francis II, it again widened to one to five, including all metals. In 1565 when Mary married her cousin Darnley the ratio widened still further to one to six. The third issue of lions and half lions was dated 1553 to 1557 and the fourth issue, in 1555, 1557 and 1558, was of ryals and half ryals. In 1558 the queen, at the age of sixteen, had married the dauphin Francis; the French seized this opportunity to improve their position and obtained a marriage treaty whereby Francis shared the throne as King of Scotland in spite of much opposition from the Scots. The gold coins after the marriage were ducats in 1558, while more gold *écus d'or* were probably issued after the death of Francis in 1560. A large silver issue, the coins being eleven parts fine silver to one part alloy, was struck in testoons and half testoons from Mary's accession (1542) until the end of her widowhood in 1565. The first testoons of 1553 were the first Scottish milled coins. These, however, were struck in France, where this new method had just been introduced.

During her marriage to Darnley silver ryals and divisions of two-thirds with the names Henry and Mary on them were issued from 1565 until 1567. The same denominations were issued after Darnley's death but in Mary's name only. Of the billon coins there were three issued before Mary's first marriage: these were bawbees, half bawbees, pennies, hardheads (or lions) and placks. The remaining issues were circulated after her first marriage and were nonsunts (or 12d groats) and hardheads (or lions). The new nonsunts take their name from the Latin inscription '. . . non sunt . . .' which appeared on the reverses.

Maundy Money

The Tudor records, particularly those of Queen Elizabeth, are the earliest detailed accounts we have of the Maundy ceremony but less complete records go back many years. The ceremony is probably derived from the actions of our Lord at the Last Supper: 'He riseth from supper . . . poureth water into a basin, and began to wash the disciples' feet, and to wipe them with the towel wherewith he was girded' (John xiii, 4, 5). The washing of feet was always part of the ceremony in early Christian days. The first evidence of the Maundy in Britain dates from the late sixth century, when it is referred to by St Augustine, whose mission from Rome arrived in Kent in 597. Further evidence exists that King John (1199-1216) distributed money to the poor. The intense humility, piety and stoicism of these early Christians is exemplified by the Maundy service of 922, which was conducted with everyone on their knees, even while crossing the hall—an almost acrobatic feat. The great physical exertion on a (presumably) stone floor was too much for the aged St Oswald, Archbishop of York, who, according to the report, 'passed to the Lord'. Detailed reports of the ceremony show how the Tudor and Stuart monarchs—sometimes accompanied by their queen consorts —carried out the ceremony with all the pomp of that period, attended by the higher nobleman and prelates. Henry VIII in one of his tyrannical moods forbade his queen, Katharine of Aragon, to 'keep her Maundy'. Nevertheless the queen made him qualify this order and so she was allowed to take part in the ceremony as a private person.

The amount of money distributed before the Tudor period is uncertain, though there is ample evidence to show that coins were given as well as food, wine and clothes. The records of the Tudors show that the number of poor persons selected for the ceremony was equivalent to the monarch's age; so that, for example, the quantity of silver made up annually into silver pennies for the Maundy service from 1574 to 1578 gradually increased. An account of 1554 states that Queen Mary distributed her Maundy with great reverence, performing the ceremony 'from one end (of the hall) to the other ever on her knees' while washing the women's feet. After inspecting the forty-one women (the queen's age) for the most deserving to receive her personal gown, which was of the finest cloth with a fur lining and sleeves 'so long and wide they reached the ground', the queen gave it to the oldest; then 'she gave to each a leathern purse containing forty one pennies, according to the number of her years. . .'

When Queen Elizabeth (1558-1603) came to the throne much of the base coinage of Edward VI was still current. For a time it continued in circulation but the two worst types of testoon, which had

The Tudors

been circulating at considerably less than their face value, were collected at appointed places in various towns and devalued. Some were marked with the Tudor portcullis and revalued at 4½d, while others were stamped with a greyhound and revalued at 2¼d. In 1561, however, they were made illegal. To cope with this large quantity of base silver a special section was reserved in the Tower mint for melting it down. The workmen engaged on this task nearly all 'fell sick to death with the savour' and they were advised, presumably by a doctor of that period, 'to drink from a dead man's skull for their cure'. A warrant was obtained for permission to remove the skulls from London Bridge, where the heads of those who had suffered hanging for their crimes were exhibited on pikes, and to use them as cups for drinking. It is said that some of the workmen found a cure, but most of them died! We know now, of course, that certain fumes from metals can be very poisonous, and fatal if inhaled in excess.

More denominations of coins were struck in Elizabeth's reign than in any other period of the English coinage. These included sovereigns valued at 30s, ryals at 15s, angels at 10s (with half and quarter angels), pounds at 20s (and half pounds) and crowns (and half crowns) struck in both gold and silver (*Figs 10 and 11*). The lower values in silver were shillings, sixpences, groats, threepences, half groats, three-halfpenny pieces, pennies, three-farthing pieces and halfpennies.

The 30s sovereigns, ryals and angels, and divisions of them, were all struck in 23 carat 3½ grains (standard gold), but the remainder of the gold coins were struck in 22 carat (crown gold). The silver coins were struck in 11oz fine silver from 1558 to 1560, but after 1560 the silver content was increased to 11oz 2dwt. The pennies were first issued at a weight of 8 grains, but this was later slightly reduced. The scarcity of small change around 1574 caused token coins in lead and tin to be circulated illegally by shopkeepers among their customers. It had been a continual problem for people to find sufficient small change throughout the Middle Ages. There had been no serious attempt to remedy this deficiency by the Crown, presumably because the smallest denominations were less profitable to strike than the larger coins. The government contemplated producing copper halfpennies and farthings from 1574, but these coins probably never passed beyond the pattern stage. In 1577, however, the City of Bristol was given a licence to strike copper token farthings, which were square and stamped with the city arms.

Milling

During Elizabeth's reign there was an attempt to introduce the newly designed French screw press for improving the edges of coins, which became known as 'mill money'—'milled money' being a commonly used misnomer. At that time watermills and horsemills supplied the power to operate a press for rolling out sheet metal to a required thickness, a cutting punch for cutting out the metal discs, and a screw press for stamping the discs from dies and containing them at the edges so as to produce a perfectly circular coin, unlike the hammered coin with its uneven edges. But about 1560 Eloye Mestrelle, an employee of the Paris mint, obtained employment in the Tower of London mint and proceeded to strike coins immeasurably superior to the existing ones, by this new milling process. Alas for Mestrelle and his new machine! Just as, many years later, workmen rioted against new machinery which they feared would spread unemployment, so the mint workers evinced such hostility that the new machinery was rejected and Mestrelle himself dismissed. In 1578 the tragedy was made complete when Mestrelle, having found no recognition for his talents, turned counterfeiter and was hanged for this crime at Norwich. Another counterfeiter named Philippe Mestrelle, also a Frenchman and possibly a relative, is sometimes confused with the mint worker. Philippe had been hanged and quartered at Tyburn nine years earlier, in January 1569, for counterfeiting gold coins.

The need for introducing the new three-halfpenny and three-farthing pieces, with the Tudor rose behind the queen's head, is difficult to understand in view of the issue of halfpennies and farthings in previous reigns. A possible reason was the earlier devaluation of the base half groats and pennies to three halfpence and three farthings respectively, which had given the public an opportunity to accustom themselves to these denominations. The unpopularity of the tiny three-farthing piece at that time is perpetuated in Shakespeare's *King John* (1, 1, 141), when Philip Faulconbridge disparagingly compares his brother's personal appearance to this extremely thin and small silver coin by vowing that he would rather forfeit his heritage than look like him:

> My arms such eel-skins stuff'd, my face so thin
> That in mine ear I durst not stick a rose,
> Lest men should say, 'Look where three farthing goes!'

The Scornful Lady by Beaumont and Fletcher has a passage which shows how similar were the penny and the three-farthing pieces and how common a trick it was to impose on the ignorant the smaller coin with the rose erased instead of the larger. In scathing words the writer refers to the usurer and his punishment:

> He had a bastard, his own toward issue,
> Whip'd and then crop'd for washing out the roses
> In three-farthings, to make them pence.

In 1562 rumours spread regarding the devaluation of the coinage, in spite of government proclamations to the contrary, and economic pressure finally forced the coinage to be devalued by one-third. No later proclamation restoring the coinage is to be found and one must conclude that it remained devalued until 1572, when a new coinage was issued at the old values.

Ireland under Elizabeth

Ireland theoretically came under the sway of the Established Church again when Elizabeth became queen in succession to her catholic sister Mary. Garrisons and English law gradually extended in spite of severe opposition from the feudal Irish lords. In 1561 Jesuit missions began to fan the existing religious discontent, which culminated in a papal bull of 1570, excommunicating Elizabeth and releasing her Irish subjects from obedience to her. Nine years later there was a widespread rising against 'Elizabeth, pretended queen of England', but the leader of the rising, Fitzmaurice, was killed in a small affray and the insurrection failed, being stamped out in pitiless and bloody massacres. Many lands were forfeited and newcomers—Raleigh was one of them—shared 200,000 acres of land. Ireland after this was so crushed for a time that she hardly showed any interest in current affairs, even when the great Spanish Armada sailed and was destroyed. In 1585 the Irish chiefs and gentry of the west were assured of their estates provided they paid rents to the Crown and recognised English tenure, an arrangement which helped to keep the peace and loyalty of Connaught under its Gaelic and Norman proprietors.

In 1598 the English under Essex were severely checked and defeated by the three most powerful Irish lords who had combined forces, overrunning Connacht and Munster. Their numbers in 1600 totalled over 20,000 men with an additional force sent to aid them from Spain; but this large army was defeated and the country conquered systematically and Celtic and Norman Ireland ceased to exist. Now a new Irishman, catholic in religion, a mixture of Irish and English in breed, and in the main Irish-speaking, came into being. It was difficult indeed for a protestant government to rule such a race.

The first Irish coinage of Elizabeth was issued in 1558, coined from the base money of England in shillings and groats, a commission being granted to Sir Edmund Peckham to coin £12,000 of base English money into £24,000 of Irish at the Tower mint. Later, in 1561, the base current money was altered to harp shillings and groats, £8,000 of this money, at 3oz fine, being coined from £4,000 English.

Sir James Ware in 1560 wrote that the mixed money of England, being no longer current, was brought into Ireland in great quantities. 'The Bungalls', the two types of testoon demonetised in England in 1561 and so called by the Irish, went for 6d and the broad pieces at 12d at first, but afterwards the former went for 2d only and the latter for a groat. After they were refused elsewhere they continued to pass in Connacht, the former at 1d and the latter at 2d.

The second issue, in 1561, was of good silver, struck in shillings and groats. After many years of base coin it caused favourable comment. One reference appears in this ballad in praise of the queen:

The Tudors

> Let bone-fires shine in every place,
> Sing, and ring the bells apace;
> And pray that long may live her grace,
> To be the good queen of Ireland.
>
> The gold and silver, which was so base
> That no man could endure it scarce,
> Is now new-coyn'd with her own face,
> And made go current in Ireland.

The third issue 1598-1602, however, when shillings, sixpences and threepences were issued, together with copper pennies and halfpennies issued in 1601, fell back again to the base metal. A writer in 1598 mentions that five sorts of money for Ireland were being minted: Irish twelvepence, the half shilling for sixpence, quarter shilling for threepence, the penny for one penny Irish and the halfpenny for a halfpenny Irish. These coins were sent over and issued for payment to the army in Ireland.

At the end of Elizabeth's reign, 1602-3, another writer gives a description of the coinage in circulation, concluding with the current issue which he describes as 'adulterate coin', and listing the various groats of earlier years as follows:

> Firstly, broadfaced groats coined originally for four pence now worth eight.
>
> Secondly, cross-keele groats, stamped with a triple crown, which were coined likewise for fourpence, but at better value at that time. These were either sent hither of old by the popes, or for their honour had this stamp set upon them.
>
> Thirdly, dominion groats of a like fineness, coined by such English kings as styled themselves Domini Hiberniae.
>
> Fourthly, Rex groats, of those who took the title of kings of Ireland which had such a mixture of copper that their intrinsic value was not above twopence.
>
> Fifthly, white groats of so base a mixture that nine were given to an English shilling. They had also brass harpers which were as big as a shilling but went for no more than one penny, and farthings of the same metal called 'smulkins'.

James VI of Scotland

Mary Queen of Scots escaped from her prison in Lochleven Castle in 1568 and fled to England hoping to find refuge. She only found imprisonment. This meant the complete triumph in Scotland of the Protestant Church, which had been legally recognised by Parliament the year before. The claims of the Church caused James VI (1567-1625) to oppose it continually and he established control over it before he became king of protestant England. The rise in power of the French catholics caused him to repent his intrigue with them, and realising that any continuation of it would anger his protestant supporters he decided that the best route to the English throne was through the friendship of Elizabeth. Even the threat against Mary's life, she was still Elizabeth's prisoner, did not make James sever his English friendship. With the threat of a Spanish invasion aggravated by continuous acts of English piracy and the plundering of Spanish merchant ships, Mary was deemed to be a dangerous prisoner and the inspiration for plots against Elizabeth, so she was executed in 1587. This caused great indignation in Scotland, but James managed to weather the storm and keep the peace. Because he was the least of several alternative evils the English tolerated his claim to the throne. In the last year of Elizabeth's reign relations improved greatly. James had acquired considerable control over the Church General Assembly and even gave seats in parliament to the bishops whom he appointed. He was, however, continually in financial difficulties and though there was much reorganisation in 1596 by eight leading statesmen known as the 'Octavians', the exchequer's need was greater than the Crown's revenues.

After Mary Queen of Scots had abdicated in favour of James many new types of Scottish coins were struck. The gold coins were as follows:

> Twenty-pound piece, the largest coin ever struck in Scotland, issued 1575-6 (Fig 12).
>
> Sword and sceptre (£6) and its half, issued 1601-4, taking its name from the sword and sceptre in saltire on the obverse.
>
> Thistle noble (£7 6s 8d), named after the thistle which is shown in the design on the side of a ship, issued in the fifth coinage in 1588.

The Tudors

Rider (£5) and its half, issued 1593-1601.

Ducat, or bare-headed noble (80s), issued 1580.

Hat piece (80s), with its Latin legend *Spera Meliora* meaning 'Hope for better things', referring to the king's claim to the English throne. It was issued from 1591 to 1593 and takes its name from the high hat worn by the king on the design. It is said to have been issued 'for the purpose of harmonising the Scottish currency with the English, and to lessen the inconvenience caused by their disagreement'.

Lion noble (75s) and its divisions of two-thirds and one-third, which is sometimes called the Scottish angel. The two-thirds is named the Scottish crown and the one-third the Scottish half-crown; issued 1584-8.

The silver coins were made up as follows:

Sword dollar, 1567-71, Scots, and its divisions of two-thirds and one-third of similar dates; value 30s, 20s, 10s Scots.

Two merk (or Thistle dollar) 1578-80. In 1578 coins of an earlier date were called in. They were then countermarked with a crowned thistle and reissued at a higher value, 26s 8d. An example is a silver ryal of Mary (former value 30s) raised to 36s 9d.

Merk 1579-80; half merk (or noble) 1572-7, 1580; quarter merk (or half noble) 1572-7, 1580; values 13s 4d, 6s 8d and 3s 4d Scots.

Sixteen-shilling piece 1581, and its divisions of half, quarter, and one-eighth of similar date.

Forty-shilling piece 1582-8, and its divisions of thirty-shilling piece 1582-5, twenty-shilling piece 1582-4, ten-shilling 1582-4.

Balance half merk 1591-4, and its half division of balance quarter merk 1591, 1592, value 6s 8d and 3s 4d Scots.

Ten-shilling piece 1593-5, 1598, 1599, and its half divisions of five shillings 1593-5, 1598, 1599, quarter division of thirty pence 1593-5, 1598, 1599 and 1601, and tenth division of twelve pence 1593-6.

Thistle merk 1601-4, and its half and quarter divisions of half thistle merk and quarter thistle merk of similar date, and eighth division of eighth thistle merk dated 1601-3; values 13s 4d, 6s 8d, 3s 4d and 1s 8d Scots.

The billon pieces were made up of placks (8d), half placks, saltire placks (4d), twopence (or hard heads) and half hard heads; there was also an issue of copper twopences and pennies. Both the merks and the saltire placks were new coins. The former originated from the medieval mark, which in the first place was a weight. Later this coin became a money of account and finally a coin of Scotland in 1591. In the same year balance half merks were struck, followed by thistle merks in 1601. The saltire placks were so named from the sceptres in saltire (ie crossed) united by a thistle on the coin's design.

1 The magnificent Tudor designed sovereign of Henry VII. Greyhound and dragon on pillars type
2 Henry VII silver testoon c 1508. The first silver coin to display the monarch's portrait
3 Gold crown of the double rose with crowned initials H (Henry) R (Rex)
4 The base testoon of Henry VIII containing only one third silver. Tower mint

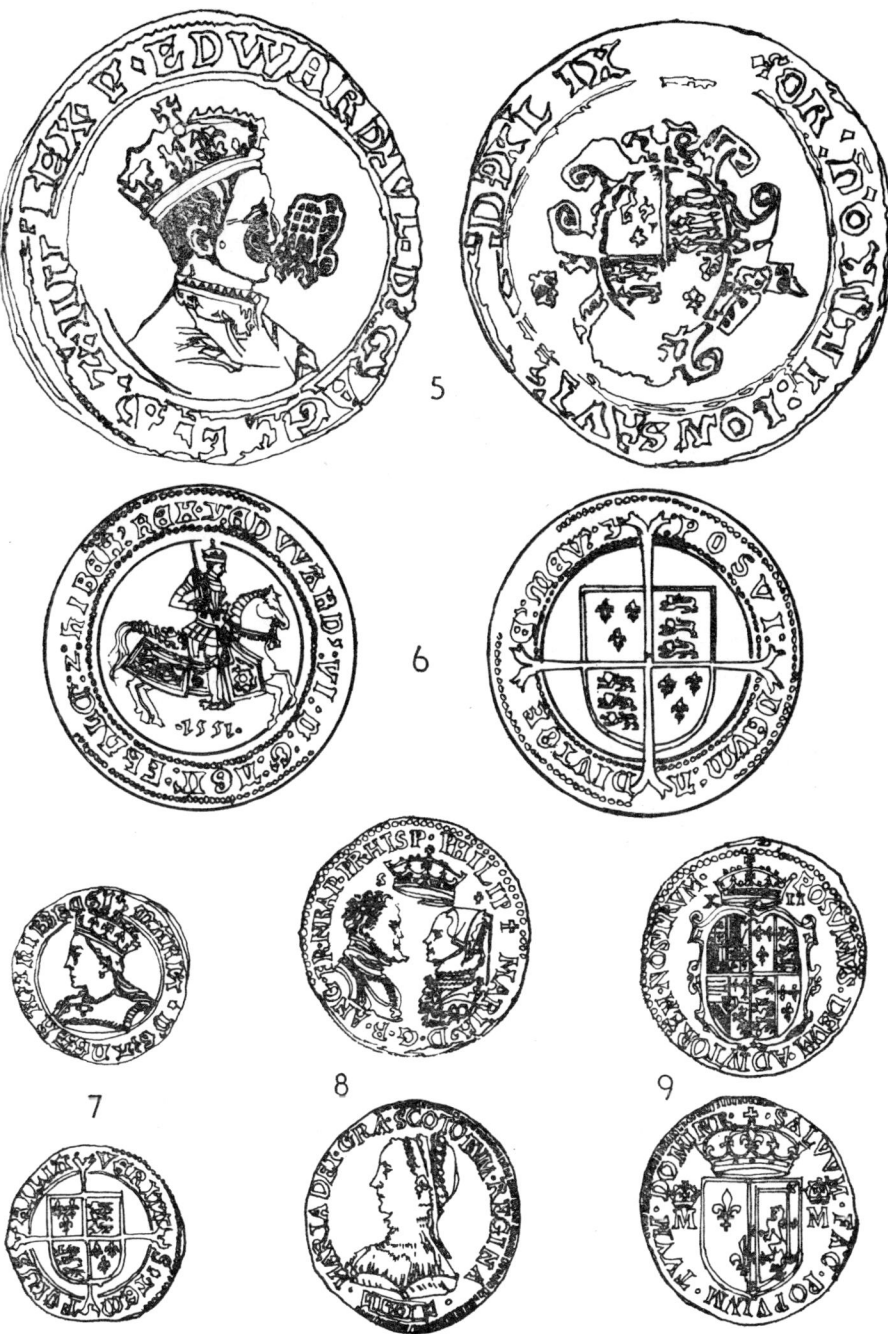

5 Edward VI countermarked testoon, of the lowest silver content ever, one quarter silver, c 1549 Southwark
6 The first silver crown dated 1551. Edward VI
7 Mary's silver groat with the reverse inscription VERITAS. TEMPORIS. FILIA (Truth, the daughter of time)
8 The silver shilling of Philip and Mary, with its unusual facing portraits
9 The Mary Queen of Scots testoon 1561 (Scottish value 5s)

10 Enlarged obverse of Elizabeth I gold half pound 22 carat (twice diameter of coin)
11 Elizabeth I silver crown, showing the much used reverse inscription POSUI DEUM ADJUTOREM MEUM (I have made God my helper)
12 James VI of Scotland twenty pound piece c 1576. The reverse shows clearly the Scottish leopard rampant (twice diameter of coin)

VII
STUART AND COMMONWEALTH

James I

When James, son of Mary Queen of Scots and Henry Darnley, became King of England (1603-25), rebellious Scottish barons and discontented Scottish preachers lost a valuable ally in the English Crown, which had been the usual refuge of agitating Scots for generations. The absence of any foreign support now made an uprising in Scotland a dangerous expedient, giving the king greater despotic power than before.

The first after-the-union Scottish issue, with the reverse showing the shield with the arms of Great Britain, and similar to the corresponding English coins with a variation in the form of the crown worn by the king, was in 1604. Gold coins named sceptres or units (£12) were struck—the equivalent English coin is spelt 'unite' (*Fig 1*) —and double crowns (£6), britain crowns (£3), half crowns and thistle crowns (48s). At the same time silver coins were issued in denominations of 60s, 30s, 12s, 6s, 2s, 1s and ½s. A second issue of gold and silver coins similar to those of 1604 was made in 1610, though the arrangement of the arms on the reverse differed. The designs of the thistle crown, two shilling, one shilling and half shilling, however, were not changed but continued to be struck with their 1604 design until the end of the reign.

The copper coins named turners (or twopences) and half turners (or pennies)—a corruption of the French 'tournois', which originated from a coin minted in the town of Tours—were first issued in 1613, with a second issue in 1623. The two issues differed in minor points only—in legend and weight—with the former the heavier of the two issues.

English coins had reached by now twelve times the value of the

Scottish coins of the same name, an example being the Scottish shilling, which was equal to the English penny. Since 1355 when the two coinages were equal, the Scottish coinage had gradually lost ground to the English until James VI ascended the throne in 1603. This ratio of coin values between the two countries remained until the reign of Anne when the articles of the Act of Union provided that the coins should be the same standard and value throughout the United Kingdom.

GOLD

Twelve-pound piece Scottish	or English unite
Six ,, ,, ,,	,, ,, double crown
Three ,, ,, ,,	,, ,, britain crown
Forty-eight shilling piece Scottish	,, ,, thistle crown
Thirty-shilling piece Scottish	,, ,, half crown

SILVER

Three-pound piece Scottish	or English crown
Thirty-shilling ,, ,,	,, ,, half crown
Twelve-shilling ,, ,,	,, ,, shilling
Six-shilling ,, ,,	,, ,, sixpence
Two-shilling ,, ,,	,, ,, twopence
One-shilling ,, ,,	,, ,, penny
Sixpenny ,, ,,	,, ,, halfpenny

The first English coinage of James I was similar to that of Elizabeth, both in metal, quality, weight and denominations. James's Scottish title was added and the royal arms was altered to include the shields of Scotland and Ireland. Gold issues were circulated in 1603, 1604, 1605 and 1619, silver issues in 1603 and 1604 and copper in 1613, when Lord Harrington was given a patent to strike token farthings, for which privilege he was obliged to pay.

The gold coins were sovereigns, half sovereigns, gold crowns and half crowns struck in crown gold, and the silver coins were crowns, half crowns, shillings, sixpences, half groats, pennies and halfpennies, all issued in 1603 for circulation in England only.

The second issue in 1604 consisted of unites, double crowns, britain crowns, crowns, half crowns and thistle crowns, again struck in crown gold; the silver coins (11oz 2dwt fine) of this issue were crowns (*Fig 2*), half crowns, shillings, sixpences, half groats, pennies and halfpennies. The gold coins were issued at a reduced weight to allow for the disproportion between gold and silver, which had caused some inconvenience when Scottish gold coins of a slightly higher gold content were declared equal in value to the English. In 1605 there was another issue of gold coins—rose ryals (30s), spur ryals (15s) (*Fig 3*), angels and angelets; but these were struck in standard gold.

The reduction of the weight of the gold coins did not have the desired effect and in 1609 a commission was appointed to inquire into the causes and to suggest a remedy. As a result, in 1619 a third coinage was issued, with the gold coins still further reduced in weight. Rose ryals, spur ryals and angels were struck in standard gold, while new types of unites (known as 'laurels' because of the laureated head on the obverse), with halves and quarters, were struck in crown gold; the silver denominations were as before.

In 1613 James decided to issue token copper farthings as a remedy for the acute shortage of small change. Lord Harrington, as mentioned previously, was given the sole right to issue them in England, Ireland and Wales, sharing the profits with the king. An exchange was set up in the City of London—evidence of which remains today in the name of Tokenhouse Yard, adjacent to the Bank of England—where 21s worth of farthings was exchanged for 20s, while they were redeemed in a similar manner with the seller obtaining 20s for his 21s worth of farthings. As Lord Harrington died in the year he received the patent, his widow is believed to have sold it in 1615 to the Duke of Lennox and Richmond; when the Duke died in 1624 the patent passed likewise to his widow, the Duchess of Richmond. The farthings varied in size, which gave rise to a belief that the smaller ones were half farthings. Another type was created, oval in shape, at the end of James's reign, which is believed to have been intended for circulation in Ireland (*Fig 4*). There was considerable opposition to these coins in certain districts, and in parts of northern England they were refused altogether. There were four types: the two 'Harrington' issues, which were small and oval; and the later 'Lennox' types, one of which was normal sized, and a second striking, which was oval.

There is an interesting report on token farthings in a book entitled *The Maintenance of Free Trade*, published in London in 1622, which comments on their issue in favourable terms:

> There was an intention to bring in the use of copper moneys within the realms; which tokens are found to bee very commodious and necessary, whereby the waste of much silver is prevented, the meere poore relieved, and many of their lives saved, and the commonwealth cannot be without them, unless leaden tokens were made againe in derogation of his majestie's Prerogative Royall.

During James's reign a good deal of silver was refined from the lead mines near Aberystwyth, which were leased to Sir Hugh Middleton in 1621. This metal was sent to the Tower mint where silver was coined with small Prince of Wales feathers over the royal arms, denoting the place of origin.

Irish Peace

James I's policy in Ireland failed in its attempt to defeat catholicism. In Ulster, however, he restored the two earls of Tyrone and Tyrconnell, but eventually nearly 100 chiefs left the north in 1607, dealing a vital blow to the catholic and Gaelic tradition. James's plantation of Ulster with protestant settlers from England and Scotland left it the most British of the provinces. In spite of much opposition to these settlements Ireland began to enjoy the early fruits of a period of peace, whereby improved agriculture, enterprising settlers and new industries made their mark on the country.

Now that rebellion was suppressed the reasons for circulating base coinage no longer existed; accordingly, instructions were given in 1603 for the issue of shillings and sixpences (9oz fine) for circulation, and the base metal money of Elizabeth was reduced to one-third in value. In the following year another issue of shillings and sixpences was made, while the English base money was reduced still further to one-quarter of its face value. This issue continued to be struck until 1607. In 1606 the Irish harp shilling was made equal to 9d English, making the English shilling equal to 16d Irish. When the token farthings were issued in 1613 many were put into circulation in Ireland.

Stuart and Commonwealth

Charles I

Charles I (1625-49) was temperamentally unsuited to rule England at a time when the people were looking for a greater say in the affairs of the nation. As an artist and a scholar his reputation was high but, probably influenced by the despotic rule of the Tudors, he failed to understand that the country would not now accept the doctrine of the Divine Right of Kings. The philosopher Hobbes, who witnessed the effects of a divided nation, wrote in his *Leviathan*:

> A philosophical treatise to substantiate the need for Absolutism in government whereby the people vested an absolute authority in their chosen leader.

At length Charles found himself in conflict with a very determined Parliament, which refused to give way to his demands to exercise complete authority over it; and by a number of foolish and unstatesmanlike acts he roused a good deal of public antagonism against himself.

His coinage is the most extensive of all the English monarchs—due mainly to the Civil War. It can clearly be divided into three groups, firstly the coins issued by the Tower mint (including those of Nicholas Briot); secondly those struck by the provincial mints during the Civil War; and thirdly the coins struck by towns besieged by Parliamentary forces. The Tower mint group (*Fig 5*) can also be divided into three—those of 1625-6 when the King wears the robes of the Garter, of 1626-31 when he wears a ruff and armour, and of 1631-46 when he substituted a falling lace collar for the ruff, with armour worn as before. In this last period, however, the King's authority virtually ended with the outbreak of the Civil War in 1642.

The gold coins following Charles's accession were unites, double crowns, britain crowns and angels; and in silver, crowns, half crowns, shillings, sixpences, half groats, pennies and halfpennies. Additional denominations were struck at the provincial mints. There were three-pound pieces in gold, twenty-shilling and ten-shilling pieces, groats and threepences in silver. The gold coins were made of crown gold except for the angels, of which a small number were struck in standard gold for the ceremony of 'Touching for the King's Evil'.

The angels served both the Tudors and the Stuarts at this ceremony, when the coins were hung by the sovereign round the necks of the sick—sufferers from a tubercular skin disease called scrofula, a complaint prevalent in those days. The ceremony was believed to have been started by Edward the Confessor in 1058 when he was supposed to have healed a woman by touch, and the disease was afterwards known as 'the King's disease'. This health service grew so popular that Charles I in 1635-6 obtained 5,500 copper discs from the mint to use for admitting people to the ceremony at 2d a time. The angels were no longer minted after the Civil War and smaller gold replicas in 22 carat took their place. The magical means of healing certainly lost none of its popularity during the reign of the Stuarts, as Charles II was credited with 'touching' 90,000 people; the ceremony, however, seems to have been on the wane after the sceptical Dr Johnson was touched by Queen Anne and from George I's reign onwards it is not mentioned.

The issue of token farthings continued under new control. The Duchess of Richmond in 1634 passed the patent to Lord Maltravers, who, in 1636, to counteract the large number of forgeries, added a brass centre to each farthing. These may be divided into five types, the 'Richmond' and the 'Maltravers' both being issued in round and oval coins, while a fifth issue of a later date, the Rose farthing, was named after the design.

In 1625, the year that Charles became king, a Frenchman from Lorraine, Nicholas Briot, formerly engraver general of the Paris mint, obtained employment at the Tower mint. Three years later in 1628 his ability as a designer became recognised and he was commissioned to design portraits for coins and medals; in the next few years he produced beautiful patterns, which were to become famous. These included his designs of the rose and the anchor, which were used as privy marks (mint marks) on coins. He reintroduced the latest mill and screw press from France, and though he succeeded in producing many beautiful coins by this method, ignorance, prejudice and jealousy among his colleagues at the mint prevented its general introduction. This press exerted an even greater pressure by the screw, and the use of a collar around the flange not only prevented the metal spreading unevenly, as with a hammered coin, but gave a fuller and more even impression of the die.

Briot's ability was not solely artistic. He was also possibly the finest die-cutter of the English coinage, apart from Alexander of Brugsal, the German graver to Henry VII in 1494. From 1635 Charles I appointed him master and engraver of the Edinburgh mint in spite of much opposition from the Scottish Privy Council and the mint itself; but after his daughter had married John Falconer, both Briot and his son-in-law were accepted as joint masters in 1637. Briot, however, returned to his post at the London mint in 1638 at the request of the King. Unfortunately the Civil War denied the country the opportunity of having a coinage from such a gifted artist and die-cutter, since he died in 1646. His coins of the London mint in two periods of 1631-2 and 1638-9 were gold angels, unites, double crowns and crowns; while his silver coins were crowns, half crowns, shillings, sixpences, half groats and pennies.

Silver continued to be extracted from the lead mines in North Wales, and struck into crowns, half crowns, shillings, sixpences, groats, threepences, half groats and pennies, with the feathers of Wales over the royal arms. In 1637 it was decided that it would be advantageous to have a mint near to the mines to avoid unnecessary transport, and so one was established at Aberystwyth under Thomas Bushell, the lessee of the mines.

Early Banknotes

During this period the development of trade often made payment by coin inconvenient and sometimes one party to a transaction would give a written acknowledgement and a promise to pay to the other. This form of promise to pay became accepted in settlement of debts by other parties not concerned in the original transaction, eg Mr Jones receives six sheep from Mr Smith and gives in return a written receipt and a promise to pay. Mr Smith can then use this promise to pay in order to buy corn from Mr Brown. Much of the same practice took place in Scotland and Ireland.

Charles I has been held responsible for the development of these early notes, because of his belief that the king could do no wrong, even when he compulsorily borrowed money to relieve his financial embarrassment. In 1640 it was customary for merchants to keep their gold and silver in the Tower mint in the absence of better facilities. A large consignment of bullion had been sent there from overseas for safe keeping; but Charles, being in great need of money —having recently lost a very large sum on speculations in pepper— gave orders for it to be seized. This caused great alarm to merchants and others, who informed the king that if this bullion were removed it would jeopardise future supplies from overseas. Finally the King agreed to borrow £40,000 only out of the total of £120,000, depositing security and paying interest. After this the merchants doubted the safety of the Tower mint and began to deposit their money with the goldsmiths, of whom there were a number in London, Edinburgh, Dublin and other cities. From about this period these goldsmiths began to act as bankers for the public by accepting deposits of money, for which a form of receipt note was issued giving the depositor an opportunity of drawing cash from his deposit in part or as a whole. From these early notes our present-day paper money has been gradually evolved.

Civil War

The King continued to take the law into his hands by levying taxes without the consent of Parliament and by dissolving that body when it protested. The position was further aggravated by his intolerance (aided by Archbishop Laud) to the Puritans and other sects of the Low Church. The final spark that set off the Civil War (1645-51) was Charles's attempt to arrest five members of Parliament for opposing him. The City of London, where they took refuge, refused to give them up and the King, fearing an armed rising in London, withdrew to raise his own army.

The first of the provincial mints of the Civil War was at York. Many of the coins struck there, which were half crowns, shillings, sixpences and threepences, were designed by Briot, who made secret

Stuart and Commonwealth

journeys from London while still working for the Parliament mint in the Tower. After the Battle of Marston Moor, in 1644, York surrendered to the Parliamentarians.

In 1642 the Aberystwyth mint was closed but moved to Shrewsbury (*Figs 6 and 7*) where the following coins were struck:

gold	triple unites
silver	pounds
	half pounds
	crowns
	half crowns
	shillings

Following this move the drawn Battle of Edgehill was fought, and the King closed the Shrewsbury mint, setting up a new mint at Oxford, his new headquarters, which lasted until 1646. Early in 1643 the Oxford mint, followed by Bristol, began production of the following gold and silver coins:

gold	triple unites (Oxford only)	
	unites	
	double crowns	
silver	pounds	⎫
	half pounds	⎬ (Oxford only)
	crowns	⎭
	half crowns	
	shillings	
	sixpences	
	groats	
	threepences	
	half groats	
	pennies	

Although still working in the Tower mint Briot is known to have made secret visits to Oxford to assist in the coin production.

In addition to these mints, Lundy Island, Combe Martin, Salisbury, Truro (*Fig 9*), Exeter, Weymouth, Worcester and Chester opened mints for the King at varying periods between 1643 and 1648, where the undermentioned coins were struck:

gold unites—Truro and Salisbury only
silver half pounds—Truro only
crowns
half crowns
shillings
sixpences   issued by mints
groats   as listed on pp 286-8
threepences
half groats
pennies

The gold and silver obtained for provincial mints came largely from plate generously given in response to an appeal by the King, who promised to pay 8 per cent interest on it. At the same time Parliament, also in need of bullion, appealed to the public at the same rate of interest. The response was so great in London that it took two days for the many donors to hand in their contributions at the Guildhall.

The increasing number of forged token farthings caused the patentee much anxiety, but new ones continued to be struck until the forgeries became so numerous that the exchange in 1644 refused coins on the ground that they were forgeries. Parliament in 1649 decided to stop the issue of token farthings—then the Maltravers 'rose' types—which left many unfortunate people with a large number of these coins on their hands. Many of them were women, often with young children, who obtained their living by selling fruit, herbs, fish, etc, and who had all their takings in farthings; and a large number applied to the House of Commons for relief.

The disappearance of small change soon had the effect of bringing back token coins. From 1648 the shopkeepers issued 'traders', a practice which soon spread very widely. Almost every town and village was circulating halfpenny and farthing tokens of varying shapes—and sometimes pennies—struck in brass or copper and bearing a tradesman's name and address. Often municipalities issued tokens, some stating on them the reason why they were being struck. The government made no attempt to stop this illegal practice as it supplied no alternative coinage until 1672, when Charles II issued a regal copper coinage.

Siege Pieces

Sheer necessity created the odd-shaped coins issued by the besieged royalists in their strongholds. These coins today are known as 'siege pieces' or 'obsidional coinage tokens'. Royalist strongholds under siege from Parliamentary forces were compelled to find a means of exchange since the regional mints were no longer accessible. Emergency issues of their own making were needed to pay both garrison troops and provide for the everyday commercial transactions of the townsfolk. Accordingly, all available plate was taken and odd-shaped pieces were crudely struck; these complied with the usual coinage only in their weight/value ratio. The estimated value was stamped on, accompanied by an identifying design, usually of the fortress of the relevant town.

A number of these was issued by Newark, situated on the River Trent, which held out until May 1646 (*Fig 10*). Many are easily distinguishable by the hole whereby they were worn as keepsakes or badges. The coining included half crowns, shillings, ninepences and sixpences, all on diamond or lozenge-shaped flans, bearing a crowned monogram CR (CAROLUS REX), with the relative value in pence below. In May 1646 Newark yielded to the Scottish army, which was later to betray Charles himself.

The King's disastrous defeat at Marston Moor in 1644 placed the rest of loyalist Yorkshire in jeopardy. Scarborough Castle, by virtue of its high and isolated position, provided an impregnable fortress from within which the Governor, Sir Hugh Cholmley, issued a sizeable quantity of tokens, irregular in shape, not in accepted denominations but in over twenty different values ranging from 5s 8d to 4d, including the odd amounts of 3s 4d, 1s 1d and 7d (*Fig 11*). Some pieces, besides the castle and value mark, bear the optimistic legend CAROLI FORTUNA RESURGAM (The fortune of Charles will rise again). The irregularity of these coins and their values results from the fact that they were manufactured from clipped fractions of silver plate, taken from household utensils, bowls, tankards, etc. Hence there is no common denominator in thickness; pieces of the same value were larger if the plate was thin and smaller if the plate was thick. Shears were used haphazardly for sizing, hence the arbitrary naming of pieces. Occasionally plate marks and patterns of the original objects are visible.

Carlisle suffered similarly, being starved into submission in June 1645. It was not until the latter months of the siege, that the Governor utilised his citizens' silver plate. Out of 1,162oz and 6dwt a ready supply of three-shilling and one-shilling pieces was coined (*Fig 12*).

Civil War II

The first Civil War terminated in 1646, and in 1647 the Scots, to whom Charles had surrendered himself, exchanged their prisoner for the handsome sum of £400,000, arrears of pay from the English. This was the unfortunate conclusion to the disastrous defeat of Charles at Naseby in 1645. At the end of the year Charles's escape to the Isle of Wight triggered off new Royalist outbreaks, causing the second Civil War of 1648-9. Colchester, the centre of the new Royalist rising in the eastern counties, was besieged in 1648 by Fairfax. A variety of pieces were struck there, including shillings, ninepences, etc, in round and octagonal shapes. These pieces were uniface, ie, stamped on one side only, with a five-towered castle in the centre and the motto reiterating that of Scarborough used three years earlier. Outstanding in this issue is the uniface gold half unite, unlike any other valid piece except the unite produced by Pontefract.

Pontefract was besieged by Cromwell and Lambert, during which time it issued obsidional shillings and two-shilling pieces on octagonal and lozenge-shaped flans (*Fig 13*). The rest of this issue bears the royal cypher CR surmounted by a large crown with the poignant legend DUM SPIRO SPERO (While I live, I hope). The reverse shows a castle defended by a hand-held sword. Charles was at this time prisoner at Hurst Castle. The Pontefract coinage has one extraordinary distinction: after receiving the news of Charles I's execution, it struck tokens from the new dies *in the name of Charles II*. The gold unite was significantly altered to show a cannon, a symbol of force, protruding from the castle, rather than a sword in a clenched fist as shown previously. The shilling, similarly altered, is distinguished by

Stuart and Commonwealth

the new legend and inscription HANC DEUS DEDIT (This God hath given) and POST MORTEM PATRIS PRO FILIO (For the son after the death of the father). Although the date may be a trifle misleading, this piece is usually classified within the Charles I issues.

As we know it, Charles I was executed in January 1649, but since the official New Year did not begin until 15 March some coins issued directly after his death still retained the date 1648.

Scotland under Charles I

The struggle in Scotland between Church and Crown had continued into the reign of Charles I. When the King was crowned in Edinburgh in 1633 he brought Archbishop Laud with him: he had been considerate with regard to the clergy's stipends and was responsible for the building of many schools but in the matter of worship he was intent on uniformity throughout Scotland and England and was determined to carry this through with a high hand if necessary. But in 1647 the Scots refused to accept Charles as their King and handed him over to the English, and the Glasgow Assembly of 1656, the first free assembly for thirty years, effected the 'second Scottish Reformation' in the Church, sweeping away the reforms he had previously imposed on them.

The Scottish gold coins during Charles I's reign were in two issues, the first struck before Briot's arrival at Edinburgh as master of the Scottish mint, and the second after his arrival. The first coinage was similar in all respects to James's last coinage and included his portrait as well. After Briot's arrival in 1635 steps were taken to produce a new coinage resembling the English style, with the portrait facing right. In 1636 Briot made the dies with the assistance of his son-in-law, John Falconer, who produced some of them during Briot's absence. As in the reign of James VI the current exchange rate between English and Scottish money remained 12 to 1, the unite or twenty-shilling piece English being equivalent to £12 Scottish. Both issues were of crown gold. The first issue (1625) consisted of units, half units and quarter units (or britain crowns). The next gold issue (1637) was similar, with one-eighth units (half crowns) added.

The silver coinage consisted of four issues as follows:

First issue 1625	60 shillings
	30 shillings
	12 shillings
	6 shillings
	2 shillings
	1 shilling
	½ shilling

These coins followed in type the last issue of the previous reign.

Second issue 1636	half merks
	forty-penny pieces
	twenty-penny pieces
Third issue 1637	60 shillings
	30 shillings
	12 shillings
	6 shillings
	half merks
	forty-penny pieces
	twenty-penny pieces

This issue was produced by the mill process introduced by Briot and engraved by him and Falconer.

Fourth issue 1642	3 shillings
	2 shillings

Briot was responsible for this engraving, aided by his assistant engraver Charles Dickeson. The silver content throughout the four issues was made up of 11 parts silver to 1 of alloy.

The copper coins were turners (or twopences) and half-turners (or pence). Of the turners there were three issues, all varying in type, dated 1629, 1632 and 1642. The turners of the last issue are commonly known as bodles, while the half turners belong to the first issue only.

Ireland and Rebellion

Charles I's early policy in Ireland was to make the country pros-

Stuart and Commonwealth

perous and then use Irish manpower in the royal interest against the Puritan opposition, at the same time reducing or altogether removing the power of the anti-Irish faction in Dublin and giving religious concessions in exchange for an army which could be used, if necessary, in England. These schemes, however, finally collapsed when the Royalist cause failed. After the inevitable rising in Ulster under the O'Neills, the Irish catholic leaders who wanted the anti-catholics and the English government removed, many of the English and Scottish settlers were massacred, while others fled to safety. For the suppression of this 'Irish War' an army was sent; but the opposition resisted strongly in the knowledge that their lands would be confiscated and their religion suppressed by the Puritans. After a confused campaign, in which there sometimes appeared to be more than two sides, Dublin was surrendered to the Parliamentarians in 1647. A final attempt was made to recapture Dublin in support of the young Charles, but it was defeated. When Cromwell landed as Lord Lieutenant the campaign was virtually at an end, though resistance continued until 1652. Resettlements in the next few years inevitably followed and resulted in new English and Puritan landlords.

The rebellion of 1641 in Ireland and the maintenance of an army there to pacify the country created an immediate need for extra money with which to pay it. As an expedient, plate from which rude and irregular coins were produced was collected from private persons and soon acquired the name of 'money of necessity'. This money was struck at various times between 1642 and 1647 and in various places in Ireland. The following are the names given to the various 'monies of necessity', which were struck in silver except for two or three pieces of gold known as double pistoles and pistoles struck with the first named: Inchiquin money (1642), Dublin money (1642), Blacksmith's money (1642), Ormonde money (1643), Rebel money (1643), and Cork money (1647). Copper coins were struck at Bandon, Cork, Kilkenny, Kinsale and Youghal.

The Inchiquin money consisted of crowns, half crowns, shillings, ninepences, sixpences, groats and threepences in irregular shapes (*Fig 14*). Although so named, no evidence can be found of Lord Inchiquin, who was vice-president of Munster in 1640, being in any way connected with these coins. The crowns and half crowns which are known as Dublin money cannot be exactly dated, but probably 1642 is fairly accurate as they resemble Inchiquin money.

The half crowns, referred to as 'Blacksmith's money' because of their extreme crudeness, were struck in Kilkenny by order of the Confederate catholics and imitate the Tower half crowns of the king on horseback holding a sword (*Fig 15*). Ormonde money was composed of crowns, half crowns, shillings, sixpences, groats, threepences and twopences and was named after the Duke of Ormonde, who was Lord Lieutenant of Ireland in 1643. Crowns and half crowns, in imitation of the Ormonde coins, were supposed to have been struck by the rebel chiefs pretending that they acted under the king's authority. The Cork money was not struck until 1647, when it is believed that Lord Inchiquin, who retired there, struck shillings and sixpences.

The copper money of this period was very crudely produced: Bandon struck irregularly shaped copper farthings; Cork struck copper halfpennies and farthings (believed to have been issued at the time of the Cork silver); and Kilkenny issued very imperfect copper halfpennies and farthings meant to imitate the copper farthings of Charles I, issued in 1625. These were ordered by the Confederate catholics. Kinsale struck square copper farthings and Youghal produced several copper varieties of the same denomination.

Since no coinage was struck during Cromwell's occupation a large number of tradesmen's tokens found their way into circulation, as had happened in England, filling a great need for small change among the poorer classes.

The Commonwealth

After Charles I's death in 1649, the first acts of the House of Commons were to vote that the House of Peers was useless and dangerous, that the office of the king was obsolete, and that both should be abolished. This came to pass in March 1649.

The Commonwealth coinage which followed distinguished itself by its extreme austerity. The lack of contrived artistic design was

Page 121 Specimen notes of the nineteenth century

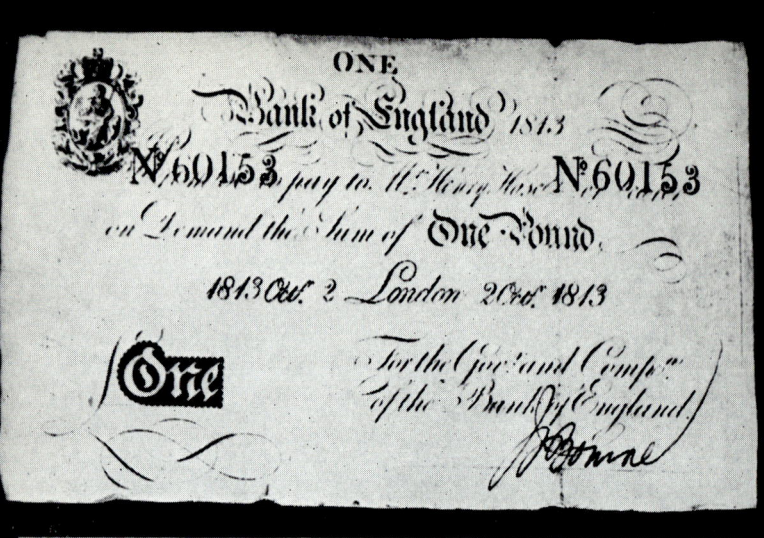
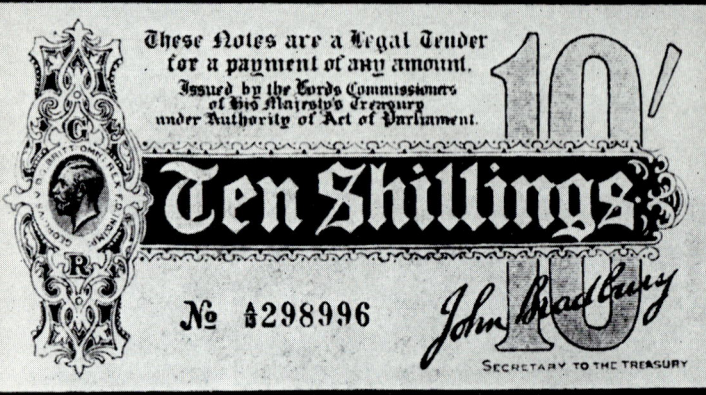
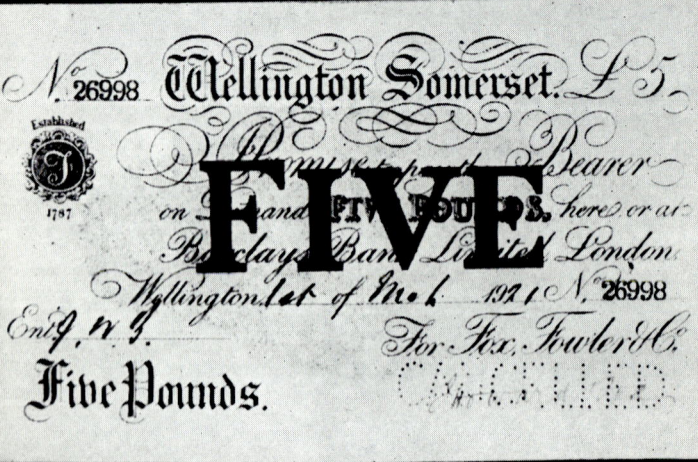

Page 122 (*above*) A £1 Bank of England note, dated 2 October 1813, and individually signed by hand; (*centre*) the ten shilling currency note withdrawn in World War I; (*below*) the last £5 note to be issued by a private bank, dated 1 March 1921

Stuart and Commonwealth

in accordance with the ideals of the Puritan Government who considered that excess in decoration and image-making was really self-indulgence and consequently unacceptable. The coinage consisted of three gold denominations named broads (or 20s pieces), half broads and crowns; and seven silver denominations of crowns, half crowns, shillings, sixpences, half groats, pennies and halfpennies (*Figs 16 and 17*). All except the halfpenny conform to one type design; this coin has a single shield on both sides, being the plainest and the last of its kind. Because of this emphasis on strict simplicity the coinage lost most of its aesthetic appeal. It became purely utilitarian, well deserving the nickname of 'Breeches money', after the double shield on the reverse of the coinage which at a short stretch of the imagination simulated the broad waisted breeches of that time and as Lord Lucas was to observe later, it was 'a fit name for the coinage of the Rump' (the Commonwealth Parliamentary assembly). The Puritans also set a precedent in that the first ever English inscriptions were introduced; Latin legends, they argued, were too much part of the papal tradition. The reverse inscription of GOD WITH US and the obverse THE COMMONWEALTH OF ENGLAND was subject to the Royalist jibe that God and the Commonwealth were on opposite sides: later the device was to be ridiculed as follows:

> A pair of breeches neatly wrought
> (Such as you see upon an old rump goat
> Which emblem our good grandsires chose to boast
> To all the world, the tail was uppermost).

The smaller coins have only their values marked; legends and mint marks are omitted (*Fig 18*). After the death of Charles in 1649, the sun mint mark was used constantly until Cromwell's death in 1658. During the last two years of the Commonwealth rule, when Richard Cromwell was Protector, the mint mark was an anchor. The gold unite and shilling bore a similarity to each other which swindlers could hardly resist. Hence, many shillings were gilded and the XII easily changed to XX.

In 1649, a Parisian engraver, Pierre Blondeau, joined the Tower mint, bringing with him a machine made for coining, inscribing legends and graining. This innovation provided an answer to the troublesome practice of clipping hammered coinage, which had only been counteracted previously by careful weighing. As with most new inventions, it meant a change from the status quo, encountering considerable opposition from the 'hammerers' and mint officials. In 1651 Blondeau made a series of patterns. Two different edge legends appear on his half crowns: IN THE THIRD YEAR OF FREEDOME BY GOD'S BLESSING RESTORED 1651' and 'TRUTH AND PEACE 1651 PETRUS BLONDEAU INVENTOR FECIT. The shilling and sixpenny patterns had grained edges. An alternative pattern series was created in 1651 by David Ramage, an English engraver. His work, however, was not so refined as that of Blondeau. Reluctance by the mint officials to acknowledge Continental superiority caused Blondeau to be given an early pension in 1656.

Cromwell and Protectorate

Before Blondeau's retirement, however, some beautiful patterns were made on his machinery for the newly appointed Lord Protector of England, Oliver Cromwell. This outstanding general was recognised as a potential national leader by the Puritans. His appointment resolved the division between liberal and militant Parliamentary factions. That no coins were struck in his name for circulation was validated by the withdrawal proclamation made later by Charles II, which makes no mention of any current Cromwell coinage. Blondeau's patterns were designed and produced in conjunction with Thomas Simon, the most gifted English die-engraver of his time, and they consisted of gold fifty-shilling pieces, broads (20s pieces) and half broads (10s pieces); silver crowns and half crowns, shillings and sixpences, and copper farthings; many of these were sold as souvenirs (*Fig 19*).

Not being of royal birth, Cromwell appears in the apparel of a Roman emperor, wearing the laurel wreath; on the silver coins he wears draped robes, but is bare-shouldered on the gold. The reverse legend significantly states PAX QUAERITUR BELLO (Peace is sought by war). The two edge inscriptions reflect both the ingenuity of technical invention and the stern severity of the Puritan ethos.

Stuart and Commonwealth

On the fifty-shilling piece the edge reads PROTECTOR LITERIS LITERAE NUMMIS CORONA ET SALUS (A protection to the letters [on the face of the coin] the letters [on the edge] are a garland and a safeguard to the coinage); and on the crown and half crowns—HAS NISI PERITURUS MIHI ADIMAT NEMO (Let no one remove these letters from me under penalty of death). The crown die broke early on in the minting and most strikings show a crack across the Protector's neck.

Apart from authentic originals, the Cromwell crown has two series following at a later date, one made from false dies, struck in the Netherlands, and known as 'Dutch crowns'; on these the neck is short, and the back hair curls are too long. Also, about 1740, one of the chief engravers at the mint, John Sigsmund Tanner, was persuaded to make copies of Cromwell money, since the dies in the Tower were suffering badly from corrosion. These then were 'well engraved colourable imitations', distinct from the originals by stops after the wording in the inscriptions and also having an irregular weight. The striking of coins after Cromwell's death continued at the Tower mint by the old hand-hammering method, the mill machinery standing idle until after the Restoration.

1 James I gold unite. The I and R on the reverse represents Jacobus Rex
2 The James I second coinage silver crown 1604 with the changed reverse inscription QUAE DEUS CONJUNXIT NEMO SEPARET (What God hath joined together let no man put assunder)
3 The James I second spur-ryal of the reign struck in standard gold
4 The oval Harrington farthing, showing one variety of the crowned harp
5 One of the Tower mint variety of silver crowns, Charles I
6 The Shrewsbury type of the famous declaration crown 1642. The declaration is stated on the reverse
7 The extremely rare gold triple unite, Charles I
8 One variety of the Oxford crown with the town named in the background
9 The Truro crown (perhaps struck in Exeter)
10 A Newark 'siege piece' with Roman numerals beneath for value
11 Scarborough 'siege pieces'—crudely cut squares of silver, depicting castle with the value below, stamped on one side only
12 Carlisle 'siege piece'—besieged 1644-5
13 The octagonal shilling 'siege piece' of Pontefract, showing the castle gateway with flag dividing letters p c
14 The irregularly (stamped) shaped crown piece, usually crudely octagonal or squared, named Inchiquin money

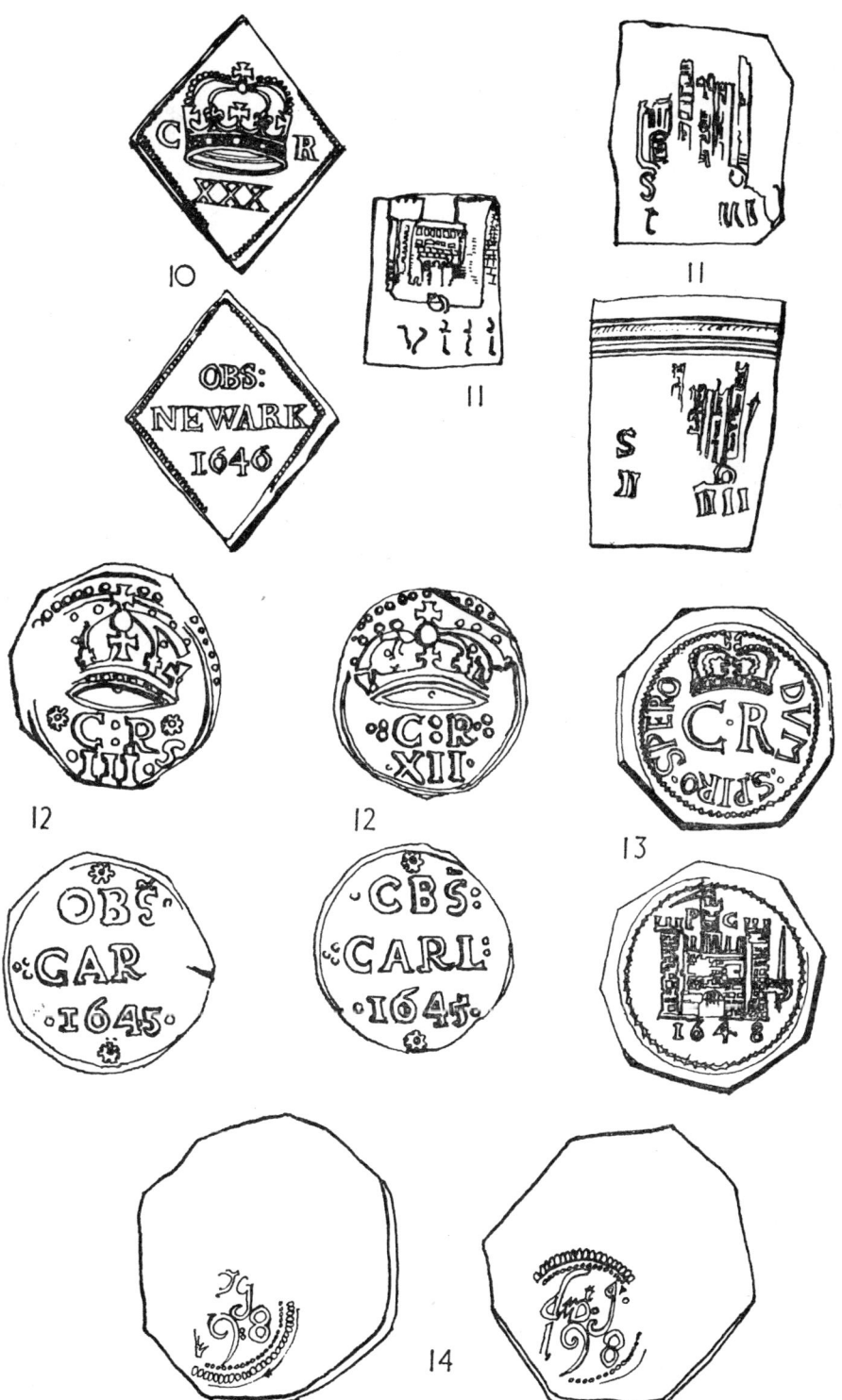

15 Coin issues by the Confederate catholics known as 'blacksmith's money'. A crude variety of half crown
16 The inartistic Commonwealth crown with the two shields of St George and Ireland joined
17 The Commonwealth shilling, showing the value in Roman numerals above the shields on the reverse
18 The Commonwealth penny without inscription or mint mark
19 The Cromwell pattern crown. Was it ever circulated?

VIII
RESTORATION AND CHANGE

Charles II

At the time of his father's execution, Charles the younger was safe in France, whence he departed in 1650 to Scotland, at the request of the Royalists there, to be crowned King of Scotland. He brought an army south to Worcester hoping to strengthen his cause en route; but there his army was routed and Charles became a refugee with a price on his head. He escaped dramatically to France where he remained until the end of the Commonwealth. In 1660, a counter-revolution managed by General Monk reinstated Charles with his rightful title as King of England (1660-85). The first coinage of the Restoration was produced by hammering, since the much desired mill machinery lacked trained operators. Thomas Simon was responsible for the first gold coins, which have a fine wigged and uncrowned portrait of Charles II; these included the unite, double crown and crown, which were of the same weight and value as the Commonwealth coins. A rise in the market value of gold in 1661 necessitated a revaluation of the unite to 21s 4d instead of 20s. With the introduction of milled coins the hammered unites became known as 'broads', since they were thicker than their predecessors.

For the 'touching for the King's Evil' ceremony, as presided over by Charles II, no angels were struck, individual gold medalets being ordered instead; these were holed for wearing as they were no longer legal tender.

No hammered silver crowns were actually issued, though they were authorised *(Fig 1)*.

It was decided in 1662 to strike future coins with the mill press under the management of Pierre Blondeau, who had been requested to return from his premature retirement in France and take charge

(*Fig* 2). The preparation of the dies was entrusted to Jan Roettiers, a Dutchman, in preference to the loyal Thomas Simon, not through artistic merit, for Simon's work was considered the superior by many, but because Roettiers' family had helped Charles financially during his exile and it was a convenient way of showing his gratitude.

The following extract from Samuel Pepys' diary records the mock trial between the two artists:

> There dined with us today Mr Slingsby of the Mint, who showed us all the new pieces both gold and silver (examples of them all) that were made for the king, by Blondeau's way; and compared them with those made for Oliver. The pictures of the latter made by Symons, and of the King by one Rotyr [Roettiers], a German I think, that dined with us also. He extolls those of Rotyr above the others; and indeed, I think they are better, because the sweeter of the two; but, upon my word, those of the Protector are more like, to my mind, than the King's but both very well worth seeing. The crowns of Cromwell are now sold it seems for 25 shillings and 30 shillings apiece.

Indignant at his displacement as chief engraver, Simon produced his famous 'petition crown', of which there are about fifteen known specimens (*Fig* 3). The 'petition' was unusual since it was engraved round the edge of the beautiful pattern crown and reads as follows:
THOMAS SIMON MOST HUMBLY PRAYS YOUR MAJESTY TO COMPARE THIS HIS TRYALL PIECE WITH THE DUTCH AND IF MORE GRACEFULLY ORDERED AND MORE ACCURATELY ENGRAVEN TO RELIEVE HIM.

Other rare pattern crowns of his design are those known as the 'Reddite' crowns, the edge inscription reading REDDITE QUE CAESARIS CT. POST (Render unto Caesar those which are Caesar's, etc). Simon's petition was unsuccessful and in a couple of years he was transferred to the Edinburgh mint; later he was pensioned off at £50 per annum, only to die in the Great Plague of 1665.

The mill coinage consisted of five, two, one, and half guineas struck in gold; and crowns, half crowns, shillings, sixpences, groats, threepences, half groats and pennies struck in standard silver (*Fig* 4). The last four coins were used together for the first time as money for the Maundy ceremony, earlier reigns having kept to silver pennies only. It is, however, not certain whether these coins were struck exclusively for use in the Maundy ceremony or were part of

Restoration and Change

the ordinary issue. The latter seems to be more likely as they show more wear than known Maundy issues of later years, and have, therefore, probably been in general circulation. Others argue that as silver pennies only were used in the Maundy service before 1670, it is too great a coincidence that the additional 2d (half groats), 3d and 4d (groats) were added in the first year of the new issue. From this period there was a tendency gradually to alter minor parts of the Maundy ceremony and to adjust them to current requirements. For a long time no monarch had personally conducted it until Charles II resumed many of the ancient ceremonies; he achieved much popularity through his personal participation in this service at a time when by appearing in public the King ran the dire risk of contracting the plague.

An amusing sidelight in thrown by a chronicler of this period on the reason for an alteration in the ceremony. It had been the custom to give clothing to the female recipients, who often disrupted the service by excited whispering and much rustling as they discarded the old and donned the new apparel with indecent haste. This resulted in the decision that measures of cloth should be substituted for individual garments.

A new coin is here introduced into our history: the guinea piece, which derived its name from Guinea, that part of the Gold Coast now called Ghana in West Africa, whence the gold was transported by the 'Company of Royal Adventurers of England trading in Africa'. This company was encouraged to bring over gold by being allowed, as stated in its charter, to have its stamp on the coins; the stamp was originally an elephant and later (after 1675) an elephant with a castle on its back. This privilege ceased in the reign of Queen Anne. The inscription on the edges of the five- and two-guinea pieces, crowns and half crowns—DECUS AT TUTAMEN (an ornament and a safeguard)—is meant to show that the lettering is ornamental as well as being protective. John Evelyn has the credit for introducing this popular 'edge' lettering to our coinage. He observed it on Cardinal Richelieu's Greek Testament vignette and advanced the suggestion that it would be an excellent inscription for use on the edges of the coinage as a prevention against clipping.

The Welsh mines again began to produce lead from which silver was extracted for coins bearing the Prince of Wales' feathers on them, while a rose shown on the obverse side of other coins denoted silver extracted from the lead in the West of England lead mines.

The Mint experimented for some time with the proposed copper coinage, and the technical difficulties encountered are borne out by the number of copper coins which escaped into circulation before the first year of the official issue in 1672, for which five coin presses had been installed—four to produce farthings and one to produce halfpennies (*Fig 5*). These difficulties caused the Mint to purchase a large number of blank copper discs from Sweden, leaving only the stamping of the coins to be done. A proclamation forbidding the use of tokens was generally obeyed.

The reverse side of these new copper coins showed the figure of Britannia seated, resting on a shield, a design taken from the Roman sestertius of Antoninus Pius, which commemorated a victory over the Britons in the second century; it is, however, modernised in that the Duchess of Richmond (formerly Frances Stewart), considered a beauty of her time, sat as the model for Britannia. An extract from Pepys' diary of 25 February 1667 states:

> At my goldsmiths did observe the king's new medall, where in a little there is Mrs Stewart's face as well done as ever I saw anything in my whole life, I think; and a pretty thing it is that he should chose [sic] her face to present Britannia by.

Until 1937 all our copper coins bore a modification of this reverse, but from that date pennies only retained the design, which was continued until the introduction of the decimal coinage in 1971, though 1967 was the last year in which pennies were dated; nevertheless, a modified effigy of Britannia was given to the reverse of the fifty new pence dated 1969. This coin was one of the three decimal denominations introduced to accustom the public to their appearance (and for use at the non-decimal values).

The cost of purchasing copper flans from Sweden caused the Mint to look for something more economical and substitutes in tin were made. These were issued as farthings in 1684, with a copper plug through the centre to make counterfeiting difficult. They were a little thicker than the previous copper farthings and were similar in design, though on the edge the year date and 'Nummorum Famulus'

Restoration and Change

(meaning 'a minor coin') were impressed. Unfortunately, this metal is subject to corrosion and it is most unlikely that any perfect specimens now exist.

Two Scottish Issues

No separate coinage was struck in Scotland during the period of the unpopular Commonwealth and the Protectorate. The Civil War and Cromwell's campaigns had reduced the country to a serious economic state. The Scots took no direct part in the Restoration and merely accepted it as an accomplished fact. It was not until after this change that the Mint resumed work on the Scottish coinage. The dies of the first coinage were made by Thomas Simon and it was issued from 1664 to 1675; it consisted of silver four, two, one and half merk pieces, marked with their respective values and year dates. The letter F which occurs on this issue represents the initial of Sir John Falconer—now a knight and Warden of the Scottish Mint.

The second issue (1675-82) was given a new name, the dollar; dollars, half dollars, quarter dollars, one-eighth dollars and one-sixteenth dollars were issued. The dollar was equal in value and weight to the four-merk piece of the first issue, and the merk was equal in value to 13s 4d English. The main difference between the first and second issues was the change in the king's head, which was turned to the left in the second issue instead of to the right as in the first. The copper coins comprised bawbees (or 6d pieces Scots) and turners (bodles or 2d pieces Scots), the latter being struck in 1663 and 1677 and the former in 1677 (Fig 6).

Ireland under Charles II

Although the monarchy in Ireland was restored when Charles II became king, he found it almost impossible to make the Cromwellian party give up the royalist property they had confiscated, and though Catholics outnumbered the Protestants by five to one, the latter maintained their supremacy despite all Charles could do.

The only coins struck in Ireland after the Restoration were two regal and several token issues in copper, two prominent token issues being 'St Patricks' coinage and 'Dublin' coinage (*Fig 7*). The first regal issue of 1660 consisted of token farthings struck under a patent granted for twenty years to Sir Thomas Armstrong. 'St Patricks' money was of halfpennies and farthings struck about 1672-4 in Dublin under permit from the Dublin Corporation. Most of these had a milled edge and a reverse showing a brass spot. 'Dublin' money is believed to have been issued by the Dublin Corporation and was of halfpennies only. This was followed by the second regal copper issue in halfpennies, struck under letters patent granted to Sir Thomas Armstrong and Sir George Legge in 1680.

James II

As Charles II had no legitimate male heir the next in line of succession was his brother James (1685-8), Duke of York, but as he was a catholic his ascent to the throne was not popular with most of the community. This unpopularity was further aggravated by James II's belief in the Divine Right of Kings and his determination to make the country catholic by giving the important government and army appointments to those who followed his faith. A rising led by Charles II's illegitimate son, the Duke of Monmouth, failed.

James's coins resembled those of Charles II and were of the same denominations (*Fig 8*). The tin farthings continued to be produced, plus halfpennies made from the same metal.

In Ireland more freedom was allowed and the army was remodelled and officered by catholics. Administrative appointments were given to James's supporters on the council and on the corporations. In England, however, the protestants formed a strong opposition, and when a son and heir was born to James they appealed to William, Prince of the House of Orange, a Dutch protestant and the King's own son-in-law, to come and take the throne. When William landed on the south Devon coast in 1688, James fled first to France and later to Ireland, where he took command of an Irish army,

Restoration and Change 137

served by officers, money and arms supplied by Louis XIV, with the sole object of regaining the throne.

Ireland and Scotland under James II

James's Irish coins were struck in two periods, before and after his flight. In the first period the only coins struck were copper halfpennies issued from 1685 to 1688. The second issue was struck during James's struggle in 1689-91 to recover the throne, with the same object as the 'money of necessity' in Charles I's reign. The coins consisted of crowns, half crowns, shillings, sixpences, groats, pennies and halfpennies in mixed metal, white metal, pewter and brass.

The mixed metal coins (1689) were known as 'gun money', as they were made from the metal of old guns, and comprised half crowns, shillings and sixpences (*Fig 9*). A second issue with the addition of crowns was struck in 1690 when all the denominations except the crowns bore the month as well as the year of minting. The white metal coins (1689 and 1690) were issued when the supplies of copper and brass had failed. The Irish named this white metal coinage '*uim bog*' which means 'soft copper' or 'worthless coin'—an expression from which the term 'humbug' is said to have originated. The gunmetal, brass and copper were collected from every possible source and even kitchen utensils were taken from private citizens to be utilised for money; it is estimated that each pound of metal produced £5 of shillings, sixpences and half crowns.

In the Battle of the Boyne, James suffered defeat and once more fled to France. His catholic supporters retreated to Limerick where they were penned in by the protestants. During the siege (1691) they struck copper and brass money which became known as 'Hibernies', the reverses portraying the representative figure of Ireland, Hibernia holding a harp. Some of these coins were restruck from the 'gun money' shillings.

James's Scottish coinage (he was known as James VII in Scotland) was of silver coins only, in forty-shilling and ten-shilling pieces. These coins were both dated and have the marks of value. A very limited number of sixty-shilling pieces were also struck at a later date but it is unlikely that they were ever circulated (*Fig 10*).

William and Mary

When the protestants invited William of Orange to dislodge James from the throne their intention was that William's wife, Princess Mary, who was James's daughter, should become Queen of England. Despite her father's faith, Mary was a protestant. William, however, would not accept the offer to be just consort to the Queen, and decided to return to the Dutch republic if he were unacceptable as king. After James's abdication, however, Parliament eventually acquiesced and William was invited with Mary (1688-94) to be joint sovereign of the land.

The same denominations were struck as with James II but the designs were altered, with the heads of king and queen conjoined and facing right. This is the one and only time conjoined heads appear on the English coinage—it is a particularly well balanced design on the crown. The ornamental shield on the reverses of the five and two guineas differed considerably from that on the guineas and half guineas, which in turn also differed from that of the silver half crowns. Some of the coins were still made from gold imported by the Africa Co and showed the usual elephant and castle badge.

From 1691 all the silver coin reverses were redesigned, showing the four shields forming a cross, with each angle having the royal monogram, the initials W and M (*Fig 11*). The importation of copper flans from Sweden ceased and home-produced metal for halfpennies and farthings was used instead. The tin halfpennies and farthings, contrary to expectations, were extensively counterfeited and were abandoned in 1692 in favour of all-copper halfpennies and farthings, issued in 1694, and struck at forty-two halfpennies to a pound avoirdupois instead of forty halfpennies as in Charles II's reign.

The price of silver at the beginning of this reign was 5s 2d per fine oz, but its export value was 5s 3½d, with the result that enormous quantities of coin were shipped overseas to France and the Dutch republic, leaving the meagre supplies in this country either very worn or badly clipped.

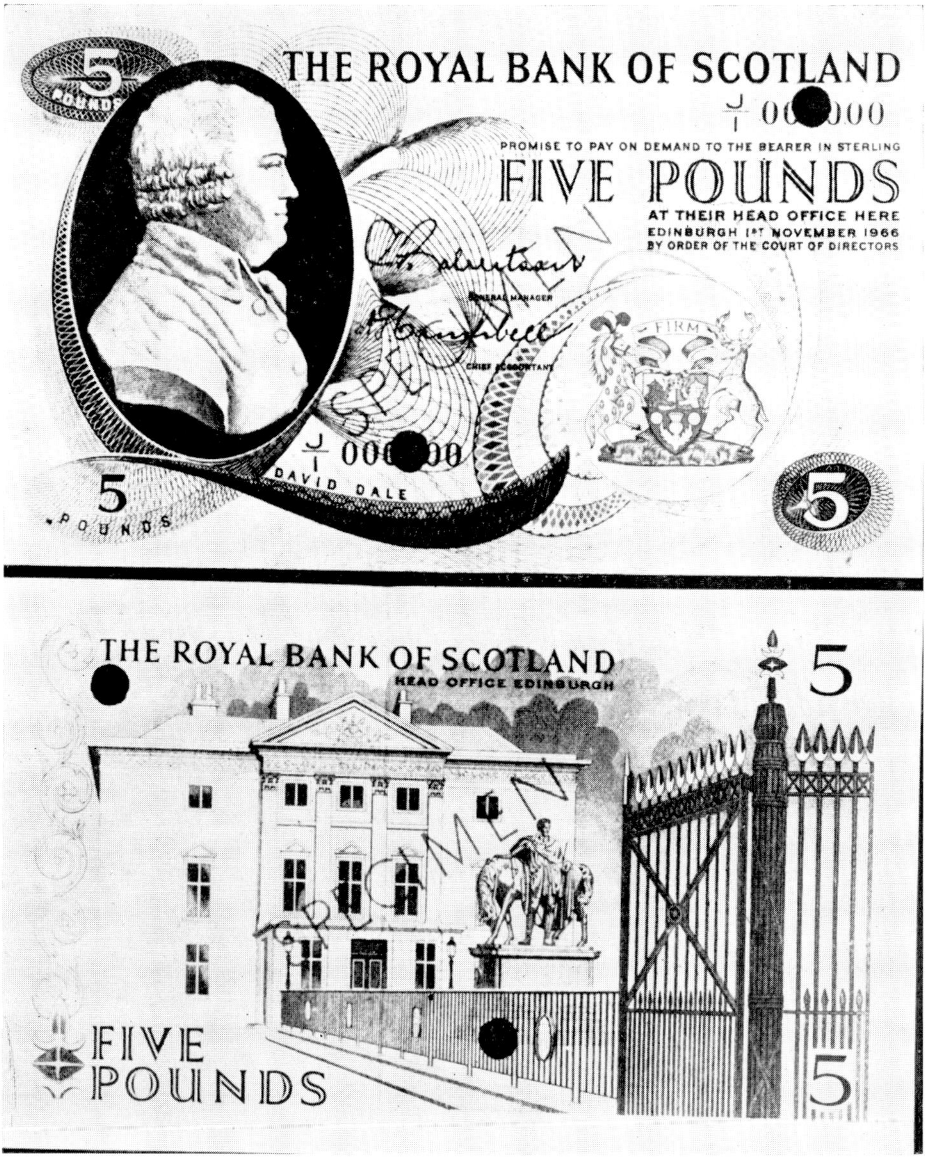

Page 139 The £5 banknote of the Royal Bank of Scotland—new type, first issued 1 January 1967

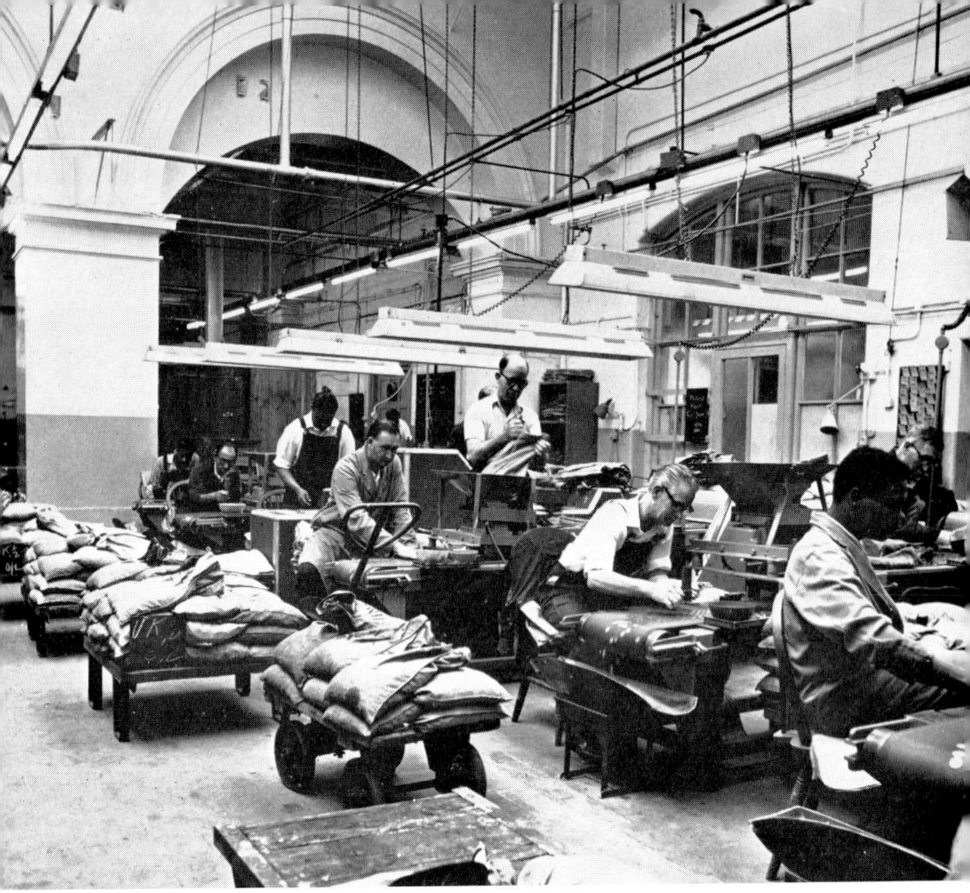

Page 140 (*above*) Newly minted cupro-nickel coins being scrutinised for faults at the Royal Mint, Llantrisant, South Wales; (*below*) the Royal Mint, Llantrisant, South Wales—an exterior view of the coining block

Restoration and Change

When the Queen died of smallpox in 1694, William (1688-1702) continued to rule alone, completely redesigning his coinage. Gold continued to be imported from Guinea and silver was supplied from the lead mines of Wales and the West of England, the mark of origin being shown on the coins minted from these supplies. The denominations, however, remained the same as before (*Fig 12*).

So long as its face value remained below Continental market value, silver continued to find its way out of the coinage on to the Continent, where it was sold at a profit. To ensure that gold did not disappear in a similar manner the guinea was revalued at 30s in 1694, raising it above the Continental value. From this time, however, the gold value was reduced gradually by statute until it reached 21s 6d in 1698.

In 1701 and 1702 Sir Isaac Newton, as Master of the Mint, issued economic reports showing that the guinea was up to 1s higher than the Continental valuations of gold and its value was fixed at 21s, a figure at which it remained until it was abolished in the recoinage of 1816 and its place taken by the sovereign. It has been widely used as a monetary measure for subscriptions and professional fees until decimalisation was introduced in 1971.

The public were becoming increasingly aware of the irregularities caused by clipping and debasing the coinage, and there were many instances in 1694 of the Government being called upon to apply strong measures to root out these malpractices. In the Guildhall Mr Fleetwood, who later became Bishop of Ely, preached a sermon demanding the removal of the evils of clipping and debasing, a sermon which attracted attention in Government circles. He took as his text:

> And Abraham weighed to Ephron the silver which he had named in the audience of the sons of Heth, four hundred shekels of silver, current money with the merchant (Gen xxiii, 16).

In 1695 the silver remaining in circulation was so clipped and defaced that the Government decided on a recoinage. Foolishly it agreed upon a limited period in which to pay the full value of the old coins whatever their condition, with the result it lost a large sum of money through further clipping by the public before the latter exchanged its silver for new. For a short period, before the coins were finally withdrawn, unclipped silver coins were permitted to circulate if they had been submitted for a hole to be officially punched in them. The recoinage, however, brought to an end the circulation of hammered silver.

Window Tax

It was the aforementioned loss in revenue which caused the Government to levy a tax in 1695 on the number of windows in each inhabited house. Each window was assessed at 2s per annum, while an extra 4s was levied on houses with ten to nineteen windows. In the first year of this tax the sum of £1,200,000 was raised, a huge amount for those days, and this no doubt was why the tax, first imposed as a temporary measure, was to remain for more than a century and a half.

Scotland and Ireland under William and Mary

William and Mary's Scottish coinage resembled that of James VII. Coins of three denominations, silver sixty, forty and ten shillings, with additional twenty-shilling pieces, remained similar to those of the previous reign except for the conjoined portraits of the King and Queen (both facing the same direction) with an inscription on the edges of the first two denominations. The five-shilling pieces were similar to the larger coins but had a crown over the shield on the reverse with V below, the mark of value. The bawbee (or 6d Scots) and the bodle (or turner) were both struck in copper dated 1691-4. After Mary's death all these coins continued but the portrait of William alone was substituted. New gold coins named pistoles and half pistoles were struck. These were the last gold coins of Scotland, their current values being £12 and £6 Scots, and they were made from gold brought from Africa by a ship named *The Rising Sun*, owned by the Darien Co. The coins were of crown gold.

The only Irish coins of William and Mary, and afterwards of William, were halfpennies.

Restoration and Change

In 1699 the English Parliament confirmed the Irish settlement in which 750,000 acres passed to new owners; thus through deprivation of their rights, voluntary exile, or death many famous names disappeared from Irish history. The catholics generally were refused admission to trades and professions and denied electoral votes, educational rights, etc.

Bank of England

When William Paterson in 1691 submitted a plan for the creation of a national bank in England he could have hardly visualised that it was the beginning of the greatest banking institution in the world. By 1694 an Act was passed by the terms of which 'the Governor and Company of the Bank of England' was formed, and a sum of £1,200,000 was raised by subscribers who were granted stock. While the Bank of England's primary duty was to raise money to continue the war against France, it soon became the only joint-stock bank in England. As the bank grew the issuing of banknotes became an important part of its duties.

Paterson was strongly in favour of retaining gold in order to back the issue of a safe paper money; if his advice had been more closely followed many private banks and business houses would have been saved from disaster in the late eighteenth and the early nineteenth centuries. His appointment as a director of the Bank of England was an acknowledgement of his ability and integrity, but the other directors were not entirely in favour of guidance from a Scot who had so many financial interests besides his bank directorship. Undoubtedly the bank would have avoided much trouble if his more cautious theories had been applied.

End of the Tally System

With the advent of paper money it was understandable that the cumbersome wood-tally system, which had been a popular auxiliary currency for nearly 600 years, should fall into disfavour. Pepys in his Diary referred to payments at the Exchequer made to him by tally and his dislike of the system because of its slowness in completing a transaction. The estimated value of the wood tallies in 1694 was £15,000 but from that date they began to decline in popularity. When the bank increased its capital in 1697, a large number of the shares were purchased with wood tallies.

Some of the tallies represented payments to government departments, including some abnormally large ones. One of these, retained at the Bank of England Museum, is 8ft 6in long, and represents the maximum amount to which any one tally was restricted—£50,000. It owes its existence to the fact that it had never been returned to the Exchequer, as the payment represented a government debt which had never been paid!

In 1783 the use of tallies was abolished by statute and the existing indented cheque receipt method expanded. This law, however, was not enforced immediately, and tallies continued to be used until 1826.

The indented cheque receipt was a form of deed (or 'check' as it was sometimes known). It was issued by the person who was paying a sum of money to another, each retaining the half which had been separated by an irregular division in the blank space in the middle where the word *chirographum* was written. When the check was presented at the bank (or goldsmith's) the two parts were matched to prove that the presented part was genuine.

Finally in 1834 the large accumulation of old tallies was burned in the furnaces that heated the House of Lords; unfortunately, this fire accidentally started another, resulting in the destruction of the old Houses of Parliament. With the destruction of these tallies disappeared much of the already scanty evidence available. Fortunately this loss was partially counteracted in 1909 by the discovery of a number of wood tallies in the Chapel of the Pyx, Westminster.

Banknotes

The first Bank of England notes were printed in 1695, when 12,000 notes in six denominations from £10 to £100 were authorised, with

Restoration and Change

the date, bearer's name and cashier's signature written in by hand. From this time onwards the problem of forgeries escalated, for within two months of the notes being issued a forged £100 note appeared. In an attempt to eliminate this problem the directors of the bank went to great trouble and expense. In 1697 an Act was passed to prevent any other organisation setting up as a bank and issuing notes, thus restricting the opportunities for the forger, while in 1708 and 1709 acts were passed which limited the issuing of notes to firms with six partners or less (apart from the Bank of England).

The problem became more acute with the increase of footpads and highwaymen. The Treaty of Utrecht in 1713 has been blamed for this, as it indirectly caused large numbers of disbanded soldiers to adopt the precarious profession of robber in lieu of honest labour, which they were unable to find.

As the only method of transporting coins and notes was by coach, many easy opportunities were open to robbers, who had merely to choose a suitable time and place to stage their hold-up. To protect travellers on mail coaches from exposure to this violence the Bank of England issued bills that were only payable three days after the date of issue, enabling anyone who was robbed to stop the payment. A period of three days, however, was found to be insufficient, so in 1738 the Bank issued bills payable seven days after issue.

The story told by Robert Walpole, prime minister 1721-42, lends colour to some of the sordid highway robberies. One November the prime minister was driving through Hyde Park when he was held up by two highwaymen. Accidentally, in the excitement of the moment, the pistol which threatened Walpole went off, stunning him and marking his face. The highwayman concerned, who was none other than the notorious James Maclean, was caught. Walpole's comment after Maclean's arrest was: 'He says, if the pistol had shot me, he had another for himself. Can I do less than say —I will be hanged if he is?'

The formal beginning of banking in Scotland came in 1695 when the Bank of Scotland was founded; but a form of banking had been carried on by goldsmiths and merchants even before this date. The new bank was granted the exclusive right to operate for twenty-one years, issuing in 1696 banknotes for £100, £50, £20, £10 and £5 in order to lend money to industry and trade, the borrowers being mostly merchants of some substance.

Throughout the eighteenth century, governments, completely failing to understand the new situation created in Scotland as well as in England and Ireland by the continual expansion of trade and employment, did not provide an adequate silver and copper coinage for the people. The failure to supply a metallic currency led to the mushroom growth of numerous private banks whose very existence depended on their notes not being cashed too quickly. When these banks inevitably failed, gloom, mistrust and hardship spread, destroying that confidence which is an essential basis of trade.

The wretchedly worn and mixed silver of all ages and nations must have been a nightmare for those who had to make calculations before the advent of paper money. When this new facility was provided, Scotland very slowly began to emerge from the distress caused by almost continual war and misrule, though it was to be many years before trade and new industries could remove the extreme poverty of the Scots. From 1695 to 1704 nothing smaller than £5 notes was issued, but in 1704 the Bank of Scotland issued its first £1 notes. These notes were accepted at the same value as their English equivalent, not at one-twelfth of the English value as was the case with other Scottish money; this old valuation was finally abolished at the time of the union in 1707.

The early notes were printed on one of the old-fashioned printing presses used for engraving, and were an enormous boon to the people, as the metal currency was totally inadequate for everyday use. The first experience of a run on the bank—an ever-present danger in those early days of banking—came at the end of 1704 when, through a rumour of a proposed increase in the nominal value of the coinage caused by its great scarcity, the Bank of Scotland had to close its doors through temporary inability to cash all the presented notes.

Anne

Meanwhile, in 1702, William III died and was succeeded by his

Restoration and Change 147

sister-in-law Anne (1702-14), daughter of James II and his first wife Anne Hyde. Her consort, Prince George of Denmark, took no part in public life. Anne's first act was an unsuccessful attempt to fulfil William's deathbed wish of a union between England and Scotland. Ultimately, the union was recognised as desirable for both countries and was successfully effected in 1707.

Except for certain issues of 1702-3, her coins were of the same denominations in both gold and silver as the previous reign, with the addition of two-guinea pieces after the union, though the reverses were altered. Those before and after the union have the reverse shields arranged differently, the arms of England, Scotland, France and Ireland being in a different order and of a different pattern.

Many of the early silver coins of this reign owe their existence to the Anglo-Dutch expedition of 1702 under Sir George Rooke during the War of the Spanish Succession, in which the Spanish towns of Cadiz and Vigo were sacked and a number of Spanish treasure ships seized in Vigo Bay. The booty brought back to England totalled over 11,000,000 silver 'pieces of eight'. To commemorate the event silver coins in 1702-3 were struck with the word Vigo on the obverse of each coin. Also a small quantity of gold was seized, brought to the Mint and made into a limited number of gold Vigo coins with the date 1703. Maundy money during Anne's reign was not struck in complete sets every year, 1704, 1707, 1711 and 1712 being incomplete. The continued demand for copper coins remained, but nothing was done until the last year of the Queen's reign, when the attractive pattern farthing of 1714 was produced. It did nothing, however, to alleviate the shortage of copper coins. For a pattern coin a considerable number must have been struck, as at no time has this coin reached a comparative value with other rare pattern pieces. Many of these coins found in collections show undue wear and are believed to have circulated sufficiently to dispose of the rumour of great rarity ascribed to it.

In Scotland silver coins only were struck, the first issue before and the second after the union. The former were ten and five shillings Scots, similar to those of the previous reign. The coins of the second issue, which was the last coinage to be struck by the

Edinburgh mint, were identical with the English coins except for an E showing that they were struck in Edinburgh, the last date being 1709. The denominations were crowns (*Fig 13*), half crowns, shillings and sixpences. The quality of the silver in the first issue was 11 1/12th fine silver and 11/12ths alloy, while in the second issue it was 11 1/10th fine silver and 9/10ths alloy, conforming to the English standard. These were the final issues for the coins of Scotland.

During Anne's reign no coins were struck in Ireland.

Good Queen Anne was noted for her piety and moral ways, evidence of which is demonstrated on her coinage where she insisted, in spite of her predecessors, that she should be modestly robed in her portrait. Also we see a well clad Britannia on the copper coins showing only a modest ankle.

1 The 'hammered' shilling of Charles II. The inner circle and value mark are omitted
2 Charles II first 'milled' crown with small bust and no symbol beneath it
3 The famous Petition crown with its beautiful design by Thomas Simon (twice diameter of coin)
4 The early 'milled' shilling of Charles II, without symbol
5 The first issue turner of Charles II; the numeral II is omitted
6 The new copper halfpenny with metal discs imported from Sweden displaying an armoured and laureated bust and Britannia seated
7 Charles II 'St Patrick's Coinage' halfpenny. The saint with cross and crozier preaching to the multitude, alongside the Arms of Dublin; on the reverse King David playing the harp, crown above
8 The laureated and draped bust of James II crown. The four shields form a cross on the reverse
9 'Gun Money'
10 The rare and unauthorised sixty shilling piece of James II. This may have been struck at a later date for collectors

149

11 The William and Mary crown, showing their draped conjoined busts. The monograms W M are seen in the angles on the reverse
12 William III crown with a laureated and draped bust. No symbol is shown
13 The Scottish crown of Anne—the letter E representing the Edinburgh mint

IX
HANOVER TO VICTORIA

George I

On the death of Anne the heir to the throne was her half-brother, the Jacobite Prince James Edward Stuart, but he was a catholic and therefore unacceptable to Protestant England. Thus George Ludwig, Elector of Hanover, a great-grandson of James I, became George I of England (1714-27). He was a rather morose and silent man who spoke only German, and spent most of his time in his German territory. Because of this he left most of his British affairs in the hands of his prime minister, Sir Robert Walpole, who was virtually ruler of the country.

To include the arms of the Electorate the royal arms now had to be changed. The gold coinage continued the denominations of the previous reign except that in 1718 there was added a quarter guinea, which, proving unpopular, was not issued again in George I's reign. Silver crowns (*Fig 1*), half crowns, shillings, sixpences, fourpences, threepences, twopences and pennies were also struck, the last four having large Arabic numerals indicating the number of pence on each coin. The initials S.S.C. and W.C.C. found on a number of silver coins represent 'South Sea Company' and 'Welsh Copper Company'. These were trading companies supplying the Mint with silver bullion; in return they were allowed to have their initials imprinted on the coins made from their supplies. A third company known as the 'Company for Smelting down Lead with Pit-coale and Sea-coale' was privileged to have roses and plumes on the reverses of those coins for which they supplied the silver. Copper halfpennies were struck in 1717 and 1718, and farthings in 1717; the latter were nicknamed 'dumps' because they were slightly smaller and thicker than usual.

Hanover to Victoria

The scarcity of silver in George I's reign had several causes. The first was the purchase and collection of silver plate by private persons; the second was the large-scale export of bullion and plate to the East Indies. Records show that over 3,000,000oz of fine silver were exported by the East India Company in 1717, which far exceeded the total imports of silver bullion, pointing to the fact that a large number of coins must have been melted down to produce this quantity. A third reason was the illegal export of gold and silver to Germany, Holland and other countries.

Irish Coinage Revitalised

Ireland under the first two Georges was an oppressed country largely ruled by a few large protestant landowners. The native catholic population and the presbyterian settlers of the North suffered equal discrimination. The bad state of the Irish currency was made worse by the development of private banks whose banknotes were allowed to pass without any restrictions. The original goldsmiths' notes in England were adjudged illegal in 1704 but were allowed as late as 1709 in Ireland. A number of issuers of banknotes were merely shopkeepers and private persons, many of whom were totally ignorant of even the elementary rules of trading and of note-issuing. The practice of merchants and traders acting as bankers, issuing notes whenever they wished, was full of danger to both the public and the whole economic structure.

The great scarcity of coin in Ireland during the reign of Anne and in the early part of George I's reign caused much inconvenience and hardship. To relieve this situation a patent was given to the King's sister—the Duchess of Kendal—to produce copper halfpennies and farthings. This patent, lasting for fourteen years, was passed on in 1722 to William Wood, a mineowner in a position to provide both the metal and the means to produce the coins. These, struck in two types of halfpennies and farthings, were of superior quality and design to those of the same period struck by the London mint, but there was an immediate outcry against them in Dublin (*Fig 2*). The reason does not seem clear except that the coins were underweight and that the agitation was for political reasons. This led to the publication of Dean Swift's *Drapier Letters* in the Dublin press, which harshly condemned Wood's coinage. Feeling was provoked to such an extent that the Lord Lieutenant of Ireland considered it necessary to offer a £300 reward for the discovery of the author. Finally the government cancelled Wood's patent in 1724, but in the following year compensated him with a substantial pension of £3,000.

By 1723 the need for money had grown so acute in Ireland that numbers of manufacturers were obliged to pay their men with tallies or card tokens signed on the back for exchange into money at a later date. Counterfeit coins in common use called 'raps' were made of such base metal that what passed for a halfpenny would not have been valued at half a farthing.

George II

George II (1727-60), like his father, was more interested in German affairs than in Great Britain, though he could speak some broken English. He had little to recommend himself as a king: he was vain and pompous, fond of show and mean. Like his father, he also left the affairs of the country in the hands of Sir Robert Walpole and afterwards of William Pitt the Elder.

George II's coins were struck in two different designs with variations to each: the earlier coins bore a young head, but an older head appeared on the later ones, beginning with the gold coins of 1739. The gold denominations consisted of five, two, one, and half guineas, all of which were given a new reverse, a single crowned shield (*Fig 3*).

This change of reverse was influenced by the gilding and altering of George I's shillings by forgers. It was found to be comparatively easy to engrave four sceptres in the blank quarter spaces of the reverse and then to gild the coin to resemble a guinea piece. Some of the coins were made from the gold brought to England by the East India Company and bear the letters EIC on the obverse. Gold and silver coins are also to be found with the word 'Lima' on the

Hanover to Victoria

obverse, commemorating Admiral Anson's three-year expedition round the world from which he returned with bullion in gold and silver said to be valued at £500,000, captured partly from a Spanish treasure ship and partly taken from Peru, where he had raided the port of Lima. A proportion of all denominations of gold and silver coins were struck from this Lima bullion except the small Maundy coins and the gold two guineas.

The silver denominations consisted of crowns, half crowns, shillings and sixpences, retaining the young head design until 1743 (*Fig 4*), after which they bore the old head; but the Maundy coins (4d, 3d, 2d and 1d) remained unaltered throughout the reign, though all Maundy denominations were not issued every year. The copper halfpennies and farthings changed to the old head design in 1740 (*Fig 5*). From this period the silver and copper coins became scarce because of the falling off in supplies of metal.

The problem of banknote forgeries continued to trouble the Bank of England and much thought was given to means of defeating the forger. The quality and type of paper, the engraving and the watermark were all considered, altered and reconsidered many times. These countermeasures, however, did not check the activities of the forger, who was quick to take advantage of this new field of operation. Acts of 1724, 1725, 1729, 1734 and 1763 were passed, making it a felony to forge banknotes, bills, etc; these Acts so completely covered all forms of forgery that, Blackstone stated, 'there is hardly now a case possible to be conceived wherein forgery, that tends to defraud, whether in the name of a real or fictitious person, is not made a capital crime (*Private Wrongs*, 1768).

The first printed Bank of England notes were for £20, £30, £40, £50, £60, £70, £80, £90, £100, £200, £300, £400, £500 and £1,000, issued in 1725, though there is some doubt as to whether the £60, £70, £80, £90 denominations were ever used. The little-used denominations were discontinued in 1803. In 1743 there was a new issue of £50 notes; in 1752, £20 and £30; and new denominations of £10 and £15 in 1759 and £25 in 1765. The issue of the last three was probably influenced by the shortage of gold and silver coin and the increasing note issues by private banks since 1750. Nevertheless, there was a shortage of currency because of the export of specie during the Seven Years War (1756-63).

Copper under George II

Since the industrial productivity of the country was greatly increasing it was essential for the output of money to keep pace with it, but little coin was struck apart from gold, as only a limited quantity of silver was obtained from the Welsh and West of England lead mines until they became worked out in 1747. From 1758 no silver was struck for nearly thirty years. Copper coins were extremely scarce and none was struck to alleviate this situation because of the high price of this metal; from 1754 until 1770 the supply of copper completely ceased. With no silver or copper minted it is understandable that an acute shortage of small money developed. In the meantime a large number of forged halfpennies, very similar in appearance to the coins of George II, arrived on the scene. Many of these, commonly called 'Bungtowns', also found their way to the American colonies and were circulated there. The probable origin of their name was the slang expression 'to bung' (to deceive).

Unlike counterfeiting in gold and silver, which was a treasonable offence, imitating copper coins was but a misdemeanour of which the Government took little notice, with the result that many firms circulated their own copper coins. An Act was passed in 1742, however, increasing to two years' imprisonment the punishment for counterfeiting 'brass or copper money commonly called a halfpenny or a farthing'.

Nevertheless, coins that did not imitate official copper too closely were legal. Forgers naturally turned to this method of reproduction in the early 1730s. It is recorded in *Some Cautions concerning the copper coin* (published for R. Baldwin in 1751):

> There are now almost infinite sorts. Every town and village has its mints where many of our master manufacturers get them coined as cheap as they can for their use to pay their workmen with.

In 1750 these halfpence sold at a standard price of thirty to the shilling, while twenty years later they were quoted at thirty-six.

Page 157 Victorian decimal patterns

Page 158 (*left*) Finished coins collected by conveyor system, for bagging prior to counting and packing, at the Royal Mint, Llantrisant; *below*) coining room at the Royal Mint, Llantrisant, showing mechanical handling equipment feeding blanks to six lines of presses and collecting finished coins

Hanover to Victoria

The number of these coins in circulation was estimated on various occasions to be from two-thirds to one and a half times the quantity of legal copper in circulation.

Hammered gold coins were withdrawn in 1732, thirty-seven years after the withdrawal of hammered silver; this was probably little more than a formality, since there could only have been a very limited number of coins in circulation such a long time after the last hammered gold had been struck.

Tanner and the Sixpence

During 1738 John Tanner, the chief graver at the Mint from 1741 to 1775, is alleged to have copied Thomas Simon's pattern coinage of 1656, a deplorable act for a man with his official authority. The possibility remains, however, that the pattern dies made by Simon escaped destruction; for although instructions were given that all puncheons and dies that had found their way into private ownership must be destroyed, it is known that at least the Commonwealth dies made by Simon for the Drury House mint, in which Briot worked, remained intact and were brought back in 1700.

Opinion has it that from John Tanner the slang expression 'tanner' for a sixpence originated. Another, less probable, theory is that it may be a corruption of the gipsy word 'tano' meaning 'little coin', ie 'little' in comparison with a shilling. From the end of the eighteenth century tanner is accepted slang for sixpence. An entry in *A Dictionary of the Underworld* by E. Partridge states that from 1797 until 1860 the word may have been cant, but probably it had been low slang for a generation or more before this date. Sixpence is given as 'the tanner' in *A New Dictionary of All Cant and Flash languages*, 1797, while in the Sessions Papers at the Old Bailey in 1810, and again in 1824-33 (Trial of Thos Mayer), reference is made to counterfeiters using the expression bob for a shilling and tanner for sixpence; and Dickens himself used tanner in *Martin Chuzzlewit*.

Yet another theory is that London's cabmen gave the sixpence its nickname. From Bermondsey on the south bank of the Thames the businessmen of the tanning industry would travel every market day to Leadenhall Street for their weekly trade discussion, at which they freely wined and dined. The only transport available at that time was the hackney coach or an old chariot, either of these costing an extra sixpence. Thus the sixpence may have been named tanner through its association with the tanners of Bermondsey.

Scottish Banks under George II

The monopoly of the Bank of Scotland expired in 1716, but it did not apply for a renewal of its licence, probably considering this unnecessary as it was so well established. The first opposition did not begin until the Equivalent Company obtained a royal charter to operate as the Royal Bank of Scotland in 1727. The two banks developed tremendous rivalry and no little ill-feeling, but after a few years they acknowledged each other's right to expand.

At first the new bank began to collect the Bank of Scotland's notes in exchange for its own, while the Bank of Scotland endeavoured to make a similar collection of its rival's notes, the object being to present a large accumulation of notes to be exchanged for gold and silver and exhaust the rival's reserve of metal currency. It is amusing to imagine two banks today deliberately trying to exhaust each other's supplies of money.

In 1746, a third bank, the Edinburgh Linen Company Partnery, was granted a royal charter, opening as the British Linen Company in 1747. This bank created a valuable service as it was the first to establish successfully a network of branches in Scotland and so to extend the circulation of trustworthy notes throughout the country, a great boon to those remote towns and villages that had been virtually without currency with which to trade and make their everyday purchases.

Many of the early private banks of the eighteenth century in Scotland issued notes far in excess of their resources, with the result that they had to use every measure possible to prevent the notes being presented too soon, in order to avoid financial embarrassment. This led the two large banks to search for a more reliable method of controlling money for circulation, especially in times of panic;

they also refused to accept the many notes of other banks which were circulating in Edinburgh. This decision unfortunately meant

> a loss to the people of Edinburgh who when they became possessed of notes of private bankers, in which indeed most of their wages were paid, were obliged to keep them dead sometime on hand or pay 1½d every 20s for changing them (Scots magazine).

Around the middle of the eighteenth century the issue of notes by new private banks began to assume tremendous proportions. Some examples show how the quantity of paper money became a menace.

In 1755 the Aberdeen town council at a meeting decided to reject every note issued by the Glasgow banks. An example of the total unreliability of Glasgow notes was shown by one bank, Murdock and Co of Glasgow, which went to great trouble to avoid cashing its own notes except under considerable pressure. At the same meeting banknotes in general came in for much criticism, the exception being those of the Edinburgh banks, whose reliability compared favourably with the dubious financial positions of the smaller banks. In Perth six new banks opened in the year 1763. It was fortunate that the Restriction Act of 1765 caused them to merge into one respectable bank, the Perth Banking Co, which in later years became the Union Bank of Scotland. This Act, among other decisions, forbade the issue of notes for less than £1.

Ireland under George II

From 1728 to 1736 great numbers of silver and copper tokens were issued in Ireland by private persons, but in spite of these token issues the shortage of coin became steadily worse. Finally the British Government in 1736 gave orders for 50 tons of copper to be made into Irish halfpennies and farthings at the Tower mint (*Fig 6*). These coins had the king's head on the obverse, and the inscription 'Georgius II Rex' with the Irish harp and 'Hibernia' above it on the reverse. They were much criticised for the omission of the inscription 'Dei Gratia' (By the Grace of God). The *Gentleman's Magazine* of July 1737 contained the following epigram in reply to the criticism of a previous publication:

> While you behold th'imperfect coin,
> Received without the Grace of God,
> All honest men with you must join,
> And even Britons think it odd.
>
> The Grace of God was well left out,
> And I applaud the politician;
> For when an evil's done, no doubt,
> 'Tis not by God's Grace, but permission.

The exchange value between Irish and English coin at this time continued as before (the Irish pound equal to 18s 5½d English, and the English pound equal to 21s 8d Irish). The coin circulating in Ireland continued to be English gold and silver (gold guineas, half guineas; silver crowns, half crowns, shillings and sixpences) and Irish copper. The supply of the first two metals was hopelessly inadequate for commercial needs, while copper coins were generally unsatisfactory after William III had abolished the large supplies of brass money. Although local commercial transactions were made at the Irish value, payment was officially completed at the English rate. Nevertheless, local transactions were often ruled by the coins actually available, two instances being found in *Faulkner's Dublin Journal* in 1740 and *The Freeman's Journal* in 1775. The former advertises a dance at Clontarf costing 'one English halfcrown', and the latter an exhibition of a 'mermaid' at Essex Quay, Dublin, for the price of 'one British shilling'. The ill-educated must have been completely confused when calculating the exchange rates between the Irish and English coins.

The production of the copper coinage for Ireland continued until 1755. Then striking was discontinued until 1760, when 50 tons of copper was allocated for the Irish coinage, but this contract was not completed until 1762. From 1755 to 1760 another flood of token coins inundated Ireland—twopenny pieces struck in Northern Ireland, and, in 1760, halfpenny tokens known as 'Voce Populi' money, struck in Dublin and so named because of the wording of the inscription (*Fig 7*). The latter are said to have been made by a man named Roche, who manufactured metal buttons for the army, the obverse bearing the head of Prince Charles Edward, the Young Pretender.

The chaotic state of the Irish currency in the earlier part of the eighteenth century—English gold and silver and Irish copper (13d English equalled 1s Irish) being in short supply and in bad condition —was further aggravated by the growth of many small and unstable banks, which were permitted by law to circulate unofficial paper money in whatever quantity they thought fit. The original goldsmiths' notes, which were transferable, can be said to have been the origin of the enormous number of notes that swamped Ireland in later years. A large number of these private bankers were merely small traders and shopkeepers, totally ignorant of the dangers of unrestricted note issues and often believing that the cash they received for their notes was profit to themselves.

Banking business was necessarily kept within the district in which a banker operated, and any upset to local trade—such as a bad harvest or a bankruptcy—would cause a panic; and even merchants who were well established and kept their note issues well within reasonable bounds would become victims of a sudden mad rush to obtain gold or silver in exchange for notes. After several Acts designed to protect the currency, an Act was passed in 1756 prohibiting bankers from engaging in any other business than banking. Unfortunately it still allowed traders to issue their notes, though they were compelled to have their names on them.

As was to be expected, crashes occurred usually through panic withdrawals. One panic, in 1754, caused three important banks in Dublin to close, the partners absconding from two of them and the third defaulting because of fraud within the firm. After these failures the public's lack of confidence in banks was not surprising and it became more acute when two of the remaining five banks in Dublin failed in 1759. These failures caused great panic and wild scenes, which forced the remaining banks practically to cease business for a time, though they kept open officially.

George III

The great industrial upheaval in the second half the eighteenth century continued more intensively into the nineteenth; and it is perhaps as well that George III (1760-1820) had few of the country's affairs under his control. Although a grandson of George II (his father, Frederick, Prince of Wales, died in 1751), he was born and educated in England. Fortunately for the country he had neither the character nor the strength to attain his ambition of increasing the power of the throne. He was, however, an extremely obstinate man, an unfortunate trait that had a profound bearing on the loss of the American colonies. He attempted to bribe his way in Parliament by titles, gifts, etc, and built up a party known as 'the King's Friends'.

From the early part of his reign to the turn of the century banknotes largely took the place of gold coinage, while the issue of silver and copper coins was almost negligible because these metals were so expensive.

The first gold coins issued were the guineas in 1762. Until 1786 the reverses remained unaltered, though the King's effigy showed four types. The quarter guineas were discontinued after one year. From 1787 the shape of the shield on the reverse of the guineas and half guineas was completely altered, becoming known as the 'spade' type (*Figs 8 and 9*). This issue continued until 1800. From 1797 to 1800 one-third guineas were issued for the first time, no doubt because of the acute silver shortage. From 1801 a new design was used for the half guineas—a 'shield in garter' type—omitting the arms of France, which had been retained as part of the arms of England since the victories of Creçy and Poitiers over the French some 450 years before.

This change of design in the arms coincided with the Act of Union in 1801, which was intended to secure Ireland's loyalty and prevent her from becoming a centre for French support against England. The Act of Union united the English and Irish Parliaments, transferring 100 Irish members to Westminster. The Treaty of Amiens which followed in 1802 was an uneasy peace, though a number of English and French wartime colonial conquests were confirmed; but war broke out again in 1803. Not until 1813 were 'shield in garter' guineas struck, and they became known as 'military guineas' because they were used during the Peninsular War for paying the British army campaigning in Spain and Portugal. The one-third guineas were also continued throughout the period 1801-13, though the design of the first issue was twice modified.

With the great recoinage of 1816 the guinea and its divisions was replaced by the sovereign and half sovereign. Both denominations were issued in 1817, continuing until the death of the King in 1820. The larger coins displayed Pistrucci's design of St George and the Dragon, while the half sovereigns showed the redesigned crown shield, which omitted the lilies of France.

The origin of the St George design can be traced to a shell cameo 'Bataille Coquille' in the Duke of Orleans' collection, which displays a Greek horse and rider. The substitution of St George for the rider was made and adapted by an Italian employee of Brunets Hotel, Leicester Square—long since demolished—where the forty-year-old Pistrucci stayed after being brought to England by the Prince Regent in 1814.

George III Silver

George III's silver coins comprised six issues. The first issue, in 1763, was of shillings, generally known as 'Northumberland shillings', struck for special distribution by the Earl of Northumberland as Lord Lieutenant of Ireland. Because of the shortage of metal currency there had been an unsuccessful attempt in 1780 to place the coinage under the control of the Bank of England. The second issue in 1787 consisted of shillings and sixpences similar to the last issue.

In 1798 a firm by the name of Dorien and Magens took the law into its own hands and sent bullion to the Mint to be made into shillings; this, however, was discovered to be illegal and the Government made the typical statement that 'no coinage is lawful without the sanction of a royal proclamation', so the coins were melted down again, notwithstanding the urgent need for them.

The high price of silver led to its being little used in the coinage during the first half of George III's reign. Although some silver was coined, the amount was quite insufficient to meet the pressing need. In 1797, in an attempt to relieve this situation, the Bank of England utilised dollars of the Spanish-American colonies from Mexico, Bolivia, Peru, Guatemala and Chile, and others from Spain, America and France, which were stamped with the head of George III, similar to the goldsmiths' hallmark, and circulated at the value of 4s 9d in a third issue. These coins cut in half were similarly stamped and circulated. The Government lost over 4d per coin on the issued value, as the English valuation of the Spanish dollar at that time, allowing for the slightly inferior silver content, was only 4s 4¾d. This issue, however, legalised a situation under which foreign dollars had been circulating because of the great shortage of silver. Two years later an octagonal countermark was substituted for the King's head on these dollars to check counterfeiting of the original hallmark (Fig 10).

The price of silver continued to rise during the French Wars (1793-1815) owing to a general shortage in Europe and a disturbed political situation. The Bank of England called in all the dollars and instructed Matthew Boulton to overstrike them with a completely new design on the powerful press at his Birmingham foundry. They were then reissued at a value of 5s. Further issues of these overstruck dollars took place in 1810 and 1811 with the same 1804 dies, even though the price of silver had risen still more, causing the dollars to circulate at a further loss. This became the fourth silver coin issue (Fig 11). New Bank of England coins were issued for 3s and 1s 6d, from 1811 to 1816 in a fifth issue. These were token coins, issued to relieve the silver shortage, as the silver content was less than the required silver standard for regal coins, but in 1813 all private silver tokens were made illegal.

The overstamped and countermarked Spanish-American dollars and the Bank of England silver tokens were withdrawn from circulation in 1818. The dollars had been subject to much ridicule, one well known comment being 'Two kings' heads not worth a crown'; while another, also referring to the countermarking of George III's head on the neck of the Spanish king, was:

> The Bank of England, to make their dollars pass,
> Stamped the head of a fool on the neck of an ass.

Although the dollar has not been current since 1818, it left behind its name as a popular slang word for 5s. The word itself is generally accepted as originating from the name *thaler*, which was given to coins struck by the Count of Schlick around 1525 from the silver mined in the district of Joachimstal in Bohemia.

This confusion in the coinage influenced the Government to withdraw all silver from circulation and issue in exchange the sixth new issue coinage of 1816, the date from which our silver is legal tender today. The denominations struck in the first year were half crowns, shillings and sixpences, followed by crowns (*Fig 12*) and Maundy coins. Prior to this great operation the public was invited to exchange ten guineas' worth of silver for ten £1 notes and ten 1s pieces, while eight Bank of England dollars were exchanged for eight times 5s 6d.

When £2 million had been collected, the new coinage was issued, but after three months the old coinage became out of date and was redeemed by weight only. The weight of the new silver coins was reduced (a shilling was reduced in weight from 93 grains to 87), since silver was to become a token coinage while gold remained standard. In February 1817, twenty booths in London—the Bank of England, South Sea House, Guildhall, Goldsmith's Hall and 16 auxiliary stations—were opened to exchange the new coinage for old, which in turn was melted down and turned into new for further exchange.

George III Copper

The copper coins comprised four issues. The first, in 1770-75, was in halfpennies and farthings, but the supply was not nearly enough for public requirements and after a period of great shortage provincial coins and tradesmen's tokens began to appear in 1784 (*Fig 13*). Some of the better known of these were well designed and executed. One example is the Anglesey penny, which bore a Druid's head on the obverse with the letters P.M. Co., signifying the Parys Mountain Company. The copper for these coins came from the company's own mines and they were struck by Matthew Boulton and James Watt at their Birmingham mint by the new steam presses invented by Watt, who was, of course, an extremely versatile inventor.

The second issue of regal copper coins appeared in 1797. This issue included twopenny pieces, circulated for the first and only time, and pennies; because of their size, they became known as the cartwheel pennies and twopences (*Fig 14*). These coins are of particular interest as the lettering is in incuse, a complete reversal of the normal practice of lettering in relief. These also were struck by Boulton and Watt, who were granted a Royal Mint warrant to strike them after a number of unsuccessful attempts to obtain Government contracts. The twopenny pieces were soon found to be too large for ordinary use—they weighed 2oz—and were discontinued. The pennies continued for another two years with the same date but gave way to the smaller denominations of the 1799 issue. The demand continued to outstrip the supply and, therefore, in 1799 the third issue of halfpennies and farthings was struck; but the supply was still insufficient and in 1806-7 a fourth issue of pennies, halfpennies and farthings was struck. In 1811 the copper shortage had become so acute that private firms once again began to circularise tokens. By 1817, however, the Government's recoinage was under way and tokens were made illegal, though nothing was done to meet the demand for regal copper until 1821, when farthings were struck.

Banking under George III

The successful circulation of the Bank of England's printed notes of 1725, 1743, 1752, 1759 and 1765, aided by the currency shortage in the second half of the eighteenth century, encouraged the established country banks, as well as a fast growing number of new firms, to issue their own notes. The Bank of England notes, however, could hardly have been circulated for general use by the public as the smallest note was £10, whereas the £1 notes of the country banks must have been eagerly accepted in the almost complete absence of metal currency. This was the situation before 1777, when forgeries forced the withdrawal of banknotes under £5. To show how worn the remaining coin was, a test was carried out in which three well

Hanover to Victoria

known London goldsmiths were asked each to send £100 of current silver for the purpose of testing the average weight of the coinage. This amount of coinage should have weighed 1,200 troy oz but in fact weighed only 624 oz—a loss in weight of almost 50 per cent. The loss in weight today of £100 of circulated silver would not exceed £2 in value.

It is understandable that this discrepancy in the weight of the coinage, as well as the defacement through wear, caused considerable chaos. Rarely was any transaction made without an argument, and no trader would sell goods without stipulating the weight of the coins in which he was to be paid; quarrels over money values were continuous; market days and fairs were regularly scenes of brawls, while wages paid by employers to their workmen were the cause of many Saturday night disputes regarding the value of their money. Such was the result of the apathy and ignorance of the Government in so neglecting the currency.

Each town was virtually the centre of its own industries, agriculture and local trade, with practically no outside trade or communications affecting the normal routine of a district; the horse was still the only means of transport. With agriculture in most areas in a very backward state, the roads, sometimes only tracks, became virtually impassable at certain times of the year; with footpads and robbers lurking in these areas it was understandable that money, particularly in bulk, could not be transported with safety. Metal currencies were almost non-existent and the people readily accepted the very much more convenient paper money which, though leaving the problem of small change unsolved, was generally sufficient for normal trading.

Small traders such as grocers, drapers, tailors, etc, and even private individuals of doubtful financial stability, took advantage of the opportunity allowed by law and issued their own notes. The only requirement appeared to be the confidence of the public. This surprising state of affairs was permitted notwithstanding the ever-present danger of an economic crisis, which might cause noteholders hurriedly to demand gold in exchange. This deluge of paper money offered considerable scope for the forger, and many people complained of forgeries. The Act of 1775 in which notes for £1 or less were prohibited, and the Act of 1777 which raised the smallest legal value for a note to £5, did little to check this activity, though they considerably simplified the note issue.

Banking during this period was for small firms a highly speculative business. Many of them issued notes to many times the value of their capital, relying on a large proportion of these always being in circulation and hoping that a large number would not be presented for cashing at one time. There was one instance of a country bank, started by four partners who each subscribed £500, issuing in a few months nearly £14,000 in notes. Twenty years later this bank, with an increased capital of only £8,000, had expanded its note issue to £180,000.

About 1790 many of these banks began increasingly to cash their bills through London agents. This practice had the ultimate effect of embarrassing London tradespeople, and caused country bills to be discredited. With the destruction of public confidence an inevitable run on the country banks took place, and many, having a note issue greatly exceeding their capital, were soon in difficulties. In 1793 about 100 of them closed their doors, while a further 300 had great difficulty in weathering the storm.

The first £5 Bank of England notes appeared in 1793 to meet the public need and attract more gold to the banks. (The first wholly printed notes were not issued until 1854, though in 1809 notes were printed unsigned, leaving only the signature for completion by hand before issue as a cheque would be signed today.) The first issue coincided with the start of the war with revolutionary France and the beginning of a gold famine, which worsened as the war continued, inflamed by public fear of French invasion under Napoleon. In the next two years a reissue of banknotes of the higher values of £100, £200, £300 and £500 was increased to absorb some of the demand for gold; but the public was still in a nervous state when a raid at Fishguard on the Welsh coast by French troops set wild rumours circulating about an invasion. The Government took steps to check a run on the Bank and ordered the directors to prohibit cash payments, 'until the sense of Parliament can be taken on that subject'; in the same year the Bank Restriction Act was passed, restricting the payment of cash by the Bank for the time being, but it was later retained until 1820. This necessitated the issue of notes, and the Act of 1777 was amended in 1797 to allow the issue of £1 and £2 notes to replace the withdrawn gold. This had the effect of relieving the financial strain caused by the Napoleonic Wars, whereby traders required to be paid in cash. From 1807 a period of improved trading began and many more new country banks were formed, with a further increase in country notes. From 1797 to 1810 the number of these banks increased from 270 to 720, with a country banknote issue of £30,000,000.

Unfortunately the proportion of forged notes began to increase alarmingly, a probable reason being that the smaller value notes had a circulation among less educated persons who had rarely been accustomed to banknotes and were easy victims for the forger. In 1800 the number of forged notes had grown to 4,000, and in spite of all efforts to check these spurious products the numbers increased still further, until in 1817 the surprising figure of 31,000 was reached—all believed to have been produced from not more than ten engravings. Laws were harshly applied in an attempt to reduce this alarming figure, but only those who passed the notes were approached. In this same year thirty-two persons were hanged for passing forged notes, making a total of 313 since the restrictions of cash in 1797, an injustice which rightly inflamed public opinion.

Some time later George Cruikshank, returning from his office to his home in Fleet Street, passed Newgate Prison and saw two women hanging from gibbets outside. Their only crime was that each had passed a forged £1 note. Incensed at this harsh treatment, he went home and sketched a banknote advertising this cruel injustice. It was published and displayed in the shop window of William Hone of Ludgate Hill, causing great public interest, so much so that the lord mayor had to send for the police to disperse the large and angry crowd that had collected. Whether this public agitation had a direct result cannot be ascertained, but the death sentence for forgery was abolished in 1832.

The question was often raised of the disposition of forged notes after their detection. Before 1818 they were retained by the Bank of England, but an incident which proved embarrassing for the Bank caused the procedure to be changed. Towards the end of 1818 an engraver named Ranson paid a man named Mitchener a £1 note which, having been presented at the Bank of England, was declared a forgery and retained. Mitchener thereupon informed Ranson and demanded payment in place of the forgery, but Ranson refused unless the note were returned for his inspection. The Bank of England, through an inspector, charged Ranson with possessing a forged banknote. He was held in prison pending trial, but as the Bank failed to produce anyone to give evidence Ranson was found not guilty. He then sued the inspector for wrongful imprisonment and received damages for £100. It afterwards transpired that the note was genuine and that the Bank of England had failed to identify one of its own notes! From that time forged notes were stamped 'forged' by the Bank and returned to the presenter when requested.

Two opponents of the death sentence for forgery were Sir Samuel Romily and Sir James Macintosh, who did much to enlist public opinion in their support. The legislators began to appreciate that prevention was better than cure. Harsh punishment was no deterrent when most of the true criminals and the engravers appeared to have escaped detection.

Expansion and Development of the Mint

Throughout the eighteenth century the production of coins had been considered unsatisfactory; in 1787, therefore, the Privy Council appointed a committee to inquire into the methods and organisation of the Mint, but it was not until 1798 that the committee commissioned two Fellows of the Royal Society to find out if the durability of coins could be improved by an adjustment of fineness. After many experiments they reported that pure gold and silver were both too soft, but an addition of an alloy in the proportion of one to twelve or one to thirteen gave a good colour together with reasonable durability. Their recommendations, which were adopted, meant that the premises in the Tower were too limited to accommodate the development and expansion necessary for the proposed recoinage. Also the encroachment of the military authorities on the build-

Hanover to Victoria

ings used by the Tower mint increased the need for finding a new location.

Accordingly a piece of land adjacent to the Tower, then known as Little Tower Hill, occupied by Government tobacco warehouses, was selected for the new building. This site had also been used as a victualling yard by the Royal Navy for over 200 years. In preparation for the great recoinage of 1816 the Government had already planned to replace the out-of-date equipment of the Tower mint. Boulton and Watt were given the contract to supply improved machinery while the buildings were erected on the new site. These buildings, designed by James Johnson and completed by Robert Smirke, were erected between the years 1806 and 1811, and still house the Royal Mint today. Soon, however, the main production will be transferred to Llantrisant in South Wales.

The new coining presses were still of the screw type, but were driven by steam with many mechanical improvements. The blank metal discs were exactly centred before being struck by a powerful hammer that contained the die producing the reverse side of the coin, while the obverse side was impressed on the blank by a fixed die underneath. At the same time the blank was held by a collar which impressed the graining on the edge of the coin as it expanded under the impact of the hammer.

The process is much the same today, though many technical advances have been incorporated; the output of coins since those early days has increased many times over, the process now working at a speed of over 100 blows a minute. In 100 years the Mint has increased its output of coins from 25,000,000 annually to the present figure of 500,000,000.

The buildings used for this tremendous expansion have long since been outdated and much improvisation has been necessary. With the introduction of a decimal coinage in 1971 the premises of the Royal Mint on Tower Hill, London, are now considered far too cramped and economically unsuitable for the very large expansion envisaged. As a result, the gradual process of moving to Llantrisant is in progress, and already much of the coinage is being produced there.

Eighteenth-century Banking in Scotland

From 1760 there was a marked change in agricultural methods in Scotland, which until that time had been in a very backward state; and a number of banks were formed to finance the improvements. Some continued successfully until they were merged with larger banks, while others came to an untimely end. The most notorious of the latter was Douglas, Heron & Co of Ayr, which failed through an over-issue of notes and a rush by the public to cash them into gold and silver. This bank, with grim but unconscious humour, issued their notes with their name and the town with the phrase, 'Banking in Air' (Ayr was spelt thus at that time).

About 1770 the notes of the Bank of Scotland and the Royal Bank almost disappeared, causing a great outcry by the public, who suffered as a direct result.

The successful British Linen Co began to withdraw from the linen industry in 1763, having established a number of agents in various parts of the country to assist in a better distribution of notes, and from that time devoted itself more and more exclusively to banking. By 1793 the British Linen Co had twelve branches and another six opened shortly afterwards; these were a great boon, for in the days when communities were connected to one another only by the most primitive communications a note circulation was of inestimable value, enabling all classes to conduct their business with greater convenience.

The commercial expansion of 1783-92 in Scotland was halted by the effects of the French war on trade; there was an excessive cashing of notes for gold and silver and consequently several well established banks shut down through failure to meet this demand. Four of these were prominent banks in Newcastle-on-Tyne, where Scottish notes had a considerable circulation. It was fortunate that public confidence was quickly restored by British naval successes, clearing the vital shipping routes from French aggression, so that trade increased more than it had ever done before during a foreign war.

The scare of a French invasion of Ireland, with gold supplies still low from the troubles of 1793, caused the Scottish banks great

Page 175 (*above*) Blanks arriving by conveyor at the coining room after blanching and washing at the Royal Mint, Llantrisant; (*below*) obverse for all denominations of decimal currency. Arnold Machin's design of the queen, already displayed on a number of Commonwealth coins, is excellent. The draped shoulders add to a pleasant feminine look. A minor criticism is of the placing of the date which unbalances the left side inscription

Page 176 (*left*) The fifty new pence note of the Isle of Man; (*below*) the first gold coinage of the Isle of Man —unlikely ever to be seen in circulation

Hanover to Victoria

anxiety lest they should be unable to meet the demands. When in 1797 news arrived that the Bank of England had suspended payment of gold, the Scottish banks had hardly any option but to follow suit. It was reported that from 1 March until the end of the week there was great uproar and confusion, particularly among the poorer classes, with 'fish women, carmen, street porters and butchers men all bawling out at once for change, and jostling each other in their endeavours who should get nearest the table'. Small change became a great problem and tallies, tokens, etc, were freely used; £1 banknotes cut in halves and quarters were accepted by the banks and assisted to some degree in solving the problem.

Finally, the Government amended the Act of 1777 and notes of £1 and £2 were again issued. A large number of Spanish-American dollars similar to those released in England and Ireland were circulated by the Government, valued at 4s 6d. These coins had the same punch mark on the obverse as those circulating in England. The three large Scottish banks and other banks that had issued notes before 1797 were then authorised to issue paper money of any denomination under £1—an Act which was later extended to include those banks that had issued notes before July 1799. These smaller notes—a popular value appeared to be 5s—soon began to be freely used by the public, many of whom brought out gold which they had hitherto hoarded.

From 1800 numerous private banks opened, but most of them either amalgamated or were closed down after a short life. By far the most important of these was the Commercial Bank of Scotland, opened in 1810 and sponsored by an Edinburgh tanner and leather merchant, and built up by Liberals who disagreed with the methods of the older banks. Competition between the banks in the provinces became very keen, which was one of the reasons why the Bank of Scotland closed a number of its branches; in 1800 it had possessed twenty-six branches, but by 1820 only thirteen remained.

Although eighty-six people were prosecuted for forgery in Scotland between 1806 and 1825, it never reached the same proportions as in England. Nor did the law operate so severely, as only eight out of this total were executed, though, as in England, these were not the actual engravers but merely people who had passed the notes.

1.

From 1816 all the existing gold and silver coinage was withdrawn, the silver coins being very little better than worn discs, and replaced by the new coinage, which was well struck and was very well received by the Scots, and probably reduced the numbers of smaller notes in circulation.

Eighteenth-century Banking in Ireland

In the eighteenth century Ireland was probably the worst governed country in Europe, controlled by a few great protestant families. Both the presbyterians of the North and the catholics of the South were excluded by law from holding civil, military or municipal offices. The natural result was the revolt of 1798, followed by William Pitt's wise measure of 1801, the Act of Union.

After the crisis of 1759 only two new banks were established in Dublin until the formation of the Bank of Ireland in 1783. This was almost a century after the establishment of national banks in England and Scotland; a strong Irish claim for free trade and a period of acute depression (1770-80), caused by too many restrictions, had been the prime factors for its creation. Under the style and title of 'the Governor and Company of the Bank of Ireland' it was given a virtual monopoly, since the members of other corporations and partnerships were not allowed to exceed six in number.

When the Bank of Ireland opened on 23 July 1783 its organisation and methods were based on those of the Bank of England, with whom the Irish bankers had been in close contact. The first notes were made by Joseph Portal, whose family had made paper for the Bank of England notes for fifty-nine years. These notes were of the same quality and size as their English counterparts but with a different scroll and device. They were issued in values of £10, £15, £20, £25, £30, £40, £50, £60, £70, £80, £90, £100, £200, £300, £400 and £500 to a total of 12,700 notes amounting to £882,500 Irish.

It was only a few months after this issue that the directors decided to print their own notes. Accordingly, plates were prepared —with only part of the design on them, the remainder of the note being stamped on. These notes were in similar denominations to the first issue with guinea notes of 5, 10, 20, 30, 40, 50, 60, 70, 80, 90 and 100, all at Irish valuation. To facilitate calculations the English equivalent was printed on each note.

As in England forgery became a great problem and the Bank of Ireland spent large sums in attempting to eliminate it. Finally an Act of Parliament was passed making the possessor of a plate for copying notes liable to transportation, later increased to the death penalty. An additional protection, similar to the English system of postdated bills, was introduced, reducing the risk of robbery; these bills were not payable until seven days after issue, giving travellers time to withhold payment in the event of a mail-coach hold-up.

Now that an increased number of gold coins was circulating in Ireland, many underweight guineas began to appear. They had obviously been 'clipped' or 'sweated' (the latter being a practice of rubbing the coins together in order to collect the gold dust from them), and the banks refused them. By 1787 the habits of 'clipping' and 'sweating' constituted a national menace, and after considerable dispute as to who should bear the cost these coins were withdrawn.

From 1790 the Bank of England was almost continuously being pressed for gold because of the political conditions on the Continent, and from 1793 until 1797 there was a steady drain of gold from the Bank, aggravated by rumours of a French fleet at sea and of invasion of the Welsh coast; these factors all helped to undermine the monetary structure, and the Bank was compelled to suspend cash payments. On 2 March 1797, when this news arrived in Dublin, the Irish Privy Council also suspended cash payments at the Bank of Ireland; the other Irish banks followed suit. Unlike Edinburgh, where there was great excitement, Dublin took the news calmly.

The silver coinage in Ireland in 1804 was scarce and badly worn. Even the best preserved silver was only valued at 9s, for the face value of 21s, while the silver coins of a lower grade, which contained base metal, were valued at only 5s for 21s face value. Crowns and half crowns were almost non-existent, while sixpences of any type were extremely rare.

Irish copper was more plentiful than silver, though much of it was struck in token halfpennies with a device instead of the king's head. Some of these, known as Cronebane halfpennies, with the supposed head of St Patrick on them, were issued by the Irish Mines Company of Dublin about 1789 (*Fig 15*). Others known as Camacs after the copper-mine proprietors Camac, Kyan & Camac of Dublin, were mainly issued in 1792.

Silver coin was almost non-existent in southern Ireland, but its place was taken by 'silver' notes issued by private bankers and traders and made payable to the bearer after twenty-one days. These notes were low in value, with denominations from 3s to 6s. This state of affairs caused the Bank of Ireland to buy silver dollars from the Bank of England and issue them at a value of 6s Irish. These dollars were the same as those issued in Britain for 5s British, though the Irish dollars had the device of the Bank of Ireland on the reverse instead of the Bank of England marking. It was agreed that the arrangement whereby these dollar pieces were overvalued in Ireland should be a temporary expedient only. At the beginning of 1805 large quantities of both 10d and 5d token pieces, also issued by the Bank of Ireland, went into circulation. At the same time Matthew Boulton entered into an agreement to manufacture 1,200 tons of copper into copper coins, half being for Ireland, half for Great Britain. This second issue—following a first issue of halfpennies in 1766—was in pennies, halfpennies and farthings, dated 1805 and 1806. Two further issues of token silver coins by the Bank of Ireland took place in 1808, when 30d tokens were circulated, and in 1813, when there was another issue of 10d tokens.

In 1817 the Bank of Ireland was authorised to pay gold and silver on all its notes under £5 provided they were dated before 1 January 1812. This represented a partial removal of the cash restrictions which had been imposed since 1797; but in 1819 the gold stocks of the Bank of England began to decrease and these cash payments were again suspended both in Britain and Ireland for almost another two years.

George IV

George III's son acted as Prince Regent twice during his father's

Hanover to Victoria

bouts of insanity (or porphyria, according to the latest research), but this experience failed to stand him in good stead, for when he became George IV (1820-30) he remained an incompetent and dissolute ruler, having very little interest in the affairs of the country, which fortunately was firmly under the control of his ministers.

His coins, however, continued to be well designed and well struck. A new denomination of gold £2 pieces was issued as well as sovereigns and silver crowns, all with Pistrucci's St George and the dragon design on the reverse (*Fig 16*). The first issues of half sovereigns, half crowns, shillings and sixpences were by another designer, Johann Merlen; as the sixpence resembled the half sovereign in appearance it was decided to replace the latter with coins of another design. A second type soon followed with half sovereigns, half crowns, shillings and sixpences with changed designs on the reverses. These coins became known as the Laureate issues.

In 1824 Pistrucci was commanded by the King to copy Chantrey's royal portrait, as he was dissatisfied with the portrait on the earlier designs, but the artist refused on the ground that it was beneath him to copy another artist's work. The assignment was, therefore, given to William Wyon, who produced the beautifully designed head by Chantrey in another issue in which all the reverses were redesigned by Merlen (*Fig 17*); the denominations being sovereigns, half sovereigns, half crowns, shillings and sixpences. These last two are known as lion shillings and sixpences because of the reverse designs, but the whole group is now known as the Bare Head issue (*Fig 18*). The only copper coins issued during the first five years were farthings of two types. Pennies and halfpennies were issued in 1825 with the obverse designed by William Wyon.

After the partial but premature removal of the cash restrictions in 1817 and their reimposition two years later, an Act was passed in 1821 once again removing them, this time completely, and the issue of £1 and £2 country notes ceased. It was not long, however, before the ample gold reserves of 1821 began to be reduced through gold exports and increased internal demands. Nevertheless Parliament did not see the danger, for in 1822 it gave 500 small country banks the right to issue unlimited quantities of £1 notes, with the result that from 1821 to 1825 the total number of banknotes rose from

4 to 8 million. These notes were payable either in gold or in Bank of England notes; but as the Bank had withdrawn its £2 notes and most of its £1 notes, which had been habitually exchanged for country notes, the public, unable to obtain Bank of England notes, asked for gold coin. Thus more gold was drawn from the country banks, which had little in reserve. Towards the end of 1825 the position of the Bank of England itself became difficult through the run on gold and through cashing country notes, etc. Finally it ran short of its own notes and but for a find in the vaults of £700,000 of pre-restriction £1 notes, which were put into immediate circulation, the situation could have become dangerous. In the words of a Bank of England director at the time:

> They worked wonders; one box containing a quantity of one-pound notes had been overlooked, and they were forthcoming at the lucky moment. As far as my judgement goes, it saved the credit of the country.

By the end of the year inevitable crashes occurred in London and the provinces. The Government very reluctantly assisted a few, but a number of the small banks were compelled to close their doors. In three weeks sixty-one country and six large London banks ceased payment. Finally the Government was forced to take steps to end the extremely precarious situation. They informed the Bank of England that it must pay out to all, advance money freely and generally restore confidence. Gold was purchased from all sources to replenish the low reserves, and the Mint worked twenty-four hours a day to turn gold bars into coin. Confidence gradually returned.

During the following year, two years after a similar Act in Ireland, the issue of banknotes for less than £5 was prohibited, a restriction largely attributable to the problems created by the unlimited £1 and £2 note issues given to the country banks in 1822. At the same time joint-stock and private banks with more than six partners were allowed to operate 65 miles outside London provided they had no London office. This helped offset the difficulties caused by the closing of banks in the previous year and generally benefited country districts, where banks which often had insufficient capital had been left to meet local needs.

Hanover to Victoria

In 1824 and 1825, 624 companies were started in England, but by 1827 these had been reduced to 127 through failures and financial difficulties. The panic, however, did not affect Scotland to anything like the same degree as England, though it caused a depression that lasted for several years. Apart from the failure of three small banks there was considerable strain, anxiety and caution without actual distress. The unfortunate English banks, of which eighty failed, having practically no customers' deposits to fall back upon, depended almost entirely on note issues. Although the immediate cause of these failures was the over-issue of small notes, the Government was really to blame because it had failed to see the dangerous implications.

Cheques

From 1825 cheques began to be used, very slowly at first, as few people kept banking accounts; as the public became aware of the convenience of this system more and more cheques came into use, taking the place of a proportion of paper money. The reason why the public was reluctant to use cheques—as they were when the money orders were first introduced in 1792—was the lack of a system for clearing or cashing them when held by persons remote from the bank on whom the cheques were drawn. With the gradual introduction of improved communications and transport their value in replacing cash became recognised. No doubt the legislation introduced in 1826 and 1833, which permitted the formation of joint-stock banks, encouraged the use of the cheque system. Cheques are indispensable today; with the many hazards of modern life they are undoubtedly a safe, efficient and simple method of settling accounts, relieving the public of the need to use banknotes except for daily personal expenses. To show how widely adopted the cheque has become, the public in 1960 issued cheques in Britain to a value of £225,417 million, and in 1969 the figure had risen to £699,192 million.

Between 1819 and 1830 forty-eight new branch banks were opened in various parts of Scotland, and in the ten years following the seven large Scottish banks opened another 110 branches, making a total of 300 branches in 1840. Undoubtedly £1 notes (and £1 1s 0d notes) must be given the main credit for enabling a uniform currency to spread over the whole of Scotland, filling the inevitable need created by the absence of a metal currency. Their great advantage was that they were not too large a sum for normal transactions, not too heavy nor too bulky, and above all easily transportable; in addition they were not so obvious to thieves, who had many easy opportunities of robbing any prosperous looking traveller.

Growth in Irish Banking

The last separate issue of Irish coins to be produced under British rule were the George IV copper pennies and halfpennies issued in 1822 and 1823. During the 1820s and 1830s there was much agitation against the restrictions imposed on the Irish catholics. Concurrently Ireland was making considerable industrial progress. Her imports and exports quadrupled in the period 1800-40, creating a need for more banking facilities to assist trade generally. Agriculture developed with improved methods of cultivation. Great activity occurred in grinding, malting, brewing and distilling, while the linen trade was prosperous. Although some small industries disappeared, the general improvement in trade more than offset the losses. In 1824, the Government curtailed the monopoly of the Bank of Ireland by removing the ban under which no Irish bank could issue notes if it had more than six partners. It now permitted banks with partners exceeding that number to issue notes provided that they were at least 50 Irish miles from Dublin. This opportunity was immediately used to advantage and the Northern Bank opened in Belfast in the same year and became the first joint-stock bank to be established after this Act, though it had been a private bank since 1809. Its opening was on 1 January 1825—a date postponed from 1 September 1824 because of a legal hitch. The Provincial Bank of Ireland began business on 1 September 1825, locating its head office at Cork because it was not permitted to open in the capital, Dublin, and retain a right to issue notes. Nevertheless, shortly afterwards, it appointed the private bank of La Touche as agent in Dublin.

The Hibernian Joint Stock & Annuity Company began business at this same period and was actually the second joint-stock bank to become established after the Northern Bank, changing its title later to The Hibernian Bank. It was formed by Dublin businessmen who resented the discrimination shown by the Bank of Ireland against catholics.

In Belfast two private banks—Gordon & Co, formed in 1808, and Tennant Callwell & Co's Bank, formed in 1809—merged in 1827 to form a new joint-stock company called The Belfast Banking Company. Several years elapsed before the National Bank of Ireland commenced business, in January 1835, to become the fifth joint-stock bank. This bank adopted the unusual course of placing each of its branches under the control of a subsidiary company, with half its shares owned by local customers and the remainder held by the parent branch. Later in the same year the Royal Bank of Ireland, based in Dublin, was formed from the private bank of Sir Robert Shaw & Company—originally, in 1798, known as Leighton, Needham & Shaw. Based in Dublin only, it was not permitted to issue notes in competition with the Bank of Ireland.

In Belfast a third joint-stock bank opened for business on 1 July 1836, taking the name of the Ulster Banking Company. Finally the Munster and Leinster Bank Ltd was formed as late as 1885 to take over the business of the defunct Munster Bank. These eight banks, together with the Bank of Ireland, represented the whole of Ireland's joint-stock banking interests except for the National City Bank Ltd, established in 1920 to take over the business of the National Land Bank, which had been founded to cater for the needs of farmers.

During the nineteenth century the Irish fought for Home Rule, but independence came to all intents and purposes to Southern Ireland in 1922. In 1926 the first Currency Act was passed, giving Eire a separate coinage, followed by the Currency Act 1927, which permitted the Currency Commission to issue notes of 10s, £1, £5, £10, £50 and £100. After this Act the British Treasury negotiated with the Irish banks for a separate issue of banknotes for Northern Ireland. This led to the Bankers (Northern Ireland) Act 1928, which enabled the six Northern Ireland banks to retain a note issue.

William IV

The Duke of Clarence, George III's third son (Frederick, the second son, died in 1827), came to the throne as William IV (1830-7) at 64 years of age. He had gone to sea at the age of 14, and it is said that his manner was that of a sailor, bluff and hearty, though as a ruler he was blundering and irresolute.

There was little opportunity for variety in the coinage of such a short reign. The coins were similar to those of the last issue of George IV, but bore the head of the new king, designed by Chantrey and engraved by William Wyon. The exceptions were the crowns, which never went beyond the pattern stage (*Fig 19*), while only sovereigns and half sovereigns were issued in gold. The old silver groats (or 4d pieces) were reintroduced, with Britannia on the reverse. Not since the reign of Charles I had these coins been issued, if the 4d pieces of Charles II to George II are accepted as Maundy money only. William IV's groats are quite distinct from the Maundy 4d pieces issued at the same time. Joseph Hume, the philanthropist and an MP, was responsible for their introduction, and it was after him that they were scornfully nicknamed 'joeys'. London cab drivers were particularly derisive, finding that their customers gave groats as tips instead of the usual sixpences. At a later date when the groats were no longer issued the nickname 'joey' was transferred to the silver 3d pieces. Of the copper coins, the pennies, halfpennies and farthings were similar to those of the previous reign, while the half and third farthings, which are sometimes found, were struck for use not in Great Britain but the former in Ceylon and the latter in Malta. The little silver three-halfpenny pieces were also for use in the colonies and have no relation to the Maundy coinage.

Victoria

Neither George IV nor William IV, first and third sons of George III, left an heir to the throne (*Fig 20*). Queen Victoria (1837-1901) was the only child of Edward, Duke of Kent, fourth son of George III, and of a German princess. To describe her upbringing as

Hanover to Victoria

Victorian would be a truism that a later generation would understand; the result proved, nevertheless, to be outstanding. After the incompetent rule of the Hanoverians she restored the Crown to the highly respected position it has since held. Apart from her devotion to duty as head of the state, she gave a shining example of happy family life. During her memorable reign society advanced with giant strides.

Three separate major issues were made in the coinage. The first issue, dating from 1838, was known as the 'Young Head', which also includes the attractive Gothic designs of crowns and florins (*Figs 21 and 22*). All the coins of the first issue, which bears the royal arms, omitted the Hanoverian shield as, under Salic Law, a woman could not mount the throne of Hanover. This design of the royal arms exists today. Salic Law excluded females from inheriting lands. The so-called French Salic Law was a fundamental pact, by virtue of which males only could inherit the throne. Its origin is traced from the archaic principle of the lifelong tutelage of women, whether of their own family or of the husband. It is safe to presume that in turbulent times, when heirship of land or a throne entailed the performance of military duties, males alone could be chosen. Denmark, among other countries, has a Salic Law today.

The florins of the 'Young Head' issue were the first silver coins of this name, taken from the Dutch and Austrian florins current at the time; though florins originally were issued by Florence. These coins, first issued in 1849 as one-tenth of a pound, were struck as an experiment to test public opinion on a decimal system (*Fig 23*). They were popularly referred to as the 'Godless' or 'Graceless' florins because of the omission in the lettering of 'DG' or 'Dei Gratia' which it is said displeased the Queen, who asked for new coins to be struck (*Fig 24*).

The remaining coins of the 'Young Head' issue were sovereigns, half sovereigns, shillings, sixpences, groats, and threepenny pieces (first issued in 1845). Half crowns were first issued in 1839, while crowns were struck for three years only in 1844, 1845 and 1847; the attractive Gothic crowns were issued in 1847 only, followed by Gothic florins, which were first issued in 1851 and continued until 1887 (*Fig 25*). The keen observation and delight for detail shown in this ornate coin typifies a trend in the art of that period which harked back, with some nostalgia, to the fine workmanship of the English Gothic period.

In the latter years came the second issue, appropriately struck to celebrate the Queen's Golden Jubilee of 1887. This issue was composed of the five pounds, two pounds, sovereigns and half sovereigns in gold, 'milled' crowns, four-shilling pieces (or double florins) (*Fig 26*) and all the smaller denominations of the previous issue with the exception of the silver groats. Most of the designs of the reverses were altered but it was soon discovered that sixpences, being similar to the half sovereigns, lent themselves to gilding; the previous design for the reverse was therefore readopted in the following year. Neither crowns nor four-shilling pieces were popular, though the former had Pistrucci's St George and the Dragon design on the reverse (*Fig 27*). The latter were issued for three years only.

The design of the 'Jubilee' issue was never considered good and Victoria's reign witnessed a third change, this time to the so-called 'Old Head' coins (1893-1901), on which the portrait of the Queen was much improved (*Figs 28 and 29*). In the issue the denominations remained the same, except that the double florin was discontinued. The legend 'Decus et Tutamen' (an ornament and a safeguard) was again revived and reappeared on the edge of the crowns.

The first issue of the copper coins followed the design of the early copper issue of George IV and was struck in pennies, halfpennies, farthings and half farthings, with third and quarter farthings struck for the colonies only; it is difficult today to visualise anything that could be bought with coins of such minute value! The following epigram by Thomas Hood on the merits of the 1843 half farthing indicates that even in his day, when the purchasing power of money was many times greater, its value was criticised:

> Too small for any marketable shift,
> What purpose can there be for coins like these?
> Hush-hush, good Sir!—Thus charitable Thrift
> May give a mite to him who wants a cheese!

In 1860 the former copper coins began to be struck in bronze, a copper alloy with 95 per cent copper, 4 per cent tin and 1 per cent zinc; they were thinner and lighter than the earlier issue. This is the

Hanover to Victoria

first year for which current 'copper' (really bronze) coins are legal tender. The change to bronze, oddly enough, can be traced to the French Revolution. When the revolutionary mob tore down the church bells they could find no market for the bell metal, and eventually it was sent to the Paris mint for conversion into money after copper had been added. The coins made from this alloy became popularly known as 'sous des clochers' (belfry halfpennies). A few years later Napoleon had much of this large accumulation melted down. As the supply dwindled, more copper was added until a point was reached at which a workable mixture was found. This alloy was made legal in France in 1825 and was adopted by Great Britain and many other countries a few years later. Unlike the gold and silver denominations, bronze was not struck with the 'Jubilee' head, but pennies (*Fig 30*) and halfpennies were issued with the 'Old Head' in 1895, with farthings—darkened to avoid confusion with half sovereigns—following two years later.

There is a story that when the Royal Mint was contemplating the 1860 bronze coinage it sent one of the penny proof specimens to Queen Victoria for her inspection. The Queen is said to have given her approval. The coin was then returned by post; but unfortunately it was never received at the Mint. It is said that a postman, feeling a coin in the package, opened it but disgustedly threw it away when he found it to be no more than a penny. The final comment on this story was that whatever the postman's hobbies were, coin-collecting was not among them!

Victorian Banking

In 1844, to avoid further danger of inflation, the Government passed the Bank Charter Act, which restricted the issue of banknotes by private and joint-stock banks and gave the Bank of England a monopoly in the London area and a share with the banks of not more than six partners which were lawfully issuing notes on 6 May 1844 within 65 miles of London.

The output of notes from these banks was permitted up to their average issue for the twelve weeks ending 26 April 1844. No new note-issuing banks were permitted, the Government recognising the need for paper money to be a national responsibility. Outside this area the Bank retained a share with other banks which were lawfully issuing notes on that date. When a bank opened an office in London or allowed its right of issuing notes to lapse, the right was transferred to the Bank of England. This act was very unpopular with the country banks, which protested strongly against the restrictions imposed on them. Nevertheless the relentless 'squeezing-out' process continued. Between 1844 and 1854 thirty-seven banks closed down. Meanwhile more Bank of England notes circulated in country districts and were accepted by country banks in place of their curtailed issues.

At the time this Act was passed 279 banks were authorised to issue notes, but eighteen years later the number had dropped to 216 and by 1900 sixty banks only were issuing their own notes. In 1921 the last bank, Fox, Fowler & Co of Wellington, issued its last £5 note and surrendered the right to issue notes by amalgamating with Lloyds Bank.

In 1880 the Government authorised the printing of postal orders on the Bank of England printing machines. These were issued in comparatively small numbers in ten denominations ranging from 1s to 20s, and were printed in similar colours to our postal orders today. As the demand grew, various intermediate denominations were added, until in 1905 there were forty-one. By 1910 the total annual issue had reached 312 million. After 1939 the number of denominations was reduced to twenty-seven, including one for 21s; the 40s postal order was added in 1951 and the higher denominations of £3, £4 and £5 in 1956.

Scotland and the Stamp Duty

The stamp duty on Scottish banknotes was originally levied in 1783 for notes over 21s; in 1800 the duty was changed to 2d on notes of all denominations to meet war expenditure brought about by the threatened invasion by Napoleon. After this it was twice raised, first in 1808 and then in 1815, when the £1 note carried a stamp duty of 5d compared with 8s 6d on the £100 note. These stamp duties were very unpopular with the Scottish banks, which finally sent a deputation in 1853 to interview the Lords of the Treasury with a view to obtaining a better method of taxation on banknotes. Eventually, it was agreed to charge 3s 4d per annum for every £100 of notes in circulation, to be paid in half-yearly instalments, an arrangement which exists to the present day. After the Act of 1844 restricting the note issues of banks in England and Wales, it was extended in 1845 'to regulate the Issue of Bank notes in Scotland and Ireland'. Scottish banks were limited to a fixed annual issue of notes based on their issue for one year from 1 May 1844. On this figure each bank was permitted to issue an 'authorised circulation', but in addition to this a further note issue was allowed which had to be backed by an equal amount of gold and silver coin kept at two approved offices of each bank.

In 1808 a law was passed requiring a licence for issuers of banknotes in Scotland. Each note-issuing office paid £20 annually for this privilege. In 1815 the charge was increased to £30, but the maximum number of licences required to be held by one bank was four, note-issuing offices above that figure being exempted from further payment. In 1844 the present licensing laws were introduced. These required all note-issuing offices (with certain exceptions) to hold a licence, each licence costing £30.

The collapse of the Western Bank of Scotland on 9 November 1857 and the temporary closing of the City of Glasgow Bank two days later was Scotland's first experience of a bank failure since the preceding century, and caused a severe loss of public confidence. There was a large 'run' by depositors, who demanded gold, and later as the panic grew they were joined by note-holders, who were equally anxious to exchange their notes for gold. The Glasgow magistrates after the first day asked the military authorities to stand by in case of a disturbance and at the same time instructed the tax collectors to take Western Bank of Scotland notes in payment. After two days, when the other banks accepted Western Bank notes, over £1 million in gold was paid out in exchange, allaying the panic but causing the Government to suspend the 1845 Act on 12 November 1857. This enabled the Bank of England to increase the number of unbacked notes, effectively checking public alarm, as Bank of England notes were held in complete confidence. During the next two weeks the fiduciary issue of notes was £2 million over its normal limit. On 14 December 1857 the City of Glasgow Bank reopened to continue its career (as results afterwards showed, one of recklessness and folly) until it failed in 1878.

The failure of these two banks aroused considerable public excitement. The leading Scottish banks loaned a large sum to the Western Bank but they refused further assistance when more severe losses appeared later owing to improvident lending. The City of Glasgow Bank failed because of overlending to speculative companies followed by falsifications in the accounts of the note issue; nearly £500,000 more had been issued than its permitted maximum. There was some panic in localities where private banks were holders of the City of Glasgow Bank's shares. In the island of Burra in the Shetlands the islanders made sure of their gold by carrying it off from the Lerwick banks in December 1878. In the following spring, however, it was returned by the 'caretakers' to its proper home! This collapse showed the need for new laws giving greater protection to the shareholders, who were committed to the principle of unlimited liability: these unfortunate people had to make good £5 million. New laws came about in 1882, placing the note issues of Scottish banks on a more solid basis.

Ireland—Famine and Instability

The 1844 Act to regulate the issue of banknotes in England was extended in its application in 1845 to Scottish and Irish banks. In Ireland it restricted the privilege of note issue to those bankers who had been issuing notes during the year ending 1 May 1845, and prohibited the issue of notes for less than 20s and notes for fractional sums. With the abolition of small value and fractional amounts it was obvious that coins would need to be greatly increased. Accordingly, negotiations began with the Mint for a supply of silver coin, and £575,000 worth was supplied in 1845. The former monopoly of the Bank of Ireland, in that it was the only issuing

Hanover to Victoria

bank with more than six partners within a distance of 50 miles of Dublin, was withdrawn, but future issuing banks were compelled to obtain a certificate from the Government stating the value of notes permitted. Over and above this total, however, banks were allowed to issue notes, provided they were covered by an equivalent holding of gold and silver. As a result of this Act six banks were permitted to issue notes in Ireland.

The following period was troubled by a catastrophic famine caused by the partial failure of the potato crop in 1845, followed by an almost total failure in 1846 and 1847. Many people died from starvation and disease, while many left the country, reducing the population from 8 to 6 million. At first a sum of £80,000 was raised and dispatched in September 1846 aboard H.M.S. *Comet*, and by January 1847 over £1 million had been sent from London. A loan was raised in England of £8 million and a number of relief schemes were started. This relief was sent largely in silver and copper coin, but even after ten shipments from London there was still a serious shortage and the Mint was instructed to supply all the Irish joint-stock banks. The great demand for coin was caused by the collapse of many credit facilities and the public's lost confidence in banknotes. Then came a big drop in the price of wheat, which created an economic collapse. The banks were subjected to intense pressure through panic by the public and turned to the Bank of Ireland for assistance. This was given, though the latter was obliged to import £200,000 of gold, while a suspension of the Bank Charter Act enabled a greater number of notes to be issued. Eventually conditions returned to normal in 1849.

The 1857 crisis, though severe in Ireland, particularly in Belfast where trade almost ceased for a time, was not felt to the same extent there as elsewhere. The demand to change notes into coin was met calmly; neither were there bank failures as in Scotland. With the great increase of industry and trade generally there had been much speculative investment in all three countries without the necessary credit to fall back on in difficult times, with the result that when some of these firms collapsed lack of confidence and panic spread quickly among the public.

Instability among the smaller Irish private banks was precipitated by a Government decision against them in 1866 in the report of a specially appointed select committee; this started a 'run' on cash, which affected all banks. Finally all sections of the public began to make continuous withdrawals of cash until even the larger banks were compelled to obtain loans to help them over their difficulties, so that the 1844 Act had once more to be suspended, this time for three months.

The difficult period of the 1870s, with the fall in the price of wheat owing to the development of wheat-growing land in America, the severe reduction in the value of the potato crop from £12 million in 1876 to a mere £3 million in 1879, together with a general agricultural deterioration, affected the Irish banks to a marked degree. Fortunately the harvests of 1881 and 1882 were excellent and normal conditions were restored for those unfortunates who almost literally depended on the harvest for their lives. In 1885 the Munster Bank found itself in difficulties and after a lawsuit and much adverse publicity was forced to suspend payment. A number of the shareholders and depositors decided to take over what assets were left and the present-day Munster and Leinster Bank Ltd was formed in the same year. This was the last failure of an Irish bank.

Between the years 1864 and 1883 all the Scottish joint-stock banks opened branches in London and the National Bank transferred its head office there from Dublin. These moves caused considerable protest by many of the English country banks, which were compelled by law to abandon their rights of note issue in exchange for an office in London, whereas the banks outside England and Wales had no such restrictions; nevertheless the evidence collected by the select committee of 1875—even though its report was inconclusive —showed some justification for the Scottish and Irish banks retaining offices in London.

Hanover to Victoria

1. George I silver crown, showing roses and plumes in the reverse angles, a privilege granted to the private company that supplied the silver
2. 'Wood's Halfpennies.' The patent given to William Wood to strike halfpence for circulation in Ireland, but cancelled because of local prejudice
3. The 'Young Head' type of George II's five guineas
4. The earliest type of 'Young Head' crown, showing roses and plumes (reverse)
5. George II 'Old Head' crown. LIMA beneath the bust denotes the origin of the silver
6. The Irish halfpenny, much criticised because of the omitted 'Dei Gratia' in the legend, was issued to counteract a shortage and a spate of token coins
7. The well circulated 'Voce Populi' token halfpenny, believed to have been produced by a Dublin button manufacturer named Roche.
8. The earliest gold guinea of George III, issued 1761
9. A later, older, laureated bust with the altered 'Spade' type reverse. This coin was frequently forged
10. The countermarked dollar of Charles IV (IIII) of Spain, used to supplement the scarce silver of the time. (Note the worn patch on the reverse caused by the obverse countermark)
11. The completely overstamped Spanish American 8 reals, creating the new Bank of England (design) dollar
12. The first crown after the 1816 recoinage, with the laureated king's head and the famous Pistrucci St George and the Dragon
13. A well known token copper halfpenny of Coventry—Lady Godiva. This was one of many issued privately to overcome the scarcity of small change
14. The only twopenny copper coin ever issued, frequently known as the 'Cartwheel' twopence because of its size and weight
15. Co Wicklow token halfpenny, known as the 'Cronebane Halfpenny', issued by the Associated Irish Mine Co in 1789. The head is believed to be that of St Patrick
16. The first silver crown of George IV, type one
17. The second type crown with the king's portrait by William Wyon. Pistrucci was originally commissioned to do it but he refused to make the die and to copy another artist's work
18. The 1826 shilling with the well received lion on crown reverse design
19. The proof crown of William IV dated 1831, with the draped arms of the United Kingdom on the reverse
20. This political counter expresses the people's dislike for Queen Victoria's uncle, the Duke of Cumberland, represented by the triple-headed dragon. He was to inherit the Hanoverian throne. This counter is more widely known as a 'Cumberland Jack'
21. The 'Young Head' Victorian crown—a fine example of simple portraiture with the minimum of decoration
22. The Gothic crown broke from tradition by showing the date in Gothic numerals in the reverse inscription. It has the reputation of being one of the best designed coins in the British coinage; the enlarged obverse clearly shows the finer details

23 One of a number of pattern pieces produced in an early endeavour to introduce a decimal currency
24 Another pattern piece of gold; the magnificent £5 piece with Una and the Lion reverse by William Wyon—probably the most valuable coin of modern times
25 The Gothic florin—unlike the crown—was in general circulation from 1851 to 1887
26 The four shilling 'Jubilee' piece (double florin) lasted for four years only, the design being adversely criticised. The five examples illustrate accepted numismatic gradings, ie Fair, F (fine), VF (very fine), EF (extremely fine), and Unc (uncirculated)

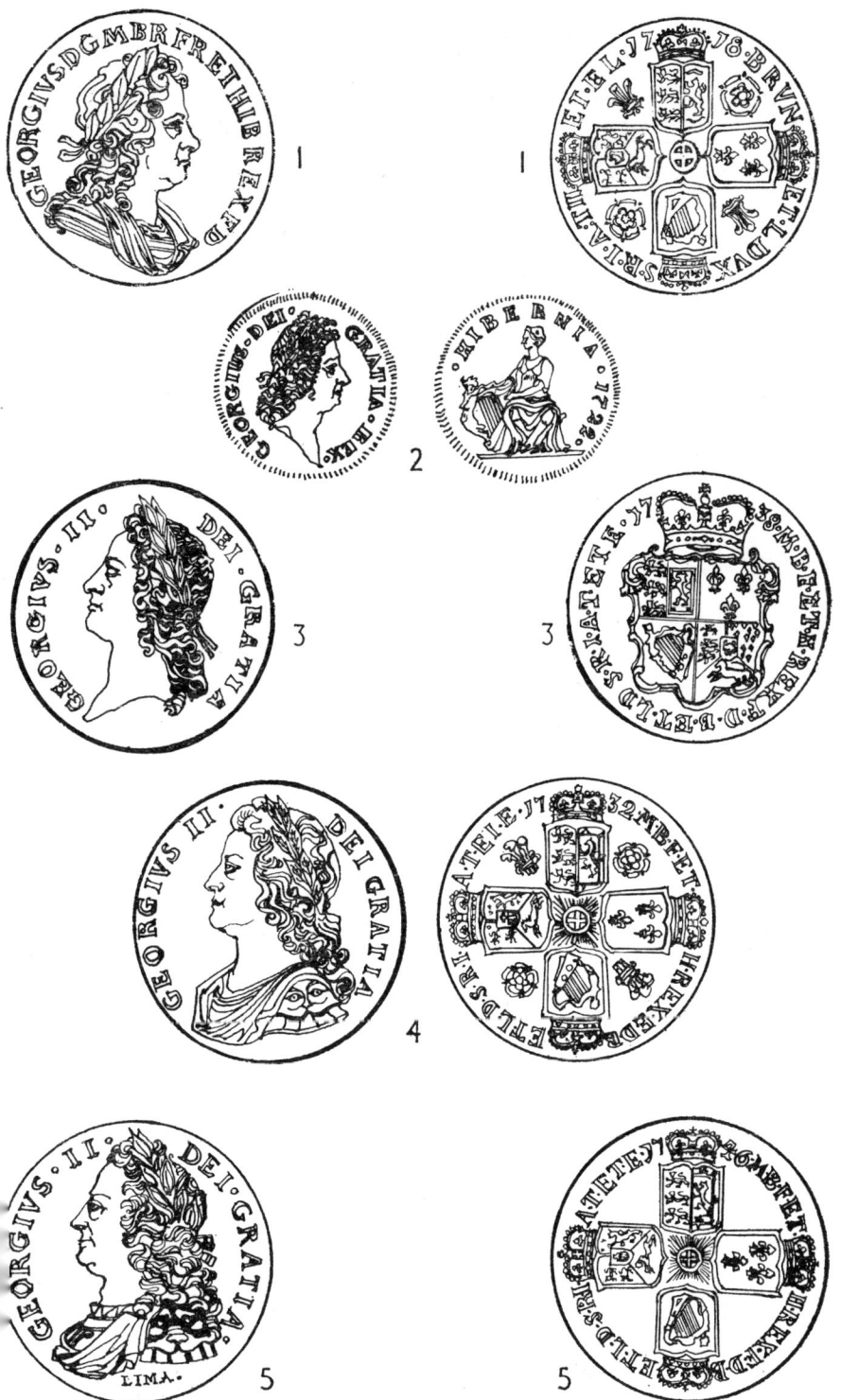

27 The five shilling piece of the same obverse was also criticised, mainly for the positioning of the queen's crown
28 The 'Old Head' crown shows a much more pleasing portrait of the ageing queen with the ever popular St George and the Dragon reverse
29 The enlarged sixpence affords a better opportunity of seeing the design that lasted, with minor variations, from 1831 to 1910
30 The well liked Britannia as displayed on the last farthing of Victoria—a coin that succumbed to the rising cost of living in 1956, after a very long life

X
TWENTIETH-CENTURY MONARCHS

Edward VII

Edward VII (1901-10) proved to be a promoter of much international friendliness, earning him the title of Edward the Peacemaker. His knowledge of international politics and his personal contact with foreign statesmen made him of genuine assistance to his ministers. He and Queen Alexandra won the real affection and confidence of the people.

The design ultimately approved for the coinage was a profile portrait of the King, facing right, with no decoration of any kind. The style and titles were announced in a royal proclamation on 4 November 1901. As the Latin rendering was too long to be practical, an abbreviated form was substituted. This in full ran as follows: 'Edwardus VII Dei Gratia Britanniarum Omnium Rex, Fidei Defensor, Indiae Imperator'.

The design for the reverse of the half crown was altered to a shield bearing the royal arms, surrounded by the garter, and not the collar of the order as before (*Fig 1*). The reverse design of the florin was less formal than expected; the windswept figure of Britannia stood on a ship's prow, her right hand grasping the trident, the shield resting at her side (*Fig 2*). The model for Britannia was Lady Susan Hicks-Beach, the daughter of the Master of the Mint. On the shilling the royal crest was substituted for the three shields bearing the arms of England, Scotland and Ireland, a similar design to the George IV 'lion' shillings of 1826. Both the half crown and the shilling show the inscription starting on the obverse and finishing on the reverse; the florin, however, has the inscription on the obverse (*Fig 2*). The remaining coin reverses were unchanged—the five and two-pound pieces, the sovereigns and half sovereigns, and the crowns—retaining Pistrucci's St George and the Dragon (*Fig 3*). The first two and the last named, however, were not issued after 1902. The smaller coins—the sixpence, threepence and Maundy coins—also remained unchanged; the bronze coins continued as previously. Farthings still had to be darkened to avoid any possible confusion with the half sovereigns.

The United Kingdom steadily improved its financial position and scientific methods of farming were spreading gradually to the remoter parts. Branch banks sprang up in increasing numbers, giving much assistance in the form of credit to the agricultural community. At the beginning of World War II well over 9,000 branch banks and agencies were available to the public. The extreme poverty of the nineteenth century with such appalling tragedies as the potato famine slowly became more remote as each year went by. With the extension of railways and the advent of motor transport, even the most isolated villages came in for a share of development, a circumstance in which the improved circulation of money played a major part.

George V

George V (1910-36), the son of Edward VII, was a kindly man, who was respected and loved by his people. He continued the policy of constitutional rule handed down by his father and grandmother. World War II caused him to change the family name to Windsor, after the royal castle of the same name, thus formally ending the connection with Saxe Coburg, the name of his grandfather, Prince Albert.

During his reign sovereigns were struck from 1911 to 1917 and half sovereigns from 1911 to 1915. It is known, however, that a number of foreign countries, particularly those of the Middle East, freely used British gold coins well after this time. Since then sovereigns dated 1925 have been struck but for the Bank of England's internal use only, though many have found their way into coin collections. Gold made up in this way was more conveniently handled and transported; at the same time it allowed the Mint to

Twentieth-Century Monarchs

retain its proficiency in striking coins in a metal that was little used.

Today the curious position exists whereby sovereigns are legal tender in Great Britain but the public are not allowed to possess them unless they are licensed collectors. This protects the sovereign from becoming obsolete, which would allow forgery abroad to be a much simpler affair.

The first silver issue (1911-19), which retained all the denominations with the exception of the crown, was the last in which our coins had a content of 92.5 per cent silver and 7.5 per cent alloy (*Figs 5 and 6*). In 1920, the coinage was debased to contain only 50 per cent silver. The high price of fine silver had reached 89.5 pence per fine oz, making the silver value of our coins greater than their face value (a half crown was worth 3s 4d). To have minted 'true' silver coins at this price would have offered too obvious a temptation to unscrupulous persons (*Fig 7*). The decision was regarded in some quarters as hasty, for the price of silver dropped soon after the change. Since then, however, the tremendous international demand for silver, for industrial use, has caused the price steadily to rise, reaching around 15s per fine oz early in 1970.

This debased issue of 1920, the second issue of George V, contained 50 per cent silver, 40 per cent copper and 10 per cent nickel, which gave the Mint considerable trouble at first. The coins struck from this new alloy in 1920 and 1921 acquired a brownish tint. The fault was partly rectified in 1922 by omitting the nickel and increasing the copper content to 50 per cent; by 1928 the Mint had overcome the difficulty and a third issue was struck with the improved alloy of 50 per cent silver, 40 per cent copper, 5 per cent nickel and 5 per cent zinc.

From this time the Royal Mint took a great interest in promoting numismatic art. An advisory committee of artists and connoisseurs was formed in 1923 for the improvement of designs, coin metals, etc. The immediate result was the fine 1928-36 coin issue, producing not only excellent designs but a great improvement in the lustre and general appearance. Although dated from 1928 for circulation, there was a proof issue in 1927. The 1927 shilling piece, however, was the exception and was actually circulated.

Included with this issue was the attractive milled 'wreath crown', introduced largely through the efforts of Sir Charles Oman, an MP and president of the Royal Numismatic Society (*Fig 8*). These crowns were never intended for circulation as the total number issued for the nine-year period until the King's death in 1936 was merely 50,893. In 1935 special crowns were substituted to celebrate the King's silver jubilee; these bore a modernised version of St George and the Dragon, with the inscription 'Decus et Tutamen' on the edge of the coins, and their design provoked much criticism (*Fig 9*).

The bronze coins remained unaltered except for a modified design of the King which began in 1925, but after 1915 farthings resumed their proper colour; after 1927 the effigy of the King was reduced in size.

Although no pennies were issued for circulation, in 1933, the Royal Mint struck a few specimen pieces from dies engraved from a normal production; these were similar to the 1927-35 type. The pattern obverse, engraved by the French artist André Lavrillier, has A.L. alongside the truncation letters B.M. Seven pennies from the normal pair of dies are known to exist; the Royal Mint holds two in its museum, while the British Museum possesses another. A fourth was sold at Glendinings in London, March 1969, for £3,600; a fifth, sixth and seventh are under the foundation stones of London University, St Mary's Church, Kirkstall, Leeds, and the Church of St Cross, Middleton, Yorks.

Although 'four specimens are believed to exist' of the Lavrillier penny, only one is officially known and this is held in the Royal Mint museum (*Fig 10*). The exceedingly high value of these offers great temptations to forgers, who have been active in attempting to foist spurious 1933 pennies on collectors, and will, no doubt, continue to do so.

End of Gold Coinage

After the murder of the Archduke Franz Ferdinand of Austria on 28 June 1914 by an agent of a Serbian secret society, the political situation rapidly deteriorated. On 1 August it was found that, through continuous withdrawals from every quarter, the Bank of England's gold reserve was dangerously low. The same danger had developed in Scotland and Ireland. Once again it was decided to suspend the Bank Charter Act of 1844, and the Currency and Bank Notes Act was rushed through, permitting the Government to issue new currency notes for £1 and 10s. These notes were legal tender anywhere in the United Kingdom. Similarly all Scottish and Irish notes were made legal tender in their respective countries as a temporary measure and postal orders were made a currency to meet the immediate demands of the public. This arrangement existed until 1920.

Britain, as a guarantor, immediately honoured her obligations once the Germans entered Belgian territory. This attempt to invade France by a surprise route, culminated in Britain declaring war on Germany on the day after August Bank Holiday, Tuesday, 4 August 1914. For the remainder of that week the banks and the Stock Exchange remained closed. There was much foreboding on the possibility of runs on the banks when they opened the following Monday, but the situation remained surprisingly calm and after a few hours it was seen that the fears were quite unfounded. The Currency and Bank Notes Act proved a successful measure. Although in theory all these notes were convertible to gold, the patriotism of the people caused them to be accepted even though the majority had not seen paper money before; as banks transferred gold to the Bank of England and accepted paper money in payment, gold virtually disappeared from circulation. In Scotland and Ireland likewise the banks paid in notes only. Nevertheless, it was known that a large quantity of gold coins was still in the hands of the public, which, it was suspected, was hoarding them in the expectation that sovereigns would be of greater value than the currency notes. It was decided to make the melting down of coin an offence and various shipping restrictions were imposed, making it unremunerative to send gold abroad.

The Government issued an emergency paper currency of 2,500,000 £1 notes and the suspension of the Bank Charter Act was authorised; sufficient paper money, however, was available and the authority to issue an excess of unbacked notes was never used. These treasury notes (issued by the Treasury, as banknotes under £5 were illegal) were commonly known as Bradburys after John Bradbury, the Chief Clerk of the Treasury, whose signature they bore. A few days after the issue of £1 notes, 10s notes of identical design followed.

These notes had been hastily printed and it was found that they needed small alterations. A few months later a second issue of both denominations was produced in a slightly larger sized note. Both the £1 notes were printed in black, the first issue dating from 7 August 1914 and ending 22 October 1914, the second issue from 23 October 1914 to 21 March 1917, and a third issue of £1 notes beginning on 1 February 1917. The 10s notes were printed in red, the first issue commencing on 14 August 1914 and ending 20 January 1915, the second issue on 21 January 1915 and ending 30 December 1918, and a third issue beginning on 2 November 1918. The supply of these notes enabled Parliament to cancel the use of postal orders as a currency. On 11 June 1920 the first and second issues of both denominations were withdrawn from circulation.

The £1 notes of the third issue were printed in green, bearing the brown coloured heads of George V and St George. The 10s notes were printed in the same manner except that the figure of Britannia was substituted for St George and coloured green, with the text in brown. These continued to circulate until the first issue of the new £1 and 10s Bank of England banknotes was released on 22 November 1928 in green and brown respectively in accordance with the Currency and Bank Notes Act of 1928. From this date the notes became 'banknotes' and the name 'treasury notes' of earlier issues ceased, the third issue being finally withdrawn on 31 July 1933.

At the end of hostilities in 1918 there was reckless spending and borrowing. Many firms and private persons indulged in speculation. There was great activity in most industries at home and overseas, and easy money made during the war found its way to the Stock Exchange, where new companies, many of a doubtful character, issued shares. Almost every trade and industry was booming until the peak period of March 1920. From then on this artificial prosperity fell away, and though it is impossible to give a particular reason for the collapse, hundreds of post-war firms disappeared and much hardship was caused.

The Republic of Ireland

On 22 December 1920 the Government of Ireland Act provided two parliaments in Ireland; one was to represent Northern Ireland with its seat in Belfast, while the other, its seat in Dublin, represented Southern Ireland. Since the 1918 elections, when the Sinn Fein party was swept into power with an overwhelming majority in the South, there had been much agitation for severing connections with Great Britain. On 6 December 1922 Southern Ireland became the Irish Free State with dominion status within the Empire; the inhabitants were entirely free to choose their destiny and the country finally became an independent state, now the Republic of Ireland. Northern Ireland, however, elected to remain part of the United Kingdom.

World War I undoubtedly delayed Home Rule for Ireland as, in 1914, the Bill was already on the statute book when war broke out. Following the Anglo-Irish Treaty of 1921 when the Irish Free State came into existence, a new constitution was born and the Free State became a sovereign republic with the name of 'Eire'.

The first coins were issued as the Irish Free State in 1928 in denominations of 2s 6d, 2s, 1s, made of 75 per cent silver and 25 per cent copper similar in size and weight to their British counterparts. The two lower denominations, 6d and 3d, were proportionately larger than those of Britain, being made of pure nickel. The bronze coins were similar in size and weight to the 1d, ½d and ¼d of Britain. The designs on the reverses of these newly produced coins by Percy Metcalfe are particularly pleasing, and represent life from the Irish countryside. The harp which has been accepted as synonymous with Irish coins was automatically accepted for the obverse. This design has been the Irish symbol on coins since the Tudors.

When the new constitution of 1937 was declared the name 'Eire' took the place of the Irish Free State inscription on the next coinage issued in 1939, with minor alterations to the harp and the reverses of the 2s 6d and penny. After a very limited issue of the higher value coins in 1943, coin production, except for the bronze, ceased until 1950 when coins of 6d and 3d began production followed by 2s 6d,

2s, and 1s, all in cupro-nickel of 75 per cent nickel and 25 per cent copper. To commemorate the 1916 Easter rising a special 83 per cent silver 10s piece was issued in 1966 with the portrait of Padraig H. Pearse on the obverse and the statue of the legendary hero Cuchulainn on the reverse. Since 1928 the designs except for minor alterations remained the same until the decimal coinage of 1971 when redesigned coins of similar denominations as those of Britain (50, 10, 5, 2, 1 and ½ new pence) followed being equal to them both in size, weight and metal content.

Northern Ireland

In Northern Ireland today £20, £10, £5 and £1 notes of the Bank of England, as well as banknotes of the eight Irish issuing banks, circulate, but the Bank of England notes are not legal tender. They are, nevertheless, extensively used by farmers and dealers at the cattle markets in Northern Ireland. The currency of the Republic is not legal tender in the North, though Central Bank notes and Republic coins circulate freely there; it would be impracticable for any other arrangement to operate in view of the constant flow of traffic and trade across the border, and the situation is generally accepted by all banks, post offices and shops. It is illegal, however, for banks in Northern Ireland to issue Republic currency, with the result that cashiers separate these notes for returning to Dublin. Practice varies with the coins. Some banks separate the two coinages, but many for want of time reissue them, this being made easier by the fact that both coinages, all but the sixpence and the threepence, weigh the same.

From 31 December 1953 the eight Irish note-issuing banks— Bank of Ireland, Hibernian Bank Ltd, National Bank Ltd, Northern Bank Ltd, Munster and Leinster Bank Ltd, Provincial Bank of Ireland Ltd, Royal Bank of Ireland Ltd, and Ulster Bank Ltd—ceased to issue banknotes in the Irish Republic. Their notes have now been withdrawn and replaced by the note issue of the Central Bank of Ireland formed in 1943, which now issues notes in the Republic in a similar capacity to the Bank of England in the United Kingdom. Although

British notes and coin (and Northern Ireland banknotes) circulate freely in the Irish Republic and are accepted generally, under the Eire Coinage Act of 1926 (repealed by the Coinage Act 1950), the Currency Act of 1927 and the Central Bank Act of 1942, they are not legal tender; nor are the banks in the Irish Republic allowed to pay out British notes, except to travellers going to destinations outside the republic. The method of collecting soiled notes is the same as in the United Kingdom; the banks return the notes via the Central Bank of Ireland.

Edward VIII, the Uncrowned King

Edward VIII's very short reign ended in abdication. He was best known as the popular Prince of Wales, who by his democratic ideas won the respect and admiration of the working classes. He surrendered the throne in order to marry the woman he loved.

No coins were circulated in his reign, though new dies were prepared, dated 1937; those coins which were struck, with the exception of a few sets retained by the Mint, were all melted down. It is known, however, that a few, probably less than a dozen, of the new twelve-sided threepenny pieces escaped destruction (*Fig 11*). The effigy on this coin, contrary to tradition, faced left instead of right —the usual custom being for a monarch's effigy to face the opposite direction to that of his predecessor's. If we acknowledge these few unofficially circulated threepences, three monarchs, George V, Edward VIII and George VI, all faced left. A full series of silver coins was struck in 1936 with the head of George V; many numismatists consider that this series belongs to the reign of Edward VIII. On the other hand, coins of 1910 are not considered as belonging to George V, nor are coins of 1901 considered among those of Edward VII.

George VI

Our late King, George VI, though physically ill-equipped for the trials and responsibilities of monarchy, nobly achieved a success which endeared him and his queen to his people. He never spared himself in times of stress, particularly during World War II, when he worked indefatigably, a fine example as monarch of the state and as head of an honoured and respected family.

The King's reign began at the end of 1936, and in 1937 a full set of silver and bronze coins was struck (*Figs 12 and 13*). Two changes were made: additional shillings complementary to the existing ones bore a newly designed reverse, copied from an old Scottish design (*Fig 14*), in honour of Queen Elizabeth (now the Queen Mother); and new twelve-sided yellow threepenny pieces made from an alloy composed of 79 per cent copper, 20 per cent zinc and 1 per cent nickel were circulated (*Figs 11 and 15*).

These had been intended as an innovation in Edward VIII's reign. The thrift plant on the reverse was similar to the intended coin of the previous reign but redesigned. This new coin was intended to replace the silver threepence but after its novelty had worn off it temporarily dropped out of favour with the public and the banks reported large unissued quantities. This was soon remedied, however, but the little silver threepenny pieces continued to be very popular in Scotland, which was why the Royal Mint continued their production until 1941. In the three years following, silver threepences continued to be struck, but these were all shipped overseas to the West Indies and Bermuda. More were minted in 1945 but instructions were given for the melting down of the whole issue together with the unissued 1944 coins—the latter being estimated at about one-third of the 1944 output.

Crowns were again 'milled', with a completely new reverse—the royal arms supported by the lion and the unicorn (*Fig 16*). The designs of the halfpennies and farthings no longer conformed to that of the pennies. The portrait of Britannia was retained, with slight modifications, showing in the background what was reputed to be the Eddystone lighthouse. The design of the halfpennies was inspired by Drake's famous *Golden Hind*, the first English ship to sail round the world (*Fig 17*), while the farthings showed one of the smallest of British wild birds, the neat little wren.

The entry of Japan into World War II curtailed the supply of tin,

Twentieth-Century Monarchs

which was normally shipped from Malaya for use in our bronze coinage. In 1942 these coins contained only ½ per cent of tin instead of the previous 3 per cent of that metal, 95½ per cent copper and 1½ per cent zinc. The metal content of the bronze coinage, however, has varied at different periods since it was first issued in 1860. Today it is made up of 97 per cent copper, ½ per cent tin and 2½ per cent zinc.

After the first years of World War II (1939 and 1940) pennies ceased to be issued, but production was resumed in 1944. This was only the second time since the first bronze issue in 1860 that the annual date sequence had been broken. The first period, also 3 years, was in 1923-5. Around 1941-2 it was found that the newly minted pennies were not circulating normally; presumably they were being hoarded because of their bright colour and glitter. In 1946, therefore, the Mint used special methods to give them a dull finish.

Cupro-nickel

In 1947 for the first time ever, our 'silver' coinage contained no silver, being made instead from a mixture of copper (75 per cent) and nickel (25 per cent); but it was not the first time that the Mint had made cupro-nickel coins, for in 1869 it had supplied Jamaica with such coins. Before this, about 1857, experiments had been made by the Americans and the Swiss, but no coinage had been issued until the Belgians produced three denominations of cupro-nickel coins a few years later. The final debasement of our coinage from silver to cupro-nickel is, however, only the logical outcome of the need to avoid the fluctuations in the value of fine silver.

In 1816 the weight of a shilling was lowered from 93 grains to 87, to reduce it to a token value, while in 1920 the silver value of the coinage rose above its face value, causing it to be reduced to a 50 per cent silver content. It is really just as reasonable to make our silver coins from 100 per cent alloy as it was to make them from 50 per cent alloy. We are not now pretending they are silver.

Undoubtedly cupro-nickel in the proportions of 75-25 is far more durable than a 50 per cent silver and a 50 per cent alloy and as a consequence must have a longer circulating life. Cupro-nickel, however, cannot compare in appearance, lacking that soft lustre which is noticeable in the last silver coins issued, 1928-46.

In 1949 the dies were again changed. India and Pakistan in 1947 acquired a new status within the Empire, so it was necessary to remove the inscription 'Ind Imp' ('Emperor of India'). On the sixpence 'GRI' ('Georgius Rex Imperator') was changed to 'GR VI'.

After the 1937 issue, no crowns were struck until 1951, the Festival of Britain year, when Pistrucci's design of St George and the Dragon was brought back. The tremendous demand for them as souvenirs at home and abroad resulted in over 2,000,000 being minted (*Fig 18*).

The criticism of these crowns struck in cupro-nickel was inevitable, but it must be borne in mind that there were technical difficulties in minting a coinage from the hard metal and no critics have identical viewpoints. For this very reason the relief on the coins is shallow when compared with pre-1947 silver issues; nevertheless they are generally considered a good clean design.

George VI died in February 1952 and the only coins to be struck in that year were nickel threepenny pieces, halfpennies and farthings. Occasionally, 1952 sixpences are to be found in circulation as approximately 1⅓ million were struck for use in the West Indies, but some found their way back to the United Kingdom.

World War II Notes

During World War II emergency issues of banknotes were prepared in £1 (blue), 10s (mauve), 5s (pink) and 2s 6d (light blue), but only the first two were circulated, on 29 March 1940, the last two being printed merely for circulation in the event of invasion—paper money being more readily transportable than silver. A noteworthy incident concerning these was related by an employee of the bullion department in one of the big London banks. Apparently the 5s and 2s 6d notes were distributed to all the joint-stock banks in great secrecy, as a precaution against a possible Hitler invasion. While these were being unloaded one of the 'mystery' boxes burst open,

Twentieth-Century Monarchs

and the notes were strewn all over the bank steps. Panic ensued; each note was carefully collected, sorted numerically and then double checked by two high officials. One can only comment that, if any present were banknote collectors, picking up these notes must have been quite hurtful! Later, of course, the notes were returned to the Bank of England for destruction. Although this issue of £1 and 10s notes ceased in 1948 and a second issue was made of green £1 notes and brown 10s notes, the emergency notes continued to be circulated as the Bank of England held considerable quantities of them.

On 1 May 1945 banknotes of £10 and over ceased to be legal tender, as did, on 1 March 1946, £5 notes dated 2 September 1944 or earlier. The issuing of these had been discontinued in 1943 and 1945 respectively. The reason given by the Chancellor of the Exchequer, was 'to simplify production and handling of the Note Issue and provide a handicap to those who contemplate breaches of the Exchange Control and other regulations'. Although it was generally believed that this measure was to check black-market activities and to make income-tax evasion more difficult, undoubtedly the words 'other regulations' referred to the very large number of forgeries circulated by the Nazis. So accurate were these spurious banknotes that they were indistinguishable from genuine notes except by highly trained specialists. At one time £1,000 in five-pound notes, which may or may not have been genuine, was offered on the black market for £900.

It was not until a Bank of England cashier, in the earlier days of the war, discovered two banknotes with identical numbers that suspicions were aroused. From 1943 onwards large numbers of forged notes were found in circulation. Many were traced to Lisbon, Stockholm and Zurich. It was then discovered that the Nazi Government were the master forgers.

The first of these forged notes were made in a concentration camp near Berlin, where 140 expert engravers, printers, die-makers, etcetera, were forced by well known Nazi methods to produce banknotes. A special research laboratory was even set up to produce Bank of England notepaper with its intricate water-marks. The bombing of Berlin by the Allies caused the plant to be removed to a cave in the

Austrian Alps, where it was discovered at the end of hostilities, but not before Himmler had destroyed the plant and millions of notes. Nevertheless, records were found which showed that over £100 million in forged banknotes had been produced as well as numerous other forged items. The finest of these were used to pay spies abroad and for making purchases in neutral countries. A slightly inferior banknote was used by agents to buy information and for payment to foreign collaborators. Forgeries of a still lower quality were stored for dumping by plane on the British Isles with the object of causing internal disorganisation.

In the place of the notes withdrawn in 1946 new thick five-pound notes with a metallic thread running through the paper were issued on 18 October 1945. These were found to be inconvenient and new flimsy notes of the same denomination with the metallic thread, dated 1 January 1947, were issued on 9 September 1948. There was no further alteration in the £5 notes until February 1957, when new notes, predominantly blue in colour, slightly larger than the current £1 notes, were issued. They were completely redesigned by the late Stephen Gooden, RA, and represent a complete break with the traditional black and white 'fivers'.

Post-war Banknotes

It was further planned that an entirely new series of £5, £1 and 10s notes should be issued. Of these the long expected new series of £1 notes was issued in March 1960, to be followed by the 10s notes in October 1961. They are smaller than the banknotes they replaced and omit the conventional figure of Britannia, substituting a portrait of the Queen—another new departure for the Bank of England; the only other note to bear a portrait of a reigning monarch was the third treasury issue of 1918-28 which showed a portrait of George V.

In 1844 and 1845 the issue of notes was regulated by the Bank Charter Act; the face value of each note issued was backed by its value in gold deposited at the Bank of England. In addition to this there was an issue of notes—known as a fiduciary issue—unbacked by gold, which from 1844 to 1928 was £14 million plus up to two-

Twentieth-Century Monarchs

thirds the value of the lapsed issues of the country banks. By 1928 the figure was £19¾ million, with notes backed by gold at a figure of over £161 million. From that date, however, gold was dispensed with as backing for notes and the issue became a completely fiduciary one of £260 million. The Second World War caused the value of the note issue to be greatly inflated, rising to the figure of £1,450 million in 1946 and to £2,261 million by the end of 1959. Ten years later at the close of 1969 the figure had reached the colossal total of £3,617 million.

To attempt to explain these complex economic adjustments in our monetary system would be beyond the scope of this story. Nevertheless it shows how money has become a mere symbol of the value it represents. It also shows that the public, by their acceptance of an unlimited supply of unbacked notes, have faith in our ability to balance our import trade with our exports.

The number of banknotes issued today depends on the requirements of the public; these are estimated by means of the orders given to the Bank of England by the banks, who require notes for their various branches. Not all these notes are new, as new notes are generally issued only in place of withdrawn dirty notes.

It will be apparent that some branch banks must collect more notes from their customers than they need for reissuing. These are dispatched to their respective centres for pulping down or for reissue to those branch banks requiring a further supply. In addition to these a limited number of new notes are put into circulation; but these are never enough, for almost everyone wants new and not reissued notes.

It is unfortunate that we are denied the opportunity of seeing our earlier banknotes as easily as our coins, but the life of paper money is necessarily short, and the law does not allow us to give reproductions of Bank of England notes. As a result the public have no opportunity of comparing our present issues with earlier ones except in museums or private collections. Figures given in 1955 showed that £1 notes remained in circulation on average rather more than one year, while 10s notes were unfit for circulation after half this period; £1 notes outnumbered 10s notes by seven to one. No comparison is available between the current £10, £5 and £1 notes, but a consensus of opinion suggests that the life of a £5 note in relation to the £1 is five to one; the life of £10 notes is very much longer in proportion as it is in very little demand with the average member of the public. As the proportion of new banknotes issued is continually changing these figures can only be regarded as approximate. Nevertheless, they give an idea of the life of our paper money.

Of recent years there has been a marked increase in those interested in banknote collecting. Unfortunately the lives of banknotes are short unless preserved; nevertheless, a surprising number of eighteenth- and nineteenth-century notes still exist. The Institute of Bankers in London holds a unique collection, which reveals many of the past note-issuing firms, who have either been absorbed by the banks of today or have failed. It is unfortunate that no book has been written on the early British, Scottish and Irish note-issuing banks, but at least one attempt is being made to collate the scanty knowledge available. If successful this will be the first of its kind to be published and will be a much needed guide to present-day note collectors.

Travellers' Cheques

In 1891 a system known as 'travellers' cheques' was introduced by the American Express Company. These enable a traveller to obtain cash in whatever country he finds himself. He must first sign these cheques as holder in the presence of a bank and when requiring cash signs one or more in the presence of the bank where he is cashing them, obtaining whatever currency he requires at the ruling rate of exchange. This method has so many obvious advantages that its use has become universal.

Scottish Banknotes

The right to issue notes in Scotland today is held by the three Edinburgh and Glasgow banks, these being all that remain of the nineteen banks of 1844 and 1845 which were then given the legal right to issue notes. The present three banks are the Bank of Scotland (with which the Union Bank of Scotland Ltd and the British Linen Bank are amalgamated), the Royal Bank of Scotland (with which the National Commercial Bank of Scotland is amalgamated) and the Clydesdale Bank Ltd. The only legal tender among notes in Scotland, however, are the notes of the Bank of England. Each bank is permitted to issue or reissue both its own notes and those of the Bank of England, but not other Scottish banknotes, which are handed over to their respective issuers at the exchange.

The issue of Scottish banknotes today remains much the same as laid down in 1845, though in 1928 the Currency and Bank Notes Act made certain amendments. The banknotes now circulating have expanded many times since 1845 but the 'authorised circulation' based on the 1845 figure is the same. Notes issued in excess of this have a backing of Bank of England notes held at the Bank of England together with silver coin held by the Scottish banks themselves. When a bank wishes to increase its note issue it deposits Bank of England notes at the Bank of England, which issues certificates for the amount deposited. When the note issue contracts at certain times of the year these certificates may be cashed in exchange for withdrawn Scottish banknotes.

Scottish banknotes are returned and exchanged through exchanges which exist in all towns of Scotland where there are two or more banks, each bank in turn taking charge of the exchange for a given period. There a bank receives its own notes from the other banks and hands over notes belonging to them, an account being kept of their mutual debits and credits. Where a bank is not represented its notes are sent to Edinburgh for exchange.

Scottish notes, though not accepted for circulation in England, have found their way south of the border on many occasions, specially since 1946 when the sixpenny commission charged for collecting and returning these notes was removed. All English and Welsh branch banks return Scottish notes to their London offices. The notes are then forwarded to the various head offices of the Scottish banks in Edinburgh, which in turn send them to the exchange house.

Coin Distribution

Coin is necessarily distributed differently from paper money, as it is heavier and not so easily transportable. At the present time banks return a proportion of their silver coin weekly to the Royal Mint, which, with the aid of mechanical sorting machines, separates it into various denominations. Then the coins are passed through an electronic sorter that attracts those with a silver content away from the remaining cupro-nickel 'silver'.

The coins containing silver are completely withdrawn from circulation and melted down, while the remaining cupro-nickel coins are reissued in £100 bags together with new coins to replace those withdrawn.

In the first twenty-three years of cupro-nickel coins—1 January 1947 to 31 May 1970—£308 million coins were issued, excluding crown pieces and demonetised half crowns. This figure includes the 50, 10 and 5 new pence issued in 1968 and 1969. In this same period coins with a silver content, which had been removed from circulation, totalled approximately £149 million. At the beginning of 1970 it was estimated that there were silver coins still in circulation equal to 3 per cent of the total, which excludes the 50 new pence and the demonetised half crowns. The value of silver and cupro-nickel coin in circulation in early 1970 was estimated at £397 million.

Authoritative estimates of the life of our silver coins state that sixpences have an average life of twenty-five years and half crowns three times as long. It remains to be seen, however, how much longer our new and more durable coinage made of cupro-nickel will last.

Because of the bulk and weight of copper coins—£5 of copper coins weighs roughly the same as £100 of silver—transportation is avoided as much as possible and banks in each district often help one another out to avoid unnecessary costs. With the introduction of the 2, 1 and ½ new pence in February 1971 these weight and cost problems have been considerably reduced.

Elizabeth II

When the youthful and popular Princess Elizabeth ascended the

Twentieth-Century Monarchs

throne in 1952 she could hardly have had more goodwill and genuine affection bestowed on her by her people. She was accepted as the ideal queen, and the British nation looked to her, her husband and children as the perfect family to whom they could express their loyalty.

The Government requested the Royal Mint Advisory Committee, under the presidency of the Duke of Edinburgh, to produce new designs. Six artists were invited to submit designs for the obverse from which two were selected. The only stipulations made were that the head should be in profile and facing to the right, and preference was shown for a head and shoulders portrait. The final choice was made by the Queen herself, who chose the work of Mary Gillick, a 71-year-old London artist; the design appears on all the silver and copper coins except the Coronation crowns, the obverse of which, designed by Gilbert Ledward, is a complete break with accepted tradition (*Fig 19*). It shows the Queen on horseback, a design taken from the familiar portrait of Her Majesty as Colonel-in-Chief, Grenadier Guards, at the ceremony of Trooping the Colour. Not since the reign of Charles I (1625-49) has a mounted monarch been shown. The reverse of the crown carries four quarterings of the royal arms each in a separate shield. The spaces between the shields contain the national emblems—the double rose, the thistle, the sprig of shamrock and the leek—with the date 1953 underneath. On the edge of the coins is the inscription 'Faith and Truth I will bear unto you', which is taken from the Oath of Homage in the Coronation service.

An opportunity was given to anyone who wished to submit heraldic designs for the reverses. Many talented artists competed; but the difficult problem of selection was left to the committee, who reduced the competitors to seventeen, then chose the designs of E. G. Fuller for the crowns, half crowns, florins and sixpences, and those of W. Gardner for the English and Scottish shillings and the nickel threepenny pieces.

Except for the crowns, the conventional head of the Queen appears on the obverse. The reverse of the half crowns bears the shield of the royal arms between the letters E and R surmounted by the crown; the florins have a double rose in a circlet of radiating thistles, shamrocks and leeks (*Fig 20*); the English shillings have a shield containing a quartering of the royal arms, which displays three lions surmounted by the crown; the Scottish shillings have a similar arrangement but the shield displays the lion rampant; the sixpences show a rose, a thistle, a sprig of shamrock and a leek all interlaced, with the inscription FID DEF (Defender of the Faith) above 'sixpence' with the date 1953 underneath. The reverse design of the twelve-sided nickel threepenny pieces incorporates a portcullis with chains ensigned with a royal coronet, this being the badge of Henry VII, later adopted by Parliament as a symbol of the Palace of Westminster (*Fig 21*). Artistic merit was not the only factor which had to be considered; the design had to avoid undue strains on the dies, which might cause constant renewals through cracking.

While it is difficult to fault these beautiful pieces of artistry, one cannot help feeling that there is too great a contrast between the obverses and reverses of these coins. The former are modern with a minimum of decoration, while the latter draw inspiration from the past for their traditional designs. More homogeneous designs, with uniform lettering, would surely enhance their beauty.

Now the coins of eight monarchs are in circulation, though the earlier ones dating from 1816 are rarely seen today except as collectors' pieces.

The same denominations continued in 1954 with the exception of the crowns, but the inscription on the obverse was changed: the BRITT OMN (BRITTANIARUM OMNIUM) meaning, when translated with REGINA 'Queen of the British Empire', was omitted; REGINA was of course retained. The alteration conformed to the wishes of certain Commonwealth countries. This change in design after the first year gave the 1953 coins a scarcity value and they became doubly sought after—as Coronation year coins and the solitary year of issue. This is reflected in both the Royal Mint Coronation Set issues—the plastic sets of which 1,308,400 were specially issued, and the 40,000 proof sets issued in a jewel-type case. The former were sold in the banks for 7s 6d per set (without the crown piece) while the latter could be purchased, if available, for 25s. These sets until recently freely changed hands at £15 and

£45 respectively. Further evidence of the great public interest in coins is seen in the isolated 1954 penny which until it was discovered was declared a 'none issued' year. Undoubtedly this coin was a trial piece struck to test the die, as it is customary to produce dies each year whether coins are struck from them or not. This coin was sold to an American firm—the Paramount Coin Corporation—who offered it for resale at $30,000!

No further new types of coin were struck until the autumn of 1960, when crowns were again issued. The obverse has the conventional head of the Queen, while the reverse design is similar to that of its predecessor (*Fig* 22). The lettering, however, is all on the obverse except for the year date. These crowns were displayed and a large number sold at the New York Exhibition as souvenirs, but the main purpose of the issue was to give the public another coin of a higher value. There was, however, very little demand for these coins at the time.

End of the Farthing

After four years, the time-honoured farthings were considered too small a value to have any monetary use and after 1956 they ceased to be issued; they were withdrawn on 1 January 1961. This left halfpennies as the smallest coins of legal tender.

Today's Maundy Money

The present Maundy service is conducted with much of the ancient ceremony; it has frequently been held in Westminster Abbey but it has also taken place in the provincial cathedrals of Rochester, York, Selby, Colchester, etc. In 1970 the ceremony was again held in Westminster Abbey; the Queen Mother took the place of the Queen, who was in Australia. Of recent years the capital has been fortunate in having a high proportion of these colourful annual ceremonies, including services in St Paul's and Southwark cathedrals. The Maundy gift itself has been subject to minor alterations in modern times. In 1837, in William IV's reign, a cash sum of 30s was given to each recipient instead of the customary supply of provisions, since these had often been sold for trifling sums of money. Later, in Queen Victoria's reign, the men recipients were given a cash allowance instead of cloth, since they were often unable to afford to have the material made up into clothes. This custom has been continued to the present day. Before 1890 the ceremony was held for many years in the Chapel Royal, Whitehall, as is shown on the 1773 engraving by Grimm.

For the present ceremony an equal number of men and women are invited—usually pensioners or persons with low incomes, who together number twice the monarch's age. For 1970 each was given Maundy coins to a value of 44 pence (made up in sets of 1d, 2d, 3d and 4d—a total of 10d per set), the total pence per person equalling the official age of the Queen. Each recipient, therefore, received four sets and four silver pence (44 pence) in a white leather purse with red thongs, and £2 10s 0d in a red leather purse with white thongs, representing the Sovereign's gown worn on the day of the distribution and cash in lieu of provisions. A third purse, white with green thongs for the men, containing £2 5s 0d, and green with white thongs for the women, containing £1 15s 0d, is the allowance now substituted for clothing. This service of Royal Maundy distribution is one of the most interesting and colourful of religious services, incorporating ancient ceremony with the distribution of alms, and symbolising the charities provided by the sovereign, including pensions, education grants and gifts.

A Past Money Survey

Looking back over 2,000 years of British money it is comparatively easy now to spot the errors in our system. Perhaps the most apparent was the notion that one could devise penalties whose deterrent powers would outweigh the greed for easy money. Fearful punishment was inflicted on the moneyers of the Anglo-Saxon and Anglo-Norman periods; but after a short time it ceased to make any impression on those who contemplated making base coins, light coins, etc. Many useless Acts of Parliament have been passed, such as those to prohibit the export of money, to enforce the import of bullion, to have its value fixed by the Mint, etc. These restrictions unfortunately showed ignorance of the general principles of trade.

To allow coins of similar value and denomination of differing weights to circulate together was confusing to the public, as well as being wasteful and unnecessary. An example of this foolishness can be seen in Matthew Boulton's copper coins, which were in circulation with the Tower mint copper coins, the latter about half the weight of the former. Another example is the recently withdrawn halfpenny, two of which exceed the weight of a penny (£5 of halfpence weighed 30lb avoirdupois while £5 of pence weighs 25lb). Fortunately the decimal bronze coins are linked in weight so that banks are able to weigh bronze coins as well as cupro-nickel. The discrepancy between the price of imported bullion and the face values of coins made from it in the reign of William III did not deter his government from continuing to strike silver coins, with the result that a large issue of silver coins disappeared from circulation and found its way to other countries where a better price was obtained.

Fortunately those who control the circulation of money today have learnt the lessons of the past. The complete substitution of paper money for gold has at one stroke removed the temptation to forge gold coins, and the cupro-nickel coinage presents too great a problem for the forger to solve except by the tedious and unremunerative method of moulds.

This method begins when a genuine coin is placed on a hard smooth surface and enveloped with plaster of paris. The coin is then reversed and the process repeated. The two plaster casts are tied together, with a hole representing the outline of the coin in the middle. The projecting flanges of one half of the plaster are rubbed down so that the space inside the two halves is equal to the thickness of the coin. A hole is bored at the junction of the two casts and melted pewter or a similar metal poured into the space in the middle. After the metal has cooled the mould is opened. Another method, which requires pressed sheet metal to be struck in the same manner as by the Royal Mint, is far too difficult for the normal

P

crook. The only successful forgeries by the latter method in this country were perpetrated by Messrs Ramsey & Steel in Edinburgh in 1920. They managed to produce some thousands of half crowns before being caught. Nevertheless, the great scientific advances and the use of cheap metals must surely offer a challenge to the criminal mind. The absence of forged notes today—in spite of the Nazi forgeries produced regardless of cost—is evidence of the triumph of scientific methods in producing banknotes.

Undoubtedly the relegation of our money to a token status is correct, but from a sentimental point of view many of us regret the substitution of paper money for gold and cupro-nickel for silver. While most of us have either long since grown accustomed to the disappearance of gold, or perhaps cannot remember its use as legal tender, many will recognise the colour of real silver coins struck up to 1919 and certainly the half-silver coins struck up to 1946. Economists point out the benefits of a token monetary system, while paper money is far easier to carry, but those of us who like to feel that coins should contain their full value in precious metal are reluctant to accept valueless 'silver' coins.

Decimalisation

The decision to introduce a decimal system in 1971 recalls several previous attempts. During Charles II's reign, in 1682, Sir William Petty wanted to introduce a new monetary system, dividing the penny into five farthings, 'to keep all accompts in a way of Decimal Arithmetik'. Following this, the architect Sir Christopher Wren (1632-1723) advocated that the coinage should be based on 1oz of silver in divisions of 100. Queen Anne took up Sir William Petty's ideas and attempted to put them into practice. The last serious attempt to introduce decimals promoted the 1849 florin, inscribed as 'one tenth of a pound', so worded to sound public reactions on decimals. This was instigated by a general agitation, causing Parliament to appoint two Commissions in 1838 and 1843 to examine the possibilities of changing the currency, both of which reported in favour of a decimal system. In 1847 Sir John Bowring—a staunch advocate of the system—obtained surprisingly strong support in Parliament for his proposal to introduce the two-shilling piece at one-tenth the value of the pound, and to consider introducing smaller decimal denominations at a later date.

The name florin was probably taken from the popular Dutch and Austrian florins circulating at that time, though an English gold florin of Edward III existed in 1344.

The events leading to the present-day decision to decimalise were many. A number of public bodies, including the British Association for the Advancement of Science and the Association of British Chambers of Commerce, as well as many private individuals, agitated for a move in this direction. In December 1961, Selwyn Lloyd, as Tory Chancellor of the Exchequer, answered favourably questions in Parliament on the subject. A Committee of Enquiry, led by Lord Halsbury, was set up, and it made specific recommendations in 1963. In March 1966 the Labour Chancellor of the Exchequer, James Callaghan, fixed the date of 15 February 1971 for the adoption of the new decimal currency to be based on the £ unit. This was finally announced in the White Paper published in December 1966. In this the Committee came out firmly on the side of a £ - new penny - ½ system in spite of powerful voices raised in favour of a 10s unit, successfully adopted in South Africa, Australia and New Zealand; others advocated the £-mil currency as used in Cyprus.

The present decimal coins began with an open competition for artists to submit reverse designs instituted by the Royal Mint Advisory Committee under the presidency of the Duke of Edinburgh. Fifteen designs were selected from eighty-two entries. Finally all the designs of Christopher Ironside were accepted, his design for the 50 new pence following later.

Confirmation of the Committee's decision to adopt the £ - new penny - ½ system was settled by the Decimal Currency Act of 14 July 1967, which fixed the date of 15 February 1971 as the day for the changeover. Four days before this the banks were allowed to close to enable them to prepare for a period of heavy work.

Traders were given the option of changing immediately to the decimal form of accounting or temporarily remaining on the old

£sd system; this was left to individual decision. Whichever currency was used first, prices in the alternative currency were also to be displayed.

One of the biggest problems to solve was that of stock-piling. Bank safes aren't limitless; to build up a large quantity of the new currency as well as keeping sufficient of the old was like pouring a pint of beer into a half-pint glass. Fortunately the Decimal Currency Board removed two denominations, the halfpennies, which were demonetised on 1 August 1969, and the half crowns on 1 January 1970. As the two-shilling and one-shilling pieces are identical in size and value to the 10 and 5 new pence—already in circulation—there was no urgency to remove them; the threepence and pence, however, became redundant on 15 February 1971. They continued in shops for the time being, but when they reached the bank they were not reissued. The sixpences have been given a two-year reprieve because of public agitation, and will remain as $2\frac{1}{2}$ new pence. If at the end of this period it is decided that these coins are necessary then they will be incorporated into the system.

This task of withdrawing the three denominations was a sizeable one, the approximate number in circulation being estimated at $4\frac{1}{2}$ thousand million. Sixpences exceed 2,000 million, which, in terms of £100 bags to be returned to the Royal Mint, is 500,000; threepences exceeded 1,000 million, normally made up by the banks in £20 bags, which would number 625,000; while the current circulation of pennies had passed the 1,500 million mark, even allowing for quantities which had already been withdrawn. The number of £5 bags that these must be made up into will be 1,250,000.

In mentioning this prodigious movement of money out of the banks, a very heavy burden had to be borne by the railways in transporting the coin to the Royal Mint in South Wales as well as dispatching the new decimal coinage. At the same time one cannot help wondering how the Royal Mint in its new premises copes with this vast quantity of bulk metal with all the necessary security measures.

The Decimal Currency Board, the Royal Mint and the banks wisely made this changeover period as long as possible. The tremendous work involved in the transition stages has required much planning by the various sub-committees, primarily affecting the Royal Mint and the banks. In April 1968, 14,500 branch banks in the United Kingdom were supplied with a token quantity of the newly issued 10 and 5 new pence as specimen supplies; the first major step was accomplished in June, two months later, when the distribution of the 6 million specimen decimal sets to the public began. The Post Office also took part in this distribution. On 1 August 1969 halfpennies were demonetised, involving the withdrawal of over 405,000,000 coins in the first nine months, representing 2,250 tons in weight.

In the following October, 50 new pence coins were introduced to the public in place of the 10s notes, which were gradually being phased out of circulation. By May 1970, 164,000,000 of these coins exceeding 2,100 tons had been minted and were either in the hands of the public or awaiting issue in the banks. In the same period 140 million 10s notes were withdrawn. On 1 January 1970 half crowns were demonetised, involving a withdrawal for the first five months of over 400 million coins exceeding 5,500 tons. While these withdrawals were proceeding, the distribution of 2, 1 and ½ new pence for stock piling continued in preparation for 15 February 1971. The total of all decimal coins distributed together with those awaiting collection and storage amounted to over £260 million or in actual coins minted, 4,000 million, weighing some 30,000 tons.

It is obvious that the change in the cheque system within the banks and the Banks Clearing House has involved major alteration and expansion to cope with the vast number of cheques handled daily.

Another major and costly alteration is the conversion of an estimated 5 million machines. These include accounting machines, cash registers, price-computing scales, cigarette- and chocolate-vending machines, amusement machines, parking meters, public telephones, coin meters, railway ticket-issuing machines, etc; and most of these machines were required to operate under the £sd currency system until 14 February.

The five decimal coins authorised by the Decimal Currency Act of 1967 were the 10, 5, 2, 1 and ½ new pence. Not until May 1968 was the 50 new pence announced by the Decimal Currency Board.

These six coins, unlike the old three-unit system (pounds, shillings and pence) utilise only two denominations, pounds and new pence. The shilling is lost to posterity like Henry VIII's testoons, though perhaps the name may continue.

The three higher values, 50, 10 and 5 new pence, are of cupro-nickel in the same proportions as previously, ie 75 per cent copper and 25 per cent nickel. While the 10 and 5 new pence have milled edges, the 50 new pence has a plain edge similar to the three lowest values—2, 1 and ½ new pence—though it is seven-sided. These last three are struck in bronze identical to the old bronze penny, ie 97 per cent copper, 2.5 per cent zinc, and .5 per cent tin.

The obverses, showing a portrait of the Queen, have been well received. Arnold Machin certainly achieved success with the portrait, which is already well established on other Commonwealth coinages. There is, however, one point which must surely have occurred to Mr Machin as well as to most of his critics. Why unbalance the left side inscription with the date?

In all other respects it is difficult to fault this excellent traditional effigy, which compares favourably with the superb 'Young Head' portrait of Victoria.

The reverse designs of the coins generally have been favourably accepted, though it would be impossible to satisfy every artistic taste. The 50 new pence (equal to 10s) is a completely new innovation in terms of shape (*Fig 24*). It is officially known as an 'equilateral curve heptagon', ie a seven-sided figure whose breadth between parallel lines remains constant. As a coin it is unique in this respect. Its design shows a pleasantly relaxed and seated Britannia, facing right, an olive sprig in her left hand, a trident in her right. A partially revealed lion rests obediently behind, and the shield is a natural part of the composition. Beneath are the numerals '50' and, above, NEW PENCE, which appears on the 10, 5 and 2 new pence also. This coin was first introduced on 14 October 1969.

The 10 new pence shows a well modelled lion, passant guardant, wearing a precariously placed crown, reminiscent of the Victoria Jubilee crown, so criticised for its unnatural position (*Fig 25*). The solitary lion has the distinction of being the first ever to be displayed on a British coin. This coin, together with the 5 new pence, was

Twentieth-Century Monarchs

introduced into the circulating coinage on 23 April 1968, partly as a substitute for florins and shillings, which would have to be discarded later, and also to accustom the public to the appearance of decimal coins. The 5 new pence represents the badge of Scotland—a thistle royally crowned (*Fig 26*). The two leaves divided by the flower, a symbol of the Scottish Stuart era, make an attractive well balanced pattern, with the numeral 5 below.

The 2 new pence displays the 'badge of the Prince of Wales—three ostrich feathers enfiling a coronet of crosses, pattée and fleurs-de-lys' (*Fig 27*). The scroll flowing on either side contains the Prince of Wales's motto ICH DIEN (I serve). As on the 5 new pence the artist has achieved satisfying balance. A further 2 new pence will be issued to represent Northern Ireland; the reverse design as yet has not been announced.

The new penny is shown with the portcullis and chains, royally crowned, once the badge of Henry VII, seen on the old threepences (*Fig 28*). It is also associated with the Palace of Westminster. The design is not impressive.

The first impression of the ½ new pence is of the extraordinary use of a fraction sign on a coin (*Fig 29*). The design, a centrally placed Royal Crown with ½ below and NEW PENNY above extended into an outer circle by an unsuitable decoration, is disappointing. Perhaps the Royal Crown should have been larger with another type scroll for decoration.

It is of interest to numismatists to observe that the nominal value of the Maundy coins will be in new pence as stated on the coins but they will remain unaltered in design. The change, however, will have no bearing on the collector value of these coins, as Maundy coins today are, absurdly, still legal tender. The 1971 coins will have a value of 2.4 pence (for the 1d), 4.8 new pence (2d piece), 7.2 new pence (3d piece) and 9.6 new pence (4d piece).

Twentieth-Century Monarchs

1. The Edward VII half crown divides the king's long titles between obverse and reverse; the shape of the royal arms shield is altered
2. The enlarged Edward VII florin (reverse) is of particular interest, showing a windswept Britannia on the prow of a ship; the model for the figure was the daughter of the Master of the Mint
3. The obverse of Edward VII's 1902 crown exemplifies clear design devoid of excess decoration; the reverse needs no introduction
4. 1910 pattern crown of George V—only ten reported to have been struck
5. The florin (reverse) design was undoubtedly inspired by Simon's Petition crown design and its inferior copies, such as the Victorian double florin reverse
6. An unsuccessful trial half crown of George V with divided titles on both sides of the coin
7. The ever popular lion over crown reverse design of the shilling—the last year of the standard silver coins
8. The wreath crown of George V was the result of Sir Charles Oman's efforts for a crown piece of limited numbers to interest numismatists
9. The jubilee crown issued in the years of the wreath crown suffered from inferiority; the modernised version of St George and the Dragon failed to achieve its objective
10. The 1933 penny differs in no way from the remainder of this issue except that only seven specimens of it are known
11. The Edward VIII twelve-sided nickel brass threepence should be non-existent but for the few that escaped destruction when the king abdicated
12. The George VI florin (reverse) showing the central English rose beneath the crown, flanked by the Scottish (flower) thistle and the Northern Ireland shamrock leaf
13. The Maundy fourpence (reverse)—a coin design which has changed little over the years
14. The shilling (reverse) designs introduced in 1937, the English (above) and the Scottish (below)
15. An enlarged reverse of a George VI nickel brass threepence—a modification of the same coin of Edward VIII
16. The 1937 George VI crown—the reverse showing the crowned arms of the United Kingdom, supported by the lion and unicorn
17. The 1937-52 halfpenny reverse based on Drake's famous *Golden Hind*, the first English ship to sail round the world
18. The cupro-nickel 1951 crown—the first of this denomination to be struck in this metal; a commemorative coin to celebrate the centenary of the 1851 Exhibition
19. The Elizabeth II coronation crown with its unusual obverse equestrian design, the first since that of Charles I. The reverse shows the four shields set at angles of 45°, the national symbols between them
20. The florin (reverse) shows a central rose encircled by thistles, shamrocks and leeks
21. The nickel brass threepence (reverse) revives the portcullis with chains, ensigned with a royal coronet
22. The 1960 crown was struck as a commemorative piece for the British exhibition at the New York Fair. The reverse is similar to the 1953 crown; enlarged it clearly shows the floral emblems

23 The Churchill crown commemorates the passing of a great statesman and leader; his portrait on the reverse shows him in a stern mood wearing his wartime 'siren' suit
24 The 50 new pence immediately attracts attention by reason of its unique seven-sided shape. The Britannia compares favourably with the sterner figure of earlier issues
25 10 new pence. The crowned lion on the reverse is part of the United Kingdom crest but the crown does not fit too well!
26 5 new pence. This coin displays the badge of Scotland—the thistle royally crowned. It is an attractive design, ideally spaced
27 2 new pence. An excellently balanced reverse with the three feathers of the Prince of Wales
28 1 new penny. The portcullis design compares unfavourably with the 5 and 2 new pence. The centre piece is too small for the space it occupies while the chains seem unwieldy
29 ½ new penny. The impression formed with this reverse is the absence of an appropriate design; a bigger crown without the gothic scroll would have improved it

235

XI
THE CHANNEL ISLES AND THE ISLE OF MAN

The Channel Isles

The Battle of Hastings caused the Channel Isles to be joined to England, though the islanders do say that William the Conqueror was their Duke and, in consequence, England really belongs to the Channel Isles!

The earliest period from which we glean numismatic information was the mid-first century BC when the Armoricans fled before the Roman legions, taking refuge in the Channel Isles. This is confirmed by the large hoards of Armorican coins found in Jersey and a small number of coins in Guernsey (*Fig 1*). The fact that these hoards were buried points to probability that these Armoricans were later driven from the Islands or even eliminated by the Romans.

The coats of arms for Jersey and Guernsey bear the three leopards of Edward I (1272-1307), or in heraldic language three leopards passant guardant. The Channel Isles adopted this coat of arms when Edward I loaned the Royal Seal to the bailiffs of the two main islands for use on legal documents. A similar coat of arms is used by the Duchy of Lancaster, but the two are unconnected.

The proximity of the French coast inevitably influenced the island's early coinage. For many generations French money circulated with the complete agreement of the British Government.

The first record of a local coinage was during Edward I's reign, when a so-called 'freluque' valued at a quarter double, or 1/32nd of a penny, was mentioned. Freluques were again recorded in 1623, when an order was given for their issue. None now exists, nor is there any record of their characteristics. Livres tournois, however, are frequently referred to, a denomination used for higher sums of money. Evidence of this is shown by the 'Extent of the revenues of the Crown in Guernsey and its dependencies' drawn up in the second year of Edward I's reign. The annual income amounted to 900 livres tournois; Guernsey rated at 765, Sark 80 and Alderney 55.

Another Guernsey entry states that in Edward III's time (1327-77), the constable guarding Castle Cornet was paid 2 sols a day in wartime, but in peacetime he was paid 16 deniers only (4 deniers at that time=1 penny). Incidentally, mention is made that a quarter of wheat cost 6 sols and that two chickens cost 100 eggs or 16 sols—revealing figures when compared to present-day prices.

Until the reign of Henry VII (1485-1509) the Islands had always been treated as a whole, but after this time Jersey and Guernsey separated, each governed by their own independent parliament. Not until 1660 was Alderney excluded from the warrant of Guernsey, though the Alderney Court continued to remain subordinate.

The first officially known reference to a Channel Isles' coinage was made in the 1533 ordinance of the Royal Court, when the French écu d'or was given a fixed value; other coins had similar treatment in 1537 and 1553. One coin of the latter date was a brass 'pallyn', a certain Collas Guilemotte having the sole right to produce them. Another Royal Court ordinance in 1581 gave a value to all coins current in the Islands.

The Royal Commission of 1607 decreed that the Channel Isles' currency should be the same as Normandy's, though the British Government left itself the right to change this when necessary. At the same time, a tax called 'Fouage' or 'moneage' was levied to meet the costs of shipping French money to the Channel Islands.

Records state that a mint was established at 'La Guerdainnerie', Trinity, Jersey, in the time of Charles I; here adulterate money was made. Colonel Smyth, the mint master, acting on a highly dubious warrant, produced in the summer of 1646 a Jersey coin known as St George's money, stamped with the effigy of the king on horseback with drawn sword. The reverse shows roses and a harp interlaced with lilies. This money appeared in denominations of 2s 6d and 1s. There were also small numbers of gold coins worth 20s inscribed with the name of Jacobus. The coin output ceased after the Seigneur of Jersey, Sir George Carteret, intervened.

According to a current Jersey account, Colonel Smyth, 'etant a

The Channel Isles and the Isle of Man

Jersey, fit de la monnaie'; this implies that the adulterate money was circulated. Unfortunately there is no existing confirmation of this fact.

In the early seventeenth century doubles (or liards de France)—copper coins circulating in Normandy—were shipped from France to the Channel Isles in such large quantities that an order had to be given in 1626 to the effect that no one was obliged to take more than two sous' worth. The value of the doubles in 1655 was fixed at the Normandy value of four per sou; a penalty of 150 livres tournois was imposed on anyone passing them for less.

During the latter part of the century French crowns and half crowns were recommended during a public meeting on Guernsey (the date is not given), to be adopted as 6s 6d and 3s 3d coins respectively. An army court-martial of 1699 is evidence of their acceptance in that three soldiers of the Royal Fusiliers, garrisoned in Guernsey, were convicted of 'coining and uttering false French half crowns'. Again in 1781 a certain Stewart Kelly was similarly convicted of the same offence, but was later pardoned.

Dealings between the Royal Mint and the Channel Isles first occurred in 1730, whereby a fixed rate of exchange between the French and English coinage was settled. This caused considerable ill-feeling amongst the islanders, who disputed the values fixed. Nevertheless this laid the foundation for Guernsey and Jersey coinage in the nineteenth century. Guernsey retained the name 'double' (connected with the Continental denier), which became a neglected coin through continual debasement and was finally worth nothing. One use of the word denier lingers on, redeemed by the Guernseymen; this is their adopted 'penny', the 8 double deniers tournois, or in more abbreviated form 'double tournois' or just 'double'. The 'tournois' ending originates from the French town of Tours, where a mint existed. Frequently 'tournois' is used after 'livres' and 'deniers'. Eight doubles are the equivalent of sixteen old French 'pence' and when introduced in 1834 they were equal to 12/13ths of an English penny.

The intrinsic value of silver coins was an acute problem at this period, as often this had been fixed previously when the silver metal price was lower. In consequence the coinage disappeared, being illegally melted down, leaving the islanders various copper types of coin from France and the mainland. This encouraged the use of private banknotes, which rarely had a backing of any substance, and relied on a large percentage of the notes always being in circulation. In times of stress such issues could not be redeemed.

Attempts to correct this occurred in 1741 when doubles were revalued. Again in 1763 they were adjusted to six per sou as against only four per sou in 1655. Three years later, in 1766, French three-livre pieces and five-sou pieces were permitted to be used for all types of payment.

From 1775 to 1789 the Guernsey coin in circulation (and one assumes that a similar situation existed in Jersey) consisted of guineas and French six-livre pieces (equal to about 5s). Little is known of the banknotes that existed and less is known about small change.

That some of the islanders were wealthy cannot be doubted, privateering being one very remunerative source of income; from 1778 to 1782 the prizes taken by the Guernsey privateers alone were valued at nearly 1 million pounds. This dubious source of income recalls another equally questionable affair. In 1794 the British Government instructed a Birmingham engraver to prepare plates for the production of French banknotes. These were duly printed and were strewn at night by two agents (one from Jersey and the other from Guernsey) along the French shore for peasants and fishermen to find in the morning. The object of this exercise was to cause confusion in the enemy's finances, and embarrassment among the French Treasury officials. Unfortunately—so the story goes—this gave the engraver ideas, and he is said to have engraved a plate copying a Bank of England note, which ultimately landed him in Van Diemen's Land (Tasmania). One cannot help wondering how narrow was the gap that kept the Ministers of the Crown from joining him!

In a letter of 1826 to Sir Robert Peel, Daniel Brock, the Guernsey Bailiff, complained that it required 27s in paper money to buy a gold guinea, and 6s 6d to obtain a silver crown piece. He urgently requested that the guinea should be reduced in value and the crown likewise so that paper money and coins would have the same values.

The Channel Isles and the Isle of Man

Collectors cannot assume that all the ancient coins found in the Channel Isles actually belong there. Sheer necessity caused the inhabitants on occasions to accept whatever coins were available. Coins circulating in Normandy, however, were accepted by the British Government as legal tender in the Channel Isles, but it was not always clear which Norman coins belong to which period.

Apart from the various Armorican coins found in hoards, odd coins have been found, such as carolusis, vaches, pistoles, double ducats, double millerays, groats, Spanish reals, French crowns, French nobles, oboles, croisades, half testons, francs, half francs, etc. Many, if not all, were probably used as currency at some period.

In 1797 the French six-livre pieces were fixed at 5s 5d, and Spanish dollars were issued by the Bank of England at 5s 9d; in 1798 these pieces were cancelled due to the war with France. In 1802 the 1797 livres were reintroduced only to be withdrawn shortly afterwards.

In the same year that the prices of the French coins were fixed, Hugh Godfrey & Co opened the first Channel Isles bank at their wine store in St Helier, Jersey; it soon became known as the Jersey Old Bank, ultimately becoming a branch of the Midland Bank in 1887. In Guernsey the only two established banks, the Bank of Guernsey (Bishop de Jersey & Co) and Brock & Le Mesurier, both issued £1 notes for circulation. The former also issued token 5s pieces, dated 1809, minted by Boulton & Watt of Birmingham (*Fig* 2). Both these banks failed in 1811 with a combined total of approximately £60,000 in circulation. The 5s piece attracts attention because of its rarity, and the fact that it was the only silver token coin issued in Guernsey. An ordinance of 2 October 1809, prohibiting the issue of these coins, was implicitly obeyed; and as its silver value exceeded its face value, it soon disappeared.

The current rivalry between Jersey and Guernsey is well illustrated by another States of Guernsey ordinance (9 March 1813) forbidding the circulation of the token Jersey coins in Guernsey (3s and 1s 6d silver and the several types of token copper coins).

In 1813 the desperate need for a silver coinage caused the Jerseymen successfully to request a supply of silver coinage. Accordingly, £10,000 of silver bullion was bought, and £13,620 of 3s and 1s 6d tokens produced from it by the Royal Mint (*Fig* 3). This supply had been agreed upon by the Council of the States of Jersey in a letter of November 1812. These two coins were still in circulation on 1 October 1834, when English money became the sole legal tender on the island; but they are today collector's pieces only.

With the British Government supplying only the silver denominations, small change remained in short supply, with the result that small local firms issued numbers of token pennies, either dated 1813 or undated (*Fig 4*). Most of these were engraved and struck by Thomas Halliday of Birmingham; others were produced in co-operation with the engraver Turnpenny. Halliday also worked for a Birmingham firm of medallist and die makers named Morgan & Co. Between them these engravers produced eight main types of pennies, which included several 'mules'. One of these was intended for circulation in Jersey, Guernsey and Alderney and bears the names of all three islands on the obverse; an identical but smaller version was produced as a halfpenny.

After 1813 the metal coinage practically disappeared and a huge quantity of low notes from 1s to £1 was circulated by people who had little regard and less understanding of the implications of such an action. As a result the local authorities passed a law prohibiting all notes valued at less than £1 and compelling all issuers to have a regular office. This increased the number of note-issuing offices in Jersey from five in 1814 to over 100 in 1817, though in the following years, particularly in 1818, a large number closed their doors. Of the original five, three were banks in St Helier, which together with private individuals issued banknotes for £1 and 24 livres French (the equivalent of £1), but the disappearance of the silver coinage forced them to issue 5s and 10s notes, presumably with the sanction of the local authorities. By 1831 the law had tightened its grip and note-issuers were obliged to produce two guarantors and to keep office daily from 10 am to 4 pm. Failure to comply with this law exposed the offender to a fine of 1,000 livres.

In 1834, in spite of many objections from the conservative Jerseymen, the French livre tournois, the pièce de deux sous, the sou and the pièce de deux liards were officially abolished, and the English currency established. The £1 was made equal to 26 livres, and as there were 20 sous to a livre, a shilling was equal to 26 sous.

The Channel Isles and the Isle of Man

The Jersey penny (or pièce de deux sous) became 1/13th of a shilling, the Jersey halfpenny (or sou) 1/26th of a shilling, and the farthing (or pièce de deux liards) 1/52nd of a shilling. The earliest regal Jersey copper coins were struck in 1841 during the reign of Queen Victoria, when coins were struck in fractions of a shilling—1/13th, 1/26th and 1/52nd, representing an English shilling at the value of thirteen Jersey pence (*Fig 5*). These coins had the usual head of the Queen, but with a different type of ribbon fastening the hair, a design produced by William Wyon. The reverse had a square shield with the arms of Jersey—three leopards passant guardant—with the words States of Jersey 1/13 of a shilling (or 1/26 or 1/52).

In 1866 a second issue was produced for values of 1/13th and 1/26th of a shilling. The metal for these was changed from copper to bronze, to correspond with the British bronze coins of 1860. They were, however, slightly smaller than the British coins, remaining at thirteen to the shilling.

A third issue with an altered obverse and reverse followed in 1877. The changed values brought the coinage in line with the British coins in value and size. The 1/12th, 1/24th and 1/48th part of a shilling corresponded to the British penny, halfpenny and farthing. Although these new dies were engraved by the Royal Mint, the 1877 coins were contracted out to R. Heaton & Son of Birmingham.

Throughout Victoria's reign there was little change in the types of coin, though there were three distinct alterations. The original 1841 obverse was the Queen's head with an ornamental fillet by William Wyon; the reverse, supplied by the Jersey authorities, was the coat of arms granted by Edward I in 1279. The second issue of 1866 showed the Queen wearing a coronet, but the reverse was very little altered except for the spacing of the legend. Th third had a similar obverse to the second issue, but the date was transferred to the reverse, which had a redesigned shield.

In Guernsey the circulating silver coinage was exceedingly worn, and included the British coins which were no longer legal tender. Because of continual complaints from the Guernseymen the British Government sent a representative in 1817 to investigate the situation. Consequently, £8,455 British silver was exchanged for new coins, which did not include French coins.

In 1829 francs and centimes became the new coinage of Normandy, making all the old coinage there obsolete. This meant that the Channel Isles' coinage, based on the same values as the French coins, would have to be adjusted. Guernsey reacted in 1830 by issuing its first official copper coins of 4 and 2 doubles. Four years later, in 1834, the 8 doubles was also circulated. No further coins with a new date were issued until 1858, when all three denominations were issued. Except for those of 1830 and 1834, minted by Boulton & Watt, the remainder were produced by Henry Jay & Co. The French coinage continued to circulate, officially accepted as legal tender. It is interesting to note that the spelling on the coinage is GUERNESEY—the French spelling—as against the English (without the middle E). The exception to this is the very rare token 5s piece of 1809, which is spelled GUERNSEY, setting the pattern for all coins minted after George VI's reign.

From 1848 until 1850, British coin and banknotes became legal tender in Guernsey with the British pound equal to £1 1s 3d Guernsey. This arrangement, halted for twenty years by unsettled conditions on the Continent, was resumed in 1870 after Guernsey had rejected the British Government's suggestion that it should use British money only.

Great Britain changed its copper coinage in 1860 to bronze, and the Guernseymen followed suit in 1864. This issue in bronze included the 8 and 4 doubles struck by Henry Jay & Co. Then followed issues in 1868 and 1874 struck by Partridge & Co of Birmingham. After this, the production of Guernsey bronze coins was entrusted to R. Heaton & Son of Birmingham. Their initial H may be found centrally on the reverses of the coins—the H on the 8 doubles being below the ribbon on the wreath and on the 4, 2 and 1 doubles below the date.

From 1870 the exchange rate remained at 21s Guernsey equal to 20s British. Until 1921 Guernsey retained a dual monetary system in both British and French currencies. In March 1921, however, British sterling became the only legal currency and 240 Guernsey pennies (8 Guernsey doubles per English penny) equalled £1.

The Jersey coins of Edward VII were issued in two denominations of pennies and halfpennies for one year only (1909). His crowned

The Channel Isles and the Isle of Man

portrait, designed by G. W. de Saulles, appears, as on many other colonial coinages. An outstanding feature of this issue is the change from the Latin to an English legend on the obverse.

King Edward's Guernsey coins retain the same rather colourless designs on obverse and reverse, though it is interesting to observe that Guernsey was one of the few countries of the British Empire that neither mentioned nor displayed the reigning monarch on its coinage. All the denominations (8, 4, 2 and 1 doubles) were issued, and they were produced by Heaton's of Birmingham in various dates.

George V's Jersey coins were in three types with 1/12th and 1/24th denominations issued. The first issue, which attracts attention because of its reversion to a Latin inscription on the obverse, is continued throughout the reign, with an unaltered design. The reverses remain similar to those of Edward VII.

The 1923 second type has a completely redesigned reverse, incorporating another Kruger Gray design. The coins of this date are not made of the normal British bronze but from the withdrawn French bronze coins that had gradually infiltrated over the years, which were melted down and restruck for this issue.

The third and last type were similar to the second but with minor alterations. The reverse shield and legend were modified, the design again being by Kruger Gray.

Guernsey coins continued to be struck throughout the reigns of George V and VI, the 8, 4, 2 and 1 doubles with the former monarch, and the 8, 4 and 1 doubles with the latter. The designs of these remain unchanged except for minor details.

George VI's Jersey coins are of two types. The first type (1/12th and 1/24th of a shilling) shows the crowned king as he appears on the obverse of other Commonwealth designs. The reverse follows the last issue of George V and has the dates 1937, 1946 and 1947. The second type, a Liberation Commemorative issue, recorded the liberation of Jersey from German occupation in 1945 (*Fig 6*). Although these coins are dated 1945 they were not struck in actual fact until 1949, and again in 1950 and 1952.

In 1954 more of these coins were produced with the identical reverse as before, but with the obverse bearing the crowned effigy of Queen Elizabeth as used on other Commonwealth coins.

Besides the Elizabeth Liberation issue, a normal issue for 1/12th of a shilling was circulated, dated 1957 and 1964. This has an altered inscription—BAILIWICK OF JERSEY—instead of the previous legend. In 1960 there was yet a further commemorative 1/12th of a shilling issued; this was to record the 300th year since Charles II's accession, indicated by C II R 1660-1960 beneath the shield on the reverse, Jersey celebrating a special association with that king.

An innovation to Jersey was the circular nickel-brass fourth of a shilling dated 1957 and 1964 issued as a twelve-sided (or duo-decagonal) coin.

In 1966 another commemorative issue was produced to record 900 years of rule from the victory of William the Conqueror at the Battle of Hastings in 1066. This issue was in denominations of a cupro-nickel 5s piece—an innovation—and 1/4th and 1/12th of a shilling. These were identical in design to the ordinary issues except that the lettering of the reverse legend was reduced in size to allow the dates 1066 and 1966 to appear on either side of the shield instead of a single divided date.

Proof issues for collectors were minted in 1957, 1960 (including 1/4th of a shilling, which was not issued for ordinary circulation), 1964 and 1966, the last containing the lower denominations only, and a second with two proof crowns of 1966.

The Guernsey coins of Elizabeth II have completely new designs throughout as well as an addition to the usual bronze denominations. The cupro-nickel 3d with a scalloped edge dated 1956 is the first Guernsey coin to be issued above a penny in value (ie 8 doubles) with the first break in the doubles' coinage (*Fig 7*). This coin reveals the famous Guernsey cow on the reverse, with the original shaped shield showing the coat of arms of Edward I on the obverse; this latter design was continued on the 8 and 4 doubles. The reverses of these last two coins show the Guernsey lily with the date 1956 beneath, the 8 doubles displaying three florets, and that of the 4 doubles a single floret (*Figs 8 and 9*). The 3d and the 8 doubles were again issued, dated 1959, with the weight of the 3d increased. The earlier issue was then gradually removed from circulation.

To commemorate the 900th Anniversary of the Battle of Hastings,

The Channel Isles and the Isle of Man

Guernsey also issued a commemorative coin—a cupro-nickel 10s piece of square design, with Arnold Machin's redesigned portrait of the Queen on the obverse and a crowned monarch representing William the Conqueror on the reverse, intended to replace the 10s Guernsey banknote (*Fig 10*). Coin collectors were not forgotten with the issue of a 1956 proof set containing two of each of the three denominations (3d, 8 and 4 doubles); and for 1966, the 10s piece together with the specially struck 3d, 8 and 4 doubles were issued as a proof set, but these last three denominations were not circulated as an ordinary issue.

The smaller islands of Sark (*Fig 11*), Alderney and Herm have no coinages of their own but rely on the money of Great Britain, Guernsey and Jersey. To celebrate the 400th anniversary of Sir Helier de Carteret freeing the island of Sark in 1565 from Bréton brigands, Sark struck gold and silver medallions in 1965. They show the arms of Sir Helier de Carteret with the inscription ISLAND OF SARK on the one side and the arms of the present seigneur, Dame Sybil Hathaway, with the inscription FOURTH CENTENARY, on the other. Sark's coat of arms differs from both of these, displaying two leopards passant guardant—the ancient arms of Normandy.

The *three* leopards passant guardant, used as a crest by both Jersey and Guernsey, were adopted later, after Edward I married Eleanor of Poitou and Aquitaine.

Alderney's coat of arms displays a single leopard rampant as its seal. It is said to have been copied from the coat of arms of the Arden (or Alderne) family in Warwickshire. Undoubtedly the use of the leopard design on the seals used by the other Channel Islands must have influenced the choice to some extent. There is no record of coins or medals ever being struck for Alderney, but a fairly recent discovery of a £1 note issued by the Alderney Commercial Bank and dated 26 December 1810 recalls an interesting period of Alderney's history, when, despite the disapproval of Great Britain, it provided capital for smuggling brandy from France to England, a very rewarding source of income for the islanders.

Towards the end of the nineteenth century British banks opened branches, attracted by the prosperity of the Channel Isles, where imports and exports per head exceeded even those of New Zealand.

At the end of the First World War the problem of the currency was examined and the money ties with France ended. In 1921 new notes, reduced to the same size as the British Treasury notes, replaced the old issues.

Nazi Occupation of the Channel Islands

The occupation of the Channel Isles by the Nazis during World War II created a peculiar situation. Special issues of German paper money circulated alongside the States issues, but did not find its way into the banks. At the beginning of the occupation nearly £250,000 were in circulation in Guernsey alone, but by 1943 this had risen to £438,081, which was almost entirely in the hands of the public. The Germans removed all the silver and bronze coinage from the islands, creating an acute shortage. To remedy this they issued in Guernsey 'States of Guernsey' notes for 6d, 1s 3d, 2s 6d and 5s, as well as 10s, £1 and £5 notes, and in Jersey 'States of Jersey' notes for 6d, 1s, 2s, 10s and £1.

An amusing incident occurred during the exchange of these notes. Because of the great shortage of banknotes the island authorities requested the Germans to increase their note issue, but the Germans required the surrender of States notes in exchange. Instead, however, of receiving in exchange the notes which were normally issued to the public, the Germans were given £5,000 of States notes which had been placed in a safe before being destroyed as unfit for reissue. To satisfy the 'overlords' further these notes were cancelled back and front with the words 'withdrawn from circulation', the Germans assuming that the cancellation had been made for their benefit. When the islands were liberated in May 1945 all notes, including German, were exchanged and notes dated before 31 March 1940 ceased to remain legal tender.

Decimalisation

Until 1968 the cupro-nickel coinage of both islands was that of

The Channel Isles and the Isle of Man 251

the United Kingdom except for the Guernsey 3d (cupro-nickel), though both had their own bronze coins and Jersey its ¼ shilling (nickel-brass) as well as those of the mainland. In anticipation of 'going decimal' in 1971, they followed a similar plan to the United Kingdom by issuing their own respective 10 and 5 new pence dated 1968 and 1969. This was intended to acquaint the public with some of the future coins, their respective island designs, and the impending changes. Both Guernsey and Jersey issue their own £5, £1 and 10s notes alongside the British ones. The 10s cupro-nickel Guernsey coin, while intended as a replacement for the note of the same value, has not yet achieved its object as collectors and souvenir hunters have prevented it from circulating by seizing it whenever possible. This is an interesting situation, in that the Guernsey Treasurer has to decide whether to saturate the collector demand with large quantities (this, however, recalls the 19,600,000 Churchill crowns that have disappeared) to enable these coins to replace the 10s Guernsey notes or to abandon the idea of coins for 10s. The balance, however, is heavily in favour of the coin continuing to be minted, as it is more economical than the note. A somewhat similar situation exists with the Jersey crown, inasmuch as it has rarely circulated as currency, being a favourite with collectors, and sold by coin dealers above its face value.

With the introduction of a decimal coinage in the United Kingdom, Jersey and Guernsey also introduced their own separate coinages with identical denominations to those of Great Britain from 50 to ½ new pence. Denominations of 10 and 5 new pence were issued in 1968-70 with 50 new pence added in 1969 and 1970. The lower bronze denominations, being of different values and weights to the circulating bronze coins, were not issued until 15 February 1971. The denominations of both islands bore Arnold Machin's design of Queen Elizabeth II on the obverse. On the reverses Jersey was content with the same reverse throughout, following the previous design of three leopards passant guardant. Guernsey produced a complete set of different reverses depicting objects of local interest. The 50 new pence reverse displays the Ducal Cap worn by the past Dukes of Normandy, an excellent example of which survives today in Canterbury Cathedral above the tomb of the Black Prince. The

10 new pence shows the well known Guernsey cow displayed on the now defunct 3d piece. The 5 new pence also retains a design of the previous issue—the Guernsey 4 doubles—which is a single floret of the Guernsey lily. The bronze 2d shows the mill on Sark built by Sir Helier de Carteret in 1571 when he colonised the island for Queen Elizabeth I. The penny perpetuates the colonies of gannets, seen on offshore islets of Alderney, by displaying a bird of this breed in full flight. The halfpenny bears no particular design but gives merely the denomination and date.

The Isle of Man

Much of the early history of the Isle of Man is hidden in obscurity. It is possible, however, that the Manxmen had their own coinage at a very early date, but no evidence exists today except for reports of ransoms and fines extracted from the islanders by various invaders from Scandinavia, Scotland and Ireland.

While this does not establish the fact that the islanders possessed money, it points to the fact that they were able to pay these tributes; those made to the Scottish crown, for example, were made in kind. In 1098 Magnus Barefoot imposed a tax on the number of cattle owned, and a maintenance rate for his men when he occupied the island. From the island king he extracted 10 gold marks as a token of vassallage. In 1315 the island was pillaged by the Mandevilles, who removed large quantities of silver. Later, when the Lord of Galloway occupied the island, he left some of his men behind to collect a tribute for him.

Sacheverell in his *Island Survey of the Isle of Man* wrote in 1702 that a coinage existed which had been issued by Martholine, who was governor of the island about 1338. A number of sixteenth-century records refer to leather money, but no remnants of it exist today. In 1577 John Meyrick, who was a bishop of the island, refers to its money and strange laws. A later writer, Waldron, in 1730, mentioned the island's leather money (c 1577) but the most diligent search by historians and numismatists has failed to reveal a single material clue. Nevertheless, Waldron was quite definite that 'every

The Channel Isles and the Isle of Man

man of substance was entitled to make leather money not exceeding a certain amount', and stated that only one side was impressed, showing who the issuing party was and the date of issue.

Towards the middle of the seventeenth century reference was made to half crowns being circulated in the island. Again all the factual evidence of these is lost. Twice, in 1662 and 1663, half crowns were mentioned in lawsuits. A possible explanation is that Royalists, fleeing from Cromwell's Commonwealth, brought these coins with them. Another explanation may be that Thomas Bushell, who was a mint master of Charles I during the Civil War, at Aberystwyth and Shrewsbury, etc, took up residence for the remainder of his life near Castletown in the Isle of Man, and that his presence facilitated the distribution of Charles I half crowns, made while he was mint master, for the benefit of himself and his Royalist friends. Bushell was also an intimate friend of the Governor—the great Royalist, the 7th Earl of Derby, who was executed for assisting the Royalist cause before the Battle of Worcester.

The earliest device purporting to represent the Isle of Man is claimed to be a ship with its sails clewed, taken from the seal of Harald, King of Man, in 1245-6. The present emblem of the Island, however, shows a figure of three legs and feet joined together at the thighs, described as a 'triune'. It is shown on almost all the coins and tokens and is the accepted arms of the Isle of Man. Some consider that the device was taken from the ancient coins of Sicily, whose triangular shape is represented by the triune, the three feet emphasising the three headlands of St Vito, Rassaro and Faro. Each of these headlands points to a foreign state. The same geographical condition exists in the Isle of Man with the three sides of the island facing England, Scotland and Ireland as the three comparable foreign countries. Another theory is that the triune was an astronomical emblem before Christian or heraldic signs were introduced. As some of Sicily's coins display stars above the triune, representing signs of the zodiac placed in such positions as would denote the seasons and great religious events, it could represent the birth of Christ and the Trinity. This also would seem to apply to the Isle of Man triune. There is also a belief that the triune represented the three seasons of the year, which dates from the time when autumn was not included as a season, being part summer and part winter.

The first Manx coins known to be circulated were dated from 1668, when a Douglas merchant, John Murrey, struck token coins about the size of a modern farthing, referred to as 'John Murrey's pence' (*Fig 12*). It is probable that these were struck by a Birmingham firm, as no mint existed on the Isle of Man. In 1679, by an Act of the House of Keys, Murrey's copper pennies became legal tender. The obverse showed HIS PENNY and I . : . M in three lines within a beaded circle, while outside the circle was 1668 ::: JOHN MVRREY. The reverse displayed a small unarmed triune within a double circle with QVOCVNQVE GESSERIS STABIT outside the circle.

These coins were made of brass, but copper coins, probably forgeries, were known to exist. This issue, together with the coins of James Stanley, Earl of Derby, issued in 1709, erroneously used GESSERIS in the Latin inscription whereas the word should be JECERIS—the whole inscription reading QVOCVQVE JECERIS STABIT (whichever way you throw, it will stand).

The emblem can hardly be described as artistic and inevitably was an object of ridicule. One local rhyme ran as follows:

> With spurs and bright cuishes to make them look neat,
> He rigged out the legs, then, to make them complete,
> He surrounded the whole with four Roman feet:
> They were Qvocvnqve Jeceris Stabit.

The point about 'Roman feet' was that Roman soldiers had a four-spiked weapon, and when it was thrown one of its spikes (feet) would stick in the ground, leaving three spikes to impede an enemy attack.

About the time that Murrey's pence were circulated, coins from Ireland began to find their way to the island, where they were doubtfully received at first, but, probably because of the shortage of small change, were eventually accepted. Many of these coins were known as Patricks in denominations of one penny and halfpenny. Others were known as Butcher's halfpence, the first with the date 1672, giving it seven years to circulate legally in the Isle of Man before the Tynwald (Upper House) law suppressed it. The second was dated 1679 and therefore could not have been legally in circulation at all.

There is an interesting record of the brass Butcher's halfpence (*Fig 13*) struck in Dublin, and issued after the producer had deposited sufficient security with the Lord Mayor and Corporation of the city, and given an undertaking that he would exchange them for cash when removed from circulation. Secretly, however, he struck counterfeits of his own issue in a proportion of ten forgeries to one genuine coin. When the forgeries were presented to him he pointed out that they were not genuine and that he was under no obligation to honour them, so the Corporation had eventually to meet a loss of almost £1,000. These—both genuine brass and copper forgery—are believed to be those of the MIC WILSON OF DUBLIN circulated in the Isle of Man.

After 1679 all token coins, other than Murrey's pence and regal halfpence and farthings of Charles II, were made illegal.

In 1710 legal copper pennies and halfpennies of a very crude appearance were put into circulation by the Governor, James, 10th Earl of Derby, but with the date 1709. This rough appearance was caused by the coins being cast in moulds instead of being struck. They continued in circulation until an issue of pennies and halfpennies was struck in 1733, when a Tynwald act was passed making all coins previous to this date illegal. This drastic act became necessary because it was easy to counterfeit the last coinage of 1709. (The Tynwald is the Legislative Council—or the Upper House—comparable with the House of Lords in Britain, with the Governor representing the Crown. The House of Keys—the lower parliament of the island—is one of the oldest parliaments in the world.)

There were, however, issues of both the penny and halfpenny in 1721 and 1723, and pennies only in 1724. These were undoubtedly pattern pieces of an excellent design, believed to be the workmanship of William Wood, who was the unfortunate issuer of the Wood money of George II, whose patent to strike halfpennies and farthings was condemned in the Dublin press in the famous *Drapier Letters*. The obverse is similar in some respects to the 1709 cast issue but with a vastly improved design of the Stanley crest and its motto SANS CHANGER. The babe in this Wood design lies in a cradle with a smaller eagle standing more erect than that of 1709. In the earlier date it lies above a cap of maintenance. The reverses are similar, though that of the later date is of far better workmanship both in design and production. The Latin GESSERIS is used on both types in the legend instead of the accepted JECERIS.

The Stanley motto SANS CHANGER has never been satisfactorily defined, and as a result the legend taken from *Memoirs of the House of Stanley* is worth recording.

Sir Thomas Latham of the House of Stanley lived during the period of Edward III's reign (1327-77). Sir Thomas and his lady were both advanced in years but their only offspring was a daughter, whereas they greatly desired a son. The knight, despairing of his wife ever producing one, developed a love intrigue with 'a young gentlewoman of his acquaintance' who was kept concealed in a 'house of retirement' nearby. Soon to his great joy she produced a son, but, after reflection, he realised that it would be difficult to pass off this son as his heir.

Not knowing how to approach his wife, he imparted his secret to a valued servant in whom he had complete trust. After several rejected schemes they decided upon putting the child in an eagle's nest close at hand with the object of 'finding' it there. On second thoughts they decided to leave the babe well fed and 'richly drest' at the foot of a tree which the eagle regularly frequented, with the trusty servant hidden close by to protect the child if need be from the eagle.

The next morning immediately after the child had been 'planted' under the tree, Sir Thomas conveniently took his early morning walk past the chosen spot and found the child fully awake. He handed the babe to a not-too-distant member of his staff, and it was hastily taken to the elderly Lady Latham, who it is said was 'enamoured with it, and concluded it to be the will of Heaven', suggesting that they should adopt him as their son and heir. Understandably, Sir Thomas readily agreed. Subsequently he adopted the eagle, with wings spread and looking back as if to see where its prey had gone, as the family crest.

In 1732 Wood redesigned his previous patterns as if to remind the Manxmen that they had not yet supplied the island's coin

The Channel Isles and the Isle of Man

requirements. More pattern pennies of this date, with at least three different dies, were struck. In the following year, 1733, more dies were prepared, differing from the previous year though repeating the same design. Both pennies and halfpennies were struck in silver patterns, and a total of eighteen coins is said to bear the 1733 date.

The 1732—issued as patterns only—and the 1733 issues have the letters J.D. and the numeral 1 (for the penny) in between each of the three limbs of the reverse (*Fig 14*). These stand for JACOBUS DERBIENSIS (James, the 10th Earl of Derby). On the halfpenny the letters are similar but the numeral is $\frac{1}{2}$. Regarding the quantities of the 1733 coins issued, £300 was made into pence and £200 in halfpence. As the population was estimated at 15,000 there were eleven coins per head of population. Unfortunately this issue coincided with an equally acute shortage of low value coins along the Irish coast, and being of an outstanding design these attractive 1733 coins found their way to Ireland. The ultimate result was the forwarding of another supply of copper coins for the island with £250 for pence and £150 for halfpence, giving the population just under another nine coins per head. As the drain of money continued it became necessary to protect the coinage from this leakage, and an Act was passed requiring that 'all persons, once in a year, were to bring in to their respective captains of their parishes such brass and copper money, to be examined and counted . . .'

At this period the differences in the money values of the Isle of Man, England and Ireland must have been very confusing for people who in the main were uneducated. Outside the towns, in the local markets, Manx money values were used, but in the towns the retail shops used English money values.

Below is a table showing the comparative figures:

An English shilling equalled				1s	2d	Manx
A Manx	,,	,,		10¼d		English
An Irish	,,	,,		1s	1d	Manx
A Manx	,,	,,		11¼d		Irish
An English £1		,,	£1	3s	4d	Manx
A Manx £1		,,		17s	1½d	English
An Irish £1		,,	£1	1s	6d	Manx
A Manx £1		,,		18s	7d	Irish

R

This exchange rate continued until 1840 when the currency became the same value in all three states.

Because of the Tynwald Act of 1737 many persons came and settled in the Isle of Man from other countries, bringing their gold and silver coins with them, particularly as the exchange rate was in their favour. Copper and brass being the only circulating coinage, the higher value metal coins were accepted, benefiting the foreigners. In addition to this the 1737 Act stated that any debt or fraud incurred abroad could not be brought against any of these people. This provoked considerable criticism from abroad. One of the English journals published a skit on this refuge for persons who were taking advantage of this loophole in the law. It went as follows:

> When Satan tried his arts in vain,
> The worship of our Lord to gain;
> The earth (quoth he) and all is thine,
> Except one spot, which must be mine;
> 'Tis barren, bare, and scarce a span,
> By mortals called the Isle of Man;
> That is a place I cannot spare,
> For all my choicest friends live there.

Before the next issue of coins in 1758 the ownership of the island changed, when James, 2nd Duke of Atholl, became Governor by right of marriage. In that year, as a result of a petition to the Governor, came a new coinage consisting of 60,000 pennies and 72,000 halfpennies; these were very much inferior to the 1733 coins, and were generally known as the Atholl penny and halfpenny (*Fig 15*). The obverse shows the monogram A.D. (an abbreviation of Atholl Duke) with the ducal crown above and the date 1758 in the exergue beneath. The reverse displays the usual triune, more flexed than usual, with the accompanying island motto. Forgeries of both denominations were numerous.

The British Government bought the island in 1765 and the sovereignty and the revenues were surrendered to the Crown by the Duke of Atholl for the sum of £70,000. Later an amount of £132,944 was paid for the island's remaining assets. It is perhaps surprising that after the transfer of sovereignty no coin issue took place until 1786. The obverse of both the penny and the halfpenny displayed the laureated bust of George III to the right with the legend GEORGIVS III DEI GRATIA and date 1786 (*Fig 16*). The reverse retained the triune with the legs much less flexed than before, and the island motto as legend. Both denominations had a diagonal milling round the edge. This issue was well received and later writers give praise to the excellently designed head of George III.

Twelve years later another issue of pennies and halfpennies, dated 1798, was circulated. This was almost identical to that of 1786, except that the general pattern was of a more shallow relief. A complete departure was the incusely cut legend GEORGIVS III D.G. REX, following the type of the English 1797 'cartwheel' issue. On the halfpenny the letter U replaced the V in GEORGIUS. The reverse, which displayed the familiar triune, also has the surrounding island motto incusely cut.

The 1813 issue was identical to the 1798 issue except that GEORGIUS (with the letter U) was used throughout.

In the absence of small change in England and Ireland the Isle of Man coinage became similarly affected. These conditions had existed in the island before Murrey's pence circulated in 1668, and at the beginning of the nineteenth century until the Victoria issue of 1839. It was during this latter period that necessity created a spate of token coins as well as a very large quantity of paper money (more commonly known as card money).

The coins were issued mainly by bankers, merchants and manufacturers, who were anxious to avoid anything that would retard their various trades. Probably the best known were those called Peel Castle tokens—all issued with an 1811 date in silver denominations of 5s, 2s 6d and 1s, and copper denominations of 1d and ½d, by Littler Dove & Co of Douglas. Two other firms that issued pennies and halfpennies with a similar date were Beatson & Copeland of the same town, and Quayle, Taubman & Kelly of Castletown; those issued by the former were known as Atlas Manx tokens and those from the latter as Isle of Man Bank tokens. About 1830 more tokens were issued by a number of private persons—McTurk's Tokens, Caines' Tokens, Faulker's Bazaar Tokens, Pro Bono Publico Halfpennies, God Save the King Halfpennies, etc (*Fig 17*).

The earliest card money is believed to have been issued in 1805 by Edward Gawn, though the earliest amounts are unknown. Later issues, when Edward Gawn had taken two partners, were in values of 5s and 2s 6d. From 1805 card money grew in popularity, and eventually almost every person of any standing issued it without any control or restriction. Speculators finally became so numerous that the many types, shapes and denominations of the card monies (*Figs 18 and 19*), from as low as 3d to as high as 7s, with the accompanying problem of issuers unable to meet their obligations, compelled the Government to act. In 1817 an Act was passed abolishing card money under £1, and requiring that issuers of £1 and £1 1s 0d notes should be licensed and be able to prove their ability to meet their total issue. The licence fee was £20.

The number of card-money issuers was never recorded, though attempts to compile a list at a later date recorded fifty-eight names, most of whom were compelled to return to their everyday business after the termination of card issues. A few, however, including Littler Dove & Co, Quayle, Taubman & Kelly, George Copeland & Co, Llewellyn McWhaunell, etc, continued to issue £1 notes, and there were a number of new issuers (*Fig 20*).

From the early to the mid nineteenth century the island was greatly troubled with forged coin, card money and notes. So numerous were these forgeries that the Duke of Atholl in 1803 issued a proclamation reminding the public that counterfeiting was high treason and punishable with death.

Frequently the *Manx Advertiser* and other island newspapers carried reports of forgers being apprehended. Two men who were found to have forged a number of John Llewellyn of Castletown's notes were caught in 1807. They were taken to every town in the island and whipped. The report stated that 'Wallace, a fifer in the Fencibles, was the whipper'. Another forger, of John Moore's 5s cards, received a fine of £50, six months' imprisonment at Castle Rushen and at the end of his sentence 100 lashes at Ramsey, where he had been tried originally.

In 1834 a report appeared in the *Mona Herald* of 2 May, stating, 'We find and experience that the island is being overrun with the basest coin that could be brought from any of the lowest states of Europe'. Before the issue of Queen Victoria coinage in 1839 the

The Channel Isles and the Isle of Man

island's own coinage was completely exhausted, and many types of token and foreign coin were circulating.

The 1839 issue was the last of the series of coins on which the arms and motto of the island were shown (*Fig 21*). It consisted of pennies, halfpennies and farthings—the first and last time that farthings were issued for the Isle of Man. This issue consisted of 79,680 pennies, 214,080 halfpennies and 213,120 farthings, allowing the population of 48,000 about ten coins apiece.

In 1840, by royal proclamation, Manx currency rates ceased, making the island's currency identical to that of the mainland in value. From 21 September of that year all the Manx coins passing at the rate of 14 pence (Manx) became 12 pence (British). This alteration in the currency created much disturbance, with rioting in Douglas causing destruction of property.

This new Victorian Manx coinage was quickly absorbed but not until 1862 was the new British national coinage officially issued, with a slightly modified 'Young Head' of the Queen on the obverse. Since that time the coinage has been the same as the mainland.

Almost all banks of today have had small beginnings, and the Isle of Man banks were no exception. With their very limited scope, note issues were probably their most remunerative income—but highly speculative. It is, therefore, not surprising that when an economic disturbance, however small, alarmed the public there would, of certainty, be a big demand by bank customers to withdraw their wealth or cash their banknotes. The inevitable happened. Without ample capital to withstand these shocks many of these so-called banks succumbed. The number of island bank failures bear witness to this. In spite of this instability there was an urgent need for more money to circulate during the early part of the nineteenth century, and as paper money was in use in the rest of the British Isles it was natural that the card money issued by a number of banks and private traders should be accepted by the public, with consequent abuse, as we have seen.

A story that reveals the extreme inconvenience of a card-money system, with issuers using denominations suitable to themselves as well as an assortment of shapes and sizes, is shown by what happened to a young Manx lawyer who collected a large quantity of them from the coroner of Glenfaba, whose home was at Peel, in connection with a law case. On arriving at the coroner's residence he was presented with a large bundle wrapped in a sheet purporting to be the cash for £300. The contents proved to be thousands of card notes in a huge jumbled mass of varying amounts, which the young lawyer was asked to check. After he had completed his arduous task the card notes were placed in a sack, which was tied at the neck and in the middle and slung across his waiting horse. On arriving home he disgustedly threw the sack in a cupboard to be dealt with later. When it was eventually opened he was dismayed to find that his hard riding home from Peel had caused the sweat and lather of his horse to penetrate into the notes, which had all stuck together.

One of the immediate results of the 1817 Act was the application by five banks for licences to issue £1 and £1 1s 0d notes to a total of £33,400. The demand for guinea notes declined considerably, since none were issued after 1836. It was not until 1847 that the first £5 note was issued by the Isle of Man Commercial Bank, which after 1849 continued as the Bank of Mona. In 1865 the Isle of Man Banking Co Ltd was formed; it changed its name in 1926 to the Isle of Man Bank Ltd. A later record states that £5 notes were circulated by this bank in 1894. It is the only one of the early banks existing in the island today. In 1868 the records show that the note-issuing licences for a total of £77,000 were held by only three banks—the Isle of Man Banking Co Ltd, the Bank of Mona, and Dumbell, Son & Howard. In addition there was the Isle of Man Bank for Savings (Douglas).

Today the British joint-stock banks are Barclays, Lloyds, Midland and National Westminster—the last-named being associated with the Isle of Man Bank Ltd. Until 31 July 1961 all these banks were permitted, under licence, to issue their own notes up to a limited amount, for which they deposited acceptable guarantees with the Manx Government. These notes were in £1 units except those of the Isle of Man Bank Ltd, which was permitted to issue £5 notes as well. When unfit for further use the notes were removed from the register which was kept by each bank and burned in the presence of a Government official. In July 1961, however, the Manx Govern-

The Channel Isles and the Isle of Man

ment took over the island's note issue, circulating 10s, £1 and £5 together with those of the Bank of England. In August 1969, 50 new pence decimal notes were issued to circulate along with the existing 10s notes. This followed the pattern of the British Treasury of preparing the public in advance for the new decimal money of 1971. Isle of Man notes circulate only within their own boundaries, but are accepted at face value by banks and the Post Office throughout the United Kingdom.

Until 1955 Bank of England notes were not legal tender on the island. This surprising situation, however, was adjusted in February of that year by an Act of the Legislative Council ratified by the Queen a month later.

In 1965 (July) gold coins were issued for the first time in the history of the island in denominations of £5, £1 and 10s. Although these coins, proof and non-proof, were technically legal tender none were circulated because of their considerably higher collector value; 1,000 proof sets and 1,500 ordinary as well as a large number of the two smaller denominations in both proof and ordinary strikings were issued, and readily sold to collectors as soon as they became available. The proof coins are unusual as they were struck in 24 carat gold instead of 22 carat. All three denominations are identical except for size: the obverse shows the Queen coroneted, facing right, with the legend 'Bicentenary of the Revestment Act 1765-1965', the usual triune being centrally placed in a shield and a surrounding Isle of Man legend with the date 1965 beneath.

By late summer 1970 a number of proof silver crowns in presentation cases were available as well as handpicked specimens, selected from the main issue of a cupro-nickel striking. The remainder of these now circulate through the banks of the Isle of Man.

On 15 February 1971 an Isle of Man decimal issue with denominations similar to those of the United Kingdom was circulated. The island government are also giving consideration to the issue of 25 new pence and £1 coins. While a decision on the design of the coinage has not yet been reached, it is difficult to visualise these without the Isle of Man triune design.

1. Armorican billon stater c 75-50 BC, found in the Channel Isles and North West Gaul. Head with curly hair, reverse horse with boar below
2. The exceedingly rare token silver five shilling piece—withdrawn after its issue to the very limited Guernsey population
3. The Jersey silver token for eighteen pence, issued at the Royal Mint in a similar manner as the Bank of England eighteen pence tokens for Great Britain in 1813
4. One of the numerous token pennies in circulation after 1813, issued by a private bank in St Helier, Jersey
5. The 1/13th shilling copper piece shows the value on the reverse as a fraction
6. The Liberation bronze penny of 1949—a commemorative coin to celebrate Jersey's liberation in 1945
7. The scalloped edged Guernsey threepence showing the famous cow of that breed on the obverse. The reverse shows the square shield of **Guernsey**
8. The 1956 eight doubles displaying the attractive Guernsey lily with its three flowers and the Bailiwick inscription on the reverse
9. The four doubles (reverse) shows only the single bloom of the lily
10. Elizabeth II Guernsey ten shilling piece. This coin of unusual square design bears on its reverse the portrait of William the Conqueror in commemoration of the 9th centenary of the Battle of Hastings
11. The Sark arms
12. The John Murrey pence were private tokens when first issued in 1668, but in 1679 they became legal tender on the Isle of Man
13. The 'Butcher's Halfpence'. An early token coin imported from Dublin and which circulated at the same time as the John Murrey pence, 1672-9
14. The 1732 halfpenny of James Stanley, Earl of Derby, shows an eagle on the cradle, below the Stanley motto. The 1709 issue was cast and not struck
15. James Murray, 2nd Duke of Atholl, issued coins in 1758, showing his monogram crowned and the triune with motto on the reverse
16. The first coinage to bear the Monarch's head laureated was issued in 1786
17. A token coin of the early and mid nineteenth century
18. Token cards of 1815
19. Bowstead's 2/6d card

12 13

14 15 16

17

 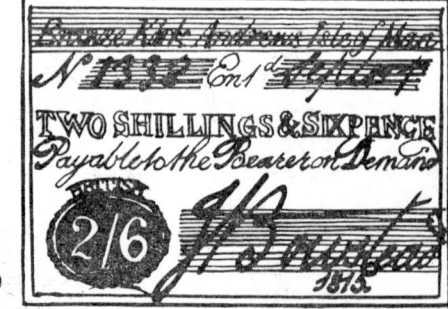

18 19

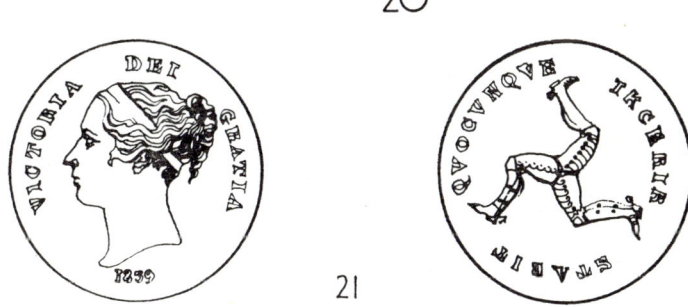

20 An early nineteenth-century Ramsey & Isle of Man Bank note
21 The well known Victorian obverse on the 1839 penny. The thighs on the triune of this issue are armoured (the last date for a Victorian issue)

BIBLIOGRAPHY

ALLEN, D. *The Origins of Coinage in Britain: A Reappraisal*
AMSTELL, M. *A Start to Coin Collecting*
ATKINS, J. *The Coins and Tokens of the Possessions and Colonies of the British Empire* (1889)
BRESSETT, KENNETH E. *A Guide to English Coins* (6th edition)
BROOKE, G. C. *English Coins* (3rd edition 1951)
BURNS, EDWARD. *The Coinage of Scotland* (1887)
CARNEY, T. F. *Roman and Related Foreign Coins in the collection of Sir Stephen Courtauld*
CLAY, CHAS M. D. *Currency of the Isle of Man* (1869)
COCHRAN-PATRICK, R. W. *Records of the Scottish Coinage* (1876)
CRAIG, J. *The Mint* (1953)
CRAIG, WILLIAM D. *Coins of the World 1750-1850*
DALTON, R. and HAMER, S. H. *The Provincial Coinage of the 18th Century*
DAVIS, W. J. *The Nineteenth Century Token Coinage* (1904)
DOLLEY, R. H. M. *Anglo-Saxon Pennies* (1964)
  The Sequence and Chronology of the 'Portrait'. Anglo-Irish Groats of Henry VII
  Sylloge of the Hiberno-Norse Coins of the British Museum (1966)
DOWLE, ANTHONY and FINN, PATRICK. *The Guide Book to the Coinage of Ireland 995-1969*
DUNCAN, JONATHAN. *History of Guernsey* (1841)
DUVEEN, SIR G. and STRIDE, H. G. *The History of the Gold Sovereign* (1962)
EXLEY, W. *Guernsey Coinage*
FEAVEARYEAR, A. E. *The Pound Sterling* (1931)
FORRER, L. *Biographical Dictionary of Medallists, Coin, Gem and Seal Engravers 500 BC - AD 1900*, 8 vols (1904-30)
FREY, A. R. *Dictionary of Numismatic Names* (1947)
FRIEDBERG, R. *Coins of the British World, complete from 500 AD to the present*

HALL, F. G. *The Bank of Ireland 1783-1946* (1956)
HAWKINS, E. *Silver Coins of England* (3rd edition 1887)
HOCKING, W. J. *Catalogue of the Coins, Tokens, Medals, Dies and Seals in the Museum of the Royal Mint* (1906)
KENYON, R. L. I. *Gold Coins of England*
KERR, A. W. *History of Banking in Scotland* (3rd edition 1918)
LESLIE, J. O. *Scottish Banking Practice—the Note Exchange and Clearing House Systems* (2nd edition 1958)
LINECAR, H. W. A. *Coins* (2nd edition 1962)
  The Milled Coinage of England
MACKENZIE, A. D. *The Bank of England Note* (1953)
MALCOLM, C. A. *The British Linen Bank 1746-1946* (1950)
MILNE, J. G., SUTHERLAND, C. H. V. and THOMPSON, J. D. A. *Coin Collecting*
MONTAGUE, H. *The Copper, Tin and Bronze Coinage and Patterns for the Coins of England* (1893)
NELSON, Dr P. *The Coinage of Ireland in Copper, Tin and Pewter, 1460-1826* (1905)
  The Coinage of William Wood 1722-1723
NORTH, J. J. *The Coinages of Edward I and II*
  English Hammered Coins, 2 vols
OMAN, C. *The Coinage of England* (1931)
O'SULLIVAN, Dr WILLIAM. *The Earliest Anglo-Irish Coinage*
PECK, C. W. *English Copper, Tin and Bronze Coins in the British Museum 1558-1958* (1960)
PRIDMORE, F. *The Coins of the British Commonwealth of Nations. Part I European Territories* (1960)
RATCLIFFE, E. E. *The Royal Maundy* (1952)
RAWLINGS, GERTRUDE. *The Story of the British Coinage* (1898)
RAYMOND, WAYTE, INC. *Coins of the World* (5th edition 1955)
ROYAL MINT. *Annual Reports*
RUDING, R. *Annals of the Coinage*, 3 vols (3rd edition 1840)
SEABY, B. A., LTD. *Coins and Tokens of Ireland*
  Standard Catalogue of the Coins of Great Britain (1969)
  Manx Money (pamphlet 1947)
  Copper Coins and Tokens of the British Isles (1949)
SEABY, H. A. *The English Silver Coinage 1649-1949* (1949)

SEABY, H. A. and P. J. *A Catalogue of Copper Coins and Tokens of the British Isles* (1949)
SEABY, P. *The Story of the English Coinage* (1952)
SEABY'S *Monthly Bulletins*
SMITH, AQUILLA. *Money of Necessity Issued in Ireland in the Reign of Charles I*
   On the Irish Coins of Henry the Seventh
SPINK & SON LTD. *Numismatic Circular*
   The Milled Coinage of England 1662-1946
STEVENSON, SETH W. *A Dictionary of Roman Coins*
STEWART, I. H. *The Scottish Coinage* (1955)
STRIDE, H. G. *The Royal Mint* (1960)
SYMONDS, H. *The Irish Coinages of Henry VIII and Edward VI*
   The Irish Silver Coinages of Edward IV
TAYLOR, F. S. *Banking in Scotland* (2nd edition 1956)
THOMSON, W. *Dictionary of Banking* (6th edition)
WILLIAMSON, G. C. *Trade Tokens of the Seventeenth Century* (1889)
YEOMAN, R. S. *A Catalogue of Modern World Coins* (5th edition)

ACKNOWLEDGEMENTS

Many kind friends and institutions have provided me with the latest information for this revised edition of *Money in Britain*, and they have my most grateful thanks. Considerable additions have been made in the 'Notes' column of the Catalogue of Coins where a concentrated summary has been made alongside the coins issued. Both the Scottish and Irish coinage have more detailed information in this section. The banknote appendix has also been carefully revised and brought up to date. For their assistance I have to thank particularly the Scottish and Irish banks, whose help and courtesy never fail.

To the curator of Williams and Glyn's Bank, Miss Ashbee, I am very grateful for providing me with a number of early banknotes and photographs, some of which are seen here.

Through the kindness of the library staff of the Institute of Bankers I have been able to see almost any books on numismatics that I have requested, and they have my most grateful thanks for their valued assistance.

CATALOGUE OF BRITISH AND ENGLISH COINS

TYPE	SILVER	BASE METALS	GOLD	NOTES
BRITISH KINGS before the Roman Invasion 43 AD	Staters and Quarter Staters	Debased coins similar to Staters and Quarter Staters	Staters and Quarter Staters	The first uninscribed Celtic coins may have been of Gallic origin but were brought to Britain by the Belgic tribes from the continent. Early British coins were struck by the Coritani, Dobuni, Durotriges. Iceni, Atrebates and Regni, Cantii, and Catuvellauni tribes
ROMAN EMPERORS First to Fifth Centuries	Antoninianus Denarius Siliqua Miliarense Argenteus Didrachm	Quadrans Semis AS Dupondius Sestertius Antoninianus Quinarius Follis Tetradrachm Small coin (minimi)	Aureus Solidus Quinarius	Many types of Roman coins circulated in Britain for over 400 years. Some were probably struck in Gaul or elsewhere overseas, but many later coins (including native imitations of Roman coins) were struck in Britain
ANGLO-SAXON KINGS Seventh Century —1066	Sceat Penny Halfpenny		Solidus Thrymsa (tremiss) Dinar Penny	The Anglo-Saxon coinage included those of the Kings of Northumbria, the Archbishops of York and Canterbury, the Kings of Kent, Mercia, East Anglia, the Vikings, and towards the end of the period, the King of Wessex and all England
ENGLISH KINGS (from the Norman period) WILLIAM I 1066-87	Penny			Over 100 mints existed during the Anglo-Saxon and Norman periods. Names of each place of mintage and the moneyer were usually shown. William I's only denomination — the silver penny— can be divided into

Catalogue of British and English Coins

TYPE	SILVER	BASE METALS	GOLD	NOTES
				eight types: Profile left, Profile right, Bonnet, Canopy, Sword, Two sceptres, Two stars, and Pax
WILLIAM II 1087-1100	Penny			William II penny reveals five types: Cross voided, Cross Pattée and fleury, Cross in quatrefoil, Cross fleury and piles, and Profile
HENRY I 1100-35	Penny			There are fifteen types of Henry I's penny showing the king's bust in full-face, three-quarter, profile to the right or left with the name and title HENRICVS REX ANGLIAE; usually an ornate cross together with roses, pellets, etc, make up the reverses
STEPHEN 1135-54	Penny			Stephen's threequarters effigy is either full-face or profile to the right. His name is used in such forms as STEF, STEFN, STIEN, STEFANUS, etc. The coins of the regal issue are in seven types. There were a number of types issued during the Civil War usually known as the Irregular Issues. Many barons set up mints in their own castles producing money on their own account
HENRY II 1154-89	Penny			There were two issues of pennies—the first from 1158-80 and the second after 1180; both showed the full-faced effigy of the king. Early ones bore the legend HENRI. R. or REX ANGL. The second issue was known as the 'short cross' coinage with the legend HENRICVS or HENRICVS REX, with the reverse showing a double cross

TYPE	SILVER	BASE METALS	GOLD	NOTES
RICHARD I 1189-99	Penny			There are no known English coins bearing Richard's name on them but the issue of the previous reign was continued. His name appears on coins of the French territories
JOHN 1199-1216	Penny			The only coins with John's name on them were pennies, halfpennies and farthings struck in Ireland. In England the short cross coins of Henry II continued, though those of John's reign are slightly smaller and of better workmanship
HENRY III 1216-72	Penny		Penny	The short cross coins ceased in 1247 and were replaced by the long cross coinage which continued—with variations—until 1278. The king's effigy was full-faced with a sceptre on the left. In 1257 a gold penny was produced copying the obverse of the Byzantium coin—the bezant—with the king seated on the throne holding the orb and sceptre in the left and right hands
EDWARD I 1272-1307	Groat Penny Halfpenny Farthing			The long cross coinage ceased in 1278 and the new 1279 (or 1280) issue produced pennies, halfpennies and farthings as well as very rare groats. All showed a full-faced bust of the king with an abbreviated legend for EDWARDUS DEI GRATIA REX ANGLIAE, with the long cross on the reverse and an abbreviated legend for DOMINUS HYBERNIAE ET DUX AQUITANAE, CIVITAS LONDON

Catalogue of British and English Coins

TYPE	SILVER	BASE METALS	GOLD	NOTES
EDWARD II 1307-27	Penny Halfpenny Farthing			The coinage of Edward II was very similar to his father's (Edward I) and differs only in small details
EDWARD III 1327-77	*1st coinage* (1327-35) Penny Halfpenny Farthing *2nd coinage* (1335-43) Halfpenny Farthing *3rd coinage* (1344-51) Penny Halfpenny Farthing *4th coinage* (1351-77) *Pre-treaty period* (1351-61) (with French title) Groat Half groat Penny		*1st period* (1344) Florin Half florin (or leopard) Quarter florin (or Helm) *2nd period* (1344-6) Noble Quarter noble *3rd period* (1346-51) Noble Half noble Quarter noble Noble Half noble Quarter noble	For the first time in the English coinage a range of silver and gold coins was struck. Groats and half groats, which were similar except for size, show a full face of the king with the legend EDWARD. D. G. REX ANGL Z FRANC. D. HY. while the reverses use the legend POSUI DEVM ADIVTOREM MEUM around the long cross. Pennies, halfpennies and farthings closely follow the designs of Edward I and II. Gold coins were introduced in 1344, but, with an incorrect ratio between gold and silver coins the weights were adjusted in 1351. The Treaty of Bretigny caused the omission of the French title but this was replaced when the French broke the treaty agreement. The first gold coins—the florin and its divisions—are extremely rare. The first named shows the king enthroned beneath a canopy, with the half-florin displaying a leopard crowned and mantled, and the quarter-florin a helmet and the cap of maintenance. The noble is believed to commemorate the English victory at the Battle of Sluys in 1340. It shows the king, full-faced, on a ship with drawn sword and shield while the half noble is similar but with a different legend. The quarter noble displays

TYPE	SILVER	BASE METALS	GOLD	NOTES
	Halfpenny Farthing *Transitional* *Treaty Period* *(1361)* (French title omitted. Aquitaine title on gold coins [except quarter noble] Groat Half groat Penny Halfpenny *Treaty Period* *(1361-9)* (French title omitted) Groat Half groat Penny Halfpenny Farthing *Post Treaty* *Period (1369-77)* (French title replaced) Groat Half groat Penny Farthing		Noble Half noble Quarter noble Noble Half noble	the arms of England and France on a shield From the Treaty period beginning in 1361, many of the nobles and divisions were struck in Calais from Continental gold, while a number of provincial mints issued silver coins in addition to London There are a large number of variations to many of the silver coins, mainly created by the use of provincial mints
RICHARD II 1377-99	Groat Half groat Penny Halfpenny Farthing		Noble Half noble Quarter noble	Except for the florin and its divisions the same denominations of gold and silver coins were issued, though the style of the lettering and an altered king's head were used in later silver issues
HENRY IV 1399-1413	*1st Issue* *Heavy Coinage* *1399-1412* Half groat		Noble	Henry IV's coins were similar to those of Richard II, though in 1412 the weights of both the gold and silver coins

Catalogue of British and English Coins

TYPE	SILVER	BASE METALS	GOLD	NOTES
	Penny Halfpenny Farthing *2nd Issue Light Coinage 1412-13* Groat Half groat Penny Halfpenny Farthing		Half noble Quarter noble Noble Half noble Quarter noble	were reduced due to the scarcity of bullion. This separated the coinage into two distinct issues known as the 'Heavy' and 'Light' coinage. The second issue showed the arms of France represented by three lis instead of a semé
HENRY V 1413-22	Groat Half groat Penny Halfpenny Farthing		Noble Half noble Quarter noble	Henry V's coins followed those of his predecessor without change, except that many coins showed privy marks to distinguish them, and the hair on the king's head is thicker and closer than that of Henry IV
HENRY VI 1422-61	*Annulet Issue (1422-7)* Groat Half groat Penny Halfpenny Farthing *Rosette-Mascle Issue (1427-30)* Groat Half groat Penny Halfpenny Farthing *Pinecone-Mascle Issue (1430-4)* Groat Half groat Penny Halfpenny Farthing		 Noble Half noble Quarter noble Noble Half noble Quarter noble Noble Half noble Quarter noble	The only means of distinguishing Henry VI's coinage from that of his father and grandfather is by certain marks denoting the various issues. On the gold coins these are the annulet, rosette and mascle, pinecone and mascle, and trefoil; on the silver the annulet, rosette and mascle, pinecone and mascle, pinecone and trefoil, pinecone and pellet, and cross and pellet. These marks may be found either on the king's bust, or among the lettering of the legends of both sides. The lis is the usual mint mark on the gold coins; while a variety of crosses are found on the silver coins, enabling them to be dated according to the type used

TYPE	SILVER	BASE METALS	GOLD	NOTES
	Leaf-Mascle Issue (1434-5)			
	Groat		Noble	
	Half groat		Half noble	
	Penny		Quarter noble	
	Halfpenny			
	Leaf-Trefoil Issue (1435-8)			
	Groat		Noble	
	Half groat		Quarter noble	
	Penny			
	Halfpenny			
	Farthing			
	Trefoil Issue (1438-43)			
	Groat		Noble	
	Halfpenny			
	Trefoil-Pellet Issue (1443-5)			
	Groat			
	Leaf-Pellet Issue (1445-54)			
	Groat		Noble	
	Half groat			
	Penny			
	Halfpenny			
	Farthing			
	Unmarked Issue (1453-4)			
	Groat			
	Half groat			
	Cross Pellet Issue (1454-60)			
	Groat		Noble	
	Half groat			
	Penny			
	Halfpenny			
	Farthing			
	Lis Pellet Issue (1456-60)			
	Groat			

Catalogue of British and English Coins

TYPE	SILVER	BASE METALS	GOLD	NOTES
HENRY VI (RESTORED) 1470-71				See after first part of Edward IV's reign (1461-70)
EDWARD IV First Reign 1461-70	*1st Issue* *Heavy Coinage* *(1461-4)* Groat Half groat Penny Halfpenny Farthing *2nd Issue* *Light Coinage* *(1464-70)* Groat Half groat Penny Halfpenny		Noble Ryal (or rose noble) Half ryal Quarter ryal Angel	Edward IV's coinage continued on similar lines to Henry VI's issues. The noble followed the same type as Edward III's, with a threequarter figure of the king, crowned and standing with drawn sword and shield, on a ship. The reverse displays an ornamental cross. New coins, the ryal (or rose noble) and its half and quarter were added. The ryal was similar to the first issue noble except for an increase in weight, and the addition of a flag to the king's right, bearing the letter E; a rose on the ship's side distinguishes it from the noble. The reverse shows a sun with sixteen rays. The silver coins included all denominations issued up to that period while in type they resemble those of the previous reign. When the recoinage began in 1464 the value of the noble of the first issue (6s 8d) had become an accepted fee in payment of accounts. A new coin, at that value, named the angel, was issued to take its place
HENRY VI (RESTORED) 1470-71	Groat Half groat Penny Halfpenny		Angel Half angel	As Henry VI's restoration to the throne was of such short duration, the coinage continued with but little change from Edward IV's issues. The angels and half angels continued but no nobles, half nobles or quarter nobles are known. The silver coins circulated were of the light standard

TYPE	SILVER	BASE METALS	GOLD	NOTES
EDWARD IV Second reign 1471-83	Groat Half groat Penny Halfpenny		Angel Half angel	During this period the variations of mint marks were considerably extended, enabling more coins to be given a more accurate date
EDWARD V 1483 April to June	Groat		Angel Half angel	The only coins of Edward V were gold angels and half angels, and silver groats. These were indistinguishable from those of his father except for the mint marks which were the halved sun and rose, and the boar's head—the latter being the personal badge of Richard, Edward's guardian and uncle. The earliest of these coins are sometimes attributed to Edward IV while some numismatists consider the later ones to be those of Richard III. All these coins are extremely rare
RICHARD III 1483-5	Groat Half groat Penny Halfpenny		Angel Half angel	Richard's coins were similar to those of his nephew, with silver half groats, pennies and halfpennies added. The mint marks were the same except that the Durham mint produced coins with an additional lis mint mark. On the Durham penny an 'S' was displayed on the king's breast representing Bishop Sherwood. Those of York mint showed a 'T' beside the neck representing Archbishop Thomas Rotherham
HENRY VII 1485-1509	Groat Half groat Penny Halfpenny Farthing Testoon		Sovereign (double ryal) Ryal Angel Half angel	Two new coins—the gold sovereign and the silver testoon—were introduced in their respective metals and were of higher value than had been previously struck. The latter is the first success-

Catalogue of British and English Coins

TYPE	SILVER	BASE METALS	GOLD	NOTES
				ful attempt at portraiture on the coinage. The king's effigy was changed on the later coins to a head in profile instead of the customary full face. The gold coins were first issued in 1485 and again in 1489 and account for several variations of the sovereign, angel and half angel. Similarly the three issues of the silver coins reveal a number of variaties on both obverses and reverses. These being the first issue, an open crown; second issue, an arched crown; and the third issue the king's bust in profile—probably the best piece of diemaking in the English coinage. The two roses design (one transposed on the other) denote the union of the houses of York and Lancaster
HENRY VIII 1509-47	*1st Coinage* (1509-26) Groat Half groat Penny Halfpenny Farthing		Sovereign Angel Half angel	A number of changes took place in this reign; type, denomination, value, weight and fineness were all adjusted and readjusted. Gold coins varied from 23 carats 3½ grains to 23 carats, to 22 carats down to 20 carats. The silver coins also came in for their share of debasement. In 1543 the ratio of silver to alloy was 5 to 1; but it was followed by a reduction to equal parts of silver and alloy, and finally the ratio of silver was one part to three of alloy. These adjustments were made exclusively for the benefit of the king, who it is believed, dissipated his father's fortune and reduced the
	2nd Coinage (1526-44) Groat Half groat Penny Halfpenny Farthing		Sovereign Angel Half angel George noble Crown of the Rose Crown of the Double rose Half crown Sovereign	
	3rd Coinage (1544-7)			

TYPE	SILVER	BASE METALS	GOLD	NOTES
	Testoon Groat Half groat Penny Halfpenny		Half sovereign Angel Half angel Quarter angel Crown Half crown	metal values of the coinage to augment his depleted income. Henry continued with his father's portrait for the first sixteen years; while after his death from 1547 to 1551 coins continued to be struck with his effigy, except the half sovereigns, which bore the portrait of the young king Edward VI. Some numismatists classify this period as Henry VIII's posthumous coinage
EDWARD VI 1547-53	1st period (April 1547- January 1549) Shilling Groat Half groat Penny Halfpenny 2nd period (January 1549- April 1550) Shilling 3rd Period (1550-53) Base-type Shilling Penny Halfpenny Farthing 'Fine' Silver type Crown Half crown Shilling Sixpence Threepence Penny		Half sovereign Crown Half crown Sovereign Half sovereign Crown Half crown 'Fine' Gold type Sovereign Angel (?) Half angel Crown Gold type Sovereign Half sovereign Crown Half crown	The first steps to raise the standard of the gold coinage were made in 1549 when 22 carat gold was reintroduced; the sovereigns, however, suffered a reduction in weight with silver coins improved to 50 per cent of that metal. Base shillings of 3oz silver and 9oz alloy were again minted in 1550; a new silver coinage was planned in 1551 with a content of 11oz 1dwt fine silver, restoring its quality to almost its previous highest standard. In this silver issue four new denominations, the crown, half crown, sixpence and threepence were added, with the last two, together with the shilling, displaying their marks of value on the obverse. Some of the gold coins were also improved further to 23 carat 3½ grains; these, however, are extremely rare and expensive. Finally a fourth issue was made with a reduced gold content of 22 carat. Since the Conquest the cross had been used for the

Catalogue of British and English Coins

TYPE	SILVER	BASE METALS	GOLD	NOTES
				coin reverses but this was replaced on the base shillings of the second issue; dates, too, were introduced
MARY (alone) 1553-8	Groat Half groat Penny Base penny		Sovereign Ryal Angel Half angel	When Mary became queen she raised the gold purity to 23 carat 3½ grains and the 22 carat gold coins were suspended temporarily, but in comparison to Edward VI's the silver coins suffered a slight reduction by 1 dwt of silver. No mints other than the Tower mint produced the coinage. The sovereign dated in Roman figures was the first gold coin to show a date. The legend on the three largest silver coins VERITAS—TEMPORIS FILIA (Truth is the daughter of time) refers to the queen's attempts to reverse the work of the Reformation and substitute the rule of Rome. The second penny issued followed the custom of the previous reign, containing the proportions of 3oz fine silver to 9oz of alloy. It is similar to the fine penny but the queen's effigy is replaced by the double rose
PHILIP and MARY 1554-8	Shilling Sixpence Groat Half groat Penny Base penny		Angel Half angel	Mary married Philip of Spain in 1554. He brought with him large quantities of gold and silver ornaments and coin. It has been said that the shortage of English coins in the latter part of Mary's reign is due to the circulation of Philip's coins, making the minting of English money unnecessary. The only gold coins known of Philip and Mary are the angel and half

TYPE	SILVER	BASE METALS	GOLD	NOTES
				angel. The silver coinage consisted of shillings, sixpences, groats, half groats and pennies, of both types ('fine' and 'base'). The groats do not show the face to face busts of Philip and Mary, but Mary's alone. The queen made several foreign gold coins legally current in England. Two of these are known to have been the French crown of the sun and the Spanish double ducat.
ELIZABETH I 1558-1603	Counter-marked Coins (1559) of Edward VI Shilling (Portcullis) Shilling (Greyhound) *Hammered Coinage* Crown Half crown Shilling Sixpence Groat Threepence Half groat Three halfpence Penny Three farthings Halfpenny *Milled Coinage* Shilling Sixpence Groat Threepence Half groat Three farthings		Sovereign (double noble) Ryal (noble) Angel Half angel Quarter angel Pound Half pound Crown Half crown Half pound Crown Half crown	Gold coins were issued in two standards—the sovereigns, angels and half angels in 23 carat 3½ grains, and sovereigns, half sovereigns, crowns and half crowns in 22 carat (crown gold). The foreign gold coins legalised by Mary had others added to the list. The milled coinage was the first attempt to supersede the hammered method; it was already established in Paris. It was abandoned until 1662 because of objections at the Royal Mint. The base shillings of Edward VI were countermarked (Portcullis shilling revalued at 4½d and Greyhound shilling at 2¼d). The silver coins were restored to 11oz 2dwt of silver in 1601 while two new silver denominations were added—the three halfpence and the three farthings
JAMES I 1603-25	*1st Coinage* (1603-4) **Crown**		Sovereign 20s	The uniting of the English and Scottish crowns caused the Scottish title and the

Catalogue of British and English Coins

TYPE	SILVER	BASE METALS	GOLD	NOTES
	Half crown		Half sovereign 10s	arms of Scotland to be incorporated on the coinage. The title soon became 'King of Great Britain'. James is the first king to show marks of value on the gold coinage. These are seen on the 3rd coinage. Gold coins of the standard type (23½ carat) and crown type (22 carat) continued to be issued. After 1612 their values were raised 10 per cent. The silver coins of the first two issues have different inscriptions on their reverses and are easily distinguished, but those of the 3rd issue are quite similar to those of the 2nd. There is no difference between the halfpence of this reign and those of Elizabeth except for the mint marks. The Royal Copper Token farthings were the result of a licence being granted to Lord Harrington in 1613 to produce them in order to meet public demand for a low value coin. Mint marks on these are said to exceed forty in number and are sometimes found on both sides
	Shilling		Crown 5s	
	Sixpence		Half crown 2s 6d	
	Half groat			
	Penny			
	Halfpenny			
2nd Coinage				
(1604-19)				
	Crown		Rose ryal 30s	
	Half crown		Spur ryal 15s	
	Shilling		Angel 10s	
	Sixpence		Half angel 5s 6d	
	Half groat		Unite 20s	
	Penny		Double crown 10s	
	Halfpenny		Britain crown 5s	
			Thistle crown 4s	
			Half crown 2s 6d	
3rd Coinage				
(1619-25)				
	Crown		Rose ryal 30s	
	Half crown		Spur ryal 15s	
	Shilling		Angel 10s	
	Sixpence		Laurel (or Unite) 20s	
	Half groat		Half laurel 10s	
	Penny		Quarter laurel 5s	
	Halfpenny			
		Harrington Type Copper Farthing (small size) Farthing (normal size)		
		Lennox Type Copper Farthing (normal size) Farthing (oval shape)		

TYPE	SILVER	BASE METALS	GOLD	NOTES
CHARLES I 1625-49	Tower mint Coinage (under Charles, 1625-43) Crown Half crown Shilling Sixpence Half groat Penny Halfpenny Tower mint Coinage Nicolas Briot's 1631-2 (gold) 1631-9 (silver) 1st Milled Issue (1631-2) Crown Half crown Shilling Sixpence Half groat Penny 2nd Milled Issue (1638-9) Half crown Shilling Sixpence 3rd Issue— Hammered (1638-9) Half crown Shilling Tower mint Coinage (under Parliament 1643-8) Crown Half crown Shilling Sixpence Half groat Penny		Angel Unite Double crown Crown Angel Unite Double crown Crown Unite Double crown Crown	This coinage is the most extensive of any English monarch, and many of the coins have a large number of variations. There are three main groups, namely, those of the Tower mint, those of the provincial mints, and crude coins struck inside the Royalist besieged towns. The first may be divided into three sections: those issued under Charles as king, those designed by Nicolas Briot, and thirdly the Tower mint issues under Parliament. In addition to these, the token copper farthings continued to be issued, though the patent to strike them had been given to the Duchess of Richmond and Sir Francis Crane in 1626. These were in five main types: 'Richmond' round, 'Richmond' oval, 'Maltravers' round, 'Maltravers' oval, and 'Rose' farthings. The licence was finally withdrawn in 1649 because of forgeries. The provincial mints are given as thirteen in number, though several are uncertain, and some of the coins cannot be assigned definitely to a particular mint. The besieged towns supporting the king, where plate was melted down for use as a coinage, were Carlisle, Colchester, Newark, Pontefract, and Scarborough

Catalogue of British and English Coins 287

TYPE	SILVER	BASE METALS	GOLD	NOTES
	Provincial Issues (1638-49) Aberystwyth mint (1638-42) Half crown Shilling Sixpence Groat Threepence Half groat Penny Halfpenny		Unite	The Aberystwyth mint mark is usually an open book but sometimes a crown
	Bristol mint (1643-5) Half crown Shilling Sixpence Groat Threepence Half groat Penny		Unite Half unite	The mint marks on the larger denominations but not so frequently found on smaller values is often a plume or the letters BR. The gold unite is similar to the Oxford type but the mint mark is Br. The originality of the penny is in doubt. It may have been issued by Exeter mint
	Chester mint (1644) Half crown Threepence			The letters CHST on the obverses under the horse identify the half crown
	Combe Martin mint (1645-8) Half crown Shilling Sixpence Groat Threepence Half groat Penny			The half crown shows an oval shield with supporters on the reverse with the CHRISTO, etc, motto. The mint mark is a crown
	Coventry mint (possibly Corfe Castle mint) Half crown			The Coventry half crown is identified by two interlocked Cs
	Exeter mint (Sept 1643-April 1646) Crown			The Exeter mint mark is a rose, or a castle, or the letters EX

TYPE	SILVER	BASE METALS	GOLD	NOTES
	Half crown Shilling Sixpence Groat Threepence Half groat Penny			
	Lundy Island *(1645-6)* Half crown Shilling Sixpence Groat Threepence Half groat			There is no certainty that the mint was here. Appledore, Barnstaple or Bideford may have been possible alternative sites, but these might have been no more than suitable landing stages where the coin was temporarily housed before circulating
	Oxford mint *(1642-6)* Pound Half pound Crown Half crown Shilling Sixpence Groat Threepence Half groat Penny		Triple unite Unite Half unite	The Oxford mint mark is a plume with a band, but on lower denominations a lis or pellet is used. The fairly frequent use of the letters OX (OXON sometimes) clearly give the place of minting. A very large number of dies were used, creating many varieties
	Salisbury mint *(1644)* Half crown		Unite	The letters SA beneath identify this mint. The most frequently used mint marks are the lis and the helmet, but a rose and others are used on some varieties
	Shrewsbury mint *(1642)* Pound Half pound Crown Half crown Shilling		Triple Unite	The mint mark is a plume minus the band distinguishing these coins from those of the Oxford mint, but sometimes Aberystwyth dies are used (mint mark an open book)
	Truro mint *(Nov 1642-* *Sept 1643)* Half pound		Unite	The mint mark, like the Exeter mint, is a rose, making it difficult to ascertain which mint struck certain coins

Catalogue of British and English Coins

TYPE	SILVER	BASE METALS	GOLD	NOTES
	Crown Half crown Shilling			
	Weymouth mint (1643-4) Half crown Shilling Sixpence Groat Threepence Half groat		Unite	Several mint marks are used —two lions, a helmet, a castle, or a helmet and castle. A number of other mint marks are used, such as a helmet and lion, a lion and a pear, a bird and lis, etc. These, however, may belong to the Salisbury mint. The gold unite has no mint mark
	Worcester mint (1646) Half crown			The mint marks of the solitary denomination is a pear (obverse) and three pears (reverse). The letters HC in the garniture below shield stand for Hartlebury Castle
	York mint (1642-4) Half crown Shilling Sixpence Threepence			The mint mark is a lion. The letters EBOR (for Eboracum meaning York) are frequently found under the horse (obverse)
	The Siege Pieces Carlisle (besieged 1644-5) Three shillings (octagonal) One shilling (circular) Colchester (besieged 1648-9) One shilling (oblong, circular and octagonal) Ninepence (octagonal)		Ten shillings (circular)	The Siege Pieces which the Royalist supporters of the besieged towns struck during the Civil War exist in considerable varieties. The metal content is sometimes suspect as dishes, salvers, etc, were melted down and from them coins were struck. Some are well made on round, octagonal, or lozenge-shaped flans but many are merely pieces of metal of irregular shape stamped with their respective values. Pontefract, though besieged before the death of Charles, continued after his death in 1649, causing some of the money to be issued in the name of Charles II

T

TYPE	SILVER	BASE METALS	GOLD	NOTES
Newark *(besieged on various dates but surrendered May 1646)* Half crown One shilling Ninepence Sixpence (all lozenge- or diamond- shaped)				
Pontefract *(besieged June 1648- March 1649)* Two shillings One shilling (all lozenge- shaped or octagonal)			Twenty shillings	
Scarborough *(besieged July 1644- July 1645)* Five shillings and eight pence Five shillings Three shillings and four pence Three shillings Two shillings and ten pence Half crown Two shillings and four pence Two shillings and two pence Two shillings (three types) One shilling and nine pence One shilling and six pence (two types)				

Catalogue of British and English Coins

TYPE	SILVER	BASE METALS	GOLD	NOTES
	One shilling and four pence (two types)			
	One shilling and three pence (two types)			
	One shilling and two pence			
	One shilling and one penny			
	One shilling (two types)			
	Elevenpence			
	Tenpence			
	Ninepence			
	Sevenpence			
	Sixpence (two types)			
	Groat (all irregularly shaped pieces)			
		Copper Royal Farthing Issues		
		Richmond Round Type Farthing (eight variations)		.
		Richmond Oval Type Farthings (eight variations)		
		Maltravers Round Type Farthing (three variations)		
		Maltravers Oval Type Farthing		
		Rose Farthing Issues Farthing (six variations)		

TYPE	SILVER	BASE METALS	GOLD	NOTES
THE COMMON-WEALTH 1649-1660	Crown Half crown Shilling Sixpence Half groat Penny Halfpenny		Unite (or Broad) Double crown (or half broad) Crown	After three years of suspension from coin production (1646-9) Parliament ordered a new coinage with an entirely new style. Inscriptions were changed from Latin to English—a reaction of the extremists who replaced the Royalists. Gold was of crown content and silver continued with the old standard of 11oz 2dwts fine and 18dwts alloy. The only coin which does not show a value is the halfpenny. Two mint marks only are used—the sun and an anchor
OLIVER CROMWELL 1653-8	Crown Half crown Shilling Sixpence	Copper Farthing	Fifty shillings Broad (or twenty shillings) Half broad	It is generally agreed that all Cromwell's coins are patterns. On the other hand certain denominations, particularly the half crowns and shillings, show signs of considerable circulation. There are also known copies of the silver coins by the Mint engraver Tanner, while others were produced in Holland. These have slight variations in the bust and in the legend. The copper farthings which bear the Protector's head on the obverse show several varieties on the reverse
CHARLES II 1660-85	1st Issue Hammered Coinage (1660-62) Half crown Shilling Sixpence Twopence Penny 2nd Issue (1660-62)		Unite Double crown Crown	Charles II's coinage may be divided into two sections—the Hammered Coinage which lasted until 1662, and the Milled Coinage. At first the gold coins showed no mark of value but in the second issue the marks of value were displayed. All these were of the same fineness as in Charles I's reign

Catalogue of British and English Coins

TYPE	SILVER	BASE METALS	GOLD	NOTES
	Half crown Shilling Sixpence Twopence Penny *3rd Issue* *(1660-62)* Half crown Shilling Sixpence Fourpence Threepence Twopence Penny *Milled* *Coinage* *(1662-84)* Crown Half crown Shilling Sixpence Fourpence Threepence Twopence Penny Maundy Set	*Copper* Halfpenny Farthing *Tin* Farthing	Unite Double crown Crown Five guineas Two guineas Guinea Half guinea	The Hammered Silver was in three issues. At first there were no marks of value, neither were there inner circles as shown in the third issue (obverse and reverse). The second and third issues have the marks of value but the second omits the inner circles. 1662 marks the great changeover to the mill and screw process for striking coins, the method universally used today. Certain gold and silver coins show an elephant, or an elephant and castle as a distinguishing mark, recording that the metal was imported by the African Company. Similarly a rose denotes West of England origin and a plume records the fact that the silver was from the Welsh mines. The first regular copper coins to circulate began in 1672, made from Welsh mines' metal, in denominations of halfpence and farthings. In 1684-5 tin farthings with an inscribed edge and a copper plug were introduced
JAMES II 1685-8	Crown Half crown Shilling Sixpence Fourpence Threepence Twopence Penny Maundy Set	*Tin* Halfpenny Farthing	Five guineas Two guineas Guinea Half guinea	James II's gold and silver coins followed exactly those of the preceding reign but no copper coins were struck—tin with the copper plug being the only metal used for halfpence and farthings. 'The elephant' distinguishing mark disappeared but the elephant and castle was still used on a small number of gold coins; none have been found on the silver coins

TYPE	SILVER	BASE METALS	GOLD	NOTES
WILLIAM and MARY 1688-94	Crown Half crown Shilling Sixpence Fourpence Threepence Twopence Penny Maundy Set	Tin Halfpenny Farthing *Copper* Halfpenny Farthing	Five guineas Two guineas Guinea Half guinea	At this period the silver coinage was in a very neglected condition, mainly through the malpractice of clipping the hammered silver which still circulated. The arms of Nassau, which is represented by the rampant lion of Orange, was added to the centre of the Royal arms shield. Tin halfpennies and farthings continued to be issued until 1692, but they were replaced in 1694 by copper denominations
WILLIAM III (alone) 1694-1702	Crown Half crown Shilling Sixpence Fourpence Threepence Twopence Penny Maundy set	*Copper* Halfpenny Farthing	Five guineas Two guineas Guinea Half guinea	Most of the early silver coinage of this reign was of badly clipped hammered coins. This caused the recoinage of 1696, when all hammered coins were withdrawn and replaced by new. The time taken to complete this operation was two years—half the estimated time. To speed up this operation mints were established in five towns, besides the Tower mint in London. Each showed an identifying letter on the coins they struck, which were half crowns, shillings and sixpences. These mints, with their identifying letters, were Bristol (B), Chester (C), Exeter (E), Norwich (N) and York (Y or y). It should be noted that any centrally pierced coins that were unclipped were officially punched and, therefore, have a place as collectors' pieces and not defaced coin
ANNE 1702-14	*1st Issue* Before Union with Scotland (1702-7)		Five guineas Guinea Half guinea	The coins of Anne were of the same denominations, values and fineness as in the previous reign, but the coinage

Catalogue of British and English Coins

TYPE	SILVER	BASE METALS	GOLD	NOTES
	Crown Half crown Shilling Sixpence Fourpence Threepence Twopence Penny Maundy Set 2nd Issue After Union with Scotland (1707-14) Crown Half crown Shilling Sixpence Fourpence Threepence Twopence Penny Maundy Set	*Copper* Farthing	Five guineas Two guineas Guinea Half guinea	divided clearly into those issues before and after the Union with Scotland (1707), the main difference being the alteration in the arms. The elephant and castle was still shown on the gold coins as they were in the preceding reign; likewise roses and plumes were continued on the silver coins. The word VIGO, found on gold and silver coins of 1702 and 1703, denotes the victory of the English and Dutch fleets over the Spaniards in Vigo Bay. Coins showing the letter E represent mintings in the Edinburgh mint which ceased production in 1709. The design of the Maundy coins remained unchanged throughout the reign, but the full four denominations were not struck every year
GEORGE I 1714-27	Crown Half crown Shilling Sixpence Fourpence Threepence Twopence Penny Maundy Set	*Copper* Halfpenny Farthing	Five guineas Two guineas Guinea Half guinea Quarter guinea	There was no change in the coinage at the accession of the House of Hanover except that a gold quarter guinea was added in 1718 for one year only. The royal arms was altered to include the arms of the Electorate, and the legend on the reverse gave an abbreviated form of the German titles. FIDEI DEFENSOR (F.D.) was included on the obverse legend for the first time. The elephant and castle mark continued on the guineas of 1721 and 1726. Plumes and roses still appeared on the silver coins, as well as the letters S.S.C. (South Sea Company) and W.C.C. (Welsh Copper

Catalogue of British and English Coins

TYPE	SILVER	BASE METALS	GOLD	NOTES
				Company). Some of the halfpennies dated 1717 and 1718, the first issued in this reign, are noticeably smaller and thicker than later ones, and the bust is smaller
GEORGE II 1727-60	*Young Head Issue* Crown Half crown Shilling Sixpence Fourpence Threepence Twopence Penny Maundy Set	Copper Halfpenny Farthing	Five guineas Two guineas Guinea Half guinea	There were two issues during this reign, but the date when the change to the second issue took place varied on the three metals—gold, silver and copper. Gold changed in 1739, silver in 1743, and copper in 1740. Sometimes the effigy alteration of the first issue of gold coins in 1739 is considered an additional issue, but this is generally accepted as an intermediate type, known as the 'Intermediate Head'. From 1729 the East India Company supplied gold to the mint which is recorded by the letters E.I.C. on all the obverses of the gold coins except the two guineas. Similarly the word LIMA, on a number of the gold and silver coin obverses, denotes a victory over the Spaniards when bullion was captured in Lima, South America. Roses and plumes were still displayed on the silver coins showing that the lead mines of Cornwall and Wales were still producing. Copper halfpennies and farthings were issued. These weighed forty-six and ninety-two to a pound avoirdupois, but these were counterfeited in large numbers creating a considerable problem. After 1754 no copper
	Old Head Issue Crown Half crown Shilling Sixpence Fourpence Threepence Twopence Penny Maundy Set	Copper Halfpenny Farthing	Five guineas Two guineas Guinea Half guinea	

Catalogue of British and English Coins

TYPE	SILVER	BASE METALS	GOLD	NOTES
				coins were issued until 1770 in the new reign.
GEORGE III 1760-1820	1st Issue (1763) Shilling	1st Issue (1770-75) Copper Halfpenny Farthing	1st Issue (1761-86) Guinea Half guinea Quarter guinea	Under George III a number of changes took place. These were not simultaneous with the three metals; thus gold, silver and copper are listed under separate issue headings. Gold coins were in four issues, but no denomination larger than the guinea was circulated. There were three different guinea issues with their divisions followed by the 1817-20 sovereigns and half sovereigns. Shortage of silver metal created a scarcity in silver coins, with little minted until the 1816 recoinage. The 1763 issue was specially struck for the Duke of Northumberland for his first appearance as Lord Lieutenant of Ireland. The 1798 shillings were made from silver sent by a firm named Dorrien & Magens but the whole striking with a few exceptions was withdrawn and melted down through an Order in Council. As an emergency measure the Bank of England countermarked Spanish and Spanish-American dollars, first with an oval punch mark in 1797 and again in 1804 with an octagonal punch. Dollars also, in 1804, were then completely overstamped, and some cut in halves. These were followed in 1811 by melted down dollars restruck as Bank of England token three shilling and eighteenpence pieces. In 1816 the recoinage began when all pre-
	2nd Issue (1787) Shilling Sixpence (Special issue of shillings dated 1798)	2nd Issue (1797) Copper Twopence Penny	2nd Issue (1787-1800) Spade guinea Half spade Third guinea guinea	
	3rd Issue (1797 and 1804) Countermarked dollars (oval countermark) Octagonal countermark 1804			
		3rd Issue (1799) Halfpenny Farthing	3rd Issue (1801-13) Guinea Half guinea Third guinea	
	4th Issue (1804) Bank of England Dollar Issue Overstamped dollar 5s Overstamped half dollar (cut) 2s 6d	4th Issue (1806-7) Penny Halfpenny Farthing	4th Issue (1817-20) Sovereign Half sovereign	
	5th Issue (1811-16) Bank of England Token Issue Three shillings Eighteenpence			

TYPE	SILVER	BASE METALS	GOLD	NOTES
	6th Issue New Coinage Crown Half crown (two types) Shilling Sixpence Maundy Set			vious issues were withdrawn. Copper issues were four in number, the last three being struck by Matthew Boulton at the Soho mint, Birmingham
GEORGE IV 1820-30	*Laureate* *Issues* *1821-6* Crown Half crown (two types) Shilling (two types) Sixpence (two types) Maundy Set (1822-30) *Bare Head* *Issues* *1824-9* Half crown Shilling Sixpence	*1821-30* *Copper* *1st Issue* (1821-6) Farthing *2nd Issue* (1825-30) Penny Halfpenny Farthing	1821-5 Sovereign Half sovereign (two types) 1823-30 Two pound Sovereign Half sovereign	Like George III issues, the dates of the gold, silver and copper coin changes do not coincide. The issue dates, therefore, are given for each metal. There were two issues in gold, the laureate head and the bare head. The latter design of the two pound (dated 1823) differs from the bare head of the other denominations and resembles the proof issue five pounds. The first half sovereign (1821) was immediately withdrawn because of the similarity to the sixpence. The silver coins are also in two issues but the denominations of the first issue, except for the crown, have two types of reverse. In 1821 the minting of farthings was resumed after an interval of fourteen years. A second issue was struck together with halfpennies in 1825, followed by pennies a year later. The farthings were minted at ninety-six to a pound avoirdupois. During this reign both half farthings and third farthings were struck with the laureate head but these were for use in Ceylon and Malta respectively
WILLIAM IV 1830-7	Crown (proof only)	Copper Penny	Two pounds (proof only)	There was only one addition to William IV's coinage.

Catalogue of British and English Coins

TYPE	SILVER	BASE METALS	GOLD	NOTES
	Half crown Shilling Sixpence Groat Maundy Set	Halfpenny Farthing	Sovereign Half sovereign (two types)	namely the silver groat—the first silver coin to display Britannia on the reverse; the gold two pound piece and the crown were not issued for general use. The first issue of half sovereigns, in 1834, was reduced in size so as not to be confused with the sixpence, but because of the public's hostility to the change, it reverted to its previous size in the following year. Silver threepences dated 1834-7 were issued for use in the West Indies, and like the silver three halfpences, which were for Colonial use only, are not included in this list

VICTORIA
1837-1901
	Young Head
	(1838-87)
	Crown
	Crown
	  (Gothic)
	Half crown
	Florin
	  ('Godless')
	Florin
	  (Gothic)
	Shilling
	Sixpence
	Groat
	Threepence
	Maundy Set
	
	Jubilee Head
	(1887-93)
	Crown
	Double florin
	Half crown
	Florin
	Shilling
	  Type 1
	  (small head)
	  Type 2
	  (large head)
		Copper
		(1838-60)
		Penny
		Halfpenny
		Farthing
		Half farthing
		
		Bronze
		(1860-94)
		Penny
		Halfpenny
		Farthing
			Five pounds
			(proof only)
			Two pounds
			Sovereign
			Half sovereign
			
			Five pounds
			Two pounds
			Sovereign
			Half sovereign
				Victoria's long reign is divided into three parts, the obverse of each showing the queen's effigy, as a young woman, an intermediate stage at her silver jubilee, and as the ageing queen. The first stage also includes the Gothic design. The full complement of denominations, similar to the previous reign, was continued. In 1843 the half farthing was included in the English coinage as well as circulating overseas. Two years later the silver threepenny piece was again added for ordinary use. Dates previous to this were issued for the colonies. This threepenny inclusion as an ordinary coin finally ended the life of the groat, which was withdrawn after the 1855 issue. The first silver florin appeared in 1849, but because the legend omitted the words DEI GRATIA

TYPE	SILVER	BASE METALS	GOLD	NOTES
	Sixpence Type 1 (reverse) Type 2 (reverse) Threepence Maundy Set (1888-92) Old Head (1893-1901) Crown Half crown Florin Shilling Sixpence Threepence Maundy Set	Bronze Penny Halfpenny Farthing (bright) Farthing (darkened)	Five pounds Two pounds Sovereign Half sovereign	it did not find favour with the public and was discontinued in the following year. Two years later, however, the Gothic florin was introduced, so named because of the lettering and date which substituted Gothic letters and numerals for those of the Roman type. These and the florins of 1849 were the first attempt to introduce decimalisation in our current coinage. Half crowns ceased between the years 1851 and 1873 (inclusive) but because of several issues appearing between these years whose validity is in doubt—a controversy has arisen among numismatists that may never be satisfactorily solved. The early copper coinage was produced at the rate of twenty-four pence to the pound avoirdupois, but the bronze pennies were issued at half this weight, forty-eight to the pound. Sovereigns struck throughout the reign had no mint mark when issued by the London mint but those of the Royal mint overseas branches show their respective mint marks. These are Melbourne (M), Sydney (S), Perth (P), and in later reigns Ottawa (C), India (I), and Pretoria (SA)
EDWARD VII 1901-10	Crown Half crown Florin Shilling Sixpence Threepence Maundy Set	Bronze Penny Halfpenny Farthing (darkened)	Five pounds Two pounds Sovereign Half sovereign	In Edward's short reign the coins followed the denominations of Victoria, but the florin reverse was completely changed, showing Britannia on the prow of a ship. The shilling, too, was altered—the royal crest replacing the re-

Catalogue of British and English Coins

TYPE	SILVER	BASE METALS	GOLD	NOTES
				verse design of Victoria which bore the arms of England, Scotland and Ireland on three shields. The half crown reverse was modified—the reshaped shield bearing the royal arms. The garter around it replaced the collar of the order as shown on the Victorian half crown. The mintage figures of this reign are very low compared to those of following reigns, consequently high prices are to be paid by would-be purchasers. The Royal mint opened its Ottawa branch in 1908, producing sovereigns (mint mark C) in addition to the three Australian mints
GEORGE V 1910-36	1st Coinage (1911-19) Half crown Florin Shilling Sixpence* (also 1920) Threepence* (also 1920) Maundy Set (also 1920) 2nd Coinage (1920-6) Half crown Florin Shilling Sixpence Threepence Maundy Set (1921-7) Modified Effigy Variety	Bronze 1st Issue 1911-26 Penny Halfpenny (1911-25) Farthing (darkened 1911-17) Farthing (bright 1918-25) Penny (1926-7)	Five pounds (proof only) Two pounds (proof only) Sovereign Half sovereign	The major adjustment in this reign was the change in metal content of silver from 92.5 per cent to 50 per cent. This took place in 1920 but the issue continued as before until 1927. In 1922, however, there was a minor alteration to the half crown die when a groove appeared between the crown and the shield, while the earlier type showed the crown touching the shield. The 1927-35 issue is generally considered one of the best productions of modern coins in both design and appearance. The 1927 dates, however, were proof only. The use of sovereigns and half sovereigns for internal use ceased in Great Britain and Ireland after 1915, though the Royal Mint con-

*A limited number of these denominations were struck with 92.5 per cent silver in 1920

TYPE	SILVER	BASE METALS	GOLD	NOTES
	Half crown (1926-7) Shilling (1926-7) Sixpence (1926-7) Threepence (1926) *3rd Coinage (1927-36)* Crown (not 1935) Half crown Florin Shilling Sixpence Threepence Maundy Set *Jubilee Issue* Crown (1935)	Halfpenny (1925-7) Farthing (1926-36) *Small Head Variety* Penny (1928-36) Halfpenny (1928-36)		tinued striking a very limited number of sovereigns in 1916 and 1917. More were used (dated 1925) for payments overseas. In addition to these, mints had been opened in India (mint mark I) and Pretoria (mint mark SA). The former produced sovereigns with 1918 date only and the latter with dates from 1923 to 1932. The last four years of these display the smaller effigy of the king. Pretoria also minted half sovereigns dated 1923 (proof), 1925 and 1926. The sovereign in particular has been singled out by international forgers as a profitable gold coin to imitate because of its high value in relation to its content. Many of these are well struck from forged dies and may easily deceive the eye and appear genuine. They usually contain the full 22 carat gold. In the years 1912, 1918 and 1919 the Royal Mint contracted out the pennies to The Mint Birmingham Ltd (formerly Heaton & Son), which shows a small H to the left of the date; and 1918 and 1919 to Kings Norton Metal Co, which shows KN in a similar position
EDWARD VIII 1936		Nickel-brass Threepence		The coins struck in 1936 are sometimes claimed as those of Edward VIII even though George V's effigy is on them. It is claimed that as George V died in early January the coins issued must have been struck after his death. As no official evidence is forthcom-

Catalogue of British and English Coins

TYPE	SILVER	BASE METALS	GOLD	NOTES
				ing to support this view the coins are of George V's reign. A full complement of denominations with the effigy of Edward VIII were struck but on his abdication all are believed to have been melted down except for a few nickel-brass threepences, which escaped destruction
GEORGE VI 1936-52	*1st Issue (1937-46)* Crown (1937 only) Half crown Florin Shilling 'English' Shilling 'Scottish' Sixpence Threepence (1937-44) Maundy Set *2nd Issue (1947-8)* Half crown Florin Shilling 'English' Shilling 'Scottish' Sixpence Maundy Set *3rd Issue (1949-51)* Half crown Florin Shilling 'English' Shilling 'Scottish' Sixpence Maundy Set	*1st Issue (1937-48)* Nickel-brass Threepence (except 1947) Bronze Penny Halfpenny Farthing *2nd Issue (1949-52)* Nickel-brass Threepence Bronze Penny (1949-51 only) Halfpenny Farthing	Five pounds (proof) Two pounds (proof) Sovereign (proof) Half sovereign (proof)	The 1st and 2nd issues, from 1937 to 1948, included the last silver coins of Great Britain issued for normal circulation, with the last two years (1947 and 1948) changed to a cupro-nickel metal. In the following year (1949) the IND IMP in the inscription was omitted. This issue lasted to the end of the reign. The interesting feature of George VI coins was the introduction of two separate designs for the shilling—the English arms on one reverse and the Scottish arms on the other. This continued until the end of the Elizabeth II non-decimal series before 1971. The only silver issues to remain were the Maundy coins. These were again struck in 92.5 per cent silver after the period of 1921-46 when Maundy coins were reduced to 50 per cent silver. The new twelve-sided nickel-brass threepence has been a useful and popular coin, but as it did not fit into a decimal system it was doomed to disappear in 1971. Silver threepences dated 1942-4 were issued for circulation in the West Indies and are, therefore, not strictly English coins. This follows

TYPE	SILVER	BASE METALS	GOLD	NOTES
	Festival of Britain Issue (1951) Crown			the pattern of colonial issues of Victoria, which were exclusively issued to colonies, though of an identical type to earlier dates circulated in Great Britain. The 1952 sixpence is also a West Indian coin, the total issue being sent there for circulation
ELIZABETH II 1952—	CUPRO-NICKEL 1st Issue (1953) Crown Half crown Florin Shilling 'English' Shilling 'Scottish' Sixpence Maundy Set (silver)	Nickel-brass Threepence Bronze Penny Halfpence Farthing		While the current coins with the queen's effigy are well known, there are numerous points that could well have escaped the eye of the coin user, if only because they become commonplace and accepted without further consideration. The Coronation crown is of interest as it displays the queen, wearing the uniform of colonel-in-chief Grenadier Guards, mounted on a horse. This is the first coin to show the monarch on horseback since the reign of Charles I. On its reverse is a well proportioned design displaying the arms of Great Britain in four separate shields. This same reverse was repeated on the crown in 1960 for the New York British Exhibition. The Churchill crown will be recalled for its tremendous mintage figure of over 19½ million. The omission in 1954 of the BRITT OMN (Britanniarum Omnium) from the legend merely reflects the general trend of certain Commonwealth nations whose growing awareness of their independence caused this adjustment. Pennies, probably because of over production,
	2nd Issue (1954-67) Crown (1960) Half crown Florin Shilling 'English' Shilling 'Scottish' Sixpence Maundy Set (silver) Churchill Commemorative Issue (1965) Crown	Nickel-brass Threepence Bronze Penny Halfpenny Farthing (1954-56)	Sovereign (1957-68)	

Catalogue of British and English Coins

TYPE	CUPRO-NICKEL	BASE METALS	GOLD	NOTES
	Decimal Coinage Issue Fifty new pence (1969) Ten new pence (1968-9) Five new pence (1968-9)	Bronze (1971) Two new pence One new pence Half new pence		were drastically reduced in the years 1950, 1951 and 1953, with none produced during 1952, 1954-60. Farthings and halfpennies ceased production in the respective years of 1956 and 1967 and were demonetised. Similarly half crowns, after the 1967 issue, ceased to be legal tender on 1 January 1970. Sovereigns again were minted in 1957 and continued annually except for 1960 and 1961, until 1968. These, however, were not for currency but for overseas government transactions, and only licenced collectors and dealers were permitted to possess them. Although decimal coins did not come into use until 1971, 5 and 10 new pence were introduced in 1968, being of identical value to the shilling and florin—presumably to acquaint the public with their appearance and to overcome some of the problems of distribution. In October 1969 the 50 new pence was circulated in place of the 10s note. The bronze decimal coins (2, 1, and ½ new pence), though available in sets along with the 5 and 10 new pence, were not used as currency until 1971. Unlike the remaining coins in circulation on 15 February 1971 the sixpence was permitted to circulate as 2½ new pence. This arrangement will last for a two year minimum to test public opinion on its need as a decimal coin.

CATALOGUE OF SCOTTISH COINS

TYPE	SILVER	BASE METALS	GOLD	NOTES
DAVID I 1124-53	Penny (or Sterling)			It was unlikely that David I produced coins before 1135—the date that Stephen became king of England—as the coins appear to be poor copies of the English king's. They are all of one denomination—a silver penny of 11 1/10th fine and 9/10ths alloy which may be divided into four types. Occasionally a legible and well struck specimen is found which has materially assisted in assigning the coins correctly
HENRY, EARL OF HUNTINGDON & NORTHUM- BERLAND 1136-52	Penny			During David's reign his son Henry, Earl of Huntingdon and Northumberland, struck silver pennies very similar in type to his father's; these may be divided into three varieties distinguished by different crosses on the reverses
MALCOLM IV 1153-65	Penny			Malcolm's pennies sometimes show a crowned bust of the king facing right while others reveal him full-face. Many of his coins closely follow those of David, and, as many do not bear Malcolm's name, there is some doubt as to whether certain coins attributed to him are really his or those of his grandfather David. Numismatists now divide these coins into five types

Catalogue of Scottish Coins 307

TYPE	SILVER	BASE METALS	GOLD	NOTES
WILLIAM I (the Lion) 1165-1214	1st Issue Penny 2nd Issue Penny 3rd Issue Penny			William's coins were in three distinct issues—the first displaying the king facing right; the second shows him turning left; the third issue, estimated to be after 1189, is in two types with the king facing right or left with a common reverse, which is a short voided cross
ALEXANDER II 1214-49	Penny			Alexander II's pennies followed closely those of William's last issue, with the crowned head facing both ways as before. Sometimes the king's head is uncrowned and sometimes a sceptre is included
ALEXANDER III 1249-86	1st Coinage (1250-80) Penny 2nd Coinage (1280-86) Penny Halfpenny Farthing			Alexander III's coins are in two main issues, the first coinage being 1250 to 1280. The second issue, from 1280 to 1286 included pennies, halfpennies and farthings. As many as sixteen mints were in use during this king's reign. All coins of this reign showed, on the reverses, either a long voided cross (first coinage) or a long single cross (second coinage). The obverses of the first coinage vary, having several varieties of head or bust, and the second issue gives the legend ALEXANDER DEI GRA or similar, with REX SCOTORUM often included. Halfpennies and farthings are similar to the pennies of the second issue
JOHN BALIOL 1292-6	1st Issue Penny Halfpenny 2nd Issue Penny			John Baliol's coinage was in two easily distinguishable issues. The first is usually known as the Rough Issue and was crudely executed with the king's bust having

TYPE	SILVER	BASE METALS	GOLD	NOTES
	Halfpenny			a particularly rough appearance. Probably the commonest reverse shows four mullets of six points each, sometimes with CIVITAS SANDRE (for St Andrews' mint). There are other variations but all appear to show REX SCOTORUM. The halfpennies are similar but very few are known to exist. The second issue is similar but the workmanship is infinitely superior, the dies cut with much more care. The halfpenny differs slightly by having two six point mullets opposite one another
ROBERT BRUCE 1306-29	Penny Halfpenny Farthing			Robert Bruce's pennies were very similar to John Baliol's second issue but were reduced in weight. The halfpennies and farthings also follow the previous reign and while the pennies are rare the smaller denominations are much more so
DAVID II 1329-71	1st Coinage Penny Halfpenny Farthing 2nd Coinage (1357-67) Groat Half groat Penny 3rd Coinage (1367-71) Groat Half groat Penny		Noble	David II's coinage, which shows considerable similarity to the English issues, was the beginning of an expansion in Scottish denominations, producing a gold coin and two higher value silver denominations for the first time. The coinage was in three distinct issues—the first consisting of pennies, halfpennies and farthings with the king's head rather crudely designed, while the reverses follow the coins of the last three reigns. The two smaller denominations show more variation on the reverses than the penny.

Catalogue of Scottish Coins 309

TYPE	SILVER	BASE METALS	GOLD	NOTES
				From 1357 to 1367 the second coinage appeared, producing the first Scottish gold coin—the noble, an almost identical coin to the English noble of Edward III, together with the first groat and half groat and the penny. These two higher value silver coins were virtually larger editions of the penny. The third coinage, from 1367 to 1371, was of the same denominations as the second but without the gold noble. The mints are shown on all the second and third issues sacrificing the lettering DEI GRA in the legend, while the latter issue had a reduction in the weight of the silver
ROBERT II 1371-90	Groat Half groat Penny Halfpenny			The coins of Robert II were virtually a continuation of David's third coinage. The majority of the coins may be recognised by a star on the sceptre handle, while others show a cross
ROBERT III 1390-1406	*Heavy Coinage* *1st Issue* Groat Half groat Penny Halfpenny *2nd Issue* Groat Half groat Penny Halfpenny *Light Coinage* Groat		Lion Demi lion Lion Demi lion Lion Demi lion	There were two types of coinage—the 'Heavy' and 'Light'. The former was in two issues and the latter in one issue only. Because of its short period of issue and perhaps metal scarcity the 'Light' is rarer than the earlier types. It is usually accepted that all the full-faced effigies of both gold and silver belong to Robert III and not to the previous reign. The gold lion and demi appear to have copied the design from the French écu à la couronne. This shows the figure of St

TYPE	SILVER	BASE METALS	GOLD	NOTES
				Andrew with a cross extending to the edge of the coin of the 'Heavy' lion, but on the 'Light' the cross is usually omitted. The two silver issues of the 'Heavy' may be separated by a roughly struck obverse on the earlier type, the second type having a much neater appearance. The bust of the king on the former is taller than that of the latter. Comparative weights of the two issues are 60 to 38 grains in the gold lion, and 48 to about 30 in the silver groat. The penny and halfpenny of the first type usually show the issuing mint, but the second type have no mint name and read REX SCOTORVM
JAMES I 1406-37	Groat	*Billon* Penny Halfpenny	Demi Half demi	The demies and half demies of James I have the arms in a lozenge-shaped shield and St Andrew's cross on the reverse. The only silver coin is the groat but the penny and halfpenny were minted with a very low silver content and are usually classed as billon coins. The coinage was produced rather late in the reign and does not appear to have had much impact on the currency. The groat is a full-face of the king with the sceptre in his right hand, otherwise resembling this coin of Robert III. The billon coins may be identified by the reverse legend, which is in one circle only and formed by the name of the issuing mint

Catalogue of Scottish Coins

TYPE	SILVER	BASE METALS	GOLD	NOTES
JAMES II 1437-60	1st Coinage (1437-51) Groat	Billon Penny	Demi	The early coinage of James II continued with his father's issues until 1451. The demies of James II, however, may be distinguished by two annulets dividing the wording of the legend. The gold coins of the second issue are similar to those of Robert III while the groat is recognised by the absence of the sceptre on the obverse. There is a second type of groat, similar but with a clothed bust. The half groat follows the style of the first type, while the penny can be distinguished by pellets in all angles of the reverse
	2nd Coinage (1451-60) Groat (two types) Half groat	Billon Penny	Lion (or st andrew Half lion	
ECCLESI- ASTICAL ISSUES c 1452-80		Copper Penny (three varieties) Farthing (three varieties)		During the reigns of James II and III, Bishop Kennedy was known to possess the right to mint coins. Pennies have been found to be plentiful in the districts surrounding St Andrews, the ecclesiastical establishment of the bishop. Farthings, however, until a hoard of them were found at Crossraguel Abbey, were exceedingly rare. The assumption has been, therefore, that the farthings may have been struck at Crossraguel, pointing to the fact that someone other than Bishop Kennedy may have produced them
JAMES III 1460-88	1st Issue Groat	Billon Penny Plack Half plack	1st Issue Rider Half rider Quarter rider Unicorn Half unicorn	Numismatists are uncertain about some coins ascribed to James III and IV. Gold, silver, billon and copper were all used in this reign. The rider of 22 carat gold, with a value of 23s and its divisions, and in a later issue the unicorn
	2nd Issue Groat	Billon Penny		

TYPE	SILVER	BASE METALS	GOLD	NOTES
	Half groat Penny			of 21 carat, with a value of 18s, and its half unicorn, were entirely new coins. The rider was named after its design— the equestrian figure of the king in armour. The unicorn achieves distinction by being the first coin of Scottish minting with a gold content below 22 carat. This coin, with its half unicorn, was probably struck for a limited period, for though it was circulated some time after the king came to the throne, it was not among the last silver issues of James III. The rider is in two types and shows the king riding to the right in the first type, and riding to the left in the second. The half and quarter rider follow type II. The earlier unicorn displays the legend EXURGAT, etc, on the reverse, but the later type show this motto on both sides of the coin. The silver coins were in six issues, all of which included the groat. In the second and third issues both silver and billon pennies were struck. For a first step in identifying the groat, the first, third and fifth issues show a crowned full-face bust of the king, and the fourth a full-face bust with a low crown; the second issue displays a three-quarter facing bust to the right, while the sixth reveals a three-quarter bust to the left. In the second and third issues pennies of both silver and billon were struck. Black farthings were originally is-
	3rd Issue Groat Penny	Billon Penny		
	4th Issue Groat Half groat Penny			
	5th Issue Groat			
	6th Issue Groat Half groat	Billon Penny		
		Copper 1st Issue Black farthings		
		2nd Issue Black farthings		

Catalogue of Scottish Coins

TYPE	SILVER	BASE METALS	GOLD	NOTES
				sued as halfpennies according to the documents of the period, but they were later reduced in value. These coins appear to be the first regal copper coins of the British Isles. The thistle design shown on the second issue of the groats represents the first time that the Scottish emblem—the thistle—was used on a coin of Scotland. About 1471 two new billon coins were introduced—the plack and half plack. Placks are estimated to have had a value of 4d
JAMES IV 1488-1513	1st Issue (1488) Groat Half groat	Billon Plack Penny	St andrew Half st andrew	The issues of James IV followed the same pattern as those of James III. The three metals, gold, silver and billon, appear to be issued independently of one another, the plack being the only coin to be continuously struck. The first gold coins commence with James IV's coronation year 1488; these were the gold st andrew (or lion) of 22 carat with the numeral IIII after the legend and a value of 14s, and the half st andrew. The unicorn and half unicorn, issued from 1496 to 1512, were similar to those of James III except for the stops on the legend (as on the new type groats). The order in which groats were issued cannot be certain but they overlap in some cases. After the first issue of 1488, which could possibly have belonged to James III, the obverse showing the only three-quarter face bust, the
	2nd Issue (1489) Groat	2nd Issue Billon Plack Half plack (?)	2nd Issue (1496-1512) Unicorn Half unicorn	
	3rd Issue (1490) Groat Half groat			
	4th Issue Groat Half groat Penny			
	5th Issue Groat Half groat			
	6th Issue Groat			

TYPE	SILVER	BASE METALS	GOLD	NOTES
				remainder are full-face. The silver penny, a very rare coin, is also full-face with mullets on the reverse but no numeral. The billon penny (first issue) shows a tall neat bust of the king with two reverse alterations, while the later issue penny has four variations. Placks were of the same type throughout, divided into two groups, the first with the letters QRA and the second group with old English lettering and no numeral
JAMES V 1513-42		*1st Coinage* (1513-26) **Billon** **Plack**	Unicorn Half unicorn	The gold, silver and billon coins of James V have, in the main, the numerals after the king's name, considerably simplifying the identification
	2nd Coinage (1526-39) Groat (four varieties) Third groat		Crown or écu (two varieties)	of his coins. Some issues defy dating while other coins so closely resemble those of previous reigns that allocating them to their correct period is sometimes difficult. Added to this there is frequently a lack of documentary evidence to support the date of issue. Unicorns and half unicorns were the first gold coins issued and were identical to those of James IV. The gold écus (or crowns) of 1526 were in two varieties; the bonnet pieces (with two-thirds and one-third divisions) were so called because of the arresting headgear worn by the king as shown on the obverse. This coin is the earliest Scottish coin to bear a date. The groats and third groats were not issued until 1526. Until then silver coin does
		3rd Coinage (1539-60) **Billon** **Bawbee** **Half bawbee**	Bonnet piece (or ducat) Two thirds bonnet piece Third bonnet piece	

Catalogue of Scottish Coins

TYPE	SILVER	BASE METALS	GOLD	NOTES
				not appear to have been much in circulation. The placks, which were issued early in the reign, resemble those of James IV. The later issues may be separated by either pellets or trefoils as stops or by a combination of both. The bawbees, and the rare half bawbees, with a crowned thistle on the obverse, have few varieties but the larger coin has either a pellet or a trefoil after the word OPPIDUM
MARY 1542-67	1st Period (1542-58) Testoon Half testoon	Billon Bawbee Half bawbee Penny Plack Hardhead (or lion)	Ecu, or abbey crown (undated) Twenty shilling piece Lion (or forty-four shilling piece) Half lion Ryal Half ryal	Mary's coinage divides naturally into five distinct personal periods: (1) As an unmarried queen from 1542-58. (2) During her marriage (1558) to the Dauphin of France. (3) As a widow (1561-5). (4) During her marriage (1565) to Henry Darnley. (5) From the death of Darnley (1567) to her dethronement. All the coins 1542-58 show the queen's name and title. The gold écus were probably first issued, being a continuation of James V's écus, after which ten years elapsed before the lion and half lion (44 and 22s pieces) were issued with the initials I.G. stamped on them. These represented James, Earl of Arran, who was the Regent and Governor. These coins have Mary's monogram on them — sometimes MARIA REGINA but usually M.R. The remaining two gold
	2nd Period (1558) Testoon (1st Issue) Testoon (2nd Issue) Half testoon (1st Issue) Half testoon (2nd Issue) 3rd Period (1561-5) Testoon	Billon Nonsunt (or 12 penny groat) Hardhead (or lion)	Ducat	

TYPE	SILVER	BASE METALS	GOLD	NOTES
	Half testoon			coins issued before Mary's marriage were the ryal and half ryal—coins so outstandingly simple and clean in design that the artist could easily have been living 400 years later. The first silver testoons did not appear until 1553. They were the first Scottish milled coins. The billon coins were bawbees (6d) and half bawbees (3d); apart from distinguishing marks they are like those of James V. Pennies were issued with a young looking front-face bust. The placks were apparently issued in large numbers dated 1557 and valued at 4d, with newly introduced hardheads (or lions) valued at 1½d. The second coinage bears the name of both Francis and Mary. The French influence is exemplified by French emblems—the dolphin, the three fleur de lis, and the cross of Lorraine shown on the coins separately or as a pair. The only gold coin was the extremely rare ducat valued at 60s. The testoons of the 1555 and 1556-8 issues are of different designs. Among the later issue the use of different dates has produced three sets of 'mules'. Only half testoons of the last type circulated. As hammered coins they were greatly inferior to those of 1553. The billon hardheads continued to be struck, together with a new coin called a nonsunt (sometimes known as a 12d groat) named after its legend. With the death of
	4th Period (1565-7) Ryal (1st Issue) Ryal (2nd Issue) Two-thirds ryal (2nd issue) One-third ryal (2nd Issue)			
	5th Period (1567) Ryal Two-thirds ryal One-third ryal			

Catalogue of Scottish Coins

TYPE	SILVER	BASE METALS	GOLD	NOTES
				Francis hardly any coins were struck except a very limited quantity of testoons and half testoons. The earliest coins of the Darnley-Mary marriage were in 1565 when obverses with two portraits facing each other were struck in silver ryals. With a second issue the design changed—more silver ryals (with divisions of two-thirds and one-third). During the last period—Mary's second widowhood—more silver ryals and the same ryal divisions were circulated. These were similar to the previous issue but with another legend
JAMES VI 1567-1603 (Before English Accession)	*1st Coinage* *(1567-71)* Sword dollar (30s) or Ryal Two-thirds sword dollar One-third sword dollar *2nd Coinage* *(1572-80)* Noble (6s 8d) or half merk Half noble Two merk (26s 8d) or Thistle dollar Merk piece *3rd Coinage* *(1580-1)* Sixteen shilling piece		Twenty pound piece Ducat (80s)	James VI's coinage was even more extensive than that of Mary's, with eight gold and silver issues, including several new denominations. As with Mary's reign the coinage may be distinctly divided, but this time into two parts—before and after accession to the English throne in 1603. The numerous denominations and a similarity in their names as well as an absence of value on individual coins tend to be confusing. As a guide, given with the list of coins and the dates of issue, the nominal values of each individual coin are shown in brackets. In almost every case the name of a coin has some connection with its design. The billion and copper coinage, however, was not so extensive's as Mary's. This coinage as a whole is considered by many to be by far

TYPE	SILVER	BASE METALS	GOLD	NOTES
	Eight shilling piece			the most artistic of Scotland's coins. James's first coins were a continuation of Mary's ryals, sometimes known as sword dollars. The second issue comprised of a few gold twenty pound pieces and silver nobles (also known as half merks) and divisions, issued from 1572 to 1580. New gold coins named nobles (or ducats) were issued dated 1580, which showed a bareheaded portrait of the young king, as well as 16, 8, 4 and 2 silver shilling pieces. The crowned lion of the gold lion noble (1584-8) may be seen on the current George VI 'Scottish' shilling reverses in honour of his Queen (now the Queen Mother) as a compliment to her Scottish ancestry. Then followed in 1588 the attractively designed thistle noble of 23 carat gold with a value of £7 6s 8d. Although no silver was produced from 1585, for the next six years a quantity of billon placks were circulated. At this time it was decided that too many varied denominations of gold and silver were circulating, resulting in much confusion. Accordingly all earlier coins were withdrawn except the thistle noble. In place of the withdrawn coins another new coin, the 1591 gold hat piece (a name acquired by the peculiar headgear of the king displayed on the obverse) was issued together with the silver balance half merk and quarter merk (a name acquired from
	Four shilling piece			
	Two shilling piece			
	4th Coinage *(1582-8)*			
	Forty shilling piece		Lion noble (75s) or Scottish angel Two-thirds lion noble One-third lion noble	
	Thirty shilling piece			
	Twenty shilling piece			
	Ten shilling piece			
			5th Coinage *(1588-90)* Thistle noble (146s 8d) or Scottish rose noble	
	6th Coinage *(1591-3)*			
	Balance half merk (6s 8d)		Hat piece (80s)	
	Balance quarter merk			
	7th Coinage *(1593-1601)*			
	Ten shilling piece		Rider (100s)	
	Five shilling piece		Half rider	
	Thirty penny piece			
	Twelve penny piece			
	8th Coinage *(1601-4)*			
	Thistle merk (13s 4d)		Sword and Sceptre piece (120s)	
	Half thistle merk			

Catalogue of Scottish Coins

TYPE	SILVER	BASE METALS	GOLD	NOTES
	Quarter thistle merk Eighth thistle merk 	 Billon and Copper Issues 1st Issue (billon) 1583-90 Plack (8d) Half plack 2nd Issue (billon) 1588 Hardhead (2d —two types) Half hardhead 3rd Issue (billon) 1594 Saltire plack (4d) 4th Issue (copper) 1597 Twopence Penny	Half sword and Sceptre piece	the design of a pair of scales above an upright sword). The seventh issue was of gold riders and half riders dated 1593, named from the design of the mounted king. Silver ten shilling pieces together with five shilling, thirty penny and twelve penny pieces were issued at the same time. These silver coins, all dated 1593, replaced the withdrawn silver coinage, which had been of many varied values and denominations. The eighth coinage of 1601 (when the gold sword and sceptre piece and its half, and the silver thistle merk and its divisions, were issued) was a result of a further rise in metal values, again requiring the withdrawal of the previous issues. No early billion coin was issued; the coins of Mary being plentiful they continued in use, but reduced in value to half their original issue price. Forgeries were numerous and the penalties harsh, but this did not appear to be a deterent; there is ample evidence of the law being enforced on culprits over long periods in the most harsh and brutal manner. The first billon coins were issued in 1583 in placks and half placks, followed by hardheads and half hardheads in 1588. The last billon issue was in 1594, when new coins named saltire placks at a value of 4d were circulated. The final small coinage before James became king of England was in 1597, when

TYPE	SILVER	BASE METALS	GOLD	NOTES
				copper pennies and twopences were issued, probably made with the aid of a new machine which cut flans from copper sheets of even thickness
JAMES VI 1603-25 Scottish coins only (After accession to the English throne)	1st Coinage (1604-9) Sixty shillings Thirty shillings Twelve shillings Six shillings Two shillings One shilling Sixpence		Unit or Sceptre (£1 English £12 Scots) Double crown (half unit) Britain crown (quarter unit) Half crown (eighth unit) Thistle crown (4s English) (48s Scots)	James VI of Scotland became James I of Great Britain in 1603, after the death of Elizabeth. His first coinage issued in 1603 was for circulation in England only, but the first coinage of the combined countries was 1604 and was the same for both England and Scotland except that the Scottish coins, almost without exception, showed the thistle mint mark. With the Scottish coinage nominally 1/12th of that in England, first impressions when comparing the two are rather confusing. The second issue for Great Britain was in 1610 and was of identical denominations to the first issue; the arms, which were on all coins except the thistle crown, two shillings, one shilling and sixpence, bore Scotland in the first and fourth quarters, England and France in the second, and Ireland in the third. The thistle crown and the three low denominations remained unaltered. No billon coins were issued but in 1613 copper pennies and twopences were issued, relieving a considerable scarcity. A second issue of twopences followed in 1623, the alteration being an abbreviation in the legend
	2nd Coinage (1610-25) (redesigned shield) Sixty shillings Thirty shillings Twelve shillings Six shillings		Unit or sceptre (£1 English £12 Scots) Double crown Britain crown Half crown	
		Copper Issues 1st Issue (1613) Twopence Penny 2nd Issue (1623) Twopence		
CHARLES I 1625-49	1st Coinage 1625-36)			There is practically no difference between the earlier

Catalogue of Scottish Coins   321

TYPE	SILVER	BASE METALS	GOLD	NOTES
	(Similar to 2nd Coinage of James VI but name and designers' initials different) Sixty shillings Thirty shillings Twelve shillings Six shillings Two shillings One shilling Sixpence		Unit Double crown Britain crown	coins of Charles I and those of his father. In the design of the king's effigy the beard is a little shorter while the name was automatically changed to CAROLUS; the only dated coin was the sixpence. These were the only changes in the first issue. The gold thistle crown, the half crown and the silver sixpence were probably omitted. The appointment of Nicholas Briot as Master of the Scottish Mint was fortunate for the coinage. His skill as a die-cutter together with the use of the mill and screw press had a very beneficial effect on the coinage, though Briot's skill was not recognised at first and he had to contend with much opposition.
	2nd Coinage (1636) (Hammered coinage by Briot) Half merk Forty penny piece Twenty penny piece			
	3rd Coinage (1637) Sixty shilling piece Thirty shilling piece (two types) Twelve shilling piece (three types) Six shilling piece (two types) Half merk Forty penny		Unit Half unit Britain crown Half crown	The 2nd Coinage was a hammered one issued in 1636 by Briot. No gold coins were issued. The 3rd Coinage which followed during the next year was much the same as before but with a number of minor variations in the legends. Some of these coins were designed by Briot while others were from dies produced by his son-in-law John Falconer. The 4th Coinage of 1642 was of two denominations only — three shilling and two shilling pieces. The earliest copper coins were similar to those of James VI, issued in 1629 in twopenny and penny denominations frequently known as turners and half turners. The 2nd Issue was a newly de-

v

TYPE	SILVER	BASE METALS	GOLD	NOTES
	piece (three types) Twenty penny piece (three types) 4th Coinage (1642) Three shilling piece Two shilling piece	Copper Issues 1st Issue (1629) Twopence (or turner) Penny (or half turner) 2nd Issue (1632) Copper Twopence (or turner) 3rd Issue (1642, 1644, 1650) Twopence (or turner, or bodle)		signed twopence, on a very small flan caused by economy measure of thirty-six coins to the oz. Of this issue there are at least six known minor variations, an issue for whose supervision Briot had been sent specially to Scotland. The copper coins of a 3rd issue were struck in 1642 in twopence only. Two more allotments of copper were used to strike more of this issue, dated 1644 and 1650. These last twopences are sometimes known as bodles
CHARLES II 1660-85	1st Coinage (1664-75) Four merks (three varieties) Two merks (three varieties)			No Scottish coin was struck during the rule of the Commonwealth and Cromwell. Not long after his father's death in 1649, Charles II was proclaimed king in Edinburgh but it was not until the Com-

Catalogue of Scottish Coins

TYPE	SILVER	BASE METALS	GOLD	NOTES
	Merk (two varieties) Half merk (two varieties) 2nd Coinage (1675-82) Dollar Half dollar Quarter dollar Eighth dollar Sixteenth dollar	Copper Issues 1st Issue (1663) Twopence (or turner, or bodle) 2nd Issue (1677) Bawbee (or sixpence) Bodle (or turner)		monwealth had crumbled that Charles II was restored to the throne. It was not until 1660 that the king really ruled the country. The first coins of his reign were copper twopences similar to those of Charles I. The numerals II found on a number of these may have been intended for a denomination number, or alternatively it may have been intended for the II of Charles II. The first full issue of silver was in 1664 when four merks, two merks, merks and half merks were struck by the mill press. All of these are in either two or three minor variations—a thistle above the head, and a thistle or the letter F below the bust (or both). All these coins bear a date between the years 1664 and 1675. A rise in the price of silver caused the coins to be revalued and a new issue of a different type circulated in 1675. These were the dollar and its divisions of half, quarter, eighth and sixteenth. The main differences of this second issue from the earlier one were the bust of the king now turned to the left instead of to the right, and on the reverse, the order in which the arms of the shield occur is varied. The first copper issue was twopences as already mentioned. A second issue followed in 1677 with a copper bawbee (6d) and a bodle (or turner)—these last names were now preferred to 'twopence'. A com-

TYPE	SILVER	BASE METALS	GOLD	NOTES
				parison of Charles II's coins show that mis-spelling is not unusual, while the variety of stops used are considerable
JAMES VII 1685-88) (James II of England)	Forty shillings Ten shillings			James II of England, known as James VII of Scotland, struck no gold or copper coins for Scotland and only forty shilling and ten shilling pieces in silver. Although sixty shilling pieces, struck specially for collectors, are known to exist, they have been issued in more recent times from dies that were made probably in 1687 or 1688. Such a regrettable action can be of no advantage to numismatists generally. All the issued coins bear dates and marks of value
WILLIAM and MARY 1688-94	Sixty shillings Forty shillings Twenty shillings Ten shillings Five shillings	*Copper* Bawbee Bodle		The silver coins omitted in James VII's reign—sixty shillings, twenty shillings and five shillings—were minted in William and Mary's reign, together with the forty shillings and ten shillings. The obverse design is of interest as it shows the conjoined busts of William and Mary facing left. On the reverse the arms of Nassau is added to the centre of the shield bearing the existing arms. The edge inscription of the two larger silver coins together with the motto PROTEGIT ET ORNAT (It protects and adorns), represents the year of reign from the coronation; for example, when PRIMO and SECUNDO occur on similarly dated coins of 1690 it merely re-

Catalogue of Scottish Coins 325

TYPE	SILVER	BASE METALS	GOLD	NOTES
				cords, in the first instance, one year of reign completed (PRIMO), while SECUNDO denotes that the king was in his second year as ruler
WILLIAM II (of Scotland) 1694-1702 (William III of England and William I of Great Britain)	Sixty shillings Forty shillings Twenty shillings Ten shillings Five shillings	Copper Bawbee Bodle (two types)	Pistole Half pistole	Although the second monarch for Scotland with the name of William and the third for England, the king used the title for Great Britain, France and Ireland which was the first of that name. Following earlier custom he omitted the numeral I after his name. Silver and copper coins continued after the death of Mary but with William's effigy only. The only alterations other than this were on the five shillings when a three-headed thistle was substituted for the previous monogram, and on the bodle where a sword and sceptre were substituted for the monogram. Abbreviation in the legend also occurs in this coin. The 1695 issue shows a sword and sceptre that slightly differ from the later years of 1696 and 1697. In 1701 the Darien Company, a trading firm operating between Scotland and the West African coast, successfully applied to have the African gold transported by their ship, the *Rising Sun*, made into coins. These were named pistoles and half pistoles showing the Darien crest—the sun rising over the horizon at sea
ANNE 1702-14	Before the Act of Union (1702-7)			The final years when a separate coinage was issued for Scotland ended in the reign

TYPE	SILVER	BASE METALS	GOLD	NOTES
	Ten shillings (two types) Five shillings (two types) *After the Act of Union (1707-14)* Crown Half crown Shilling Sixpence			of Anne, when ten shilling and five shilling pieces were issued before the Act of Union. The arms of Orange were omitted from the shield on the ten shillings and apart from the changed effigy and legend, the abbreviation REG was used in 1705, but spelled in full (REGINA) in 1706. On the five shillings, the later legends were much abbreviated with ANNA being shortened to AN. After the Act of Union, which took place in 1707, the Edinburgh mint continued working on coins identical to the London mint except for the letter E shown below the bust, to denote all coins struck north of the border. The denominations were crowns, half crowns, shillings and sixpences. Strikings are also known to exist from dies dated 1711 E of fourpences and twopences, probably from Edinburgh dies that had been produced but never used during the official period, which ended in 1709

CATALOGUE OF IRISH COINS

TYPE	SILVER	BASE METALS	GOLD	NOTES
HIBERNO-NORSE PERIOD Late Tenth Century to early Twelfth	Penny			The first coins of Ireland struck in that country were by raiding Norsemen who had settled there. The first of these known to strike coins with any certainty was Sihtric III (989-1023) in 995. Other Norse kings who may have issued coins before Sihtric were Ifars I (870-72) and Anlaf IV (962-81). Early issues followed closely the Anglo-Saxon silver pennies revealing excellently produced coins. Later coins deteriorated with blundered legends, some being quite impossible to read. Many early types copied the Aethelred CRVX type, some with the name of Sihtric; others imitated Aethelred's long cross pennies. Later ones copied the helmet type, the small cross type, and, about 1016, the quatrefoil pennies of Canute. From this period more long cross types were in evidence. These were well produced and are distinguishable from the earlier coins by pellets in the angles of the cross. Another type from this period had cruder strikings with a number of blunders in the legends. Later long cross types showed the reverses, which appear to have been struck with the die, part engraved and part punched. There are numerous imita-

Catalogue of Irish Coins

TYPE	SILVER	BASE METALS	GOLD	NOTES
				tions of Norman, Anglo-Saxon and Northern European coins from the period beginning with the Norman Conquest. Another type of Bracteate silver coins, which are very thin and have a design on one side only, were almost unknown until a large hoard was found in 1837. They were probably struck by native rulers in the late eleventh or early twelfth centuries. Those known as semi-bracteates may have been obverse and reverse types struck at different times by the Dublin mint of the Hiberno-Norsemen
PRINCE JOHN 1172-99 as Lord of Ireland [see also as King 1199-1216]	*1st Coinage* (c 1158) *Profile Issue* Halfpenny *2nd Coinage* (c 1185) *Dominus Issue* *1st Type* Halfpenny Farthing *2nd Type* Halfpenny Farthing *3rd Type* (1198-9) *Cross Pommée* Halfpenny			In 1172 Henry II handed over his newly acquired title of Lord of Ireland to his ten-year-old son John. When John first visited Ireland in 1185 he struck halfpennies with an effigy in profile facing to the right. This was followed by a second coinage of both halfpennies and farthings, issued in three types about the year 1190 and again in about 1194 to 1198, known as the Dominus issue. The third type was in halfpennies only and is known as the Cross Pommée type. These three types showed a full-face within an inner circle
JOHN DE COURCY 1177-1204 Self-styled Lord of Ulster	Halfpenny Farthing			During the issues of John, unofficial coins of John de Courcy—self-styled Lord of Ulster for twenty-six years until 1204—were circulated. He was accepted by Henry II

Catalogue of Irish Coins

TYPE	SILVER	BASE METALS	GOLD	NOTES
				in 1185. His coins were halfpennies and farthings. The former shows a bishop's crozier within an inner circle on the obverse, while the latter shows crosses—usually crosses potent or double pommée—or cross potent on both sides. The latter are in several varieties with varied inscriptions
JOHN 1172 (Lord of Ireland) and 1199-1214 (King)	Penny Halfpenny Farthing			The third issue of John was after he had become king of England in 1199 but no further Irish issues appeared until the Rex coinage in 1204. These coins are clearly identifiable by the head enclosed in a triangle with a sceptre on the right. All the reverses have a similar triangle. The denominations are in pennies, halfpennies and farthings
HENRY III 1216-72	Penny (cut) Halfpenny (cut) Farthing			Henry III allowed his brother Richard, the Earl of Cornwall, in 1248 to issue coin for twelve years in England and Ireland in exchange for a sum of money, with the brothers sharing the profits. It was not until 1251 that pennies were minted in Dublin with dies produced at the London mint. The Dublin mint worked for three years only and closed in 1254. The reverses display the long cross with the triangle enclosing the king's effigy on the obverse—not unlike those of King John (3rd Issue). To supply the requirements of halfpennies and farthings, pennies were cut in halves and quarters

TYPE	SILVER	BASE METALS	GOLD	NOTES
EDWARD I 1254 (Lord of Ireland) 1272-1307 (King)	1st Coinage *(1276-9)* Henricus type Penny 2nd Coinage *(1279-1302)* Edward type 1st Type *(1280-4)* Penny (four varieties) 2nd Type *(1294)* Penny 3rd Type *(1295)* Penny 4th Type *(1297-1302)* Penny Halfpenny Farthing			The first coinage of Edward I was a continuation of Henry III's silver pennies. This began in 1276 when the Dublin mint restarted after a twelve-year interval of no coin production. To distinguish between the coins of father and son, the hair and beard of the latter is clearly identifiable from the cruder punched dots and lines of Henry's coins. The second issue of 1279-1302 was a complete recoinage with the name of Edward (EDW) in the legend instead of Henricus, with the triangle containing the king's head inverted. For convenience these may be divided into four types, which again may be divided into varieties. The last type (1297-1302) struck halfpennies and farthings in addition and reveal a number of variations of the two larger denominations. Forgeries are sometimes found and frequently mules with the obverses and reverses of English and Irish dies mixed up
EDWARD II 1307-27				No coins appear to have been struck during Edward II's reign, though pennies with an effigy of the king-in-the-triangle type were formerly attributed to him
EDWARD III 1327-77	Halfpenny			With the exception of the two halfpennies which are considered to belong to Edward III, no coinage is known to have been issued. Possibly a very small output, to which these two specimens belong, was struck

Catalogue of Irish Coins 331

TYPE	SILVER	BASE METALS	GOLD	NOTES
RICHARD II 1377-99				No coins appear to have been struck during Richard II's reign
HENRY IV 1399-1413				No coins appear to have been struck during Henry IV's reign
HENRY V 1413-22				No coins appear to have been struck during Henry V's reign
HENRY VI 1422-61	Penny			The British Museum appear to be one of the two known holders of the only two Irish coins (pennies) of Henry VI. These coins were the result of an ordinance of 1425 authorising pennies similar in weight and fineness to those in England to be struck in Dublin. A second issue was decided in 1460 by his Anglo-Irish Parliament, but before this decision could be implemented, Edward IV had seized the throne in the following year
EDWARD IV 1461-83	*Anonymous 'Crown' Coinage (c 1461-3)* Groat (three types) Penny *2nd 'Crown' Coinage (1463-5)* Groat Half groat Penny *3rd Coinage (Central Cross on Rose*			The accession of Edward IV did not hinder the decision of the Anglo-Irish Parliament to strike a new coinage. It cannot be decided whether this coinage should be attributed to Henry VI, as it was his Parliament that decided to strike a new coinage, or to credit Edward IV with this first issue of his reign. For this reason the first coinage is sometimes known as 'Anonymous' or 'Untitled' issue. Groats and pennies were produced between the years 1461 and 1463 showing a large crown on the obverse.

TYPE	SILVER	BASE METALS	GOLD	NOTES
	1465-7) Groat Penny 4th Coinage (Crowned Bust 1467-70) Double groat Groat Half groat Penny 5th Coinage (Heavy Cross and Pellets 1470-3) Groat Half groat Penny Halfpenny 6th Coinage (Light Cross and Pellets 1473-8) Groat Half groat Penny 7th Coinage (Central Rose on Cross Reverse c 1478-83) Groat Penny	 Copper and Billon Issues 1st Issue (c 1461) Half farthing (Copper) 2nd Issue (1462) Farthing (Billon)		A second crown coinage followed in 1463-5 with the king's name and his Irish title. The denominations were the same except that half groats were now added. The next two issues suffered progressive reductions in weight—the double groat of the fourth issue being reduced to half the silver weight of the first issue with the other denominations similarly treated. The designs of these two issues (the third and fourth) were also changed to the Yorkist rose on the obverse of the earlier issue and a crowned bust on the later one. The reverses displayed the sun in splendour. The 1470-73 heavy cross and pellet coinage and the 1473-8 light cross and pellet coinage were quite similar to the existing English coins of Edward; even so the 'heavy' was slightly lighter than its English counterpart, at 41 grains to the groat, but the 'light' was reduced to 32 grains. These last two issues are conspicuous by the very large number of varieties, particularly of the penny of the 'light', which, when including the six issuing mints, exceeds thirty. These two issues with others of Edward reveal 'privy' marks (a check on the moneyers for fraud) and mint marks (a code for the issuing dates). The final issue, which took place during Edward's second reign, continued with the facing bust. The rose in the centre of the cross is con-

Catalogue of Irish Coins

TYPE	SILVER	BASE METALS	GOLD	NOTES
		3rd Issue (*1463-5*) Farthing (Copper) Half farthing (Copper) 4th Issue (c *1467-70?*) Farthing (Copper)		spicuous on the reverse. The first copper issue was in half farthings (or 'Patricks') circulated about the same time as the Anonymous coinage. A billon farthing (mostly of copper) followed in 1462, with another copper issue circulating with the second crown coinage in farthings and half farthings. The copper farthing shows three crowns within a shield, with a central rose over a sun on the reverse; its date is uncertain but probably about 1467-70
EDWARD V April to June 1483				No coins appear to have been issued for Edward V's short reign, although it has been suggested that a groat of the three crowns with an E below was his, distinguishing it from Edward IV's. It has been now established that the three crown issues began after the proclamation of July 1483 and March 1484
RICHARD III 1483-5	*1st Coinage* (*Facing Bust and Rose on Cross 1483*) Groat (two types) Half groat Penny *2nd Coinage* Penny *3rd Coinage* Groat			The coins of Richard III were of silver only, struck in a first issue of groats, half groats and pennies—the half groats being a recent discovery belonging to the first issue of the front face obverse type, with a central rose on the reverse cross. The groats are in two types—one from an Edward IV die with Richard's name (RICA) overstamping EDWA. The other type is from a Richard die replacing the makeshift one. Another issue, which minted pennies only, was of the cross

TYPE	SILVER	BASE METALS	GOLD	NOTES
				and pellets reverse type. The third issue was the three crowns issue of groats only
HENRY VII 1485-1509	1st period, Three Crowns Issues 1485-90 1st Issue (1485-7) Groat Half groat Penny Halfpenny 2nd Issue (1487?) Groat Half groat 3rd Issue (1487) Groat 4th Issue (1488-90) Groat Half groat 2nd period, Portrait Issue (1496 or 1497-1503) 1st Issue Groat 2nd Issue Groat 3rd period, Portrait Issue (c 1503-7) 1st Issue Groat Half groat Penny			The lack of documentary records relating to Henry VII's Irish coinage makes the sequence in which some of the coins occur somewhat speculative, though there is little difficulty in allocating them to Henry. Soon after his accession he had to deal with a Yorkist plot to place on the throne Lambert Simnel, supported by the Earl of Kildare —a member of the Fitzgerald family and the late deputy of Richard, Duke of York. This rebellion resulted in the groats of 1487 having the Fitzgerald arms on either side of the obverse shield of arms. The three crowns issues were continuous from Henry's earlier coins until 1490, followed by the portrait issues of about 1496 or 1497. Those of the first three crowns period (1485-90) may be divided into four types: (1) with the king's name in the legend with an H under the three crowns; (2) omission of the initial and the king's name; (3) the Fitzgerald arms added; and (4) similar to (1) but with lis and lions on the royal arms slightly altered. The second period issues occur about 1496 or 1497 until 1503 when the facing portrait of the king, either with an open or an arched crown, was substituted on the obverses and a plain cross on the reverses. The third period issues of

Catalogue of Irish Coins

TYPE	SILVER	BASE METALS	GOLD	NOTES
	2nd Issue Groat (four types)			about 1503-7 also have a facing portrait with either an arched crown without jewels or an open crown. A cross fourchée is on the reverses. This last issue is in four types with groats the only denomination
HENRY VIII 1509-47	Harp Coinage 1st Issue (1534-40) Groat Half groat 2nd Issue (1540-2) Groat (three types) 3rd Issue (1543) Groat 4th Issue (1544) Sixpenny groat 5th Issue (1544-6) Sixpenny groat 6th Issue (1546-7) Sixpenny groat Harp groat			As in his father's reign Henry VIII's documentary records of the Irish coinage are almost non-existent, though there were numerous types circulated. Only silver coins were struck. The order in which they were issued can be reasonably certain to be correct. Although Henry became king of England in 1509, no coins were produced until 1534 when the first 'harp' issue was circulated in groats and half groats. These were only slightly debased below the recognised standard. They displayed the title DOMINUS in the legend with the crowned arms on the obverse. On the reverse was a crowned harp dividing two initials h and A representing the names of Henry and Anne (Anne Boleyn) 1434-5. Similarly, other coins have the initials of Henry and Jane Seymour (h and I) 1436-7, Henry and Katherine Howard (h and K) 1540, and another in the same year (h and R) presumed to represent HENRICUS REX. The second 'harp' issue—of groats only—continued with the DOMINUS title but with a new mint mark; another type omitted the numeral VIII from the

TYPE	SILVER	BASE METALS	GOLD	NOTES
				legend, while in 1541 the legend title was changed to HIBERNIE REX in place of DOMINUS HIBERNIE. The third 'harp' issue continued with the 'Rex' legend and at the same time the silver content was improved over the second issue. Again the only coin was the groat but with a rose mint mark. The fourth and fifth issues of 1544 and 1544-6 were of 8oz fine and 6oz fine respectively. These two issues were for the sixpenny groat only, both with the lis mint mark, but with the later issue having either 'REX S' or 'REX 37' (the regnal year) on the reverse legend. The sixth issue should strictly be classed as billon as it contained only 3oz of fine silver (75 per cent alloy). These were in two denominations; the sixpenny groat bore a changed legend ending with the regnal year (38). Another type omits the regnal year. The second denomination was the 'harp' groat identified by four pellets, which was possibly a mark of value stamped on in a later reign
EDWARD VI 1547-53	*Posthumous Coinage of Henry VIII* (1547-c 1550) Sixpence (four types) Threepence (three types) Three-halfpence (two types) Three farthings			The death of Henry VIII did not immediately cause the coinage of Ireland to be changed. The harp issues, omitting Henry's regnal year at the end of the legend, continued but with a different appearance to the previous harp coins. They resemble far more the English groats of 1550-1, and repre-

Catalogue of Irish Coins 337

TYPE	SILVER	BASE METALS	GOLD	NOTES
	Edward VI Effigy Coinage (1552) Shilling			sent the final issue of a coinage from the Dublin mint until it was reopened in 1641 during the reign of Charles I. Some of the earliest coins, however, are believed to have been struck from dies made in London. There are four types of sixpences, which are the same size as the English groats. They are (1) an English style bust, (2) and (3) a large and a smaller facing bust, and (4) another turning half right. The threepence show similar busts, but without the large facing effigy; the three-halfpence suggests the early English style with a half right portrait; and the threefarthings displays the large full-face of the monarch. Of the coins showing the portrait of the young King Edward only one appears to have general acceptance as belonging to Ireland. This is the shilling of 1552, showing the young crowned bust with the legend on the reverse ending in MDLII
MARY TUDOR 1553-8	Issue before marriage (1553-4) Shilling Groat Half groat Penny			The only Irish coins struck by Mary were of silver about 6oz fine. The standard of the early issue showed an improvement on those of Henry VIII's and Edward VI's, with the weights similar to those of the English standard; many of Mary's coins, however (and later those of Mary and Philip), have been counterfeited. The first issue (ie the coins before her marriage) was of shillings, groats, half groats, and base pennies

w

TYPE	SILVER	BASE METALS	GOLD	NOTES
				specially struck in the Tower mint, with the crowned harp for use in Ireland. The shillings (MDLIII and MDLIV) are the only ones bearing a date
MARY and PHILIP 1554-8		Issue after marriage Billon Shilling Groat Penny (English type)		Following her marriage to Philip of Spain another issue of coins was struck. These showed the royal arms on the obverse. The shillings and groats are unusual in two ways: (1) the design shows a crowned king and queen vis-à-vis, and (2) the debasement of the coins was reduced to 3oz fine (75 per cent alloy) qualifying the coinage for billon only. In 1557 the circulation of the pennies was restricted in Ireland and prohibited in England
ELIZABETH I 1558-1603	2nd Coinage (1561) Shilling Groat	1st Coinage (1558) Billon Shilling Groat 3rd Coinage (1598) Billon Sixpence Threepence Copper Coinage (1601-2) Penny Halfpenny		Elizabeth's three coinages for Ireland were issued once in silver and twice in billon, while at the end of her reign, under an indenture of 1601, copper coins were struck. For much of her reign English money circulated in Ireland, as shown in various hoards. The first issue of 1558 continued Mary and Philip's base coinage of 3oz fine silver with crowned bust of the queen facing left. The reverse displayed a crowned harp dividing the crowned letters E and R. The second issue of 1561 was of good silver with similar denominations, while the reverse differed from the first issue with a shield bearing three harps. The third coinage of 1598 reverted to the base metal of the first issue. The design of the ob-

Catalogue of Irish Coins 339

TYPE	SILVER	BASE METALS	GOLD	NOTES
				verse displayed a plain shield, and the reverse a modified crowned harp in denominations of sixpence, threepence, penny and halfpenny. The copper pennies and halfpennies followed the last billon coins in design except that the harp divided the date 16-01 and 16-02
JAMES I 1603-25	1st Coinage (1603-4) Shilling Sixpence 2nd Coinage (1604-7) Shilling Sixpence	Token Copper Farthing Issue (1613) Farthing (four varieties)		James I was the first king to rule over a united England, Scotland and Ireland. His coinage was of the same metals as the previous reign with the silver (9oz fine) in two coinages of 1603-4 and 1604-7. In 1613 farthing tokens were issued under a royal licence with a patent granted to Lord Harrington. These were authorised to circulate in Ireland as well as in England. The silver coins of both issues were in denominations of shillings and sixpences but with different legends. In both issues the shilling had a second variety with the king's beard differing in each case. The token farthings were in four varieties—the first being a small coin with the obverse showing a crown over crossed sceptres. The remaining three varieties have their legends starting in different positions in relation to the design, while the fourth variety is oval in shape. All four reverses show the crowned harp
CHARLES I 1625-49				The only coins of Charles I issued as a regal currency in Ireland were the token farth-

TYPE	SILVER	BASE METALS	GOLD	NOTES
		Farthing Copper Token Coinage (1625-44) 'Richmond Issue' Farthing (two types) Maltravers Issue Farthing (six types) 'Money of Necessity' Kilkenny Money (1642) Copper Halfpenny (two types) Farthing (two types)		ings circulated under a patent granted to the Duchess of Richmond in 1625 and Lord Maltravers in 1635. The absence of a royal coinage was probably caused by the rebellion of the Irish catholics in 1641, and civil war in England. The Irish were embittered by the introduction of English and Scottish settlers who had dispossessed them of their land. This ill-advised scheme, first introduced by Mary Tudor, finally caused the catholics to burst into open rebellion. Many thousands of protestant settlers were killed in the fighting that followed. Many, however, withdrew to the defended towns of Cork, Bandon, Kinsale and Youghal, where crudely struck money was circulated. These coins were known as 'money of necessity'. Overstamped foreign coins from such countries as Spain, Spanish America, France, etc, were also pressed into service. By 1642 the two catholic factions (pro-royalists and anti-royalists) merged to form a combined group known as The Confederated Catholics, who met at Kilkenny to draw up laws for governing Ireland. There they issued copper coins based on the designs of the token farthings of 1625 and 1635, though the finish was much inferior. After General Munro had landed an army in Ulster to suppress the rebellion, civil war broke out in England between the
	1st Silver Issue Crown Half crown Shilling Ninepence Sixpence Groat 2nd Silver Issue (Number of annulets on reverse representing value) Ninepence Sixpence		Inchiquin Money (1642) Double pistole Pistole	

Catalogue of Irish Coins

TYPE	SILVER	BASE METALS	GOLD	NOTES
	Groat			king and his parliament causing Lord Inchiquin to take command of the protestant army in Munster where he was vice-president. In the years 1642-6 three issues of silver were struck as well as a few gold coins named pistoles and even rarer double pistoles; these irregular polygon-shaped pieces with the weights stamped on both sides were named Inchiquin money. Today, however, it is known that it was the lord justices of Ireland who gave the orders for their issue. The coins do not have an official legal status. Another issue was made in 1642-3 known as Dublin money. This consisted of crowns and half crowns similarly shaped but with a different value stamp. The 'blacksmith's money', showing the king on horseback, is given as 1642 and is attributed to the Confederate Catholics. The date, however, is uncertain and many consider that it was issued as late as 1649 by royalist catholics. Ormonde money issued in 1643-4 was named after the Marquis of Ormonde who became Lieutenant of Ireland in 1643. This money may also have been issued by the lord justices. The coins showed a crown above the letter C R on the obverses and the value on the reverses. Rebel money of 1643 is believed to have been issued by the Confederated Catholics in opposition to the coin production of the Ormonde money. The towns
	Threepence			
	Dublin Money Issue (1642-3)			
	Crown			
	Half crown			
	'Blacksmith's Money' (1642? or 1649?)			
	Half crown			
	Ormonde Money (1643)			
	Crown			
	Half crown			
	Shilling			
	Sixpence			
	Groat			
	Threepence			
	Half groat			
	Rebel Money (1643)			
	Crown			
	Half crown			
	Siege Money (1642-9?)			
	Cork	Copper		
	Shilling	Halfpenny		
	Sixpence	Farthing		
		Copper Farthing from Bandon Kinsale and Youghal (three varieties)		

TYPE	SILVER	BASE METALS	GOLD	NOTES
				of Cork, Bandon, Kinsale and Youghal, which were virtually isolated from outside assistance, all struck crude coins for their own use showing the town's name or its first initial. Cork issued silver shillings and sixpences in 1647 and copper halfpence and farthings with the name CORK on each coin. Bandon, Kinsale and Youghal all struck copper farthings with their own identification mark —Bandon (three castles), Kinsale (KG in a circle of pellets) and Youghal (letters Y T)
COMMON-WEALTH 1649-60				The period of the Commonwealth produced no coinage in Ireland, but the money issued in England quite conceivably was intended for Irish circulation as the Irish harp shield was given the same prominence on the coinage as the St George shield. No evidence, however, exists of the Commonwealth coins circulating in Ireland. A large number of copper token coins were circulated by merchants from the cities and towns
CHARLES II 1660-85		'Armstrong' Copper Coinage (1660-1) Farthing St Patrick's Token Copper Coinage (c 1674) Halfpenny Farthing		It is sometimes claimed that the crown and half crown of the Ormonde silver coin issues were struck after the death of Charles I in 1649, when the Marquis of Ormonde had proclaimed Charles II king of Ireland. While this is possible, there is no evidence that the date of these coins is 1649. The first coins were token copper farthings which showed a crown and

TYPE	SILVER	BASE METALS	GOLD	NOTES
		Dublin Token Copper Coinage (1676-9) Halfpenny		two sceptres. These were struck under a royal patent granted to Sir Thomas Armstrong in 1660 for twenty-one years, banning the use of all other tokens. The Irish strongly opposed this; consequently only a very small number circulated. In 1663-73 large numbers of tokens appeared but it was about 1674 that the St Patrick coinage was issued. Information regarding these coins is lacking, but it is likely that the Dublin Corporation contracted out to one of a number of token coin manufacturers in the city to produce them. They were in copper halfpennies and farthings displaying St Patrick preaching to the people with the arms of Dublin shield beside him. The reverse shows King David playing a harp beneath a crown. Most of the known specimens today have a brass plug. The Dublin copper halfpennies were probably issued in similar conditions to the St Patrick's money. These show a crowned harp on the obverse and the arms of Dublin on the reverse with the date (1676-9) above. In the following year Sir Thomas Armstrong and Colonel George Legge were granted a licence to produce halfpence for twenty-one years. The coins display the bust of Charles II on the obverse and a harp beneath the crown on the reverse. After 1680-2 the large letters in the legend ceased, while from
		Armstrong and Legg's Copper Regal Coinage (1680-4) Halfpenny		

TYPE	SILVER	BASE METALS	GOLD	NOTES
				1681 to 1684 small letters were used
JAMES II 1685-8		Regal Copper Coinage (1685-8) Halfpenny		When James II ascended the throne he handed the unexpired patent for the regal halfpennies, previously granted to Armstrong and Legge by Charles II, to the Dublin Lord Mayor, Sir John Knox. These coins were similar to those of the previous reign except that the bust of James II faced left instead of right with the issue continuing until 1688. After James had abandoned the throne and fled from England to France he collected support for his cause from the Continent and landed an army in Ireland at Kinsale. Lack of funds to continue the war caused him to produce a token coinage at Dublin and Limerick in crowns, half crowns, shillings and sixpences, dated 1689 and 1690; this became known as gun money because of its source of metal supply, which relied on the scrap metal from guns, church bells, etc. At first, in 1689, coins of a heavier weight were used, but as the supplies began to fail the 1690 issue was reduced to a smaller and lighter size, with half crowns of the first issue being overstamped as crowns. The crown obverse shows the king on horseback facing left but the remaining denominations display the laureated and draped bust of James facing left. On the reverses, apart from the
		Emergency Gun Money Coinage (1689-90)		
		1st Issue (*Larger Coins 1689*) Half crown Shilling Sixpence		
		2nd Issue (*Smaller Coins 1690*) Crown (overstamped half crown) Half crown Shilling Sixpence (similar size to 1st Issue)		
		Emergency Pewter and White Metal Coinage (1689-90) Crown (half crown size with brass plug) Groat (similar size to sixpence)		

Catalogue of Irish Coins

TYPE	SILVER	BASE METALS	GOLD	NOTES
		Penny (as large as Gun Money shilling) Penny (obv smaller head design) Halfpenny (obv king with shorter hair) Halfpenny (obv smaller head design) *Besieged Limerick Coinage (1690-1)* Halfpenny (shilling sized flan —large) Farthing (shilling sized flan —small)		crown piece, which has a central crown and the four United Kingdom arms in four shields at right angles, the remaining denominations display the value above the crown and sceptres, and the date at the top of the coin. When the gun metal, etc, ran out, white metal, pewter and brass were used. With the first two metals, crowns with a brass plug and a much improved design and striking were circulated, together with groats, pennies and halfpennies. These displayed the same obverses as the gun money, with the groat the same size as the sixpence and the penny (in two types) similar in size to the previous shilling. The halfpenny was very similar to the groat but was reissued with a smaller head and a brass plug. The reverses of these three denominations displayed the crowned harp, the groat showing the addition of numeral II on either side of the harp. The last catholic town to surrender was Limerick, which in 1691 issued halfpennies and farthings, frequently overstruck on gun money coins, the former over the large gun money shilling and the latter over the smaller second issue gun money shilling. The obverses were the normal head of James but the reverses show Hibernia seated and holding a cross

TYPE	SILVER	BASE METALS	GOLD	NOTES
WILLIAM and MARY 1688-94		Copper Halfpenny (two varieties)		Halfpennies were the only Irish coins to be issued in the name of William and Mary. The obverse showed the conjoined busts of the king and queen, while the crown-over-harp design continued on the reverse. The lower part of the crown divided the date 16-92, 16-93, 16-94. A variation shows the letter A, which occurs twice in GRATIA, without the 'crossing' (ie Λ)
WILLIAM III (alone) 1694-1702		Halfpenny (two varieties)		During the reign of William after the death of Mary in 1694, the same copper halfpenny continued, with the obverse changed to a draped effigy of William, dated 1696. Another issue of the same date with an undraped bust of the king was issued but it was of a cruder design. There were several proclamations relating to the coinage of this period but they referred to English and foreign coins circulating in Ireland
ANNE 1702-14				No Irish coinage was issued
GEORGE I 1714-27		Wood's Coinage 1722 Issues (Harp on Hibernia's right side) Halfpenny Farthing 1723-4 Issues (Harp on Hibernia's left side) Halfpenny Farthing		After a period from 1702 to 1722 without an issue in Ireland the absence of small change had become serious. George I was persuaded to grant a patent to produce copper coins, which was sold ultimately to William Wood for £10,000. The production of these began in north London, but later continued in Bristol. Unfortunately Wood provoked the Irish Parliament by producing halfpennies and farthings below the weight

Catalogue of Irish Coins

TYPE	SILVER	BASE METALS	GOLD	NOTES
				of their English counterparts, and with the Irishmen already in belligerent mood, it sparked off a rising anger and general discontent. Wood was compelled to cease production in 1724 and to surrender his patent in 1725. The coins were withdrawn and sent to America, where they circulated with the Rosa Americana halfpence—also a production by Wood. There appears to have been no attempt by the Royal mint to replace this coinage. Both denominations showed a well produced effigy of the king facing right, with the smaller coin having the more abbreviated legend. The reverses show two major types, which occur on both coins. These are Hibernia seated holding a harp at her right side in the 1722 issues and on her left side in 1723-4. There are, however, numerous minor variations of both halfpennies and farthings
GEORGE II 1727-60		Young Head Coinage (1736-55) Copper Halfpenny (three varieties) Farthing (two varieties) Old Head Coinage (1760) Copper Halfpenny Farthing		The withdrawal of Wood's halfpennies and farthings in 1724 left a void in Ireland's small change, which the British government made no attempt to fill. Not surprisingly a number of Irish tokens began to appear in circulation and were generally accepted. These may be said to have begun in 1728 in Dublin. They remained in use until 1736 when the new copper halfpennies and farthings of George II appeared. Presumably the majority were then redeemed by the issuers, in

TYPE	SILVER	BASE METALS	GOLD	NOTES
				easy stages. In Ulster the token coins were more frequently of higher values, twopences and threepences being quite normal. These were not generally in circulation until 1734. The 1736 regal issue of halfpence lasted until 1755 with issues for most years in that period. Farthings appeared a year later, but the only years of issue were 1737, 1738 and 1744. Both denominations showed the laureated bust of the king facing left with the reverses displaying the crowned harp and date beneath. The halfpennies have three varieties: (1) the legend in small lettering, (2) in larger lettering and (3) Georgius spelled GEORGIVS. The farthings have small lettering in 1737-8, and large lettering in 1744. From 1755 no regal coins were issued until 1762, creating another spate of copper tokens. A further halfpenny and farthing coinage with an older effigy of the king was prepared, but his death in October 1760 caused the issue to be held up until 1762. In Dublin a number of token halfpennies and farthings again appeared, dated 1760, an issue known by the name on its obverse—'Voce Populi'. These apparently were withdrawn after the 1762 appearance of the 1760 issue
GEORGE III 1760-1820		London Coinage (1766-82) Copper		The 1760 halfpennies and farthings (not issued until 1762) were made from 50 tons of copper, and, apart from the

Catalogue of Irish Coins

TYPE	SILVER	BASE METALS	GOLD	NOTES
	Bank of Ireland Coinage (1804-13) Six shillings Thirty pence Tenpence (two types) Fivepence	Halfpennies (three types) Soho Coinage (1805-6) Copper Penny Halfpenny Farthing		token coins, sufficed until 1766 when the first Irish coins of the new reign—halfpennies —were issued with the obverse showing the laureated bust of George III and the crowned harp with the date below on the reverse. A further issue dated 1769 was circulated. Another type, also in 1769, was struck with a redesigned bust giving a taller appearance. The third type issued in 1775 displayed the head with longer hair. The silver coinage at this period had become extremely worn and scarce, as in England, and was totally inadequate. Apart from a small issue by the Royal mint in 1787 of shillings and sixpences, no coins had been minted since 1758 (except the 'Northumberland' shillings, which were for complimentary distribution in Dublin by the new Lord Lieutenant—the Duke of Northumberland). The Bank of Ireland bought large stocks of Spanish-American and similarly sized dollars from the Bank of England, and a quantity was sent to Matthew Boulton's Soho mint in Birmingham; these were overstruck with a new design into Six Shilling Bank of Ireland tokens dated 1804. The obverse showed the laureated and draped bust of George III, and the reverse Hibernia seated, facing left, holding the harp with her left hand. In the two following years tenpenny and fivepenny bank tokens circulated with a

TYPE	SILVER	BASE METALS	GOLD	NOTES
				modified bust, and a plain inscription and date across the field on the reverses. In 1808 the thirtypence bank token was issued with a similar obverse but with Hibernia seated—as on the six shillings. In 1813 a redesigned bust was displayed on another tenpenny token issued with a similar reverse inscription and date but enclosed in a wreath. The last copper coins were in pennies, halfpennies and farthings, issued in 1805 and 1806, with another and older portrait of the king. The reverses showed a smaller crowned harp than the previous issues. These were struck at the Soho mint, Birmingham. The Act of Union in 1801, which merged England and Ireland into one realm, caused the inscription in the British recoinage of 1816 to be changed to BRITANNIARUM REX ('King of the Britains')
GEORGE IV 1820-30		Penny Halfpenny		The Exchequers of Britain and Ireland finally merged in 1817, but it was not until 1821 that the currencies were given the same value. A final issue of pennies and halfpennies was made in 1822 and 1823. Irish coins being formally withdrawn from circulation in 1826. From then until 1928 the coinage was exactly that of Britain. The last issue showed George IV's laureated and draped bust facing left, with the crowned harp reverse, this being a modification in design of the last Soho issue of George III

CATALOGUE OF IRISH FREE STATE COINS

TYPE	SILVER	BASE METALS	GOLD	NOTES
1928-37 Issue	Half crown Florin Shilling	Nickel Sixpence (1928-35) Threepence (1928-35) Bronze Penny Halfpenny Farthing		The obverse displays the Irish harp popular as the emblem since Tudor times, while the reverses illustrate life from the Irish countryside with the 2s 6d displaying a standing horse, 2s a salmon, 1s a bull; these are produced in 75 per cent silver and 25 per cent copper. The 6d displays a wolfhound, 3d a sitting hare—both struck in pure nickel; the penny shows a hen and chicks, the ½d a sow and piglets, and the farthing a woodcock in flight. These are in bronze. The issue ceased in 1937 when the new Eire constitution was declared

CATALOGUE OF EIRE COINS

TYPE	SILVER	BASE METALS	GOLD	NOTES
1939-68 Issue	Silver Half crown (1939-43) Florin (1939-43) Shilling (1939-42) Cupro-nickel Half crown (1951-67) Florin (1951-68)	Nickel Sixpence (1939-40) Threepence (1939-40) Bronze Penny (1940-68) Halfpenny (1939-67) Farthing (1939-66)		Apart from minor modifications to the harp of the obverse, the hen on the penny, and the horse on the half crown, the only major alteration was the change in inscription from SAORSTAT EIREANN to EIRE. The extremely low mintages of the 1943 silver half crowns and florins make both coins extremely rare especially the latter. The commemorative ten shilling was not taken up by the public and over half the output was withdrawn and melted down

Catalogue of Eire Coins

TYPE	SILVER	BASE METALS	GOLD	NOTES
	Cupro-nickel Shilling (1951-68) Sixpence (1942-68) Threepence (1942-68)			
Commemorative Issue 1966 (1916 Easter Rising)	Silver Ten shilling (1966)			
Decimal Issue 1971	Cupro-nickel 50 new pence 10 new pence 5 new pence Decimal coins similar to the 50, 10 and 5 new pence were also issued with the following dates: 50 new pence 1970 10 new pence 1969 5 new pence 1969 and 1970	Bronze 2 new pence 1 new penny ½ new penny		The Irish government decreed that the change to decimal currency must coincide with a similar change in Britain. Accordingly both currencies 'went decimal' at the same time, 15 February 1971. Both sets of coins are similar except in designs. Except for the bronze coins which were not issued until the officially announced date, the cupro-nickel coins of 50, 10 and 5 new pence, which were issued before 15 February 1971, were circulated with the object of acquainting the public with their appearance and to avoid congestion at the banks as much as possible. The three coins, 2, 1 and ½ new pence, display reverse designs adapted from Zoomorphic ornaments found in Irish manuscript decoration of the 7th and 8th centuries which are from original ornamental bird detail from the following illuminations: 2 new pence: The Second Bible of Charles-the-Bold (in the Bibliotéque Nationale, Paris)

TYPE	SILVER	BASE METALS	GOLD	NOTES
				1 new pence: The Book of Kells (in Trinity College, Dublin)
				½ new pence: A manuscript in the Cathedral Library, Cologne
				These were prepared by Gabriel Hayes and modelled by the Royal Mint. The three cupro-nickel coins have reverses taken from the designs of the previous issue with the 50 new pence adopting the farthing design of the woodcock in flight, and the 10 and 5 new pence using the same designs of a salmon and a bull as were shown on the 2s and 1s. The dates of the decimal coins issued before 'D' day and which actually bear these dates on the coins are:
				50 new pence 1970
				10 new pence 1969
				5 new pence 1969, 1970
				These coins circulated with the sterling values as 10s, 2s and 1s. Whether future numismatists will class them as pre-decimal period, or within the decimal era, remains to be seen

CATALOGUE OF ISLE OF MAN COINS

TYPE	SILVER	BASE METALS	GOLD	NOTES
CHARLES II 1660-85		Brass penny		This coinage began as privately struck tokens in 1668, but in 1679 it was made legal tender. The issuer was John Murrey, a merchant of Douglas, Isle of Man
ANNE 1702-14		*Copper* Penny Halfpenny		These coins dated 1709 were cast probably in England at the request of the 10th Earl of Derby (1702-36) after the Royal Mint had rejected his request for a regal issue
GEORGE II 1727-60		*1st Issue* *(1733)* *Earl of Derby* *Copper* Penny Halfpenny *2nd Issue* *2nd Duke of* *Atholl* *Copper* Penny Halfpenny		This issue, too, was sent from England on the Earl's instructions but unlike the 1709 issue it was struck. Another issue, however, was struck locally and is superior to the English production. The date of both is 1733. With a change in the ownership of the island a new issue appeared in 1758 with the monogram of the Duke of Atholl on the obverse, a ducal coronet above, and the date below
GEORGE III 1760-1820		*1st Issue* *(1786)* *Copper* Penny Halfpenny *2nd Issue* *(1798)* *Copper* Penny Halfpenny		This issue dated 1786 has an uncommon obverse design by the engraver Lewis Pingo, which shows a laureated bust of a youthful looking king. The obverse of the 2nd Issue is similar to that used on the English 1797 copper issue with its distinctive incuse lettering and date for the legend. The engraver of this

Catalogue of Isle of Man Coins   355

TYPE	SILVER	BASE METALS	GOLD	NOTES
				issue was Conrad Kuchler. Another striking was made (with minor adjustments), dated 1813
VICTORIA 1837-1901		Bronze Penny Halfpenny Farthing		This was the last Isle of Man coinage before English coins took its place. Its date was 1839 when the Manx coin values were reduced from 14 to 12 pennies to the English shilling. Soon after this (May 1840) Manx copper dated before 1839 was demonetised
ELIZABETH II 1952—	*Special Crown Issue (1970)* Five shillings (proof silver and cupro-nickel) *Decimal Issue (1971)* Cupro-nickel Fifty new pence Ten new pence Five new pence	Bronze Two new pence One new pence Half new pence	*Special Gold Issue (1965)* Five pounds One pound Ten shillings	These gold coins issued in 22 carat gold were to celebrate the bicentenary of the Revestment Act of 1765, but because of their high metal value were not circulated. These, and a proof issue of 24 carat, were for the benefit of collectors. In late summer 1970 an issue of cupro-nickel crowns was circulated, with specially selected specimens reserved for collectors. Proof crowns in restricted numbers struck in silver were available at the same time. Although not in operation as a decimal coinage until 15 February 1971 the cupro-nickel and bronze denominations were planned to give the island its own coinage again with the same denominations as the United Kingdom

CATALOGUE OF CHANNEL ISLES COINS BEFORE HENRY VII

TYPE	SILVER	BASE METALS	GOLD	NOTES
NAMES OF EARLY COINS MENTIONED	Livre (livre tournois) Ecu	Freluque (1/32nd of a penny) c 1300 and 1623 Pallyn (brass) c 1550 Sol (or sou) Denier	Ecu d'or Louis d'or	Until the reign of Henry VII (1485-1509) the Channel Isles were considered as one group, but after this period they were treated as separate islands—Jersey being one island, and Guernsey, with Alderney and Sark attached for some administrations, the other. From 1607 the British Government announced that the money of the Channel Isles was that of Normandy. Records relating to detailed use of money in the Channel Isles before this date are very few, though the proximity of the Continent had a major effect on the coinage circulating

The monetary system before 1794 was as follows:

12 deniers	=	4 liards
4 liards	=	1 sol (or sou)
20 sols (or sous)	=	1 livre
5 livres	=	1 silver écu in 1715
6 livres	=	1 silver écu in 1718
9 livres	=	1 silver écu in 1724
4 livres	:=	1 silver écu in 1724
5 livres	=	1 silver écu in 1737
6 livres	=	1 silver écu from 1740

until 1794 when 100 centimes = 1 franc

CATALOGUE OF JERSEY COINS

TYPE	SILVER	BASE METALS	GOLD	NOTES
CHARLES I 1625-49	St George's Money Half crown Shilling Normandy coins Livre	Liard (or double sou)	'Jacobus' (20s)	The gold 'Jacobus', the silver half crown and the shilling were reported to have been issued by Colonel William Smyth in 1646, struck at a mint in Jersey

Catalogue of Jersey Coins

TYPE	SILVER	BASE METALS	GOLD	NOTES
WILLIAM and MARY 1688-94 and WILLIAM (alone) 1694-1702		'French crowns' (silver écu?) 'French half crowns' (silver half écu?)		'French crowns' (possibly six- or five-livre pieces) and half crowns circulated with a value equal to 6s 6d and 3s 3d. These coins probably continued to circulate late into the eighteenth century
GEORGE III 1760-1820	Three shilling token Eighteen pence token			These silver coins were authorised by the States Government in 1812 and issued in 1813 by the Royal Mint from £10,000 of silver bullion. When English money was declared the sole legal tender in 1834, both coins were withdrawn from circulation
VICTORIA 1837-1901		1st Issue (1841-61) Copper 1/13th of a shilling 1/26th of a shilling 1/52nd of a shilling		The effigy on the obverse was engraved by W. Wyon from his own model of the queen taken from actual life. The reverse showing the three leopards passant guardant was redesigned—an alteration supplied by the Jersey Government. The dates of the issue were 1841, 1844, 1851, 1858 and 1861 for the pennies and halfpennies; and for the farthings 1841 and 1861. The Jersey penny (1/13th of a shilling) was still linked to the French livre. The reason for this odd fraction is as follows. As the exchange rate was 26 livres to one sovereign and one livre contained 20 sous, an English shilling equalled 26 sous (or 26 halfpence). It followed, therefore, that a penny equalled 1/13th of a shilling. In 1866 came the first bronze issue following the change of 1860 in Great Britain. The

TYPE	SILVER	BASE METALS	GOLD	NOTES
		2nd Issue (1866-71) Bronze 1/13th of a shilling 1/26th of a shilling 3rd Issue (1877-94) Bronze 1/12th of a shilling 1/24th of a shilling 1/48th of a shilling		dates of issue were 1866, 1870 and 1871. The value of the Jersey penny remained at 13 to the English shilling. In this issue the size of the coins was reduced to that of the British bronze coins, with 12 Jersey pennies to the English shilling. The shield on which the original arms was used in 1279 in Edward I's reign was changed to a plainer design. Heaton & Son of Birmingham were given the contract to strike the coins of the first year (1877), showing their 'H' mint mark. The remaining dates of the issue were 1881, 1888 and 1894, struck at the Royal Mint. The only year when farthings were minted was in 1877 but in 1881 most of them were withdrawn leaving only 38,400 in circulation. Those withdrawn were melted down and reissued as 1881 pennies
EDWARD VII 1901-10		Bronze 1/12th of a shilling 1/24th of a shilling		The effigy of Edward VII appeared on all colonial coins of his reign with the legend in English (obverse and reverse). The only date of issue for his Jersey coins was 1909
GEORGE V 1910-36		1st Issue 1911-23 1/12th of a shilling 1/24th of a shilling 2nd Issue 1923 and 1926 1/12th of a shilling		There were three years of issue (1911, 1913 and 1923) with the crowned bust of the new king facing left. The abbreviation BRITT in the legend is short for the plural of BRITANNIARUM — the double T correctly presenting the contracted plural. During World War I shortage of coin created an accumulation

Catalogue of Jersey Coins

TYPE	SILVER	BASE METALS	GOLD	NOTES
		1/24th of a shilling 3rd Issue (1931-5) Bronze 1/12th of a shilling 1/24th of a shilling		of French and other bronze coins in the Channel Isles. These were collected and melted down at the end of the war and made into 300,000 pennies and 72,000 halfpennies in 1923. More of each denomination were struck in 1926. The reverse was redesigned with square shield of arms. For this issue the States redesigned their shield of arms again, the main alteration being large lettering in the legend. The dates of issue for both pennies and halfpennies were 1931, 1933 and 1935
GEORGE VI 1936-52		1st Issue (1937-47) 1/12th of a shilling 1/24th of a shilling 2nd Issue (1949) Commemorative 1/12th of a shilling		Except for the new king's effigy, the design remained unchanged This is the commemorative issue for the liberation from German occupation on 8 May 1945, though the date of issue was not until four years later. In this year the IND IMP was omitted from the king's title shown in the legend. Coins continued to be issued in 1950 and 1952 with the 1945 date
ELIZABETH II 1952—		1st Issue (1954) Commemorative Bronze 1/12th of a shilling 2nd Issue (1957-64) Nickel-brass 1/4th of a shilling		A commemorative coin similar to George VI's last issue retaining the 1945 liberation date with the effigy of Queen Elizabeth on the obverse This issue produced the first Jersey 1/4th of a shilling (a circular threepenny piece) in nickel-brass, together with a bronze penny. These coins (in a case with two of each denomination) were also produced as a proof set. The

TYPE	SILVER	BASE METALS	GOLD	NOTES
		Bronze 1/12th of a shilling		issue was repeated in 1964 as ordinary and proof issues
3rd Issue (1960) Commemorative		1/12th of a shilling		This coin commemorates the tercentenary of the Restoration, the 300th anniversary of Charles II, who was a refugee in Jersey from the Roundheads during the Civil War, with the lettering 'C II R 1660-1960 E II R' beneath the reverse shield. The penny (1/12th of a shilling) was for ordinary and proof issue, but the nickel-brass threepence (1/4th of a shilling) was issued in proof only, for inclusion in the proof sets. This latter coin—with two in each cased set—had a mintage of only 5,600
4th Issue (1966) Commemorative Cupro-nickel Five shillings		Nickel-brass 1/4th of a shilling 1/12th of a shilling		The crown piece was struck to commemorate 900 years since William the Conqueror invaded England, together with the nickel-brass 1/4th of a shilling and the bronze 1/12th of a shilling. The design was similar to the 2nd Issue, but the reverse differed slightly by showing a divided commemorative date (1066-1966) on either side of the shield. The crowns were also issued in proof—two per presentation case, and the two smaller denominations similarly presented (four coins per case)
Decimal Issue (1968—) Cupro-nickel Fifty new pence Ten new pence Five new pence		(1971) Bronze Two new pence One new pence Half new pence		Although not in operation as a decimal coinage until 15 February 1971, the cupro-nickel denominations of 50, 10 and 5 new pence were issued as 10s, 2s and 1s from 1968 and 1969.

CATALOGUE OF GUERNSEY COINS

TYPE	SILVER	BASE METALS	GOLD	NOTES
GEORGE III 1760-1820	Five shillings			These coins were issued in 1809 at the time when the British Government were issuing overstruck Spanish dollars as currency. This is a similar coin, though it can only be a token, as it was ordered by private Guernsey bankers, Bishop de Jersey & Co
WILLIAM IV 1830-7		Copper 8 doubles 4 doubles 1 double		The first two coins to be circulated as Guernsey's own coins were the 4 and 1 doubles of 1830 followed by the 8 doubles of 1834 with a more ornamental shield, which was continued on the largest coin in 1858
VICTORIA 1837-1901		*1st Issue* *(1858)* *Copper* 8 doubles 4 doubles 2 doubles *2nd Issue* *(1864-99)* *Bronze* 8 doubles 4 doubles 2 doubles 1 double		These were struck with 1858 date and are an identical type to the William IV issue, but as they were issued in Victoria's reign they are classed as another issue The design of the shield on the obverse was slightly altered, with other minor adjustments. There are a considerable number of variations in the number of leaves and berries in the wreath, and a single stalk or three stalks to the leaves above the shield. The coins were not struck every year between 1864 and 1899. The only years in which all four denominations were struck were 1868 and 1885. The mint

Catalogue of Guernsey Coins

TYPE	SILVER	BASE METALS	GOLD	NOTES
				mark H in 1885 denotes Heaton & Son of Birmingham
EDWARD VII 1901-10		Bronze 8 doubles 4 doubles 2 doubles 1 double		These coins are identical to the 2nd Issue of Victorian coins but were struck during Edward VII's reign, intermittently during the 1902-10 period, with 1902 and 1903 being the only years when all four denominations were issued. All the coins were struck by Heatons
GEORGE V 1910-36		1st Issue (1911) Bronze 8 doubles 4 doubles 2 doubles 1 double 2nd Issue (1914-34) 8 doubles 4 doubles 2 doubles 1 double		This 1911 striking was a continuation of Edward's coins and was identical in every respect except for the date The shield was altered to correspond with the earliest 4 doubles and 1 double of 1830 but the wreath was continued. 1914 was the only year in which all four denominations were struck. All were produced by Heatons
GEORGE VI 1936-52		Bronze 8 doubles 4 doubles 2 doubles 1 double		These coins were a continuation of George V coins with no difference except the dates, which are (8 doubles) 1938, 1945, 1947, 1949; (4 doubles) 1945 and 1949; (1 double) 1938. All were produced by Heatons
ELIZABETH II 1952—	1st Issue (1956-9) Cupro-nickel Threepence (light type) Threepence (heavy type)	Bronze 8 doubles 4 doubles		In 1956 the Guernsey coins were completely redesigned, the threepence being a new introduction. This coin has a scalloped edge with the reverse displaying the Guernsey cow. The 8 and 4 doubles showed the Guernsey lily, the larger coin with a spray of three flowers and the smaller

TYPE	SILVER	BASE METALS	GOLD	NOTES
				a single bloom. The two larger denominations were again struck in 1959—the threepence weighing more than the 1956 issue, which was withdrawn from circulation. The three coins dated 1956 were also issued as a proof set with each denomination duplicated—a total of six coins
2nd Issue (1966) Cupro-nickel Ten shillings				This unusual square coin with rounded corners was struck to commemorate the ninth centenary of the Battle of Hastings. Apart from Arnold Machin's bust of the queen on the obverse it showed a crowned and robed bust representing the victor of that battle, William the Conqueror, on the reverse
Decimal Issue (1968-) Fifty new pence Ten new pence Five new pence		Bronze (1971) Two new pence One new pence Half new pence		Although not in operation as a decimal coinage until 15 February 1971, the cupro-nickel denominations of 50, 10 and 5 new pence were issued as 10, 2 and 1 shillings from 1968 and 1969. They were intended to relieve the pressure of too many denominations being exchanged at one time (on 15 February 1971) and to acquaint the public with their appearance

SPECIMEN SET CATALOGUE

Not until 1826 in the reign of George IV were coins issued with a special finish distinct from the ordinary issues. These coins have a far superior appearance to those struck for general circulation and may be truly defined as 'Fleur de Coin' (FDC).

The early specimen or proof sets were issued by the engraver himself and were probably complimentary. Any remuneration, no doubt, was the engraver's personal affair. He also selected the case to contain the coins, and so several differently shaped cases exist for otherwise identical sets. From 1887, however, cases were standardised and were officially issued by the Royal Mint.

George IV (1826)*
(eleven coins in the set)

This set was originally issued in an oval case; it is estimated that approximately 150 were issued. The gold coins were five pounds, two pounds, sovereign, half sovereign; the silver coins crown, half crown, shilling, sixpence; and the copper coins penny, halfpenny and farthing. The set was issued along with all the denominations completed in 1826, and is probably the rarest of the British sets.

William IV (1831) Coronation Set
(fourteen coins in the set)

The case in which these coins were issued was round. The set omitted the proof five pounds but the remaining gold two pounds, sovereign and half sovereign were included. The silver coins were crown, half crown, shilling, sixpence, and Maundy set; the copper coins were the penny, halfpenny and farthing. The number of sets issued was about the same as the George IV set.

Victoria (1839) Young Head Set
(fifteen coins in the set)

This set is perhaps the most sought after of all the British specimens. Probably the attraction of the exquisite 'Una and the Lion' five pounds is the reason. The remaining coins are sovereign, half sovereign, crown, half crown, shilling, sixpence, groat, Maundy set, penny, halfpenny and farthing. No figure can be suggested for the number issued but possibly less than the earlier specimen sets. The case is spade-shaped. This may be considered a Coronation issue as all the denominations had been completed at the beginning of Victoria's reign.

Victoria (1853)
(sixteen coins in the set)

This issue was probably to display the new silver Gothic crown and florin.

★ Coins of 1746 are reported to have a special finish.

It is also interesting to observe that the quarter farthing, which does not belong to the British series, is included. The remaining coins are the sovereign, half sovereign, shilling, sixpence, groat Maundy set, penny, halfpenny, farthing and half farthing. Various types of case may be seen containing this set. The number issued is unknown but probably was less than 500.

Victoria (1887) Golden Jubilee Set
(eleven coins in the set)

797 sets were made to commemorate the Queen's Golden Jubilee. Frequently sets made up from uncirculated coin are displayed in a variety of unofficial cases, but the officially issued case bears the Royal Mint crest. The coins included are five pounds, two pounds, sovereign, half sovereign, crown, double florin, half crown, florin, shilling, sixpence and threepence.

Victoria (1887) Golden Jubilee Silver Set
(seven coins in the set)

This set is similar to the larger 1887 set, except that only the silver coins were included.

Victoria (1893) 'Old Head' Set
(ten coins in the set)

The coins of this issue, struck as specimens to display the changed design to the 'Old Head' issue, were the same denominations as those of 1887, with the exception of the unpopular double florin, which had been withdrawn after 1890.

Victoria (1893) 'Old Head Silver Set'
(six coins in the set)

This set is similar to the larger 1893 set, except that only the silver coins are included.

Edward VII (1902) Coronation 'Long' Set
(thirteen coins in the set)

Edward VII's Coronation was commemorated by a specimen set dated 1902. The coins were treated so as to give a frosted or iridescent appearance, unlike the usual proof struck coins, which had a mirror-like shine. This surface is known as a 'matte' or 'matt' finish. The coins, contained in a red leather case, are five pounds, two pounds, sovereign, half sovereign, crown, half crown, florin, shilling, sixpence and Maundy set. 8,066 of these sets were issued.

Edward VII (1902) Coronation 'Short' Set
(eleven coins in the set)

This set is known as 'the Edward VII short set' and is similar to the 'long' set except that the five pounds and two pounds are omitted. The number officially issued was 7,057.

George V (1911) Coronation 'Long' Set
(twelve coins in the set)

George V's Coronation was also commemorated by a specimen set issued in 1911. The sets followed the pattern of the previous reign by issuing a 'long' and a 'short' set. In addition an all-silver set was made available. 'The George V long set' contained five pounds, two pounds, sovereign, half sovereign, half crown, florin, shilling, sixpence and Maundy set. They were issued in a red leather case. The number of sets made available was 2,812.

George V (1911) Coronation 'Short' Set
(ten coins in the set)

The 'short' set is similar to the 'long' set except that the five and two pounds were omitted. This, too, is in a red leather case. The number of cases made available was 952.

George V (1911) Coronation Silver Set
(eight coins in the set)

The silver set contained simply the silver coins of the 'long' set. Although some are issued in red leather cases, a number may be found in red cardboard boxes. These, like all the other proof issued sets, bear the Royal Mint crest on the lid of the box.

George V (1927) New Issue Silver Set
(six coins in the set)

This silver coin set recorded a complete change in design on both obverses and reverses. The denominations were crown, half crown, florin, shilling, sixpence and threepence. All these, dated 1927, except for the shilling, did not go into ordinary circulation until 1928, making this set particularly desirable. Some were issued in red leather cases, but most of them were in red cardboard boxes. The total number available was 15,030.

George VI (1937) Coronation Gold Set
(four coins in the set)

The Coronation sets of George VI were divided into two types—gold only, and silver and bronze. The 'gold set' contained the five pounds, two pounds, sovereign and half sovereign, and a total of 5,501 sets were issued. The case is dark maroon in colour and of leather.

George VI (1937) Coronation Minor Set
(fifteen coins in the set)

The Coronation minor set is composed of the crown, half crown, florin, 'English' shilling, 'Scottish' shilling, sixpence, threepence, Maundy set, nickel-brass threepence, penny, halfpenny and farthing. Sometimes it is in a similarly coloured leather case to the gold set, but frequently it is in a red cardboard one. The number of cases issued was given as 26,402.

Specimen Set Catalogue 367

George VI (1950) Mid-century Set
(nine coins in the set)

The official reason for the issue of this set is not stated but it is sometimes called the mid-century set. Its appearance may have been due to a combination of circumstances, though the first proof production of cupro-nickel coins is the most likely reason. It contains the half crown, florin, 'English' shilling, 'Scottish' shilling, sixpence, nickel-brass threepence, penny, halfpenny and farthing. The number of sets issued was 17,513.

George VI (1950) Festival of Britain Commemorative Issue
(ten coins in the set)

This issue is in cupro-nickel, nickel-brass and bronze and consists of the crown, half crown, florin, 'English' shilling, 'Scottish' shilling, sixpence, threepence, penny, halfpenny and farthing; it records the centenary of the 1851 Festival of Britain. 20,000 sets were struck, most of which were sold at the 1951 'Festival'.

Elizabeth II (1953) Coronation Set
(ten coins in the set)

Of particular interest, apart from being the Coronation proof issue, is that this was the only year of Elizabeth's reign when the coinage included the BRITT OMN in the legend. The denominations included are the crown, half crown, florin, 'English' shilling, 'Scottish' shilling, sixpence, threepence, penny, halfpenny and farthing. The number of sets issued was 40,000 in dark maroon leatherette.

PRINTED NOTE ISSUES IN GREAT BRITAIN

Bank of England and English Country Banks

1691 William Paterson's plan for a national bank.
1694 Bank of England formed.
1695 First Bank of England notes issued for £10, £20, £30, £40, £50 and £100, with date, bearer's name and cashier's signature written by hand and rest of note copperplate printed. They were, however, withdrawn in the same year. Notes written in manuscript were also issued on demand in varying amounts.
1697 Act preventing any organisation setting up as a bank and issuing notes, thus restricting the opportunities of the forger.
1708 Act passed to protect the Bank of England's note monopoly and to restrict the note issue of country banks, preventing firms with more than six partners—other than the Bank of England—from issuing notes. The Act was also intended to make forgery more difficult.
1724 Earliest post bills payable three days after issue used to protect travellers on mail coaches from robbery. They were replaced in 1738 by bills payable seven days after issue.
1725 First printed Bank of England notes on much improved paper, in denominations of £20, £30, £40, £50, £100, £200, £300, £400, £500 and £1,000, and probably also of £60, £70, £80 and £90. It is believed, however, that at least some of the plates from which the notes were printed were not fully engraved.
1738 Bank Post Bills payable seven days after the date of issue made available in an attempt to protect travellers on mail coaches from robbery. These bills superseded those payable three days after issue as three days were considered insufficient a period.
1743 Further £50 note (January) issues of the 1725 Bank of England notes.
1752 Further £30 note (June) and £20 note (December) issues of the 1725 Bank of England notes.
1759 £10 and £15 notes added to the 1725 issue.
1765 £25 notes added (March).
1775 Act prohibiting the country banks from issuing £1 notes or less.
1777 Act prohibiting the country banks from issuing notes under £5.
1793 Bank of England £5 notes issued for the first time. About 100 country banks failed through over-issue of notes.
1794 Further £100 and £200 note issues of the 1725 Bank of England issue.
1795 Further £300 and £500 note issues of the 1725 Bank of England issue.
1797 Act passed to permit Bank of England to issue £1 and £2 notes for the first time. There followed a large issue of these notes both by the Bank of England and the country banks.
1797-1810 Large increase in private banks. The numbers jumped from 270 in 1797 to 720 in 1810 with a total note issue of £30 million.

Printed Note Issues in Great Britain

1802 Further £1,000 note issues of the 1725 Bank of England issue.
1803 Little-used denominations of the 1725 Bank of England notes were discontinued; these were probably £60, £70, £80 and £90 of the original 1725 types.
1809 Bank of England issued notes which were wholly printed except that the signature was in manuscript.
1818 Bank of England in October issued their last £2 notes.
1821 Act passed in May ended the restriction period. £1 Bank of England notes were discontinued (apart from a number discovered—and issued —in the 1825-6 crisis).
1822 Bank of England discontinued issues of £15 and £25 notes. In the same year 500 country banks issued an unrestricted number of £1 notes.
1826 Act prohibiting notes under £5.
1844 Bank Charter Act passed. The Act in its application was extended to Scotland and Ireland in 1845.
1851 Bank of England notes for £40 discontinued.
1852 Bank of England notes for £30 discontinued.
1853 First wholly printed Bank of England notes.
1885 Bank of England notes for £300 discontinued.
1914 Currency and Bank Notes Act passed permitting issue of currency notes for £1 and 10s. Postal Orders made legal tender as a temporary measure in the British Isles.
  Currency note issues:
  First issue of £1 notes (black) on 7 August 1914;
    discontinued 22 October 1914 (withdrawn 11 June 1920).
  First issue of 10s notes (red) on 14 August 1914;
    discontinued 20 January 1915 (withdrawn 11 June 1920).
  Second issue of £1 notes (black) on 23 October 1914;
    discontinued 21 March 1917 (withdrawn 11 June 1920).
  Second issue of 10s notes (red) on 21 January 1915;
    discontinued 30 December 1918 (withdrawn 11 June 1920).
  Third issue of £1 notes (green) on 1 February 1917;
    discontinued 21 November 1928 (withdrawn 31 July 1933).
  Third issue of 10s notes (green and brown) on 2 November 1918;
    discontinued 21 November 1928 (withdrawn 31 July 1933).
1928 Bank of England again issued banknotes for £1 (green) and 10s (brown) on 22 November. This was the first occasion on which the Bank of England had issued 10s notes. Bank of England £200 notes discontinued.
1940 1928 issue of £1 and 10s notes temporarily superseded by emergency issue of £1 (blue) and 10s (mauve), with a thread running through the paper (29 March).
1943 Bank of England £10, £20, £50, £100, £500 and £1,000 notes discontinued.
1945 £5 notes withdrawn and similar notes with a metallic thread issued in their place (October). These notes were of thicker paper. On 1 May all £10, £15, £20, £25, £30, £40, £50, £100, £200, £300, £500 and £1,000 notes ceased to be legal tender.
1946 The withdrawn £5 notes ceased to be legal tender (1 March).
1948 Second issue of 1928 Bank of England £1 (green) and 10s (brown) notes,

Y

now with a metal thread running through the paper; 1940 emergency issues were discontinued, though for a time the Bank of England continued to use up a large stock of them. The thick £5 notes of 1945 were discontinued and in their place thin paper notes with a metallic thread, dated from 1 January 1947, were issued.

1957 Bank of England 1948 £5 notes discontinued and an entirely new type, blue in colour and only slightly larger than the current £1 notes, issued (February).

1960 Completely new type of green £1 notes, reduced in size and with a portrait of the Queen; 1928 £1 notes discontinued.

1961 All the £5 notes other than those of the 1957 issue ceased to be legal tender, though full value given for notes when returned to Bank of England (14 March). Later in the year Bank of England slightly modified £5 notes by substituting a redesigned £5 symbol on the reverse, printed in outline with the background showing through, in place of the heavily printed dark blue design. A third change took place when in October the 10s note issue of 1948 was discontinued and a slightly smaller note issued in its place.

1963 Bank of England issued blue £5 notes bearing a portrait of the Queen.

1964 Bank of England issued brown £10 notes bearing a portrait of the Queen.

1970 Bank of England issued an entirely new type of note on 7 July of £20, designed by Harry Eccleston of the Bank staff bearing a portrait of the Queen (on the right), a portrait of St George and the Dragon (centre) and Britannia within a circle (beneath). The back of the note shows the statue of Shakespeare taken from the Westminster Abbey memorial (right centre) and a balcony scene from Romeo and Juliet. The colour of the note is purple against a multi-coloured background mainly in blue, gold and green tints. Bank of England plan to issue new £1, £5 and £10 notes as part of a series belonging to the same type as the £20 note.

Scottish Banks

1695 Bank of Scotland formed.

1696 Bank of Scotland issued its first banknotes for £5, £10, £20, £50 and £100.

1704 Bank of Scotland issued its first £1 notes. During the period 1704-68 nine issues of notes took place similar to the first issue, with the continuation of £1 notes.

1727 Royal Bank of Scotland formed, issuing notes for £1, £5, £10, £20, £50 and £100 (8 December).

1747 British Linen Co formed, issuing notes for £5, £10, £20 and £100.

1750 British Linen Co issued its first £1 and 10s notes.

1759 Royal Bank of Scotland issued £1 1s 0d notes to relieve coin shortage.

1762 Royal Bank of Scotland adopted the option clause whereby it undertook to pay its notes on demand or in six months' time, plus interest, at the option of the directors. A new set of notes was issued for £1, £5,

Printed Note Issues in Great Britain

£10, £20, £50 and £100 and all previous issues were withdrawn as they returned to the bank.
1765 Act of Parliament passed in an attempt to overcome some of the evils of paper currencies, making notes under £1 and the option clause illegal.
1768 Bank of Scotland issued their 'eleventh set', in similar denominations to previous issues, together with £1 1s 0d notes. Royal Bank of Scotland again issued £1 1s 0d notes and they remained popular for many years, taking the place of £1 notes. British Linen Co issued £1 1s 0d notes in common with the other banks. The popular guinea notes were a means of overcoming the small-change problem (nineteen guinea notes and one shilling made £20).
1777 Royal Bank of Scotland issued new £1 1s 0d notes with the words in blue and the king's head in red, its object being to make forgery more difficult.
1788 Royal Bank of Scotland issued £1 notes again, but the practice of showing the value in Scots currency on the notes (£12 Scots equalled £1 sterling) was discontinued.
1791 Royal Bank of Scotland issued its last £50 notes.
1797 British Linen Co issued 5s notes in common with other banks. After the Bank Restriction Act was passed the Scottish banks followed the Bank of England in stopping payment of gold for notes. In Scotland, however, the ban on the issue of notes under £1 was lifted and a large number of small notes were circulated, which relieved the small-change shortage. This privilege lasted until July 1799.
1797-9 Royal Bank of Scotland issued 5s notes.
1810 Commercial Bank of Scotland formed, issuing notes of £1, £1 1s 0d, £5, £20 and £100.
1810-32 Additional notes of £2 and £2 2s 0d denominations issued by the Bank of Scotland.
1811 Commercial Bank of Scotland changed note designs.
1823 British Linen Co issued new set of notes in black ink in denominations of £1, £5, £10, £20 and £100. Commercial Bank of Scotland changed note designs.
1824 Royal Bank of Scotland issued its last £1 1s 0d notes.
1825 National Bank of Scotland formed, issuing notes for £1, £1 1s 0d, £5, £20 and £100.
1826 An Act forbade notes under £5 in Scotland but was withdrawn after protest from the Scottish banks. Scottish and Irish notes under £5, however, were made illegal in England.
1827 Commercial Bank of Scotland issued additional denomination of £10 and at the same time changed note designs.
1830 Union Bank of Scotland Ltd formed under name of Glasgow Union Banking Company.
c 1830 Commercial Bank of Scotland ceased to issue £1 1s 0d notes about this time.
1833 National Bank of Scotland ceased to issue £1 1s 0d notes.
1836 North of Scotland Banking Co formed (to become the North of Scotland Bank Ltd at a later date), issuing notes for £1, £5, £20 and £100, and adding £10 notes later.

1838 Clydesdale Bank formed, issuing notes for £1, £5, £20 and £100.
1844 Bank Charter Act restricted the issue of notes by individual banks to the 'authorised circulation' but allowed an excess of notes above this amount if gold and silver coin equal to the excess issue were held as security. It also prohibited notes for fractions of £1. The authorised circulation laid down was as follows:

	£ Sterling	
Bank of Scotland	300,485	
Central Bank of Scotland	42,933	joined Bank of Scotland
Caledonian Banking Co	53,434	joined Bank of Scotland
Union Bank of Scotland	327,223	
Perth Banking Co	38,656	joined Union Bank of Scotland
Aberdeen Banking Co	88,467	joined Union Bank of Scotland
Royal Bank of Scotland	183,000	
Dundee Banking Co	33,451	joined Royal Bank of Scotland
British Linen Co	438,024	
National Bank of Scotland	297,024	
Commercial Bank of Scotland	374,880	
North of Scotland Bank	154,319	
Town and Country Bank	70,133	joined North of Scotland Bank
Clydesdale Bank	104,028	
Eastern Bank of Scotland	33,636	joined Clydesdale Bank
Edinburgh and Glasgow Bank	136,657	taken over by Clydesdale Bank
Ayrshire Bank	53,656	failed
Western Bank of Scotland	284,282	failed
City of Glasgow Bank	72,921	failed

The Bank Charter Act, though applied to English banks in 1844, was not extended to Scotland and Ireland until 1845.
1849 Commercial Bank of Scotland changed note designs.
1853 An Act was passed releasing the Scottish banks from the necessity of stamping their notes and a tax of 8s 4d per annum on each £100 circulating was substituted.
1854 Commercial Bank of Scotland changed note designs.
1860 Clydesdale Bank Ltd adopted newly designed bank notes produced by Hugh Wilson, Glasgow. Commercial Bank of Scotland ceased issue of black and white notes and printed all denominations in colour. At the same time note designs were changed.
1861 British Linen Co changed colours of notes. They were reprinted in blue ink with red 'B.L. Co.' added, the denominations as before being £1, £5, £10, £20 and £100.
1864 National Bank of Scotland opened branch in London.
1867 Bank of Scotland opened branch in London.
1870 Thomas de la Rue & Co produced new design for Clydesdale Bank's notes. This was incorporated in note issues until 1878, when Hugh Wilson's designs of 1860 were restored, the notes being printed in black, white and red until 1922. The colour was then changed to predominantly blue with a design printed on the back. The two signatures on the notes were then lithographed.

Printed Note Issues in Great Britain 373

1874 Royal Bank of Scotland opened branch in London.
1883 Commercial Bank of Scotland opened branch in London.
1885 Redesigned note of Bank of Scotland by William S. Black issued in an effort to defeat the forger in denominations of £1 (1,000,000), £5 (80,000), £10 (20,000), £20 (20,000) and £100 (4,000).
1886 Commercial Bank of Scotland ceased issue of £10 notes and changed note designs.
1893 National Bank of Scotland ceased issuing black and white notes and issued all denominations except £10 notes in colour, at the same time changing note designs.
1906 British Linen Co changed its name to The British Linen Bank and altered the watermark of its notes accordingly.
1907 Commercial Bank of Scotland changed note designs.
1914 The British Linen Bank issued a new £1 note, with printing on back but with no watermark.
1915 The British Linen Bank issued £5, £10, £20 and £100 notes, printed on back, using a thinner paper, subsequently used on £1 notes.
1918 National Bank of Scotland became affiliated to Lloyds Bank with the Scottish bank retaining its separate identity.
1919 British Linen Bank became affiliated to Barclays Bank Ltd, though retaining separate identity. Opened branch in London.

The authorised circulation of banknotes in 1919 is listed below, but banks were permitted to issue notes in excess of these totals provided security was held equal to the excess issue.

Bank of Scotland	£396,852	
Union Bank of Scotland	£454,346	amalgamated in 1955
Royal Bank of Scotland	£216,451	
British Linen Bank	£438,024	
National Bank of Scotland	£297,024	became National Commercial
Commercial Bank of Scotland	£374,880	Bank of Scotland in 1959
Clydesdale Bank	£274,321	became Clydesdale and North
North of Scotland Bank	£224,452	of Scotland Bank in 1950

It will be observed that the figures for some of the banks show an increase over the figures shown in the 1845 table. This is because when one bank of issue took over another bank of issue it was permitted in Scotland to add the latter's authorised circulation to its own.

1920 Clydesdale Bank became affiliated to London Joint City and Midland Bank (now Midland Bank), though retaining separate identity.
1924 Drummond's Bank acquired by Royal Bank of Scotland and became a branch of the Scottish bank. Commercial Bank of Scotland changed note designs. North of Scotland Bank became affiliated to Midland Bank, retaining its separate identity.
1926 British Linen Bank introduced smaller £1 notes bearing the lithographed signature of the cashier.
1927 National Bank of Scotland, Commercial Bank of Scotland, Royal Bank of Scotland and Clydesdale Bank reduced size of £1 notes.
1929 Bank of Scotland introduced small size £1 notes with change in design.
1930 Royal Bank of Scotland acquired Williams Deacons Bank Ltd, each bank retaining separate identity. The business of the Burlington Gardens

branch of the Bank of England was acquired and incorporated into the Scottish bank's branch system.
1934 British Linen Bank adopted new coat of arms on note design.
1939 Royal Bank of Scotland acquired Glyn Mills & Co, each bank retaining its separate identity.
1944 British Linen Bank introduced smaller £5 notes. From this date all notes carried the general manager's lithographed signature.
1945 Bank of Scotland made minor change in £1 note design and reduced size of £5 notes.
1947 Commercial Bank of Scotland changed note designs.
1950 North of Scotland Bank and Clydesdale Bank amalgamated and became single bank. New design for £1 notes introduced for the amalgamated bank, followed by new design for £5, £20 and £100 notes introduced in 1951. These three denominations were also reduced in size, while all bear the printed signature of the general manager only.
1954 Commercial Bank of Scotland changed colour of £1 notes.
1955 Union Bank of Scotland amalgamated with Bank of Scotland.
1957 National Bank of Scotland changed note designs.
1959 National Bank of Scotland and Commercial Bank of Scotland merged and issues of each individual bank ceased. The new bank, the National Commercial of Scotland, issued notes for £1, £5, £20 and £100.
1960 The Scottish banks agreed that, as and when they changed their notes, they would conform to the sizes of the Bank of England notes of £1, £5 and £10 denominations.
1961 In 1961 the following Scottish banknotes were in circulation (authorised circulations as in 1919):

Bank of Scotland	£1, £5, £10, £20, £50, £100
Royal Bank of Scotland	£1, £5, £10, £20, £100
British Linen Bank	£1, £5, £10, £20, £100
National Commercial Bank of Scotland	£1, £5, £20, £100
Clydesdale and North of Scotland Bank	£1, £5, £20, £100

Clydesdale and North of Scotland Bank reduced size of £1 note to same size as Bank of England £1 note, and introduced a new design for this denomination printed in green, orange and mauve. British Linen Bank reduced the size of £5 note to Bank of England size. Bank of Scotland reduced the size of £1 and £5 notes to the same size as Bank of England £1 and £5 notes. National Commercial Bank of Scotland Ltd reduced the size of £1 and £5 notes with the £1 colour changed from blue to green.
1962 The British Linen Bank issued Series 'C' £1 and £5 notes (corresponding in size to the Bank of England notes of these denominations), the latter being a new design with the portrait of Sir Walter Scott on the right.
1963 The Clydesdale and North of Scotland Bank Ltd altered its name to Clydesdale Bank Ltd. New type £1 and £5 notes issued but basic design unchanged. National Commercial Bank of Scotland Ltd reduced the size of the £5 notes to the same size as that of the Bank of England, redesigning and printing them in blue.
1964 Clydesdale Bank Ltd issued its first £10 notes printed in brown, magenta, lilac and green. A new issue of £20 notes was made with a

Printed Note Issues in Great Britain 375

new design, reduced in size and in colours red, ochre, magenta and green. Royal Bank of Scotland reduced the size of £1 and £5 notes to the same size as those of the Bank of England.

1965 Clydesdale Bank Ltd issued newly designed £100 notes in purple, burgundy, burnt orange, dark amber and green.

1966 National Commercial Bank of Scotland Ltd issued its first £10 notes printed in brown.

1967 The Scottish banks adopted a new type of sorting machine for counting and sorting banknotes into their respective banks. A bar code known as CMC7 is applied to the backs of the £1 and £5 notes. This bar code involved the redesign of the backs of £1 notes. When fully operational this machine reads the coding of each note and automatically sorts the mixed Scottish banknotes into individual banks and counts them in batches of 100. (Scottish banks receive mixed notes of all banks but issue only their own notes.) Royal Bank of Scotland reduced the size of £1 and £5 notes to the same size as similar denominations of the Bank of England.

1968 Bank of Scotland introduced new design for current £5 notes. Royal Bank of Scotland £1 notes redesigned to conform to the proposed new size Bank of England notes. National Commercial Bank of Scotland Ltd reduced in size its £1 notes to conform to the proposed new size Bank of England £1 notes. The front of the notes was redesigned.

1969 Bank of Scotland introduced a new design for its current £5 notes. British Linen Bank issued £1 and £5 notes to conform to the Bank of England proposed 'Series D' size, bearing the CMC7 code with centre of note at back tinted. The £1 notes have incorporated in the new design the portrait of Sir Walter Scott on the left. The Royal Bank of Scotland and the National Commercial Bank of Scotland Ltd amalgamated under the title of the Royal Bank of Scotland Limited with a combined authorised circulation of £888,355. Redesigned notes of £1, £5, £10, £20 and £100 were issued.

1970 Bank of Scotland and British Linen Bank announce their amalgamation 'at some future date'.

Irish Banks

1782 Bank of Ireland founded.

1783 Bank of Ireland issued first notes in denominations of £10, £15, £20, £25, £30, £40, £50, £60, £70, £80, £90, £100, £200, £300, £400 and £500, comprising 12,700 notes totalling £882,500 Irish. These notes were printed in England. After this first issue a stamp for use as part of the design of Bank of Ireland notes was submitted by a local designer for the printing of banknotes in Ireland. The offer was accepted.

1784 The Bank of Ireland thereupon appointed an engraver, Edward Fitzgerald, to engrave the plates, while William Wilson, the bank's printer, produced the same denominations as were issued the previous year together with 5, 10, 20, 30, 40, 50, 60, 70, 80, 90 and 100 guineas, all issued in Irish currency.

1794 A 'Belfast Bank' existed as a private bank in this year, unconnected to the present bank of similar name. This bank issued notes for one guinea dated 2 June 1794, which exist today in collections.
1808 The present Belfast Banking Co Ltd formed under the name of Belfast Bank.
1809 Northern Bank commenced business as a private bank and issued notes with lithographed signatures which included denominations of £1, 30s and £2.
1816 Bank of Ireland's banknote printer, John Oldham, invented greatly improved note-printing process at far lower cost than previous issues. He took this process twenty years later to Bank of England.
1824 Northern Bank became first joint-stock bank in Ireland after 1824 Act, issuing notes for £1, £5, £10, £20, £50 and £100.
1825 By Act of Parliament in this year Irish currency became same as British (ie 13 pence Irish to a British shilling was abolished 6 January 1826). This meant that banknotes would not be issued in Irish currency from that date.

Provincial Bank of Ireland formed, opening its first branch in Cork. From 1825 to 1845 its note issues, known as 'General Issue notes', are believed to have been in denominations of £1, £1 5s 0d, £1 10s 0d, £1 15s 0d, £2, £3, £4, £5, £10, £20 and £100 as well as a number of stamped notes. They were marked payable at the issuing branch and signed by the manager. The Acts of 1824 and 1825 amended the 1782 Act (which gave the Bank of Ireland virtual monopoly of the note issue in Dublin and 50 miles around), allowing English capital to be invested in the new bank, which set up its head office in London.
1827 Commercial Bank (Tennant Callwell & Co) and Belfast Bank (Gordon & Co) amalgamated to form Belfast Banking Co and issued notes for £1, £5, £10, £20, £50 and £100.
1834 Nationalist Party founded National Bank of Ireland.
1835 National Bank of Ireland opened first branch, Carrick-on-Suir, issuing notes for £1, £5, £10, £20, £50 and £100.
1836 Ulster Bank opened in Belfast as Ulster Banking Co. Its note issue was in denominations of £1, £1 5s 0d, £1 10s 0d, £1 15s 0d, £5, £10 and £20.
1839 and 1840 Belfast Banking Co made two separate issues of notes of same denominations as 1827, the 1839 issue lasting until 1844, and the 1840 issue ending in 1848.
1845 By Act of Parliament the six issuing banks of Ireland were required to keep their note issues within the undermentioned figures unless a cover in gold or silver coin equal to the excess of notes issued was deposited:

Bank of Ireland	£3,738,428
Provincial Bank of Ireland	£927,667
Belfast Banking Co	£281,611
Northern Bank	£243,440
Ulster Bank	£311,079
National Bank of Ireland	£852,269

By Act of Parliament banknotes with fractional parts of a pound were illegal after 1845. Provincial Bank made its notes payable at a particular branch after the Act. Ulster Bank discontinued issuing notes for

Printed Note Issues in Great Britain

£1 5s 0d, £1 10s 0d and £1 15s 0d, but issued £2 and £3 notes.

1847 On 7 October, Belfast Banking Co issued new notes known as its 'General Issue', which continued until 15 April 1868 in denominations of £1, £5, £10, £20, £50 and £100.

1853 Ulster Bank issued notes in denominations of £1, £5, £10 and £20.

1856 National Bank of Ireland changed name to National Bank.

1862 Ulster Bank issued notes in denominations of £1, £5, £10, £20 and £100.

1864 Act passed authorising banknotes to have a printed facsimile signature, a procedure adopted by the Bank of England in 1811 and by the Bank of Ireland in 1820. The Act was apparently to legalise this procedure.

1867 On 8 November (printed 7 August) Belfast Banking Co issued its 'Incorporated Issue'. This lasted until 4 November 1884. The denominations were in £1, £5, £10, £20, £50 and £100. Ulster Bank, though still known as Ulster Banking Co, became incorporated.

1870 Provincial Bank of Ireland issued notes in denominations of £1, £5, £10, £20, £50 and £100, payable at any of its branches.

1880 Belfast Banking Co on 27 September produced its 'Blue Back Issue' of notes first printed on 9 October 1879. This issue was in the same denominations as the 1867 issue and lasted until 9 March 1928.

1883 Ulster Banking Co changed its name to Ulster Bank Limited and issued £1, £5, £10, £20, £50 and £100 notes under its new name. Towards the end of the nineteenth century £3 notes known as 'pig money' were circulated in Southern Ireland by the National Bank, Provincial Bank and Bank of Ireland, and so named because of their frequent use in the pork markets.

1917 Ulster Bank and Westminster Bank merged, the latter acquiring the whole of the Ulster Bank's shares, though the Irish bank retained its independent identity.

1922 Belfast Banking Co's 'new issue 1922' was circulated on 2 January in denominations of £1, £5, £10, £20, £50 and £100.

1928 The Bankers (Northern Ireland) Act required the six issuing banks in Northern Ireland to keep note issues within the undermentioned figures unless cover was held for any excess.

Bank of Ireland	£410,000
Provincial Bank of Ireland	£220,000
National Bank	£120,000
Belfast Banking Co	£350,000
Ulster Bank	£290,000
Northern Bank	£244,000

Northern Bank called in issues prior to 6 May and issued new notes of £1, £5, £10, £20, £50 and £100. National Bank issued new notes on 6 May in denominations of £1, £5, £10 and £20, as did Provincial Bank. Notes issued from 6 May were called 'Northern Ireland Issue', and 'General Issue' notes for all Ireland ceased.

1929 Ulster Bank issued new notes in the same denominations as in 1883 which were called 'Northern Ireland Issue', while the 'General Issue' notes for all Ireland ceased.

1937 National Bank made a new issue of £1, £5, £10 and £20 notes in place of the 1929 issue (1 February).

1952 Provincial Bank changed the design of £1 and £5 notes.
1954 Provincial Bank made a new issue of £1 and £5 notes in place of the 1952 issue.
1961 The following note denominations were in circulation in Northern Ireland:

Bank of Ireland	£1, £5, £10, £20
Northern Bank	£1, £5, £10, £20, £50, £100
Provincial Bank of Ireland	£1, £5, £10, £20
Belfast Banking Co	£1, £5, £10, £20, £50, £100
National Bank	£1, £5, £10, £20
Ulster Bank	£1, £5, £10, £20, £50, £100

1966 On 1 April the Irish business of the National Bank was taken over by a new Irish registered company, The National Bank of Ireland Limited, becoming a subsidiary company in the Bank of Ireland Group. Ulster Bank made a new Northern Ireland issue of completely redesigned £1, £5 and £10 notes.
1968 Provincial Bank issued new Northern Ireland notes of £1 and £5. These notes are of a similar design to the previous issues, but smaller.
1970 Northern Bank and Belfast Banking Co amalgamated on 1 July under the title of United Northern Banks; simultaneously Northern Bank issued notes in denominations of £1, £5, £10, £20, £50 and £100.

Isle of Man

1817 Act of Tynwald forbade use of card money and of paper money under £1 and all note-issuers were compelled to hold a licence. Five firms were granted licences to issue £1 and £1 1s 0d notes.
1847 £5 notes were issued for the first time by the Isle of Man Commercial Bank, which two years later became the Bank of Mona (later failing).
1865 The Isle of Man Banking Co Ltd was formed, and circulated an issue of £1 notes. This bank in 1926 became the Isle of Man Bank Ltd.
1894 The Isle of Man Banking Co Ltd issued its first £5 notes, which have been issued continually along with the £1 notes until the present day.
1900 Westminster Bank Ltd (then Parrs Bank) took over the goodwill of the private bank, Dumbells Banking Co Ltd, which had failed. From 1900 until 1961 Westminster Bank held a licence to make and issue £1 notes to a maximum of £25,000. In 1923 the size of these notes was reduced. In the same year the Mercantile Bank of Lancashire Ltd (which amalgamated with the Lancashire and Yorkshire Bank Ltd in 1904, and finally became Martins Bank Ltd) took over the Manx Bank Ltd, formed in 1882. The note issue of Martins Bank Ltd in the Isle of Man was authorised at £25,000 in £1 notes only.
1919 Lloyds Bank Ltd opened a branch in Douglas and was granted a note-issue licence 'to make and issue' £1 notes up to a total of £15,000. This bank was shortly followed by Barclays Bank Ltd, which was granted a licence for £1 notes to a total of £10,000.
1955 Act of Tynwald passed making Bank of England notes legal tender.

Printed Note Issues in Great Britain

The Isle of Man Bank Ltd (formerly the Isle of Man Banking Co Ltd) was by far the largest note-issuer of the five licensed banks, with a permitted maximum of £150,000 in £1 notes out of a total of £225,000. It was also licensed to make and issue £5 notes.

1961 These five licences, however, were revoked with effect from 31 July 1961, when the Isle of Man Government took over the note issues. The limit that each bank was permitted to issue in notes at the time these licences were revoked was as follows:

Isle of Man Bank Ltd	£150,000
Westminster Bank Ltd	£25,000
Martins Bank Ltd	£25,000
Lloyds Bank Ltd	£15,000
Barclays Bank Ltd	£10,000

Isle of Man Government issued 10s, £1 and £5 denominations, while Bank of England notes continued to circulate as before.

1969 In August, 50 pence notes were issued, equal to and to circulate alongside the 10s notes in anticipation of the introduction of the decimal currency.

Jersey

1797 The first bank was at Hugh Godfrey & Co's wine store and issued £1 notes; a number of these dated up to the year 1843 are still in existence. Later this bank was known as the Jersey Old Bank, which in 1887 was acquired by the Midland Bank.

1827-86 Between these years there were many issues of notes by banks, parishes, trading companies, etc, but only one known issue, in 1874, by the States of Jersey.

1874 The Harbour Committee of the States of Jersey issued £1 notes.

1882 and 1884 The 1874 note issue was recalled during these two years.

1940 During the German occupation of Jersey in World War II, which lasted from 1940 to 1945, most of the coinage disappeared. This resulted in notes being issued in its place for 6d, 1s, 2s, 10s and £1 to a total of £65,000. Bank of England notes disappeared, presumably hidden by the local population. German reichmarks and pfennigs were also issued as currency.

1963 The States of Jersey issued 10s, £1 and £5 notes.

Guernsey

1808 The Bank of Guernsey and Brock & Le Mesurier issued £1 notes until they both failed in 1811.

1816	The States of Guernsey issued its first £1 notes to a total of £4,000, for coast preservation and the building of Torteval church and Jerbourg monument.
1818	The 1816 notes were redeemed.
1820	More £1 notes were issued to a total of £4,500. It is probable that these notes were printed by Perkins, Bacon Ltd, London.
1826	The States of Guernsey for the first time issued £5 notes, to a total of £10,000, as well as £1 notes to a total of £20,000.
1827	A private bank opened and issued notes.
1830	The 1820 issue of £1 notes was redeemed.
1835	Another private bank opened and issued notes.
1836	The States had an issue of £55,000 but agreed with the banks of the island to restrict its note issue in future to £40,000.
c 1890	The Guernsey Banking Co in the late nineteenth century was known to have a considerable note circulation in Alderney, St Malo and Cherbourg; specimen notes for £1 dated 1918, 1921, 1922 and 1923 are held by the note printers Perkins, Bacon Ltd.
1914	The States' arrangement with the private banks ceased and their note issue was considerably expanded, including war issue notes of 5s and 10s, printed by Perkins, Bacon Ltd, the latter being the forerunner of the current 10s Guernsey notes.
1918	At the end of World War I the State note issue had risen to £142,000.
1921	A facsimile of the signature of the States Supervisor as Treasurer of the States was authorised instead of his being required to sign each note. Notes, however, were countersigned by hand as an indication that they had been entered in the register of notes issued. This countersigning came to an end in 1934.
1940	During the German occupation of Guernsey in World War II, which lasted from 1940 until 1945, most of the coinage disappeared. This resulted in notes being issued in its place for 6d, 1s, 1s 3d, 2s 6d and 5s to a total of £11,767. The States' notes of 10s and £1 as well as Bank of England notes also disappeared. German reichmarks and pfennigs were also issued as currency. At one time the note circulation reached £434,081. These notes were not, however, actually circulating and it was a rarity to see a States note at all. The public were keeping the States and Bank of England notes in their own homes.
1961	Notes issued by the States of Guernsey for 10s, £1 and £5 to circulate with Bank of England notes, also made legal currency.
1969	The States of Guernsey redesigned the £1 and £5 notes, which were printed by Bradbury Wilkinson & Co Ltd, New Malden, Surrey, and issued in March. No further 10s notes were issued, their place being taken by the 10s coin, followed by the introduction of decimal coinage in 1971.

TRANSLATION OF MOTTOES ON COINS

ANGLO-SAXON COINS	TRANSLATION
Domine Deus Rex	O Lord God (heavenly) King
Mirabilia Fecit	He hath done marvellous things
Rex Saxonum Occidentalium	King of the West Saxons
Rex Totius Britanniae	King of all Britain

ENGLISH COINS	TRANSLATION
A Domino Factum Est Istud Et Est Mirabile in Oculis Nostris	This is the doing of the Lord, and it is marvellous in our eyes
Amor Populi Praesidium Regis	The love of the people is the protection of the king
Anno Regni Primo, etc	In the first (year) of the reign, etc
Bello Et Pace	In war and peace
Britanniarum Omnium Rex Fidei Defensor Indiae Imperator	King of all the Britains, Defender of the Faith, Emperor of India
Britanniarum Rex	King of the Britains (ie Britain and British territories overseas)
Brun, Et L. Dux S. R. I. A. TH. ET EL (abbreviated for Brunsvicensis et Lunenbergensis Dux, Sacri Romani Imperii Archi-Thesaurarius et Elector)	Duke of Brunswick and Luneberg, Arch-Treasurer of the Holy Roman Empire, and Elector
Caroli Fortuna Resurgam	I, the Fortune of Charles, shall rise again
Charitie and Change	Charity and Change
Christo Auspice Regno	I reign under the auspices of Christ
Civium Industria Floret Civitas	By the industry of its people the State flourishes
Cultores Sui Deus Protegit	God protects His worshippers
Decus Et Tutamen	An ornament and a safeguard
Dei Gratia Rex Angliae Et Franciae Dominus Hyberniae	By the Grace of God king of England and France Lord of Ireland
Dieu Et Mon Droit	God and my right
Domine, Deus Rex	O Lord God, (heavenly) king (Gloria)
Domine Ne In Furore Tuo Arguas Me	O Lord, rebuke me not in Thy Indignation
Dum Spiro Spero	Whilst I live, I hope
Exaltabitur In Gloria	He shall be exalted in glory
Exurgat Deus Dissipentur Inimici	Let God arise (and) let His enemies be scattered
Faciam Eos In Gentem Unam	I will make them one nation

Faith and Truth I will Bear Unto You	
Fidei Defensor	Defender of the Faith
Florent Concordia Regna	United kingdoms flourish
God With Us	
Hanc Deus Dedit	God has given this (meaning a crown)
Has Nisi Periturus Mihi Adimat Nemo	Let no one remove these (letters) from me under penalty of death
Henricus Rosas Regna Jacobus	Henry (joined) the roses, James the kingdoms
Honi Soit Qui Mal Y Pense	Evil to him who evil thinks
Ich Dien	I serve
Inimicos Ejus Induam Confusione	As for his enemies I shall clothe them with shame
Jesus Autem Transiens Per Medium Illorum Ibat	But Jesus passing through their midst went His way
Justitia Thronum Firmat	Justice strengthens the throne
Lucerna Pedibus Meis Verbum Est	Thy word is a lantern unto my feet
Munus Divinum	A divine offering
Nummorum Famulus	The servant of the coinage
O Crux Ave Spes Unica	Hail, O Cross, our only hope!
Pax Missa Per Orbem	Peace sent throughout the world
Pax Quaeritur Bello	Peace is sought by war
Per Crucem Tuam Salva Nos Christe Redemptor	By Thy cross, save us, O Christ, our Redeemer
Post Mortem Patris Pro Filio	After the death of the father for the son
Posui Deum Adjutorem Meum	I have made God my Helper
Protector Literis Literae Nummis Corona Et Salus	A protection to the letters (on the coin face), the letters (on the edge), a garland and a safeguard to the coinage
Quae Deus Conjunxit Nemo Separet	What God hath joined together, let no man put asunder
Redde Cuique Quod Suum Est	Render to each that which is his own
Religio Protestantium Leges ⎱ Angliae Libertas Parliamenti ⎰	The religion of the Protestants, the laws of England, the liberty of the Parliament
Rex Anglorum	King of the English
Rosa Sine Spina	A rose without a thorn
Rutilans Rosa	A dazzling rose
Rutilans Rosa Sine Spina	A dazzling rose without a thorn
Scutum Fidei Proteget Eum (or Eam)	The shield of faith shall protect him (or her)
Tali Dicata Signo Mens Fluctuari Nequit	Consecrated by such a sign the mind cannot waver
Timor Domini Fons Vitae	The fear of the Lord is the fountain of life
Tueatur Unita Deus	May God guard these united (kingdoms)

Translation of Mottoes on Coins

Veritas Temporis Filia	Truth, the daughter of Time
SCOTTISH COINS	**TRANSLATION**
Christo Auspice Regno	I reign under the auspices of Christ
Crucis Arma Sequamur	Let us follow the arms of the Cross
Da Pacem Domine	Give Peace, O Lord
Dat Gloria Vires	Glory gives strength
Decus Et Tutamen	An ornament and a safeguard
Deus Judicium Tuum Regna Da	Give the king Thy judgements, O God
Diliciae Domini Cor Humile	An humble heart is the delight of the Lord
Diligite Justiciam	Observe justice
Dominus Protector Meus Et Liberator Meus	God is my Defender and my Redeemer
Ecce Ancilla Domini	Behold the handmaid of the Lord
Exurgat Deus Et Dissipentur Inimici Ejus	Let God arise and let His enemies be scattered
Faciam Eos in Gentem Unam	I will make them one nation
Fecit Utraque Unum	He has made both one
Florent Sceptra Piis Regna His Jova Dat Numeratque	Sceptres flourish with the pious. Jehovah gives them kingdoms and numbers them
Henricus Rosas Regna Jacobus	Henry (joined) the roses, James the kingdoms
His Differt Rege Tyrannus	In these a tyrant differs from a king
His Praesum Ut Prosim	I am set over them, that I may be profitable to them
Honor Regis Judicium Diligit	The power of the King loveth judgement
Horum Tuta Fides	The faith of these is whole
In Justitia Tua Libera Nos Domine	Deliver us, O Lord in Thy righteousness
In Utrumque Paratus	Prepared for either (meaning peace or war)
In Virtute Tua Libera Me	In Thy strength deliver me
Jam Non Sunt Duo Sed Una Caro	They are no more twain but one flesh
Jesus Autem Transiens Per Medium Illorum Ibat	But Jesus, passing through the midst of them, went His way
Justitia Thronum Firmat	Justice strengthens the throne
Justus Fide Vivit	The just man lives by faith
Nemo Me Impune Lacesset	No one shall hurt me with impunity
Parcere Subjectis Et Debellare Superbos	To spare the humbled and to subdue the proud
Per Lignum Crucis Salvi Sumus	By the wood of the Cross we are saved
Post 5 & 100 Proavos Invicta Manent Haec	After one hundred and five ancestors these remain unconquered
Pro Me Si Mereor In Me	For me; but against me, if I deserve
Protegit Et Ornat	It protects and adorns

Translation of Mottoes on Coins

Quae Deus Conjunxit Nemo Separet	What God hath joined together, let no man put asunder
Quos Deus Conjunxit Homo Non Separet	Those whom God hath joined together, let no man put asunder
Regem Jova Protegit	Jehovah protects the king
Salus Populi Suprema Lex	The safety of the People is the supreme law
Salus Riepublicae Suprema Lex	The safety of the State is the supreme law
Salvator In Hoc Signo Vicisti	O Saviour, in this sign hast Thou conquered
Salvum Fac Populum Tuum Domine	O Lord, save The People
Servio Et Usu Teror	I serve and am worn by use
Spero Meliora	I hope for better things
Te Solum Vereor	Thee alone do I fear
Tueatur Unita Deus	May God guard these united (kingdoms)
Unita Tuemur	These united we guard
Utrumque Paratus	Prepared for either (war or peace)
Vicit Leo De Tribu Juda	The Lion of the tribe of Judah hath prevailed
Vicit Veritas	Truth has conquered
Vincit Veritas	Truth conquers
XPC Regnat, XPC Vincit, XPC Imperat	Christ reigns, Christ conquers, Christ commands

IRISH COINS — TRANSLATION

Christo Auspice Regno	I reign under the auspices of Christ
Christo Victore Triumpho	I triumph in Christ, the Conqueror
Ecce Grex	Behold the flock
Exurgat Deus dissipentur Inimici	Let God arise (and) let His enemies be scattered
Floreat Rex	May the king flourish
Henricus Rosas Regna Jacobus	Henry (united) the roses, James the kingdoms
Melioris Tessera Fati	A token of better fortune
Posui Deum Adjutorem Meum	I have made God my helper
Quiescat Plebs	May the people remain in quietude
Rosa Sine Spine	A rose without a thorn
Salvator	The Saviour
Tueatur Unita Deus	May God guard these united (kingdoms)
Veritas Temporis Filia	Truth, the daughter of Time
Voce Populi	By the voice of the people

ISLE OF MAN — TRANSLATION

Quocunque Jeceris Stabit ⎱ Quocunque Gesseris Stabit ⎰	Wheresoever you have cast it, it will stand
Sans Changer	Without changing

INDEX

'Adulterate Coins', 99
Aethelred, 327
Aethelstan, 30
Aethelwulf, 29
Africa Company, 138
Agricola, 21
Albany, Duke of, 74
Alexander of Brugsal, 78, 111
Alexander the Great, 17
Alexander II, King of Scotland, 53
— coinage, 307
Alexander III, 53, 55
— coinage, 307
Alfred, 29
Allectus, 23
Alney, Treaty of, 31
Angel, half angel, 71
Anglesey penny, 167
Anglo-Gallic coinage, 48
Angus, Earl of, 86
Anlaf IV, 327
Anne, Queen, 146-8
— coinage, 147-8, 294, 295
Anonymous issue, 67, 331, 332
Anson, Admiral, 155
Anted, 20
Antonine Wall, 21
Antoninianus, 23
Aragon, Katharine of, 94
Argenteus, 23
Armorican coins, 243
Armstrong & Legge, 343, 344
Armstrong, Sir Thomas, 136, 343, 344
Atholl, 2nd Duke of, 257, 354
Atrebates tribe, 18, 19
Augustus, Emperor, 19
Aureus (gold), 22

Balcombe (Sussex) find, 60
Baldred, 29
Baliol, Edward, 58
Baliol, John, 55, 307, 308
Bank Charter Act, 189, 190, 369
— suspension, 207
Bank of England, founded, 143
Bank of Guernsey, 379
Bank of Ireland, founded, 375

Bank of Scotland, formed, 370, 371
Bank post bills, 368
Banking, 160-1; eighteenth-century Irish, 178-80; eighteenth-century Scottish, 160-1, 174, 177-8; growth in Irish, 184-5; under George III, 168-72; Victorian, 189-90
Banknotes, 144
— early, 111
— forgeries, 155, 215-16
Bawbees, half bawbees, 89
— in billon, 92
Belfast Banking Co, 185
Billon, 65
Bishop de Jersey & Co, 361
Blondeau, Pierre, 123, 131
Boadicea, 20
'Bob', The, 78
Bosworth, Battle of, 78
Boulton, Matthew, 166, 167
Bowring, Sir John, 227
Boyne, Battle of the, 137
Bracteate coins, 47, 328
Bradbury Wilkinson & Co Ltd, 380
Bradburys, 208
Branch banks and agencies, numbers in 1939, 204
Bretigny, Treaty of, 275
Brigantes tribe, 20
Briot, Nicholas, 110, 112, 113
Britain crowns, 106
British Linen Co, 174
Brock & Le Mesurier, 379
Brock, Daniel, 242
Bronze coinage of 1860, 189
Bruce, Edward, 55, 56
Bruce, Robert, 55
Buckingham, Duke of, 73
'Bungalls', 98
'Bungtowns', 156
Burgundy, Duke of, 66, 72
Bushell, Thomas, 253
Butchers' halfpence, 254

Caesar, Julius, 18
Caithness, Earl of, 89
Camacs, 180

Camulodunum (Colchester), 19
Cantii tribe, 19, 272
Canute, 31
— pennies of, 327
Caracalla, 23, 25
Caractacus, 20
Carausius, 23
Card money, 259, 260, 261, 262, 378
Carlisle, 116
— mint, 43
Carteret, Sir George, 240
Carteret, Sir Helier de, 252
Cartimandua, 20
Cassivellaunus, 18
Catuvellauni tribe, 18, 19, 272
Ceolwulf II, 30
Channel Isles, 239-52
— coinage, 356-63
— German occupation, 250
— note issues, 379-80
Charles I, King, 109, 110, 117, 120
— coinage, 109-11, 117-20, 286, 320-22
Charles II, King, 131, 133
— coinage, 131-6, 292-3, 323, 354
Charles IV of France, 58
Cheques, 183
— travellers', 218
Civil War, 112-14
Clarence, Duke of, 186
Claudius, Emperor, 20
Clipping, 50
Coenwulf, 29
Coin distribution, 220
Commius, 18
Commonwealth coinage, 120, 123-4, 292, 342
Confederated Catholics, The, 340
Constantine I, 23
Copper token farthings, 96
Coritani tribe, 20, 272
Cromwell, Oliver, 119, 123
— coinage, 124-5, 292
— the Protectorate, 124
Cronebane halfpennies, 180
Cross Pommée, 328
Cruikshank, George, 171
Cunobelinus, 19
Cupro-nickel, 213-14

Danbury Hill Fort, 18

Darien Company, 325
Darnley, Lord, 92, 93
David I, King of Scotland, 43
— coinage, 306
David II, King of Scotland, 58, 61, 62
— coinage, 308-9
Debased coinage, 82
De Bello Gallico, 18
De Boochose, William, 42
De Courcy, John, 47, 328
De la Rue, Thomas, & Co, 372
De Saulles, G. W., 247
De Turnemire, William, 54
Decimal coinage, 363
Decimalisation, 226, 227, 228, 229, 230, 231, 250
Demi-lions (demies), 61
Denarii, 23
Deniers, half deniers, 48
Derby, 10th Earl of, 257, 354
Dickens, Charles, 159
Dinar, Offa's, 28
Divine Right of Kings, 136
Dobuni tribe, 19, 272
Dorrien & Magens Company, 297
Doubles (William IV), 361
Douglas, Earl of, 68, 74
'douglas groats', 89
Drapier Letters, 154
Drummond's Bank, 373
'Dublin coinage', 136, 341
Ducal cap, 251
Ducats, 93, 101
Dupondii, 23
Durotriges tribe, 19, 272
'Dutch crowns', 125

'Easterlings', *see* 'Esterlins'
Ecclesiastical issues, 311
Eccleston, Harry, 370
Ecfrith, 28
Ecgberht, 29
Ecu (or crown), 86
Ecus d'or (abbey crowns), 92, 240
Edgar, 31
Edgehill, Battle of, 113
Edmund, 31
Edred, 31
Edward I, King, 40, 53, 55, 239
— coinage, 54, 155, 274, 330

Index

Edward II, King, 56
— coinage, 275, 330
Edward III, King, 56, 57, 58, 59, 60
— coinage, 275, 330
Edward IV, King, 67, 71, 73
— coinage, 279, 280, 331-3
Edward V, King, 73
— coinage, 280, 333
Edward VI, King, 72, 81, 84, 85
— coinage, 84-6, 282-3, 336-7
Edward VII, King, 203, 204
— coinage, 203-4, 300, 301, 358
Edward VIII, King, 211
— coinage, 302-3
Edward, the Black Prince, 58
Edward the Confessor, 32
Edward the Elder, 30
Edward the Martyr, 31
Edwig, 31
Eire coinage, 209, 351-3
Eleanor of Poitou & Aquitaine, 249
Elizabeth I, Queen, 91, 92, 94, 97, 99
— coinage, 96-9, 284, 338-9
Elizabeth II, Queen, 221-4
— coinage, 304-5, 355, 359, 360, 362-3
England, printed note issues in, 368
Erebald, 43
'Esterlins', 49
Evelyn, John, 133

Falconer, Sir John, 135
Farthing, 'black', 75; end of, 223; from 'feorthing', 47; forged token, 114
Fitfigerald, Edward, 375
Fleetwood, Mr, later Bishop of Ely, 141
Florin, 227
— Henry III gold, 57
Follis, 23
Forgery, death sentence abolished, 171
Freluques, 239
'French crowns', 356
Fuller, E. G., 222

Gardner, W., 222
Gawn, Edward, 260
Gaunt, John of, Duke of Lancaster, 60, 61

George I, King, 152
— coinage, 152-3, 295-6
George II, King, 154
— coinage, 154-6, 159-60, 162-3, 296-7, 347-8
George III, King, 163, 164
— coinage, 163-8, 297-8, 348-50, 354, 357, 361
George IV, 180, 181
— coinage, 181-3, 298, 350
George V, King, 204
— coinage, 204-6, 301-2, 358-9, 362
George VI, King, 211-12
— coinage, 211-13, 303-4, 359, 362
George nobles, 81
Gillick, Mary, 221
Glenfaba, 262
Gloucester, Richard, Duke of, 73
Gold coins, 50
— nobles, half and quarter nobles, 57
— penny, 42, 50
Gothic crowns, 187
Gray, Kruger, 247
Grey, Lady Jane, 90
Greyhound shilling, 284
Groats, 54
— sixpenny, 83
Guinea piece, 133
'Gun money', 137
Guernsey, coinage, 361
— note issues, 379-80

Hadrian, Emperor, 21
Halfdan, 80
Halliday, Thomas, 244
Hardheads, 92
Harold I, King, 31, 32
'Harp' issue, 335
Harrington, Lord, 107
Harthacnut, 31
Hastings, Battle of, ninth centenary, 248, 249, 363
Hat piece, 101
Heabert, King of Kent, 28
Heaton & Son, R., 245, 246, 362
Heavy coinage, 65, 276
'Helms', 57
Henry I, King, 40
— penny, 40, 273
Henry II, King, 44, 46, 48, 49

— penny, 47, 48, 273
Henry III, King, 49, 50
— coinage, 49-50, 274, 329
Henry IV, King, 60, 65
— coinage, 165, 276-7, 331
Henry V, King, 60, 66
— coinage, 66, 277, 331
Henry VI, King, 67, 72
— coinage, 66, 277-9, 331
Henry VII, King, 66, 73, 77, 78
— coinage, 77-9, 280-1, 334-5
Henry VIII, King, 80, 83
— coinage, 80-4, 281-2, 335-6
'Hibernies', 137
Hicks-Beach, Lady Susan, 203
Hood, Thomas, 188
Hume, Joseph, 186
Huntingdon and Northumberland, Henry, Earl of, 306

Iceni tribe, 20, 272
Ifars I, 327
Inchiquin, Lord, 341
Institute of Bankers, the, 218
Ireland, and rebellion, 118; banknotes issued in, 375-8; famine in, 192, 193; Northern, 210; republic, 209
Irish Free State coinage, 209, 351
Isle of Man, arms, 254; banknotes, 378-9; coinage, 252-63, 354-5; government, 379; triune, 253

James I and VI, 61, 65, 92, 100, 105
— English coinage, 106, 284-5
— Scottish coinage, 106, 317-20
James II, King of Scotland, 68, 136
— coinage, 68, 293
James III, King of Scotland, coinage, 74, 311-13
James IV, King of Scotland, coinage, 80, 313-14
James V, King of Scotland, coinage, 86, 89, 314-15
Jersey, note issues, 379
— coinage, 356-60
'Joeys', 186
John, King, 49
— coinage, 49, 274, 329

Keys, House of, 255

Kildare, Earl of, 79
King's disease, touching for, 110
Kuchler, Conrad, 355

La Touche bank, 185
Latham, Sir Thomas, 256
Ledward, Gilbert, 221
Legge, Sir George, 136, 343, 344
'Leopards' and 'double leopards', 57
Lion noble, 101
Lionel, Duke of Clarence, 59
Lions, half lions, 92
Littler Dove & Co, 259, 260
Livres tournois, 239, 240
Llantrisant, 173
Long cross coinage, 50
Lydia, 17

Machin, Arnold, 230, 363
Malcolm IV, 48
Maltravers, Lord, 110
March, Edward, Earl of, 67
Marshall, William, 49
Marston Moor, Battle of, 113, 115
Mary I, Queen, 90
— coinage, 90-1, 283, 337-8
— with Philip, 91, 283-4, 338
Mary, Queen of Scots, 89, 92, 100
— coinage, 92-3, 315-17
Massilia, 17
Matilda, 43, 44
Maundy ceremony, 133
Maundy money, 93, 147, 155, 204, 223, 224
Menapians, 23
Mercia, 29
Merks, 101
Merlen, Johann, 181
Metcalfe, Peter, 209
Mey, Castle of, 89
Miliarense, 24
Mill coinage, 132
Milling, 96
Minimi, 24
Minimissimi, 27
Mint marks, 287, 288, 289, 292
Money of necessity, 119
Moneyer, the, 39
Monk, General, 131
Monmouth, Duke of, 136

Index

Morgan & Co, 244
Mortimer's Cross, Battle of, 67
Mortimer, Roger, 56
Munro, General, 340
Murdock & Co, Glasgow, 161
Murrey, John, 254, 354

Newton, Sir Isaac, 141
Niall, 21
Noble, 71
Nonsunts, 92
Northumberland, Duke of, 297
Northumberland, Earl of, 165

Offa, King of Mercia, 28, 77
Oldham, John, 373
Oman, Sir Charles, 207
Ormonde, Duke of, 120
Orrok, Alexander, Lord of Sillebawbye, 89

Pallyn, brass, 240
Parys Mountain Co, 167
Paterson, William, 143, 368
Patricks, 67
Peckham, Sir Edmund, 84
Peel Castle tokens, 259
Penda, 28
Pennies, 1933, 206; 1954, 223; billon, 68; Canute's, 327; gold, 42, 50; William I, 39
Pepin, 28
Pepys, Samuel, 143, 144
— diary extract, 132
Perkins, Bacon Ltd, 380
Petty, Sir William, 226
Philip of Macedon, 17
Philip II, King of Spain, 90
Philippi, the, 17
Pile and trussel, 32
Pingo, Lewis, 354
Pistrucci, 165, 181
Placks, 74 ,101
— saltire, 101, 102
Pontefract, siege pieces, 116-17
Portal, Joseph, 178
Portcullis shilling, 284
Post bills, 368
Postal orders, 369
Poynings Law, 79

Poynings, Sir Edward, 79

Quinarii, 23

Raleigh, Sir Walter, 98
Ramage, David, 124
Ramsey & Steel, forgers, 226
Regni tribe, 18, 19, 272
Restoration, the, 136
Revestment Act 1765, bicentenary of, 262, 355
Richard I, King, 48
— coinage, 48, 274
Richard II, King, 60, 61
— coinage, 60, 276, 331
Richard III, King, 73
— coinage, 73, 280, 333-4
Richmond, Duchess of, 134
Riders, half riders, quarter riders, 74, 101
Robert II, King of Scotland, 61
— coinage, 61, 309
Robert III, King of Scotland, 61
— coinage, 61, 309-10
Roettiers, Jan, 132
Rose noble, 71
Royal Mint, advisory committee, 221
— expansion and development of, 172-3
Ryals, 71; double ryals, 77

St Andrews (lions), 61
St Patrick's coinage, 136
Salic Law, 187
Sark gold and silver medallions, 249
Sceats, 27
Schlick, Count of, 167
Scottish banks, notes issued by, 370-5
— under George II, 160,
Scottish banknotes, 219-20
Septimius Severus, Emperor, 21
Sharington, Sir William, 84
Shaw & Co, Sir Robert, 185
Ship halfpennies, 212
Short cross coinage, 47
Siege pieces, 115
Sihtric III, 22, 327
Siliqua, 24
Simnel, Lambert, 79, 334
Simon, Thomas, 131, 132

Sluys, Battle of, 275
Smyth, Colonel William, 356
South Sea Company, 152
Sovereign, 77, 95
Stamford Find, of groats, 60
Stephen, 43, 273
Sterlings (pennies), 48
Strongbow, Richard, Earl of Pembroke, 46
Sweyn, King of Denmark, 31
Sword dollar, 101

Tallies, 43
Tanner, John Sigsmund, 125, 159
Tasciovanus, 19
Testoons, 78
Thaler, 167
Thistle noble, 100
Thrymsas, 28
Tincommius, 19
Tower pound (Saxon pound), 81
Trente, William, 41
Trial of the Pyx, 59
Trinovantes tribe, 19, 20
Turners, 105
Twenty-pound piece, 100
Tynwald (Upper House), IOM, 254

Ulster, Richard, Earl of, 55
Union, Act of, 325
Utrecht, Treaty of, 145

Van Diemen's Land, 242
Vellocatus, 20
Venutius, 20
Verulamium, 18, 19
Victoria, Queen, 186, 187
— coinage, 187-9, 299-300, 355, 357-8, 361
Violet, Thomas, 15

'Voce Populi', tokens, 162

Wakefield, Battle of, 67
Wallace, William, 55
Walpole, Robert, 145, 152, 154
Wars of the Roses, 67
Warwick, Richard, Earl of, 71, 72
Watt, James, 167, 168
Welsh Copper Company, 152
Whaddon Chase, 18
Wiglaf, 29
William & Mary, 138, 141
— coinage, 138, 141, 142, 294, 324-5, 357
William I (the Conqueror), 32, 39, 239
— coinage, 39, 307
— crown piece commemorating, 360
William II, King, 39, 40
— coinage, 40, 273
William III, King (alone), mints, 294
— as Prince of Orange, 136, 138
— coinage, 141, 142, 294
William IV, King, 186
— coinage, 186, 298-9, 361
William the Lion, 48
— coinage, 48, 49, 307
Williams Deacons Bank Ltd, 373
Wilson, William, 375
Window tax, 142
Wolsey, Cardinal, 81
Wood tally system, 40-3, 143
Wood, William, 153, 255, 346, 347
World War II notes, 214-16
Wreath crown, 205
Wren, Sir Christopher, 226
Wyon, William, 181, 245, 357

York, Duke of, 67
York, House of, 71